T0308831

Old Sleuth's Freaky Female Detectives

Old Sleuth's Freaky Female Detectives
(From the Dime Novels)

Garyn G. Roberts
Gary Hoppenstand
and
Ray B. Browne

Bowling Green State University Popular Press
Bowling Green, Ohio 43403

Copyright© 1990 by Bowling Green State University Popular Press

Library of Congress Catalogue Card No: 89-085966

ISBN: 087972-475-7 cb
      087972-476-5 pb

Contents

Introduction:
Who Was That Androgynous, Angelic, Society Lady Female Detective?

Garyn G. Roberts
Gary Hoppenstand
and
Ray B. Browne

Welcome to the dime novel's version of "freaky" female detectives. This collection provides a concentrated sampling from several of the more popular series: the *Old Sleuth* serials. The introduction to this volume is divided into three parts. The first part discusses the history of dime novels—specifically prominent publishers, popular genres and formulas, and specific, landmark dime novel titles. Also included in the first part of the introduction is a brief discussion of the *Old Sleuth* canon from which the freaky female detective stories for this collection were selected. In the second part, three freaky female detective novels are examined, and the images of the female characteristics in them are analyzed. In addition, the second part poses several questions about the fate of the female private detective from the 1920s to the present in American popular literature. Finally, in the third part of this introduction, the leveling out of freakiness into normality is discussed.

The editors would like to acknowledge the Russel B. Nye Special Collections Division of The Michigan State University Library, Ray Walsh of the Curious Book Shop in East Lansing, Michigan, and Edward T. LeBlanc and Dan Webb—nationally renowned dime novel experts, for their invaluable assistance in putting this collection together. Stories presented herein are facsimile reprints of original dime novels. Facsimiles help provide a historical context for the tales being analyzed and celebrated and are therefore doubly valuable.

1

Perhaps the greatest truth about American popular culture studies is that the scholar, student and fan may remember the past much more

romantically than realistically. This is not necessarily good or bad. The axiom that the simpler (or so they are often perceived) times of old fuel the collective reality of a complicated contemporary society seems more truthful than ever before. Further, if we have a specific tie to that romanticized past, the axiom approaches profundity. If we as a culture are fortunate enough (and perhaps smart enough) to listen to and embrace the stories and experiences of our grandparents, then we have a very real tie to those "better" times of old. The products of our grandfathers and grandmothers, great grandfathers and great grandmothers, consequently hold special meaning to us connoisseurs of culture, for these same products are the result of lifetimes of work by people whose acquaintances we need to treasure always. These products also feed our romantic visions of the past.

At the close of the 1980s, America's first popular entertainment medium, the dime novel, is over 130 years old and has been extinct for about seventy-five years. The birth, rise and reign of the dime novel were events whose likes the world has never seen before or since. Our recent ancestors were very much part of these phenomena as literally billions of dime novels were produced and sold in the latter half of the nineteenth century and early years of the twentieth. At that time, genres and formulas of fiction abounded; some emerged anew, several flourished. In the 1860s and 1870s, frontier stories which chronicled America's expansion westward were popular. In the 1880s and 1890s, tales of mystery, crime and its detection were all the rage in dime novels. For the first time in American history, a mass audience was targeted for an inexpensive entertainment form that was physically

1

accessible to a large portion of the total populous. E.F. Bleiler writes of that dime novel industry, "The first mass-produced entertainment industry of importance, it stood in the same relation to the average young American as television does today."[1]

As might be expected, the dime novel claimed as its birthplace New York City, for over a century ago New York established itself as the publishing center of the world. "New York, during the 1850s was an awakening giant just beginning to be conscious of its strength. To the visitor...a restless, bawdy, vigorous and vulgar place, and people were already saying that it was a nice place to visit but as for living there—never."[2] The most successful and popular of dime novel (and later pulp magazine) publishers was the firm of Francis S. Street and Francis S. Smith. Street and Smith purchased *The New York Weekly Dispatch*, a newspaper, in 1855. Yet, it was not until 1889 that Street and Smith got into the dime novel game. Beadle and Company (later Beadle and Adams) was the first firm to produce dime novels on a regular basis. Charles Bragin, top authority on dime novels when he collected the same in the 1940s, 50s and 60s, claimed that Beadle and Adams dominated the field for some thirty years and that, "Wild West novels were the most popular during the period, and Beadle had the finest staff of Western writers ever to be gathered."[3] Beadle began publishing dime novels in 1860, but several irregularly formatted and published story newspapers had been marketed prior to this time.

The term "story newspapers" is a very accurate description of dime novels. The earliest dime novels, and the majority of dime novels, were printed in a very similar fashion to newspapers of the day. They were roughly nine inches wide and twelve inches tall. Text was typeset in columns—usually two or three to a page. Titles of stories resembled those of articles commonly found in newspapers. These titles attracted readers to the stories. Authors of dime novels frequently had their literary beginnings in journalism. The writing styles employed in dime novel stories, like those in newspapers, were filled with intense action and colorful wording. The dime novel was a sensual form that appealed to a variety of emotions—base and redeeming alike.

June, 1860. Now comes the point in our discussion of dime novels where we pay homage to Beadle's first dime novel—*Malaeska, the Indian Wife of the White Hunter*, by Ann S. Stephens. Seemingly all histories and studies of the dime novel cite this one particular work as the starting point for the medium. There is a degree of justification

in this since Beadle was the first major dime novel publisher and since *Malaeska* was Beadle's first published title. "Yet, *Malaeska, the Indian Wife of the White Hunter* was not a new work; it had appeared in the *Woman's Companion* magazine in 1839, and it was not especially sensational. It was not the first inexpensive book, either. There had been earlier issues, such as Ballou's, that had essentially been dime novels."[4] With the success of *Malaeska*, Beadle began to publish two titles per month. The eighth title in the series was written by a man who became one of the most prolific and published authors of all time. The novel was entitled *Seth Jones or The Captives of the Frontier* and the author was Edward S. Ellis. *Seth* appeared in October, 1860.

In 1863, there was division in the house of Beadle as Irwin Beadle and George Munro broke away from the publisher. Shortly thereafter, Irwin Beadle left the business and George Munro became the chief competition for the Beadle Company. In 1870, Norman Munro (George's brother) entered the field with his own company, and in 1878, Frank Tousey started publishing dime novels. In 1889, thirty-four years after their purchase of *The Dispatch* (1885), Street and Smith began publishing dime novels. Around 1912 when this medium moved into its twilight years, Street and Smith was the only dime novel publisher to successfully make the transition into the era of the pulp magazine. Here of course, Street and Smith flourished.[5]

Buffalo Bill and Deadwood Dick were the fictional stars of two of the most popular Western and frontier life dime novels of the 1860s and 1870s. Buffalo Bill was also, of course, the name of a real life frontier hero. William S. Cody ("Buffalo Bill") became a legend in his own lifetime largely because of the factual, fictional, always sensationalized stories of his life written by Colonel Prentiss Ingraham and others for the dime novels. Perhaps the most popular and assuredly the longest running of all dime novel series, the Buffalo Bill tales saw publication first in 1869 (Ned Buntline was the author) and was the last series in print in 1912 when the dime novel died. Edward L. Wheeler's Deadwood Dick, in addition, debuted in 1877.

Detectives with rather two-dimensional personalities and incredible superhuman strength tracked and hounded rather two-dimensional criminals in many of the dime novels of the 1880s and 1890s. Tales of Old Cap Collier, Old King Brady, Nick Carter and Old Sleuth were the most celebrated. John R. Coryell's and Street and Smith's Nick Carter, who debuted September 18, 1886 in *The Old Detective's Pupil; or The Mysterious Crime of Madison Square,* made the transition to the pulp magazines and is today still published in paperback form. Hence, Nick Carter is the longest running series detective in fiction. The Old Sleuth stories, which began in the *Fireside Companion,* later yielded the female detectives and stories of the same that are the focus of this edited collection.

While frontier stories and tales of crime and detection were the bread and butter for dime novels, other genres and formulas flourished in this medium. Edward S. Ellis produced the first Science Fiction for the dime novels in his 1865 *The Steam Man of the Prairies.*[6] The story is magnificent and was so popular, inventive and ingeniously crafted that it was imitated (more accurately, stolen) and was responsible for the launch of the most popular Science Fiction series in dime novel form—stories of Frank Reade, Jr. The invention in a good percentage of the Reade stories is a "steam man" or variation of Ellis' steam man of some sort. Frank Reade, Jr. first appeared in Frank Tousey's *Frank Reade Library,* September 24, 1892, in a story entitled *Frank Reade, Jr. and His New Steam Man; or, the Young Inventor's Trip to the Far West.* The Reade stories were heavily cannibalized years later in Victor Appleton's turn-of-the-century stories of Tom Swift. Science Fiction was even blended with science fact in the dime novels. When Thomas Edison was receiving publicity for his inventions, a new dime novel library (series) appeared which starred Edison. Horatio Alger, Jr. produced the first of his very popular tales of poverty-stricken, homeless waifs rising from "rags to riches" in *Ragged Dick* of 1867. The dime novels married Alger to his consuming public. The Frank Merriwell stories of Burt Standish (pseudonym) employed a somewhat similar formula. The nineties were the heyday for Alger and Standish. Frank Merriwell first appeared in 1896.

After some sixty years of incredible circulations and unparalleled landmarks in publishing history, the dime novel as first established by Beadle and Adams met its demise. As can be expected, the decline of the dime novel occurred because of a variety of factors. Further, America's first entertainment medium died as it was born—slowly, over a period of years. The descent began about the turn-of-the-century and continued until the beginning of World War I. Formulas simply wore out. Convention overshadowed invention. Profits had been measured by dime novel publishers by the cent and fraction of a cent. Revenue had previously been generated by marketing thousands and millions of issues at low profit margins per issue. The post office increased the postage on "novels" sent through the mail. The increase of one or two cents per issue was enough to destroy the profitability that had been inherent in dime novel publications for years. Of the dime novel publishers, Street and Smith was one of the few to alter its product so that it adhered to postal regulations and still maintained its large market. Story newspapers (now more like magazines than newspapers) retained their ten cent cover prices in many cases and were still technically "dime" novels. But, the ten cent fiction magazines that Street and Smith and new emerging companies produced no longer featured the one novel that was so offensive to the postal service. Rather, these magazines provided collections of stories, novels and short stories alike. They were still eligible for the old postal rate, and these new "dime novels"—now deemed "pulp magazines" because of the crude quality pulpwood paper on which they were printed—also were marketed more heavily on newsstands than were the old dime novels. With about as much certainty as it can be said that Beadle's *Malaeska, the Indian Wife of the White Hunter* was the first dime novel, *The New Buffalo Bill Weekly,* published by Street and Smith through 1912, can be claimed the last dime novel publication. Hence, to say that the dime novel lived from 1860 to 1912 would be generally accurate.

There were several other contributors to the downfall of the dime novel. Almost from the start, individuals emerged who condemned the content inherent in dime novel storylines. These "moralists" usually arose from the ranks of clergy and educators, but to state that all people of the cloth and teachers embraced a common revulsion for the dime novel would, of course, be erroneous. The usual point of contention was that these publications showcased ruthless violence and blatant disregard for human life of any form. Indians and villains were often "picked off" by gunfire like bottles lined up on a wooden fence. Perhaps. But, it is important to remember that dime novel publishers could ill afford to offend any portion of their market share. Subsequently, all "immoral" acts in dime novel storylines had to be justified to the purchasing public. The medium monitored itself better than any outside interest group could. Some educators found something else very disquieting about these story papers—the dime novels typically, but not always, showcased fiction that was not "L"iterature.

This so-called "Literature," as wonderful as it might be in some ways (indeed much of what educators celebrated in fiction during the time of the dime novel did having redeeming value), was simply not available to the mass market. Most people could not afford or locate books outside the realm of newspapers and dime novels. Dime novels pervaded the populous like no other medium of the nineteenth century. Philip Durham writes of the earlier dime novels, "As the demand for dime novels increased—it was reported that they were shipped to the Union troops by the freight car load—Beadle and Adams branched out..."[7] States E.F. Bleiler, "There are, of course, no figures for the total number of dime novels printed, but it is not an unreasonable guess to say several billion. Horatio Alger alone accounts for about 250,000,000 copies!"[8] Luis Philip Senarens (primary creative force behind the *Frank Reade Library*) had some forty to fifty million of his words reach print in his lifetime, estimates Bleiler.[9] Relevant discussions of the value of dime novels go on. Indeed, some of the worth of America's first entertainment mass medium is self-evident, but dime novel experts Philip Durham and E.F. Bleiler are especially poignant in their respective discussions of the topic. Durham comments on the early dime novels and Literature,

Although Beadle and Adams reprinted many English and American authors such as Milton, Byron, Dickens, Cooper, and Twain, one can see from the classification that approximately three-fourths of the dime novels deal with the various forms, problems, and attitudes of life on the frontier, and that more than half are concerned with life in the trans-Mississippi West. The breakdown also shows that there was but little of American life which escaped the pen of the dime novelist. In the pages of these fictional, semihistorical novels there is source material in abundance for the literary and social historian if he wants to add to our understanding of the significance of the settlement and development of America during the nineteenth century.[10]

Bleiler notes, "The dime novels also reflected and served to reinforce the general cultural 'myths' of the period: the ambivalence felt toward the successful criminal; admiration for the violent egotist; worship of physical strength; the Puritan ethic about wealth; the upward dynamism of progress; the righteousness of expansion; and a simplistic morality."[11]

George Munro's Sons and Munro's Publishing House, P.O. Box 2781, 17 to 27 Vandewater Street, New York City and author Harlan P. Halsey first presented "Old Sleuth, the Detective" to the public in the pages of the *Fireside Companion* in 1872. The publisher copyrighted the term "sleuth"— presumably suggested from the word "sleuth hound"—and kept rivals from using the moniker for several years. The first great dime novel detective was born. The original *Fireside Companion* stories

related the exploits of a young detective who disguised himself as an old man and pursued many a vile character through the wildest of adventures. Shortly after the introduction of Old Sleuth, Street and Smith (not yet in the dime novel game) lured Halsey to their offices. "Smith signed him up, gave him a literary christening, and a brand-new writer, 'Judson R. Taylor,' made his debut. Under that name he wrote detective stories which gained so much popularity among the *Weekly (New York Weekly)* readers that they often wrote to say how much better 'Judson Taylor's' yarns were than those featuring the Old Sleuth for *The Fireside Companion*."[12]

Public acclaim landed Old Sleuth his own dime novel series on March 3, 1885 when Munro Publishing presented the first issue of the *Old Sleuth Library* entitled *Old Sleuth, the Detective; or The Bay Ridge Mystery*. The new library sold for five cents a copy. An advertisement claimed it was "A Series of the Most Thrilling Detective Stories Ever Published," and boasted, "The books in *The Old Sleuth Library* contain twice as much reading matter as any other five-cent library." The stories featured in the *Library* were reprints from the *Fireside Companion*. The *Library* featured issues which were 8 1/2" wide and 12 1/4" tall, thirty-two pages and more in length, and showcased a black and white cover illustration. Installments were issued biweekly, then monthly and finally quarterly. The *Library* ran 101 issues in all.

Edmund Pearson recounts the famous 1889 New York County Supreme Court case of "George Munro versus Beadle and Adams."[13] Munro had kept his competitors from using the term "sleuth," but he could not stop imitations of his detective character. Munro's brother and bitter rival, Norman, started the *Old Cap Collier* Library which was scripted by Irvin S. Cobb and ran for almost 800 novels. Frank Tousey presented *Old King Brady*; however Street and Smith introduced the most popular dime novel detective of all—Nick Carter.

In 1897, J.S. Ogilvie Publishing Company of 57 Rose Street, New York picked-up Old Sleuth's character and continued the saga in *Old Sleuth's Own*. New stories were created, and this series lasted 146 issues. *Old Sleuth's Own* resembled today's mass market paperbacks in format. Novels ran 100 pages plus on paper 4 3/4" wide by 7" tall. Covers boasted illustrations and lettering in black and red ink on white or yellow backgrounds.

The fourth and final library to carry adventures of the character Munro and Halsey created was *Old Sleuth Weekly* published by the Arthur Westbrook Company of Cleveland, Ohio. Westbrook produced

203 more novels, though many were reprints. The *Weekly* ran from April 17, 1908 to May 17, 1921 and was issued biweekly until issue #15 when it was released weekly. Numbers 1 to 104 were 8 1/2" by 12"; numbers 105 to 203 were 8" by 10 3/4", and cover illustrations were done in color and had yellow borders. Like the *Library*, issues were thirty-two pages and more in length. Westbrook also issued Old Sleuth in a digest format with color covers and approximately 200 pages of text per issue.

II

Mention "private detective" and the reader's mind instantly conjures images from the pulpwood magazines of the 1920s, 30s and 40s. Dashiell Hammett's Sam Spade, for example, or Carroll John Daly's Race Williams or Raymond Chandler's Philip Marlowe: these famous gumshoes set the fictional standards of the hard-boiled formula that are still vital today. Without a doubt, this is a fraternity that stereotypes the male hero as tough, crafty, persistent and possessing a sense of personal honor. Women, unfortunately, are as often stereotyped either as *femme fatales*, using their sexual appeal as weapons against their male adversaries, or as "gal fridays," loyal to an extreme to their bosses. Whether good or bad, images of women in the hard-boiled story group into secondary, subservient roles. Private Eyes wear rumpled overcoats, snap-brim felt hats, and have the smell of stale cigarettes and cheap whiskey about them. They need a shave and they're tough with their fists. When push comes to shove, they're experts at violence, and yet vulnerability—in particular vulnerability to females—scratches their tough, unwashed exterior. Women are universally sensual, universally devious, universally virginal non-human entities who need to be protected, saved, worshipped, vilified. "Private Dicks" are archetypal male heroes in a male fantasy world. In the residences of these fictional "mean streets," the female detective need not apply. This male/female dichotomy in the private detective story appears, however, to have solely been a product of the pulp magazines. There existed a Private Eye tradition before the pulps in the dime novels. In fact, outside of Edgar Allan Poe's invention of the fictional detective hero, the dime novels did more to popularize and diversify the formula than did any other mass medium in America during the nineteenth century. The road to profit for dime novel publishers was paved with one simple word: quantity. Since per-unit profit margins of each dime novel were very small, the publishers needed to print and sell fantastic numbers of their product.

Naturally, if a series character, like a detective hero, proved to be popular, the publisher tried to give more of what the public wanted, releasing their series titles monthly, bi-weekly and even weekly. And, to keep pace with this demand, the authors of these dime novel serials had several tricks or literary gimmicks that they could fall back on when a deadline was closing and material was hard to come by. One trick that was prevalent, as you will note from the selections in this collection, was the reliance on dialogue. Characters talk and talk and talk in the typical dime novel story. This trick was used to help the author write as much material as possible in a relatively short time. Another trick was the author's reliance on writing extremely brief paragraphs (many times only a sentence in length). By keeping their paragraphs compact, less emphasis was placed on the time-consuming literary chores, like detailed character or setting descriptions.

Yet another gimmick that worked, the one that provides the most interest for the readers of this collection, was repetition. If a detective hero generated reader support, then dime novel publishers strove to duplicate this hero in a myriad of offshoot imitations. During the height of the detective dime novel era, from about 1880 to 1900, the variety of detective heroes was staggering. They came in all shapes and sizes, from all types of ethnic, economic and social backgrounds, and yet they were all cut from the same basic whole cloth. Each detective tended to be superior in strength and intelligence and each detective represented the highest moral values of that era. In no time, female detectives were added to this fictional legion, and their particular adventures provide some revealing insights into the technique of formula construction in early popular literature, and into the socially proscribed roles of men and women in late Victorian/American society.

For example, in the two-part serial from *Old Sleuth Library* included in this collection entitled *Lady Kate, The Dashing Female Detective* (1886), the female detective of the story, Kate Edwards, possesses nearly all of the skills, intelligence and strength of her male detective counterparts. Every fictional detective of the time had to be able to read the physical evidence, or clues, of the crime. Lady Kate, of course, could read them at will. In Chapter V, Kate employs a ruler to measure a stranger's footprint, and in the best tradition of Holmesian deduction, places the whereabouts of the mysterious suspect by the clay on his boots. Kate is proficient in the use of disguises (the most basic of all requirements for the dime novel detective hero in particular, and nineteenth century melodrama in general). Bounding through the adventure of the story, Kate's disguises vary from that of an old woman to a rough-edged male sailor. Lady Kate also demonstrates her great strength time and again by knocking her antagonists (in particular, her male antagonists) to the ground. In Chapter XXXIV, she is called a "magnificent female athlete" and "an expert in the use of weapons." She is said to be able to use sword or pistol with skill. While trapped on a cliff at night and during a storm, Kate lowers herself by climbing from bush to bush—a skill even Tarzan of the Apes might find hard to duplicate.

However, Kate is the well-rounded detective. Her mental *and* physical skills complement each other. In Chapter LV, the reader is told that Kate is "an excellent singer, and a good performer." When she assumes a disguise, she successfully employs the "gestures and intonations of voice" of her pretended role. She can sing and speak both French and Italian. In addition, Kate has intimate knowledge of the criminal's lifestyle and of gambling. She enters a saloon on the trail of a suspect in Chapter VII, and she recognizes the pickpockets and forgers and robbers gambling there. She is described as a quick thinker and as being cool and courageous during "critical moments."

Kate's origins also deserve some mention. In Chapter VI, we learn that she is an orphan who was placed "in a charitable institution." She ran away from this orphanage at "an early age," and she decided to remain in New York. She grew up a beautiful woman, following a type of Horatio Alger rise in social position. Described as a "self-made girl," and while saving her money earned from one occupation and investing it in the next, Kate's social climb eventually rested at the private detective plateau, where she was said to have made even more money and to have worked with such famous detectives as Old Sleuth.

In Kate Edwards, the reader is offered the typical superhuman dime novel detective. Unfortunately, this superhuman detective is a woman and her exploits were published in a socially conservative mass medium and intended for a predominately male, adolescent audience. An *independent* superhuman female was no doubt unacceptable to the audience of that time. On the other hand, a *dependent* female detective, no matter how superhuman in skill and strength, *would* be acceptable, especially if that dependence had its foundation in a love interest with a male protagonist. Thus, in *Lady Kate, The Dashing Female Detective*, the emphasis divides itself equally between adventure and social melodrama.

Indeed, the worst sort of melodrama plagues Kate's sleuthing at every point throughout the plot. She falls in love with her intended quarry early on in the story's development, and then at various points plays ridiculous games of hide-and-go-seek (both in and out of disguises). Whole chapters are devoted to her love-smitten banter with Arthur Everdell, the story's principal heroic villain. Kate's quest to solve the story's mystery is inexorably intertwined with the trite, romantic fiction motif that pits the love of a good woman against the moral crimes of a bad man. She pursues Arthur Everdell's love with fanatic zeal, not unlike her "Avenging Angel" dream of Chapter X. Convinced of Everdell's basic goodness, she disarms her fellow detectives' futile attempts at capturing him. Kate, of course, converts Arthur Everdell by story's end. She "saves" him with her love, but not before she renounces her superhuman "maleness" and quits her detective career.

That male/female dichotomy of pulp magazine detective fiction mentioned earlier appears to have embodied itself in Kate Edward's character. Note the various instances throughout the story where Kate transforms herself from man to woman. When she is using her detective skills, she's described like a man. When her love for Edwards possesses her, or when she screams at being startled, she is described as being womanly. Kate was a woman when in Chapter IV she is surprised by a mysterious face materializing in the mirror of a Gothic-like house. She calms herself, begins her transformation and then puts aside the "woman in her nature" to track the stranger who cast the reflection in the mirror. Kate, as the detective on the stranger's trail, is "cool, cunning, level-headed": a man-like detective.

Lady Kate's "Jekyll and Hyde" male/female metamorphosis can be seen, in part, as the author's attempt not to betray the traditional, masculine dominating sensibilities of the dime novel's nineteenth century audience. At a specific moment in the story, no matter how "fantastic" Kate the detective is, the very next moment she becomes Kate the vulnerable woman. No matter how many men Kate can knock to the ground, the very next moment she is love-stricken by another man. Ultimately, Kate's strengths are framed by the traditional feminine weaknesses of romantic melodrama, and her story becomes a mixed blessing for the woman's image in early popular fiction.

In the next selection in this collection, *The Great Bond Robbery, or Tracked by a Female Detective* (1885/1908) from the *Old Sleuth Weekly* series, the dilemma of the masculine/feminine detective is investigated further. The story resounds with gothic excesses. For example, the head villain, Cameron, is a bigamist and cloisters one of his unfortunate wives in a prison-like room in his villa where, like an avenging specter, she prowls the rooms of the mansion seeking vengeance against her traitorous "husband." Money and sex, of course, assume center stage in the plot. Cameron is the mastermind behind a million dollar bond theft, and yet he himself is manipulated by an evil *femme fatal*, Julia, who is euphemistically called "Mrs." Cameron and who is as close to a prostitute as the dime novel formula gets. Amidst the masquerading and the deception of identity among the preliminary characters (that are typical motifs of the dime novel detective story), there exists in *The Great Bond Robbery* a very real sense of dramatic tension. Paranoia, indeed, might exemplify how both heroes and villains view one another throughout the course of the adventure. The million dollar robbery is the primary criminal act of the story, and yet each chapter dwells upon questions of loyalty and deception so that after a while the problem of the theft becomes secondary to the problem of trust. Moral vision becomes the challenger of paranoia: the champion of this moral vision is the story's female detective, Kate Goelet.

The reader will note a number of significant parallels between *The Great Bond Robbery* and *Lady Kate, The Dashing Female Detective*. Both detective heroines are named Kate. Both Kates possess similar skills and talents, and both eventually fall in love with their respective quarries. The two men in each of these adventures, Arthur Everdell and Henry Wilbur, are more or less wrongly accused of criminal acts. Masking, unmasking and masquerading define the mating rituals of the two Lady Kates. Their unfaltering faith, their courage and their persistence eventually save the lives and reputations of Arthur and Henry (indeed, saving them from misdirected blind justice and the fallible court system). And finally, both pairs of lovers discover domestic bliss at the conclusion of their adventures. The formula of nineteenth century romantic melodrama is thus typically resolved.

Miss Kate in *The Great Bond Robbery*, again like Kate Edwards in *Lady Kate, The Dashing Female Detective*, is a multi-talented detective. In Chapter II, Kate successfully assumes the disguise of an old lady, "dressed in the most grotesque manner and looking exactly like some old farmer's wife." Later in the story, Kate adopts the role of a French maid, working for the evil Julia. In Chapter XX, the reader is told about Kate's skills as a burglar and her abilities as a gymnast. Several times Kate physically flattens Cameron and in Chapter XVI, when Julia attempts to rough-up Kate in her French maid's disguise, the reader is told: "the slender, gracefully formed maid appeared to possess muscles of steel, combined with most extraordinary activity and strength."

Kate Goelet is ultimately described in the title of Chapter VI as "The Lady Detective as a Saving Angel." This confirms for the reader the quasi-religious, moral nature of Kate's character, which proves even of more interest when one thinks of the confrontation between the romantic pairs of the central characters. On the one hand, there is Mr. Cameron and his "kept" prostitute, Julia. Their relationship is based solely on greed and sexual lust. They plot as much against each other as they do against the heroine Kate. Their dark morality serves as dramatic foil for Kate's and Henry's relationship. Henry is basically a "good guy gone temporarily bad," and Kate, through her unselfish love, indeed assumes the role of "saving angel" to both morally strengthen Henry and make him socially acceptable for a proper domestic relationship. In essence, Kate cleans up Henry's bad habits. The story itself presents a type of social textbook of nineteenth century manners. Mr. Cameron and Julia are the couple not to emulate, while Kate and Henry show the reader the valued method of how to attain familial bliss.

The most striking similarity between the two Kates featured in this anthology is their androgynous trait. Like Kate Edwards, Kate Goelet is split several times into masculine/feminine roles during the course of her adventures. In Chapter VI, Kate disguises herself as a "little Frenchman," and while she interrogates Henry Wilbur (in her capacity as detective), she responds to Henry's questioning of her entering a "resort of sporting men and 'knucks' " by stating: "Oh, I am a man now, you know." In her romantic relationship with Henry, time and again in conflict with her masculine detective skills, she assumes the traditional feminine stance. In Chapter XII, for example, the reader is told "She [Kate] was but a woman, and women are strange beings when affairs of the heart are concerned." And though Kate in her masculine detective role is physically clobbering male villains left and right, Kate the love-stricken female eventually abandons independence for a man. Ironically, at story's end when Henry has Kate firmly in tow, the reader is told: "and Kate Goelet's husband [Henry] is constantly heard to say that, if his wife had been born a man, she would have rivaled Napoleon the Grand."

Of the three short novels in this anthology, *Madge The Society Detective, Or A Strange Quest Among The Four Hundred* published in *Old Sleuth Weekly* (1911) most closely approximates the contemporary detective story. There is actually some detective work involved in the plot, especially with Alice VanCamp's relationship with the police investigation at the beginning of the story. This adversarial relationship could have just as easily appeared in a Sherlock Holmes mystery. And when Alice confronts a powerful criminal organization, "one whose ramifications and branches were too numerous to take account of," the story establishes close ties with the Doc Savage and Shadow pulp magazine adventures (featuring mastermind criminal organizations) that would follow some two decades later.

What differentiates the female detective in *Madge The Society Detective* from her predecessors in this anthology is the fact that her assumed, disguised role is that of the detective (while both Kates, in contrast, were detectives who employed civilian disguises). The "true" identity of the lady detective in question here is Alice VanCamp. Like Kate Edwards and Kate Goelet, Alice is described as being beautiful and graceful, according to the standard form. When Margaret's jewels are stolen as the story opens, "Beautiful Alice VanCamp, society favorite, brilliant women of the world" flits around looking for clues and generally acts like the lead detective. But the detective protagonist, the reader is informed by the title, is Madge. By Chapter X, however, the "mystery" is explained: "Alice VanCamp was none other than Madge, the Society Detective, known as Madge Nelson, one of the most brilliant and clever detectives in the great Metropolis." In the same chapter, the reader learns of Alice's/Madge's past. She becomes a detective (in typical Horatio Alger fashion) because it brings in the big bucks, "and it was her ambition to retain the family name and the old home on lower Fifth avenue." Alice is successful in her Jekyll/Hyde role:

Not one of the young society woman's friends suspected that she was leading what they would have called a double life. This very fact enabled her to get closer to many mysteries than would otherwise have been the case. When Madge the Detective got a society case to investigate, Alice VanCamp usually worked it up as a favored guest. Hers was a clever and brilliant mind.

Social melodrama again plays a significant role here as Alice/Madge attempts to unite Agnes with her true father, and thus return Agnes to her proper position in society. These formulaic motifs, of familial identity and romantic ideals, are so prevalent in dime novel detective fiction that

perhaps it might be safe to disagree with the majority of dime novel historians and suppose that a significant number of dime novel detective readers were women. Women readers comprised the major audience for the flood of romantic dime novel fiction that was published during this same time. Since romance formulas crossed over into a number of the detective stories, maybe their female readers crossed over as well.

The female private detective's demise concurred with the death of the dime novel. By the height of the American depression, she was nowhere to be seen. Maybe the gangster and hard-boiled formulas reassigned women characters to subservient roles. Maybe the readership of the detective pulp magazines was even more male oriented than the dime novel's audience. Certainly the sentimental elements of the detective story disappeared at the same time as the formula toughened. The hard-boiled story is the very antithesis of melodrama, as far apart as the romance novel is from the naturalistic novel. Maybe women readers jumped the literary tracks to classical, or British, detective fiction where authors like Agatha Christie and Dorothy Sayers exerted considerable influence. Read any number of "golden age" classical detective novels, and one quickly discovers where the romance and sentimentality ended up after their departure from the dime novels. Today, women writers and female detectives of all kinds comprise the backbone of popular mystery fiction. The paperback detective novel has at last come full circle from its distant dime novel ancestor. It's sad though that nothing published these days can match the "style" of those androgynous, angelic, society detectives of the dime novels: freaky females all.

III

Up until public outrage over exploitation of the physical and mental abnormalities of people, the word "freak" was common—both in public entertainment such as circuses, fairs, traveling burlesque shows, and in common everyday speech. The word could mean anything from General Tom Thumb, P.T. Barnum's very successful curiosity, to Ella Harper, "the Camel Girl," to eight-foot-eleven inch Robert Wadlaw, to anybody who looked or acted a little differently from oneself. The nineteenth and early twentieth centuries were full of these individuals and of approved concepts of the degradation of people who differed from the norm. Such degradation was natural and expected—even approved.

But in the non-technical lexicon of the time there were individuals who called themselves freaks and *were* freaks only because of their unusual talents. They were knife throwers, sword-swallowers, expert wrestlers, unusual handlers of guns. In other words, generally there is no great leap from expert to freak or from freak to expert, or for that matter from freakish to heroic or heroic to freakish. Everything in essence is in the name.

In the sense of the unusual being freakish, the female detectives of the *Old Sleuth* school surely qualify for the term. They were both normal and abnormal. They were extraordinarily talented and unusual, and at the same time normal. They could switch from one role to the other at the barest evidence of need. So they were doubly talented; no man of the time could assume the double roles women played as detective hero—hero and weakling, masterful and subservient—or had to. Men did not have to be freaky—women did.

Robert Bogdan, world renowned authority on the subject of freaks, feels quite properly that just as people are created by the world they inhabit, that world also is a result of their creation. "Freak shows," he says in the book *Freak Show*, "are not about isolated individuals, either on platforms or in an audience. They are about organizations and patterned relationships between them and us." In other words, the "freak" is "something we created: a perspective, a set of practices—a social construction."[14] Although those constructions are usually negative, they can be positive. Just as physical giants—like Robert Wadlaw—are freakish, so are heroes like Odysseus and Sir Lancelot. In our own day, there are only small differences between the heroes, say, of crime fiction and ourselves. The heroes—who surely at times seem a little freaky—are not much different from ourselves and from one another in the books. For example, Gutman, Wilmer, Cairo, Brigid, and Sam Spade, in *The Maltese Falcon*, are only marginally different; yet Spade's actions are socially and culturally (and legally) approved whereas the actions of the others might not be.

So the differences between the unusual female detectives in the stories contained in this volume and others, say, in present-day crime fiction are those of degree. Present-day female detectives have to work a little harder than their male counterparts to establish their credentials. Although equals—at least they are called "equals"—they are still considered as somewhat unusual—as being somewhat unnatural, that is, as "freaky." But just as "freaks" are being less and less viewed as being unnatural and objects of scorn, so are women

detectives. In crime fiction, perhaps more than in other genres of popular fiction, women are becoming less "freaky" and more natural; that is their natural behavior, is starting to be viewed less and less as unnatural. Through the years, women have been considered sex objects and abused as such in popular fiction, and in detective fiction where women were the equal of men they still were thought of as engaging in "freakish" activity. It is interesting that crime fiction might be the literary genre that has through the years led the way toward female liberation. Such is the persuasive push of power. In literature, as in life, power begets power. Power smooths "freakish" characteristics of individuals into normality. Women who in the past were considered to be freaky now are looked upon as normal. The stories in this collection not only show us old stereotypical images of women, they showcase the means by which women have arrived today.

Notes

[1]Bleiler, E.F., ed., *Eight Dime Novels* (New York: Dover Publications, Inc., 1974), p. viii

[2]Reynolds, Quentin, *The Fiction Factory or From Pulp Row to Quality Street* (New York: Random House, Inc., 1955), p. 3

[3]Bragin, Charles, "Dime Novel History," *Dime Novel Club* #63 (Brooklyn, New York: Charles Bragin Publisher, 1964), p. 1

[4]Bleiler, p. vii. Philip Durham, editor of *Popular American Fiction: Seth Jones* (by Edward S. Ellis) and *Deadwood Dick on Deck* (by Edward L. Wheeler) (New York: The Odyssey Press, 1966), cites the publication as *Ladies' Companion* not *Woman's Companion* on page v of his book.

[5]Charles Bragin of Brooklyn, New York published *The Dime Novel Club*—a semi-professional fanzine dedicated to the hobby and scholarly pursuit of collecting dime novels. In issue number sixty three of *The DNC*, Bargin provided a bibliography for dime novels and an informative essay on dime novel history aptly entitled "Dime Novel History."

[6]Ellis' *The Steam Man of the Prairies* is reprinted in Bleiler's *Eight Dime Novels*. The steam man, as conceived by Ellis, was a steam powered mechanism that was fashioned in the form of a man. When its wood fueled boiler produced enough steam, the legs of the man pulled a wagon much as a team of horses did. Of course, there was no practical means of stopping the contraption before the wood burned up.

[7]Durham, p. vi

[8]Bleiler, p. vii

[9]Bleiler, E.F., ed., *The Frank Reade Library*-Vol. 1 (New York: Garland Publishing, Inc., 1979), p. ix

[10]Durham, p. vi

[11]Bleiler, E.F., ed., *Eight Dime Novels*, p. ix

[12]Reynolds, p. 40

[13]Pearson, Edmund, *Dime Novels or Following an Old Trail in Popular Literature* (Boston: Little and Brown, Inc., 1929), p. 191. Remember, Beadle and Adams were George Munro's former employers.

[14]Bogdan, Robert, *Freak Show: Presenting Human Oddities For Amusement and Profit* (Chicago: University of Chicago Press, 1988), pp. x-xi

Lady Kate, the Dashing Female Detective.—First half.
By OLD SLEUTH.

This Number contains a Complete Story, Unchanged and Unabridged.

No. 30 | SINGLE NUMBER. | GEORGE MUNRO, PUBLISHER, Nos. 17 to 27 Vandewater Street, New York. | PRICE 10 CENTS. | Vol. II.

Old Sleuth Library, Issued Monthly. By Subscription, $2 per annum.
Copyrighted 1886, by George Munro.—Entered at the Post Office at New York at Second Class Rates.—September 1, 1886.
Copyrighted 1882 and 1886, by George Munro.

LADY KATE,
THE DASHING FEMALE DETECTIVE.

By OLD SLEUTH.

FIRST HALF.

CHAPTER I.

"IF I thought you were in earnest, I'd tear that mask from your face."

The words were spoken in a low, firm tone.

A laugh, sweet, clear, and musical, greeted the fierce expression as quoted in the opening paragraph of our narrative.

It was at a grand masked ball held in an elegant private mansion.

A gentleman arrayed as a brigand was seated beside a lady in the costume of the Queen of Night.

The latter had said:

"You act your part so well I am almost inclined to believe *you are a burglar!*"

The lady had spoken in a merry, bantering tone, and the man had replied in a tone of semi-seriousness.

After all, it was but a commonplace dialogue, *on the surface.* The words, under similar circumstances, might be used a hundred times, and be as meaningless as a careless laugh.

When spoken as narrated, there was a fatal significance in their use; a dark tragedy lurked in the shadow.

The lady was a wonderful character. She had attended that masked ball with a purpose; she had a deep purpose when she addressed the language to the man costumed as a brigand.

The man— Well, the lady was trying to find out who and what he was.

A few weeks previous to the occurrence of the incident narrated, the public had been horrified by the announcement of a terrible tragedy.

A supposed widow lady of wealth and culture had been murdered by a masked burglar.

She had occupied an elegant residence, had lived alone with her servants, surrounded by a shadow of deep mystery.

She had been murdered in cold blood; large amounts of personal property had been taken; and even after her death the mystery remained unexplained.

A gentleman had come forward and proved himself a distant relative, and had been appointed administrator of the estate.

The gentleman named, one Augustus Prang, had stated that there was an heir—a lost heir—a daughter.

The gentleman also stated that there was a will, which had been stolen by the assassin.

Mr. Prang had proved his relationship, and appeared to be an honorable man.

He took no steps to become possessed of the property, but merely demanded to be appointed trustee upon furnishing ample security for the faithful performance of his duty.

Mr. Prang was a well-known business man, and had once employed a lady detective to work up a case for him.

The lady had proved herself wonderfully competent for the undertaking, and had successfully carried through the job.

Some months subsequent to the tragedy, Mr. Prang sent for the same lady thief-taker.

The mystery of the murder had remained unsolved. The most noted detectives in the land had been put upon the job, and had thus far failed.

The incidents of the tragedy had faded from the minds of the general public, their attention had been absorbed in more recent tragedies.

Not one cent of the stolen property had been traced, not one article.

A large reward had been offered for the return of the will, but no heed had been paid to the offer.

The case had drifted away to be buried, as far as the public was concerned, with other dark tragedies that had lain hidden under a cloud of undispelled mystery.

Mr. Prang had tried every effort to solve the mystery, but had failed. And no will was found, no heir came forward to claim the large estate.

It was when matters had thus simmered down that Colonel Prang sent for Kate Edwards.

Kate was the lady detective whom he had once employed.

The lady detective, who was known as Lady Kate, was the heroine of a remarkable personal history.

No one knew her history save the chief of the bureau in which she was employed.

She was a remarkably handsome young woman.

She had once been employed in the New York Custom-house as a lady inspector, or secret-service officer.

It had been her duty to examine females suspected as lady smugglers, and the government officials had utilized her talents upon many occasions in particular cases.

She had lost her position because of sympathy displayed toward an accused lady, and she had left the service under a cloud.

Financially, the discharge was an advantage, as almost immediately she was employed by a detective bureau, where she made herself remarkably useful.

Lady Kate had enjoyed a varied and wonderful experience; and yet at the time of the opening of our story she was not more than five-and-twenty.

Colonel Prang did not desire to hold all the estate of his relative. He was a man of large wealth, and it was his most ardent desire to discover the real heir.

As stated, he sent for Lady Kate.

The great banker was seated in his private office, when a card was handed to him.

He glanced at the bit of pasteboard, and read the name:

"KATE EDWARDS,
"Private Detective."

The lady was shown into his presence, when the gentleman bound her to confidence, and told her a strange, weird tale.

CHAPTER II.

MRS. RAYMOND, the lady who had been murdered, was the only daughter of a gentleman who had inherited a large estate.

After the completion of her education she went with her father to Europe.

In Paris she met with a young American,

who was one of the handsomest men she had ever met.

The young lady could only boast rare accomplishments and great prospective wealth, but personally she was plain-looking.

She fell madly in love with the elegant young American. Her father announced himself as not opposed to the marriage, in case young Balfour Raymond should prove every way worthy of his child.

The young man asserted his high birth, and his education, manners, and breeding were confirmatory of his claim, but withal there was a mystery about him.

The young lady's father could not discover what the young man's previous career had been, and at the last moment proved one of the would-be son-in-law's statements concerning himself to be false.

General Renton, Grace Renton's father, was an honorable and a very proud and punctilious man, and upon making the discovery named he refused his consent to the marriage.

Balfour Raymond claimed to be rich. He certainly supported an elegant style of living, and always appeared to have abundance of money.

It was the old, old story.

Love blinded the maiden, who was proud of her conquest of such an elegant lover, and, despite her father's warnings, a secret marriage followed.

Upon discovering his daughter's mad act, General Renton determined to make the best of it, although at the very time of the marriage he had made some startling discoveries as to the former career of his son-in-law.

He learned that Balfour Raymond's parents were people of the very highest respectability. His father was a clergyman of high standing in the Episcopal Church, and his mother was the daughter of an historic family.

So far the young man had told the truth concerning himself; but beyond that his statements had been a tissue of falsehoods.

His parents were comparatively poor, and he had been a wild, harum-scarum boy, causing his father no end of sorrow.

At the age of fifteen he had come very near being sent to jail for a criminal offense; and after leaving college he had entered business, had become a defaulter and a fugitive, and still later he had been accused of being a forger and bank-burglar.

General Renton did not make all the discoveries above quoted at one time, but within a year following his daughter's clandestine marriage he learned all the facts above detailed.

Balfour Raymond proved a kind husband and really loved his wife.

He was an extravagant man, but there was something fascinating in his very recklessness.

After his marriage he was engaged in no disreputable proceedings, and the chances were that under proper circumstances he would have turned out a really grand and noble man, despite the blots upon his early career, for he was a generous fellow, brave and brilliant.

Unfortunately, a year after the birth of a son, his wife became unreasonably jealous of him, and treated him at times in an unkind manner.

The husband was too generous and independent to mind his wife's silly notions, and hoped that she would soon get over them, and be it said to his credit that he was undeserving of her suspicions.

She, however, being so plain, and he so handsome, was jealous despite herself, and as "jealousy makes the food it feeds upon," her fever increased rather than diminished.

Grace Raymond had learned of her husband's previous history; and one day, in a fit of rage and bitter anger, she had called him a thief and a forger, who had inveigled her into a marriage with him and his disreputable and infamous history.

The young man had always been a kind and loving husband, but when his wife used those words to him, a terrible look came into his face.

In calm, cold tones he said:

"You have thought it well to taunt me with my past life!"

"Yes, and had I known your previous history, you would never have bound me to you in marriage!"

"You fully understand what you are saying?"

The wife was beside herself with passion, and answered recklessly:

"I do."

"You mean every word you say?"

"I do."

"I thank you for your frankness; and now, Grace, listen to me. I was a foolish young man, indulged and spoiled by a fond father and a doting mother. I was not trained and reared to exercise control of my appetites and desires. I love wealth and luxury; and not having been reared to a strength of character to resist temptation, I fell. I met you and I loved you, and I resolved ever through the remainder of my career to lead an honorable life. It was your love that first formed my high purpose; but now the last link is broken that bound me to you or to honor! I endured your jealous reproaches, though I did not deserve them; but when you, my wife, the wife whom I loved, throw in my teeth the criminal folly of my youth, the last anchor that moored me to an honorable future is cut loose. You will never reproach me again. You have called me thief and forger! thief and forger I will be. Farewell!"

The young man turned and left his wife's presence.

CHAPTER III.

GRACE RAYMOND did not call her husband back. She thought he would "get over it," and rather gloried in having humiliated him.

"It will do him good!" she said. "He is too proud and domineering, and now he is aware that I know from what I raised him!"

It was in the morning when the scene occurred which we have related. Night came and Balfour Raymond did not return home.

The wife had recovered from her wild, unreasonable rage, and regretted her vehement and insulting language.

She remembered that her husband came of a proud race, an ancestry that had been distinguished both in the navies and armies of the United States.

She remembered the words she had spoken. How stern and handsome he looked, and yet how calm.

The night passed, and he came not.

Upon the following day her father asked:

"Where is your husband?"

The wife told her father of what had occurred.

General Renton was a passionate man. It was from her father that Mrs. Raymond inherited her temper.

"You fool!" exclaimed the father, "you have sent your husband to h—l!"

General Renton had come to admire his son-in-law. There had been many frank conversations between them.

The general had come to understand how the young man had been led into crime, and had encouraged him in his new resolves.

The father-in-law had discerned the heroic element in his son-in-law's character, and allowed for the weakness that had marred his earlier life.

When uttering his wild words General Renton did not dream how prophetic they were destined to prove.

A week passed, and Balfour Raymond did not return to his wife.

The latter began to bitterly regret her harsh assaults, and later on she had more cause to regret them.

The nurse had the child out for an airing, but returned without the infant.

"Where is my child!" demanded the frantic mother.

The nurse told her story.

The child's father had suddenly come upon her, and had taken the infant.

"Tell my wife," he said, "the child is the offspring of a *thief and a forger, but he shall never be twitted of it by his mother.*"

Every effort was made to recover the child, but without success. General Renton died, leaving his daughter his sole heiress.

After twenty years and a few months following the death of General Renton, Mrs. Raymond received a note through the mail.

The note ran as follows:

"Your son still lives, but I can not tell you where to find him!   BALF   R   D."

There was no doubting the genuineness of the note.

Mrs. Raymond knew well those peculiar characteristics that distinguished her husband's handwriting.

She sought to find her husband, and failed. She made every effort to discover her son, but failed; and she made a will bequeathing all her fortune to her son, Balfour Raymond, Junior.

Mrs. Raymond was a crushed woman; she had never entered society after the desertion of her husband, and she had led the life of a recluse.

Seven years subsequent to the death of her father she was murdered, and her taking-off became one of the mysteries of the land.

The above was the story Colonel Prang related to the dashing female detective, Lady Kate.

Upon the conclusion of the strange, sad story, Kate asked:

"What do you suspect?"

"Nothing."

"What do you want me to do?"

"Recover the lost will."

"Colonel Prang, do you think it was the son or the husband murdered Mrs. Raymond?"

The gentleman was silent.

"Which do you suspect?"

"I suspect no one."

"All you want me to do is recover the lost will?"

"Yes."

"You do not wish me to trail the assassin?"

"I give you no other instructions than to find the will: in tracing the will you will necessarily track the assassin."

"And then?"

"Matters must take their course. I've no suggestions to offer now."

"Will you answer me one question? In your own heart do you suspect either of the persons named?"

"I have no reason to suspect either of them. I have related the family history."

"Did you ever know Balfour Raymond?"

"The father?"

"Yes."

"I did."

"Could he commit such a deed?"

"I should say not."

"And the son?"

"No one knows anything about the son, save those who have associated with him during the last seven and twenty years. He was a year old when stolen by his father."

"I will find that will!" said Kate.

"I trust you may."

"To whom does the property go in case the will is not found?"

"To me."

"You are a generous man to seek an heir under all the circumstances."

"We will not talk about that, go find the will!"

"I shall do so, and I will do more."

"What will you do more?"

There was a curious look in Colonel Prang's eye as he asked this question.

"I will find the heir!"

CHAPTER IV.

KATE EDWARDS had a great work on hand. She had promised to perform a great piece of detective work, where some of the most expert detectives in the country had failed.

Kate had asked for a photograph of Balfour Raymond, senior.

She had been informed that no photographs of him were known to be in existence, but that there was a portrait painted nearly thirty years previously.

The portrait was at the mansion where the murder had been committed.

The mansion had been closed after the funeral, and left in charge of an old man who had been gardener.

Kate received a permit to visit the house and see the portrait.

It was noon when she was shown into the house.

The portrait hung in the library, a room which opened upon a broad piazza.

Kate threw the windows wide open to let in the light, so that she might have a distinct view of the portrait.

The picture charmed her.

"Indeed, he was a handsome man, if that is a correct likeness of him!" was the muttered exclamation that fell from the lips of the lady detective.

She stood a long while contemplating the painted features.

It had been a mere matter of business when she first gazed, but she was so charmed with the face she stood fascinated, gazing and gazing as though she could not withdraw her eyes.

Involuntarily she murmured:

"I fear I could love that man, even though he were a thief and a forger!"

The beautiful female detective little dreamed how much fate there was in her muttered declaration. She little dreamed how in time to come she would be brought face to face with her words, through a fearful ordeal she would be called upon to pass.

There was a large mirror in the wall built into the house, between the two doors leading from the library into the adjoining room.

The mirror depended from ceiling to floor, and was at least four feet in width, a noble piece of plate glass, environed by an oak frame which accorded with the wood trimmings of the room, and was most elaborately and magnificently carved.

Kate turned one moment from the picture and glanced into the mirror, when a most strange and extraordinary incident occurred.

With a cry of amazement the lady detective saw reflected in the mirror a face that was an almost exact counterpart of the face of the portrait.

The reflection appeared but for a moment, and it was gone.

The lady detective for a few seconds was completely dazed, but in time she recovered her full, keen sense, and with the recovery came a succession of strange, weird, and wonderful suspicions.

The mirror lay directly opposite the opened windows that led out to the piazza, and the portrait was so hung that it was a physical impossibility that the painted face of the portrait could have been reflected in the glass.

Kate was mystified.

To herself she muttered:

"I was not deceived by my own fancy!" but as she reflected she was compelled to admit that she must have been.

It was too strangely wonderful to be real that she had really seen a genuine reflection.

She dismissed the subject from her mind, and once more fixed her glance upon the portrait.

Again, after an interval, she once more involuntarily glanced into the mirror, and again caught a passing glimpse of the reflection.

"Heavens!" she exclaimed, and glanced round at the window.

Nothing met her view.

She rubbed her eyes and looked again into the mirror, and only beheld her own handsome face.

"Well, I am becoming a victim of my own imagination with a vengeance!" she muttered, and walked toward the window.

At the window the detective made a wonderful and mysterious discovery.

"Oh, my soul!" she ejaculated, "what does it mean?"

Upon the floor of the piazza were the *fresh imprints* of human feet!

Some one had been upon the piazza since her entrance into that room—some one who had just stepped in soft, clayed mud, and had left their foot imprints behind.

Those imprints were not there when Kate first opened the window.

She was too well trained not to have noticed them had they been there. No, the party making these footmarks must have stood there at the moment she was looking into the mirror, and the reflection was a counterpart of the portrait face.

Kate was a well-trained woman, but she trembled.

A whole wonderful life history was represented in that one glimpse of a human face in that mirror.

The seeing of that face there at such a moment was an extraordinary incident.

The mirror had told a fearful tale—had revealed the face of a murderer.

Of all the strange incidents of our heroine's life the adventure of that midday was the strangest.

"What am I doing here?" said Kate.

The woman in her nature had been put aside. At once she was the cool, cunning, level-headed detective.

She must find the will. She must find the murderer.

She stepped out upon the piazza, and as she did so her heart received a thrill. She saw a man's form disappearing in the shrubbery, and with a gleaming eye and iron-nerved form, *she started to shadow him.*

CHAPTER V.

KATE had not stopped to close the windows, nor explain her departure to the old man who had admitted her to the house.

She started to follow the man whom she had seen disappear in the bush.

The grounds surrounding the mansion were large.

Kate tracked the man down to the lake.

She saw that he was handsomely dressed, and bore the general appearance of a gentleman.

As yet, she had not seen his face.

The lake was an artificial pond that had been filled on the grounds, and was surrounded by a dense bordering of trees and brush.

In former days it had been well kept, but since the death of General Renton the place had been neglected.

The man wandered down by the lake, passed in the midst of the brush, and disappeared.

Kate came to a halt, to consider what she should do.

The man had not discovered that she was shadowing him.

At length an idea struck her. She made up her mind to pretend to belong to the place, and thus claim a right to inquire the man's business.

She followed into the brush, and was walking hurriedly along, when suddenly she came face to face with the stranger.

The man appeared surprised at beholding her, and Kate was even more surprised than he.

As she glanced at him she saw that he did not bear one particle of resemblance to the picture.

She had followed the wrong man.

The two stood and gazed at each other a moment, when the man broke the awkward silence by saying:

"Good-day, miss!"

"Good-day sir."

"It's a pleasant day."

"Yes, sir."

"You belong to this place?"

"I am staying here at present."

"It's a beautiful place."

"Yes, sir; it was a lovely place when it was kept up."

"The lady who lived here was murdered?"

"She was; yes, sir—assassinated in the most cowardly manner."

"Have they discovered any clew to the murderers?"

Kate was a thorough business woman, and fixing her clear blue eyes upon the man, she answered:

"Yes, they think they have discovered a clew."

"Have you heard it mentioned what was the motive of the murder?"

"No, sir."

"It is strange any one would want to murder an inoffensive old lady!"

Kate had watched the man's face.

As stated, he bore no resemblance to the portrait. It was not his face she had seen reflected in the mirror.

When she had stated that they had discovered a clew, she had expected to see the man start; but he gave no sign, and only acted as an indifferent stranger might act when making passing inquiries concerning some subject of interest.

"Are you alone, sir?" asked Kate.

"Why do you ask?"

"I thought I saw *another* gentleman."

"I am alone."

"Have you seen another gentleman on the place within the last half hour?"

"No—ah, I can't say."

The man exhibited a momentary confusion.

"Did you see any one?"

"I must answer that I did not."

"Were you up at the house?"

"No."

The last answer in a decided manner.

Kate was more and more mystified.

The man explained that he was stopping near by, and wandered into the grounds inadvertently, and said he hoped he would not be looked upon as an intruder.

Kate said she could speak for the present owner of the place, and would say it was all right.

The man thanked her, bid her good-day, and walked away.

Kate knew of no excuse for detaining him, although she would have liked to have talked with her further.

The man walked away, and Kate remained by the shore of the lake.

After the man had passed from view, the lady detective appeared in her true character.

She drew a measuring rule from her pocket, and walked along until she found a place where the footprints of the stranger had been plainly marked on the margin of the lake.

She made a critical examination, and then made a careful measurement of the footprints.

There was a mystery she could not fathom.

She had looked at the stranger's feet when first coming near him, and had observed that his boots were smeared with the same sort of clay as had marked the footprints on the piazza.

Having studied the general characteristics of the imprint, and made an accurate measurement, she returned to the house and measured the prints on the piazza.

Both measures agreed to a hair, and the general characteristics of the imprints were preserved.

"What does it all mean?" was the muttered exclamation that fell from her lips.

Here was a strange mystery.

The man had denied being at the house, and yet he had left silent evidences of the fact that he had told a falsehood.

It was the reflection of whoever had been upon the piazza that she had seen in the mirror, and the reflection was a vivid counterpart of the face of the portrait, and yet when she came face to face with the living man there was no resemblance at all.

Kate Edwards determined to solve the mystery.

CHAPTER VI.

OUR heroine was a thoroughly trained detective.

Her experience in the Custom-house had been of great service to her, and since she had become a regular detective she had enjoyed a remarkable experience. She had been associated in cases with some of the most noted detective experts. Upon one occasion she had been employed as an aid to no less a man than Old Sleuth himself, the most successful detective on complicated cases who ever shadowed a hidden crime.

Kate Edwards was a waif.

She had been placed by her parents, whoever they were, in a charitable institution. She had run away from the place at an early age, and ever since had knocked around New York.

She had grown up handsome, ay, wondrously handsome, was, indeed, a beautiful woman, and she had managed to educate herself, and had picked up many lady like accomplishments, although she had graduated from a crossing-sweeper to a newspaper vender, from the latter to a telegraph operator, and from the latter position she had gone into the Custom-house.

She was a self-made girl. She had improved every opportunity.

The money she made as a newsgirl she had expended to fit herself to become a telegraph operator, and the money earned in her latter position had been expended in the acquirement of other accomplishments.

She was a smart, brave, enterprising, beautiful, virtuous young woman, born with great natural talent and wonderful energy of character.

The moment she had received an appointment as a detective she had applied herself to become fully fitted for the position, and had become, in her way, an expert.

It has been proven that women of spirit can fit themselves for almost any vocation in life, and Kate Edwards was just one of the sort named.

When it came to the matter of disguises she was a wonder, and had got the art down so fine that she could leave a company for two minutes and return and pass unrecognized.

Having determined to solve the mystery of the reflection in the mirror, she set herself deliberately about her difficult task.

Kate completely changed her appearance—changed it before leaving the house, after having demonstrated the identity of the two sets of imprints.

The mansion where the tragedy had occurred was situated about ten miles from the city.

Kate had made up her mind that the man whom she was shadowing did not belong in the vicinity, and she proceeded first to the depot.

She carried a time table, and knew exactly at what time a train was due bound for the city.

Her calculations proved correct. She saw the man at the depot with whom she had been talking on the margin of the lake.

Kate was got up as a respectable old lady, with spectacles, leather satchel, and all.

She boarded the train, and, following the man, seated herself right beside him in the car.

She commenced at once to talk to him, availing herself of an old lady's assumed privilege.

The train ran along a point from whence the mansion, standing on an eminence, could be seen.

As the car shot past, the old lady said:

"There was a horrible murder committed in that house!"

"Was there a murder committed there?" asked the man, innocently.

"Why, laws me! didn't you ever hear of the Raymond murder?"

"I never heard anything about it," was the cool, deliberate, false reply.

Kate knew that the reply was false, because she had been talking about that very murder to that very man within an hour.

His falsehood was significant and suggestive. *Why should he deny all knowledge of it?* and why should he have denied being up at the house when he had been upon the piazza, gazing into the very room where hung the portrait of the man who should have been its master?

As Kate sat beside the man, the mystery of the reflection deepened.

She had expected to find that the man was disguised, but the closest scrutiny failed to reveal the fact.

She could not detect that he was disguised; and yet, whence had come that strange resemblance reflected in the glass?

The idea did suggest itself that, having been gazing at the portrait and seeing the reflection so suddenly, the resemblance might have been a fancy; but the suggestion was not satisfactory at all.

At the moment Kate was perfectly cool, was investigating, and had seen the reflection twice, and each time had observed the wonderful resemblance.

"You never heard about the murder, eh?"

"Never."

"Do you live in New York?"

"Yes."

"And you read the papers?"

"Sometimes."

"Well, it's strange you never heard about the Raymond murder!"

"Never read anything about it."

"What's your business?" asked the old lady abruptly and rather impertinently.

"I have no business."

"You are a gentleman of leisure?"

"Yes."

"And you never heard or read anything of the murder of Mrs. Balfour Raymond?"

The name Balfour had never in a single account been associated in connection with the name of Mrs. Raymond.

Kate had mentioned the name as an experiment, and had watched the result with keen eyes.

The stranger listened to the name in an indifferent manner, and Lady Kate thus far was baffled.

CHAPTER VII.

"THE lady's name was Mrs. Balfour Raymond?" repeated the man.

"Yes, Mrs. Balfour Raymond. She had a son she had not seen for many years, and it is believed by some that the son had something to do with the murder."

Kate had fired her biggest gun, but the statement fell upon cold, indifferent ears.

"It would be a horrible thing for a son to murder his mother!"

"Yes, it would; but he may have murdered her by mistake."

The stranger laughed, and said:

"Well, old lady, you have strange ideas."

"How so?"

"To think that a son could murder his mother by mistake!"

"Well, under some circumstances, he might."

"I can't see how he could, under any circumstances."

"Well, suppose he should not know his mother?"

"A man not know his own mother!"

"Suppose a boy were stolen from his mother when he was but an infant, and had never seen her again?"

"Well, you do make a case, but tell me, were such the facts in the case of the woman who was murdered?"

"I am only repeating just what I heard."

"Oh, it's rumor?"

"Well, yes."

The train reached New York.

At the depot Kate entered the ladies' room. It chanced fortunately to be vacant at the moment.

It was an old lady entered the room. It was a young woman who came forth.

The spectacles had disappeared, the old gown had gone, and the satchel had been transformed into a handsome reticule.

The transformation took place in a few seconds, and Kate appeared again in time to board the same car the man had taken with whom she had conversed in the train.

The man rode down town and alighted at Fourteenth Street.

Kate left the car a block lower down town.

From the car window she had seen the man enter a certain well-known resort.

The moment the lady detective left the car she hastened to her lodgings, which fortunately chanced to be near by, and half an hour later a nobby young man entered the same saloon Kate Edwards had seen the man whom she was shadowing enter.

There were a number of men in the place, and they were all bad characters.

Some of them were gamblers, some were pickpockets, some were forgers and robbers, and there were also one or two well-known burglars in the crowd.

Kate knew them all.

As a detective she had a pretty good recognition of all the prominent criminals who made their head-quarters in New York.

Kate knew the men; they did not know her.

She had a nice game to play to get at the facts she was seeking.

The men were playing a game of dice at one end of the bar; Lady Kate in her safe disguise was a looker-on.

At length one of the men got "broke," and withdrew from the game.

Kate took the man's place.

She was thoroughly up in all games of chance. There was no part of her education she had neglected.

She played several games and lost.

She had expected to lose, and got out of the game all the sooner, just as she desired.

She asked a fellow to have a drink. The man was a low-bred, treacherous fellow, who had suffered a long run of bad luck, and who was very bitter in his feelings.

He had only been down from "up river" for a few weeks.

The two drank, when Kate, who well knew the character of her chosen chum, said, speaking of one of the men:

"Ben Searle had a narrow squeeze of it."

"Yes; he's always lucky in getting out of a tight place, while better men are always 'lifted.'"

Kate made remarks concerning several of the men present. Her object was to make the man she was talking to understand that she was "one of 'em."

At length she ventured to remark, pointing toward the man she had been shadowing:

"I don't know that 'daisy.' Who is he?"

"That fellow? He's a high toner; only goes in on heavy jobs. He's an eccentric, they say, but *immense!*"

"What's his name?"

"Randolph Cummings. He calls himself a high-toned name."

"Is he a regular?"

"Yes; he's over from England. He's a dead regular; been at it all his life, but queer."

"How do you mean 'queer'?"

"Well, I can't tell you exactly; but he's very high-toned, and they say the best 'jail-jumper' in the world—a regular, natural-born Jack Sheppard."

Kate made up her mind to "lay in" with Randolph Cummings, and take his full measure.

She made several attempts to get acquainted with him, but got the "dead shake" every time. She hung around until he left to go away.

She followed him and saw him enter a hotel, and on his way he was greeted in a pleasant manner by several men whom she knew to be respectable and honorable young fellows, belonging to most excellent families.

In her talk at the resort, the man who was telling her about Cummings made the remark that the latter did not appear among the boys very often. "He's a 'double.'"

Upon seeing the man enter the hotel and speak to several young men, she "tumbled," as the saying goes, to what was meant when Randolph Cummings was termed a "double."

Kate sauntered into the hotel and lay around for points.

She was handsomely dressed, and followed the man she was shadowing into the billiard-room, where she made a singular discovery, and the mystery deepened.

CHAPTER VI.

HER man played a game of billiards with one of the assistants in the room. He was an expert player, and had left the room, when she sought and quiet in his demeanor.

Kate waited until Cummings had finished his game and had left the room, when she sought the assistant to play a game.

After playing awhile Kate asked:

"Who was that young gentleman you were playing with?"

"Mr. Arthur Everdell."

"Does he live here?"

"Oh, yes; he has boarded in the house for over a year."

"What is his business?"

"He has no business. He's living on his money; and he's plenty of it and spends it like a lord."

"He has lived here over a year?"

"Yes."

Kate had tracked her man pretty well, but as far as all practical discoveries were concerned, she was as far off from a solution of the mystery as when she started in.

She went upstairs.

Arthur Everdell was not in sight. Kate felt that she could afford to lose sight of him for awhile. She wanted to go deeper into his antecedents and present rôle.

She played her cards well, and soon managed to get on speaking terms with one of the young men to whom she had seen Mr. Arthur Everdell speak.

It is an easy matter to get on speaking terms with a man in New York. Introductions are not always essential. You are measured first by your appearance; secondly, by your style and actions.

Kate had been talking some time with the young man, when, in an off-hand manner she asked:

"Are you acquainted with Everdell?"

"Yes; I know him well."

"What kind of a fellow is he?"

"Why do you ask?"

"He looks very much like a friend of mine."

"Well, if your friend is as good a fellow as Everdell, he's a splendid man. That's all I've got to say!"

"Everdell is a good fellow, eh?"

"One of the finest young fellows I ever met in all my life. Generous to a fault, brave as a lion, and true as steel!"

"You appear to think a good deal of him?"

"Well, I ought to. He saved my life once!"

"Saved your life?"

"Yes, saved my life at the risk of his own, and he'd do it again to-morrow for a friend."

The mystery deepened.

The man whom Kate had "piped" down as a burglar, a forger, and possible assassin, was leading a double life, and in one of his lives he was recognized as a man who was the soul of honor and the very pink of virtue and manly courage!

"Under what circumstances did he save your life?"

"We were out yachting. I fell overboard in a rough sea. Everdell came over after me and supported me in the water for half an hour, until the yacht could be brought around and a boat lowered."

"You would have drowned?"

"I would have drowned surely!"

"Mebbe he is an old sailor?"

"What! Everdell an old sailor! Why, he is connected with some of the best families down South. He is a rich man, and is recognized in the very best circles of New York society!"

Kate became thoughtful.

She had struck many big bonanzas in her professional career, but it appeared as though she had struck upon the best "lay" of all her life.

There had been a number of mysterious robberies perpetrated in New York, and the whole police force had been baffled.

It was discovered that the robberies took place in mansions just after some party or *fête* had been held.

Another mystery of the occurrences was the fact that the robbers only took money or expensive jewelry.

A young lady would dazzle the eyes of her friends at some grand party with her diamonds and jewels. She would return home, and the chances were that ere morning all her gems would be stolen.

The police had resorted to every device known to detective strategy, to catch the mysterious thieves, but in every instance had failed.

Kate had demonstrated Randolph Cummings and Arthur Everdell to be one and the same person. She had demonstrated to her own satisfaction that Cummings was a skillful and daring burglar; while Arthur Everdell—Cummings under another name—was a popular society man, and had an *entrée* into the best circles.

Kate thought that accident had opened up to her the mystery that had baffled all her male *confréres*.

There was something strangely mysterious about Randolph Cummings every way he turned.

Had Kate been able to demonstrate that the man was in disguise, she would have soon solved the enigma of the reflection; as it was, the incident at the mansion remained shrouded in the deepest of veiled secrets.

Lady Kate still indulged a suspicion that in some way she might yet demonstrate that Cummings was under a disguise.

There was no question as to the fact that he had been the man on the piazza at the Renton house; and the question only remained: had Kate really seen a resemblance in the reflection to the portrait, or had she been deceived by her own fancy?

As stated in a former paragraph, the clear-headed lady detective did not believe she had been deceived, and in her own mind she felt satisfied that she had come upon the greatest villain of the age, as well as the greatest monster.

The lady detective hung around the hotel, intending to spend the night shadowing the strange man.

She did shadow him, and ere morning encountered an incident that again deepened the mystery.

CHAPTER IX.

It was about nine o'clock when Arthur Everdell came forth from the hotel and sauntered down Broadway.

Kate trailed him to a well-known gambling-den.

She did not enter the faro-room, but waited outside.

Arthur Everdell had seen, had even given a sign, that he suspected he was being followed.

Kate had thrown him off the suspicion, but in her disguise she did not dare enter the place.

She did not have to wait long, however.

Arthur Everdell only remained in the faro-room about five minutes, when he came forth.

It was a pretty cold night. The strange criminal had just stepped from the lighted hall of the faro-rooms, when he was accosted by a miserably clad girl.

"Oh, sir," pleaded the girl, "can you help me?"

Kate was standing near by, and could see and overhear all that passed.

The young man stopped and gazed at the girl a moment, and then asked:

"Are you really in need?"

"I am cold, and starving!"

"Hang it, poor creature! I've just lost every cent I had. But wait here a moment; I may raise a few dollars for you."

Arthur Everdell re-entered the gambling-room.

Kate was greatly interested to see the result of the strange incident.

A few moments passed, and the young man returned.

He bore in his hands a heavy shawl, such as gentlemen sometimes wear.

"Here, girl," he said, "put this on, and here is five dollars I've scared up for you. Take it, and may Heaven bless you!"

The poor beggar received the money and the shawl, and was about to thank him, when he said:

"Go on, now; go home! I may meet you some time when I've more to give you. Don't bother me!"

The girl went on her way, and the young man marched off up the street.

Kate had lingered a few seconds, when a party of men came from the faro-room.

"Hang it, he didn't look like a thief!" said one.

"You can't tell thieves by their appearance in New York!" was the reply.

"Well, come, he can't be far off. We will find him, hang it! I'd send up a man who would steal a shawl such a night as this!"

"Good heavens!" ejaculated Kate. "He stole the shawl!"

The young men followed up the same direction that had been taken by Everdell, and they soon overtook him.

Kate was on hand to see and hear the fun.

One of the men accosted the thief with the remark:

"Hello, stranger, I want to talk with you a moment."

"All right! What have you got to say?"

"What is your name?"

"I forget."

"What is your business?"

"I haven't any."

"What did you do with the shawl you just nipped?"

"Ah, the shawl?"

"Yes, the shawl."

"I've no shawl."

"What did you do with it?"

"Did the shawl belong to you?"

"Yes."

"And you've lost it?"

"And you were seen to take it, Mister Man!"

"How much was the old thing worth?"

"No matter how much it was worth; you had no business to 'nip' it."

"Well, I did take the shawl."

"What did you do with it?"

"I gave it to a poor girl who was freezing to death."

"That is a nice story!"

"What else would I do with the old thing?"

"The old thing did not belong to you, and we are going to arrest you."

"I will pay for the shawl."

"That won't do; you had no business to take it."

"Well, the poor girl was freezing."

"That is no excuse for the robbery."

"But can't I pay for it?"

"No; come along to the station and explain."

"Don't put your hands on me!"

There were four of the young men—great, stalwart fellows.

"Eh? will you resist?"

"Don't put your hands on me, that's all! I'll pay for the shawl; here, take my watch for security."

"No; we will take you to the station."

"Not to-night."

The man placed his hand roughly on Everdell's shoulder, and the next moment he went sprawling into the street.

The man's three companions sprung upon the thief, and were all knocked down in a trice; indeed, dropped as though they had been so many wooden men.

They hallooed for the police, when the thief took to his heels and ran away.

Kate ran after him.

Everdell did not run far.

Kate was amazed.

The man had proved himself possessed of the most noble and generous impulse, and yet it was evident he possessed no principle.

It was a generous act, the giving of the shawl, and yet the shawl had been stolen.

Arthur Everdell had saved a man's life at the risk of his own. He had performed an act of noble charity, and yet he had proved himself a careless but valiant thief.

Before daylight Kate had another evidence of the eccentric character of the strange fellow.

Arthur Everdell was walking along the street, and Kate was following him, when a scream rang out on the night air.

Everdell ran in the direction whence the scream had emanated. He came upon a man and woman struggling together.

With an oath the forger and thief dashed forward to the rescue.

CHAPTER X.

Quick as a flash, he wrenched the girl from the man's grasp.

The character of the girl was apparent at a glance.

She was loudly, but magnificently dressed.

The man who had been interfered with turned on Everdell with an oath, and demanded:

"Hello! what business had you to interfere?"

"The girl called on me for help."

"Well, it's a quarrel of our own. You go off about your business, or you will get hurt!"

"The girl called on me for help!"

"Yes, I did," said the girl.

"Well, go on, sis."

"He will follow me."

"No, he won't follow you."

"Yes, I will," said the man.

"Not to-night," came the quiet response.

The girl moved away, and the man who had interfered with her sought to follow.

Everdell stepped before him.

"Hold on, old man, you stay here."

The man drew a pistol, but was disarmed in a trice.

"I'll call the police!" he said.

"Do so, and the girl will make a complaint against you!"

In the meantime the girl had gone off.

When she had disappeared from sight, Everdell walked away.

Kate had beheld another evidence of the thief and forger's good heart.

Everdell returned toward his hotel.

On the way he encountered a man who hailed him as Cummings.

"Hello, Ran!" said the man.

"Hello, Skipsy!"

"You're just the lad I wanted to meet, Ran."

"Well, what do you want?"

"I've gone dead broke."

"So am I."

"Haven't you got a fiver?"

"Not a cent."

"It's bad."

"Yes; but I'm in for a 'lift' next week, and if you can hold out until then I can drop you a few teners."

It was no use. Kate had tried to hope even against hope that some development would be forthcoming to pronounce that Arthur Everdell was not a thief; but, alas! the evidence against him was overwhelming.

She had heard him confess to one theft, and now she had seen him hailed by a low-bred knuck, to whom he had said:

'I'll make a 'lift' next week."

The term "lift" next week meant a contemplated robbery.

Arthur Everdell passed on to his hotel, where Kate dropped the "shadow" for the night.

She knew where she could find her man when she wanted him.

Lady Kate returned to her lodgings with a heavy heart.

As a detective, she had done a good night's work, but still she was exceedingly sad and unhappy.

Kate had seen a great deal of life, although she was but five-and-twenty. She had witnessed on every hand during her brief but eventful life, the cold selfishness of the world.

She had become hardened toward the human race, and now, alas! she had met a man who had given evidence of a grand generosity—a man possessed of a kind, good heart, a careless, indifferent fellow, who, as far as she could judge, had not a selfish hair in his head, and that man was a thief.

He had periled his life to save that of a friend. He had risked jail to cover the naked shoulders of a freezing girl, a poor, miserable beggar whom he had met by chance. He had faced a pistol and a ruffian to save a poor outcast woman from the clutches of a wretch, and he had promised to divide his anticipated "loot" with a common "knuck."

The four latter evidences of a good, generous heart had been furnished in one night, and the man was a thief.

It was a strange thing, and Kate Edwards trembled as she realized that in her inmost heart there burned a sympathy for the strange young man.

He had awakened an interest such as no other person ever had

It was an interest born of sympathy and admiration for the brighter side of its object's character.

The man had two strongly contrasting sides to his strange nature; one side was bright and grand, the other dark and ignoble.

He was generous and charitable, and was a thief, perchance a murderer.

Kate, the lady detective, retired to her couch that night to become the subject of strange dreams.

She saw herself, like an avenging angel, upon the track of Arthur Everdell. Her dream was vivid, specific, and finely drawn. She dreamed in detail how she gathered item after item of evidence pointing to Everdell as a murderer, how she finally closed in on him and arrested him.

She dreamed of the trial and conviction, the death sentence, and the man's calm and brave bearing during the whole ordeal.

She started with a smothered shriek when, after the sentence, the doomed man fixed his calm, handsome eyes upon her in a reproachful manner.

Her dream proceeded, and she came to witness the final scene. Her man was upon the gallows, the black cap was about to be drawn, when at that supreme moment there was a change come over his face, and she saw the same handsome countenance which had appeared to her so mysteriously as the reflection in the mirror at the Renton mansion.

With a scream Kate awoke, only to find she had been dreaming. But, alas! as she recovered from the shock, the conviction settled upon her mind that the horrid dream had been but a weird premonition of what was to occur. It was but the "shadow of coming events cast before."

She was upon the young man's track, and if she continued the pursuit the chances were she would, in the end, bring Arthur Everdell to the gallows.

CHAPTER XI.

THE dream left an unpleasant impression upon the handsome woman's mind, and as she strained her eyes in the darkness of the room, a chill shook her frame, and in her anguish of spirit she exclaimed:

"No, no; I'll not have his blood on my hands, though he may be a red-handed assassin!"

With the returning light of day came a sense of renewed devotion to duty, and she resolved to shadow the forger, burglar, and assassin to his doom.

One resolution was taken when trembling under the prostration succeeding a horrid dream in the darkness of the night. The other resolution was made in full brightness of the day.

In the morning Kate called upon Colonel Prang.

The man was calm and kindly as ever in his demeanor.

"Well," he said, "did you see the portrait yesterday?"

"I did."

"What do you think of the picture?"

"It is the face of a very handsome man."

"Yes; Balfour Raymond was a remarkably handsome man; and one of the most *generous* men who ever lived. It was his own sense of generosity that made the ungenerous remark of his wife sink so deep into his soul."

"And yet the man was a thief and a forger?" said Kate.

"He was a thief and a forger. He was a strange man. Let me tell you something about him. He was a soldier after he had separated from his wife, and he distinguished himself. In his regiment was a man who had insulted him in the grossest manner, and yet, later on, Balfour Raymond, at the risk of his own life, saved the life of his insulter!"

"Was he a man who would brook an insult?"

"No; but he had robbed the man who had insulted him, and, as stated, later on saved the man's life. Indeed, his whole career was a series of strange contradictions."

"You say *was?* Is he dead?"

"I do not know."

"When did you see him last?"

"Twenty years ago; but the picture is a good portrait."

"I saw a ghost while I was at the mansion!"

"You saw a ghost?" queried Colonel Prang.

"I suppose I must call it a ghost. You have been in the room where the portrait hangs?"

"Many times."

"You remember a mirror hangs upon the walls facing the windows opening upon the piazza?"

"I do."

"When I entered that room I flung open the windows to let in the light."

"Well?"

"I had gazed awhile at the portrait, when I chanced to turn and glance in the mirror."

"Well?"

"It was then I saw the ghost."

"I do not understand you."

"I saw a reflection in the glass of a human face—a living face."

"Some one in the garden, possibly."

"That is not the strangest part of the adventure."

"Indeed!"

"The reflected face was an exact counterpart of the face of the portrait hanging upon the wall."

"Bah! a mere freak of the imagination—a fancy," said Colonel Prang.

"I thought so; but I saw the face twice."

"Twice a fancy."

"I tried to argue so, but facts pointed to another conclusion."

"What facts?"

"I discovered fresh tracks on the piazza, the imprint of muddied feet."

"Well?"

"The man who stood there had come *after* I had flung open the windows: *was there when* I saw the reflected face in the mirror!"

"This is a strange story!"

"It is a true tale."

"Did you not investigate?"

"I did."

"With what result?"

"I discovered a man on the grounds."

"And did his face resemble the portrait?"

Colonel Prang showed signs of deep agitation when he asked the question.

"His face did not resemble the face of the portrait."

"Then it must have been a fancy."

"Listen. I demonstrated that the man whom I met in the grounds was the same man who had been upon the piazza."

"Then the resemblance must have been a fancy!"

"I tried to think so, but I am compelled to conclude differently."

"This is indeed a strange incident."

"I have more to tell. I tracked the man whom I had seen upon the grounds."

"Did you discover who he was?"

"I learned that he was a notorious burglar."

"Oh, heavens!"

"Mark the strange phases of the mystery," said Kate.

"The man was at the Raymond mansion. Now, then, mark particularly that the man is a burglar, and the reflected face in the glass was the resemblance of the only man on earth who would have a motive in murdering Mrs. Raymond!"

"This is terrible!" ejaculated Colonel Prang.

"It is terrible, but it is true! There is but one link missing."

"What link?"

"I must establish the identity between the real and the reflected face."

"And do you hope to do so?"

"I do."

"I trust you will fail."

"Why?"

"It would be too terrible to learn that young Balfour Raymond was the murderer of his own mother!"

"I fear the establishment of that fact will be the result of my investigations."

"I would like to see the young man whom you met upon the grounds."

"You shall see him."

"When?"

"If possible, this very night."

CHAPTER XII.

THAT same night Colonel Prang and Kate, the lady detective, met by appointment.

Kate was disguised as upon the previous night, in male attire.

Kate had promised to show to Colonel Prang the face of Arthur Everdell.

They were at the hotel where the young man boarded.

The young man did not put in an appearance. Kate did not dare go to the office and inquire for him.

An hour passed, and Everdell came not.

"We will take a stroll and may come across him," said Kate.

They started for the door, and in the brightly lighted hall met Everdell coming in.

They met him squarely face to face.

The detective did not say a word.

She did not exclaim, "There he is!" She waited to learn if Colonel Prang would recognize the young man.

The colonel gave no sign.

They walked to the door, when Kate said:

"You have not seen any one who reminded you of Balfour Raymond?"

"No."

"You have seen Everdell."

"The man whom you met at the mansion?"

"The same."

"Where did he go?"

"Inside."

"Come, I will look at him."

Everdell was in the reading-room.

Colonel Prang took a seat near him. Kate remained in the background.

Colonel Prang sat for a long time studying Everdell's features, but at length he joined Kate.

The two walked away, when Colonel Prang exclaimed:

"It is strange! it is mysterious!"

"What do you think of him?"

"He does not look like Balfour Raymond as I remember the man; but he has a manner, a cold, steady gleam in his eyes that is Balfour Raymond to the life!"

"I am going to the bottom of the mystery," said Kate.

"Oh, heavens! woman, haul off the scent!"

"What do you mean?"

"Go no further."

"Why?"

"A great fear has taken possession of me."

"What fear?"

"That you may bring Balfour Raymond's *son to the gallows!*"

"If he is a murderer he should hang!"

"No."

"Sir! what has come over you, that you speak in the manner you do?"

"I will tell you. If young Balfour Raymond is a thief, a forger, and an assassin, he is the victim of a maniac!"

"You use strange words!"

"I will explain. If the young man is what I have declared, he was deliberately trained to it by a father seeking revenge in a wild spirit of maniacism."

"We have no proof that Everdell is the son of Balfour Raymond?"

"I do not believe he is. I have not any idea that he is. But if there is the remotest possibility that he may be, I pray you cease the pursuit."

"I have my duty to perform."

"You are a private detective."

"But my duty remains, all the same."

"Well, well, go on. But I hope and pray that you have been deceived."

Kate bid Colonel Prang good-night.

The colonel went to his home; the lady detective returned toward the reading-room.

At the door she met Everdell face to face.

The young man said:

"Good-evening."

Kate was taken all aback.

"I think I have seen you before," said Everdell.

Kate remained mute.

"I saw you last night. I believe you are following me. Now, what do you want?"

"I am following you."

"That is frank. Why are you following me?"

"Simply because you happen to be going in the same direction as myself when we meet."

"That is a cunning answer, not a frank one. Come, I want to have a little talk with you."

"Where would you go?"

"To my room."

"I will go."

The two proceeded up the stairs, and a moment later Kate was ushered into a handsomely furnished apartment.

The moment the door was closed she received a dash that completely upset her for a moment.

"Now, then, Sis," said Everdell, in a perfectly cool tone, "why are you on my track?"

"Oh, God!" thought Kate, "I am unmasked! This man has penetrated my disguise—discerned my sex!"

She was at a disadvantage, and made to get out of the scrape.

"If you have brought me here to insult me, I will leave your presence!"

"Oh, I will not insult you. And, as I remember, you and I have met before."

"You must be mistaken, unless you mean we met last night."

"We met before last night."

"Where?"

"On the grounds of the Raymond mansion."

Kate was taken all aback.

"Miss, will you tell me why you are shadowing me?"

Kate was completely beat.

"Yes, I will tell you why I am shadowing you."

"Do so."

"I am shadowing you because I saw you up at the Raymond mansion."

"A poor reason."

"There was a murder committed there, and I am looking for the murderer!"

The young man laughed, and then assuming a stern look, said:

"I had nothing to do with the murder of that old woman! Mark me, I swear it! So do not follow me any more, or you may come to some bad end."

CHAPTER XIII.

As the young man spoke, there was a gleam in his eye that intimated that he meant just what he said.

"You may go now, *young man!* I have warned you! now beware and do not dip too deeply into my affairs!"

Kate sneaked out of the room fairly beaten.

The mystery was deeper than ever.

How on earth that strange young man had penetrated her disguise, how he had identified her as the lady he had met on the Raymond grounds, was a problem that passed her power of solution.

She was a chop fallen lady detective as she left that hotel and passed out into the street.

There was one fact that consoled her—the game was not altogether out of her hands.

She had been under a close disguise when she had visited the Raymond mansion.

She had changed her complexion, had worn false hair, and in various ways had put herself under close cover.

He had recognized her as the young lady of the mansion grounds. He had identified her in the young man about town, but he had not yet fully identified her in her real character and appearance.

Kate changed her disguise and kept upon the young man's track.

She kept out of his sight, however. She trailed his movements more particularly, and laid in with his associates.

While in company with one of Everdell's friends, Kate learned a fact which she determined to utilize.

She was in company with the young man who had first told her of Everdell.

"Are you going to the masquerade?" asked the young man.

"What masquerade?"

"At the Dennisons."

"When does it come off?"

"To-morrow night."

"Who is going?"

"Oh, almost everybody."

"Does your friend Everdell go?"

"Oh, yes; you bet. He will be on hand."

Kate went to her home shortly after receiving the above information."

The crisis had come. If Everdell were going to the masquerade, he was going for purposes of robbery.

It is recorded in the Bible, in the book of Job, that thieves prowl around in the daytime to spot the houses they intend to rob at night.

We may not quote the exact language, but the direct intent of the declaration is indicated.

As it was in the old days, it is now: human nature—and especially thief nature—is the same.

Kate determined to set a trap for her man. She determined to set herself as a bait to tempt him to his ruin or capture; the latter meant ruin to the thief.

It was a sense of duty that urged her forward.

Despite all her knowledge of the dark side of the character of Everdell, she still felt a keen interest in him—a strange, weird interest, which she could not permit to defend itself in her mind.

She visited Colonel Prang.

"You are acquainted with the Dennisons?" she said.

"I am."

"There is to be a grand party at their house?"

"Yes."

"I wish to switch off from my late duty and follow up an old clew."

Kate was purposely misleading the colonel.

"What do you want to do?"

"You know there have been a great many mysterious robberies lately?"

"I do."

"I think I have a clew to the perpetrators."

Colonel Prang fixed his eyes upon the lady detective.

"It is an old gang of burglars I am trailing."

What she asserted was in one sense true.

"What can I do for you?"

"You can aid me."

"How?"

"In the first place, you can procure me an invitation to the ball."

"I can."

"Will you do more? I wish to sleep in that house after the ball is over."

"That is a strange request."

"Great results may follow."

"I will give you a letter to Mr. Dennison. He is my friend."

"Please do."

Kate received the letter, and went to call upon Mr. Dennison.

After presenting her credentials, she opened the conversation in a very abrupt manner.

"I think, sir, your house is about to be robbed!"

"My house robbed?"

"Yes, sir."

"By whom?"

"Thieves!"

"Ah! yes; I did not suppose by honest people; but I mean what thief or thieves?"

"That we are to find out."

"Colonel Prang in his letter informs me you are a detective."

"I am."

"And what is your idea?"

"You will remember that some strange robberies have occurred lately, and usually these robberies have happened in houses where a great *fête* has just been held."

"You are right."

"I have an idea that it may be attempted at your house."

"And what can you, a weak woman, accomplish?"

"I have done some good work in my time."

"Oh, yes; fine detective work, but what could you accomplish against a band of masked robbers?"

"I can prevent a robbery."

"You must be a very bold woman!"

"I have had experience."

"So I should believe; well, now, what do you wish me to do?"

"I wish an invitation to the ball, and after the ball I wish to remain at your house all night."

CHAPTER XIV.

Mr. Dennison was thoughtful a moment, but at length he said:

"How do I know that you are not in league with the robbers? Yours is certainly a strange request."

"You have Colonel Prang's letter?"

"Yes."

"Does he not vouch for me?"

"He does."

"Is not that sufficient?"

"Yes."

"Can I come?"

"You can."

"And remain all night?"

"Yes; under what name will you be announced?"

"I must not be announced, but I will assume the *rôle* of your daughter or niece."

"My niece will do."

Kate arranged all the details of her intended game with Mr. Dennison, and returned to her home.

It was yet early in the day, and she set to trail her man awhile.

She got herself up as a mendicant.

In assuming the disguise she had only had an idea to a perfect concealment of her identity; but as the matter turned out she met with a strange adventure.

She was in the vicinity of the hotel, when she saw Everdell coming from the building. She started to cross the street, when suddenly all was confusion; she only knew that there was a rush, a clatter, and she had been seized in somebody's arms, and the next moment there was a crowd.

A policeman was holding on to Kate.

The girl had been momentarily stunned and dazed, but recovering her senses, she asked:

"What has happened?"

"You good-for-nothing careless thing!" said the policeman. "You came as near being killed as you ever will again in all your life!"

"How was it?"

"You came near being run over by a runaway team!"

Kate had been so intent in thought on the subject matter of her whole scheme, that she had been too absorbed to notice a runaway team,

until the madly rushing horses were close upon her.

A young man had seen her danger; at the risk of his own life he had dashed forward and had snatched her from death.

The rescuer had saved the girl, but had not himself escaped.

The crowd were gathered around the man.

He had been knocked down by one of the horses.

Kate worked her way through the crowd, and her glance rested upon her rescuer's face just as he recovered consciousness.

Her life had been saved by the man whom she was tracking to the gallows!

Arthur Everdell had seen the danger of the poor mendicant and had run forward, the heroic rescuer.

As it turned out, he was not seriously injured; the rescued and the rescuer had met with a very narrow escape.

In a few moments Arthur was on his feet, and the crowd which had gathered dispersed.

Kate had been ordered away by the policeman, who finally seized hold of her to take her to the station-house as a vagrant.

Once more the young man came to the rescue.

"Hold on, officer," he said; "do not molest the poor girl; she had a narrow escape, and she has committed no crime!"

"It's against the law to beg."

"No one has seen the poor girl begging;" and stepping beside Kate, Arthur said: "Come along, sis, you shall not be arrested."

The policeman marched off, and Arthur walked away with Kate.

The latter was trembling like an aspen leaf.

There were many reasons why she should tremble.

The peril she had escaped was enough to unnerve her, but it was not the escaped peril that was the real cause of her agitation. Her trembling came of the knowledge that her life had been saved by the man she was shadowing to prison, and possibly to death!

Again Kate feared lest the keen-sighted young man might penetrate her disguise and recognize her.

"Well, girl, you had a narrow squeak of it!"

"I did."

"Poor creature! I am glad I saved you, and I wish to be able to help you."

"Help me?"

"Yes."

"How?"

"Oh, give you some money.'

"I have not asked for money."

"No; but you need it all the same."

"I never asked for alms in my life."

"Excuse me, I thought you were a beggar, and you are only poor."

"And it was a beggar's life you thought you were saving?"

"Yes; and I really wish I could give you some money, whether you are a beggar or not."

"But I have not asked for money!"

"Still I tell you that you need money; and now look here, you come to this corner day after to-morrow, and I will give you a heap of money!"

"Why should you give me money?"

"Because you are poor!"

"But you are poor?"

"Yes; poor to-day, rich to-morrow; comes easy, goes easy. I say, girl, I give away lots of money. You may as well come and get a share."

"When shall I come?"

"Day after to-morrow."

"Why shall I not come to-morrow?"

"Well, you may."

"Suppose you are not here?'

"If I am not here, girl, you may make up your mind that I need your sympathy more than you do mine."

"To-morrow night I will be here!"

"All right, and I'll have something for you any how, come what may!"

Poor Kate! What should she do?

CHAPTER XV

THE lady detective walked away, after parting from Arthur Everdell, completely dazed.

She was in the greatest dilemma of her whole life; indeed, her position was the strangest that could be occupied by a person in her vocation.

She was the bitter, relentless Nemesis and shadow of the man to whom she owed her life.

The circumstances under which her life had been saved were remarkable.

At the moment the peril came upon her she

was, to all appearances a poor, miserable mendicant; no rich young lady in satins and silks, but a poor, miserable beggar.

The man who would peril his life to save such as she must have a noble and generous heart.

And then she was compelled to remember the goodness that was displayed afterward; no bitterness of feeling because of the peril he had encountered in her behalf, but pure sympathy for her in her poverty.

"I can not run that man down!" murmured Kate Edwards. "I can not bring him to jail! and oh! what shall I do if I prove him a murderer?"

The girl remembered Arthur Everdell's words:

"If you are shadowing me because of the murder, I tell you I am guiltless; there is no blood on my hands!"

Kate hoped that he was innocent, and although he was undoubtedly a criminal, she thought it impossible that a man who was so generous could really be an assassin.

Kate had earned a great deal of money, and her peculiar profession had given her rare opportunities to purchase some rare gems.

She owned some elegant diamonds of her own, and she borrowed some from the wife of a man who had once been a noted detective.

She had not given over her determination to trail Arthur Everdell, but her motive was changed. She did not mean to run him to jail, but if possible acquire an influence over him and save him.

It was a strange resolution for a detective to take.

We are relating a strange narrative however. If it were not so, there would be nothing worth recording.

They are the strange and wonderful experiences that we select as the foundations for our tales.

Hundreds of strange incidents are occurring to-day right around, and the daily papers teem with veritable facts, almost too incredible for belief.

Kate went to her home and prepared herself for the grand *bal masque*.

She decided upon the character of the Goddess of Night, and the real diamonds which she wore on her dark robes, made her appear like a veritable Goddess come down from the starry realms.

The lady detective had put aside all her disguises and appeared in her real character.

For the occasion the latter was the best disguise she could assume, as it was only upon rare occasions that she was not in some sort of disguise.

She went without escort to the *bal masque*.

She arrived before the appointed hour, according to agreement, so as to make it appear that she was an inmate of the house.

Her room had been assigned to her, and in her jewel-case, to guard against all accidents, she placed false gems.

The company in due time arrived, and the lady detective was put to her wits' ends to identify Arthur Everdell.

At length she was asked to dance by a man dressed as an Italian brigand.

Kate was a splendid dancer, and found herself whirling around with the most graceful partner who had ever waltzed her across a floor.

When the dance was over, the man led her to a seat and stood over her, when she made the remark which called forth the exclamation with which we open our narrative:

"If I thought you were in earnest, I'd tear that mask from your face!"

As stated, the lady had answered with a merry laugh, but away down in her heart there was sorrow and sadness.

Lady Kate had found Arthur Everdell.

"How you do take a bantering remark!" said Kate. "Why," she added, "I am almost inclined now to believe that you are a burglar!"

"Can it be possible that I can discern who you are?"

"I think not, sir; you and I never met before!"

"And yet it is strange you should have used those words."

"It is stranger, sir, that you should take them so much to heart!"

"I beg pardon. I care not for the words, it was the *tone* and *manner* in which they were uttered!"

"Are you a burglar?"

"You may think I am."

"Why should I think you were?"

"I believe you have recognized me."

"What would come of a recognition?"

"I will tell you. I once entered upon the private grounds of a house that had been recently robbed. I met a queer sort of a young lady while on those grounds, and I really believe that the same queer young lady has run away with the idea that I was one of the masked burglars."

"How funny!" said Kate.

"Do you think it funny?"

"Yes."

"Why, then, have *you* made such a serious matter of it?"

"I do not understand you, sir!"

"You do not understand me?"

"I do not."

"Shall I speak plainly?"

"Yes."

CHAPTER XVI.

THE young man was silent a moment, but at length he repeated:

"Do you really wish me to speak plainly?"

"I do."

"I will."

"Well?"

"I believe you are the queer young lady whom I met that day."

Kate laughed again, and said:

"Indeed, it is very funny!"

"What is funny now?"

"That you should think I was the young lady!"

"Who are you?"

"I reside in this house. I am *known* as the niece of Mr. Dennison."

"I do not care who you may be! I still think you are the young lady I met!"

"Indeed. I must repeat that it is very funny, very funny, indeed; would you know the young lady?"

"I would."

"You are sure you would know her?"

"I am sure."

"I've a great mind to let you see what an egregious mistake you have made: but I prefer for awhile to let you think I am the young lady. It has a spice of romance about it, and may be you are a burglar!"

"You are very facetious!"

"Indeed! But you have shown such a strange sensitiveness to an idle remark."

"I have told you why I have shown such a sensitiveness."

"I do not consider your reason sufficient."

"What would you imply?"

"Nothing."

"You are seeking to tease a stranger."

"You are not compelled to remain and be teased."

"I rather like it."

"Do you?"

"I do."

"And you were really mistaken for a burglar?"

"I think I was."

"And you were innocent?"

"Miss!" ejaculated the young man.

The lady merely laughed.

"How droll it all is!" she said.

"Will you do me a kindness?" asked Arthur.

"What kindness can I do? Withdraw my charge, and proclaim that you are not a fierce burglar?"

"You are incorrigible!"

"Am I?"

"You are."

"Well, what kindness will you ask?"

"I wish to see your saucy face."

"Would you consider the granting of your request a kindness?"

"I would."

"Turn about is but fair play."

"Even so."

"If I raise my mask, will you raise yours?"

"Why should I raise mine?"

"I want to see if you are the man I met in the grounds upon that eventful day."

"Ah! do you admit that you are the young lady?"

"No."

"Then why do you say that you wish to learn if you can recognize me?"

"You appear so positive that I am the lady I may be mistaken, and a sight of your face may recall the incident of the meeting to my mind."

"You are in a merry and quizzical mood."

"I am."

"Shall I see your face?"

"Certainly, if the courtesy can be reciprocal."

"It shall."

"On your word of honor?"

"Yes; on my word of honor."

"We will walk into the conservatory—lend me your arm!"

It was a strange experience for the great lady detective to be promenading on the arm of such a man.

They reached the conservatory, when Kate said:

"Well, this is a rare adventure."

Her companion had become quite merry, and answered:

"A tragedy, a comedy, and a farce all in one night!"

"Where does the tragedy come in?"

"It will come at the last, may be."

"Well, you are a strange sort of man; but listen; suppose you discover that you have made a mistake, and have given your confidence to a stranger?"

"I can not recall what I have said."

"Who will unmask first?"

"You shall."

Kate raised her mask and showed her truly beautiful face.

As the real Kate Edwards, she did not at all resemble the lady detective.

Her strange companion gazed at her a moment, a look of surprise upon his countenance was betrayed by his attitude, although it could not be seen upon his mask-covered face.

"Well," demanded Kate, "am I the wonderful lady of the castle grounds?"

"You are not."

"Oh, pshaw! I am so disappointed!"

"Disappointed?"

"Yes."

"Why?"

"I did hope that you would recall to my mind that we had met before."

"Why do you wish we had met before?"

"You are such a strange, romantic, sensitive young man."

"I should say *you* were a strange, romantic girl."

"You have seen my face."

"Yes, thank you."

"You are convinced you never saw it before?"

"I am."

"I am not the lady you met, you are sure?"

"I am."

"Now let me see your face."

"Will you not release me from my promise?"

"Why would you be released?"

"It will be so piquant to carry on the little mystery awhile."

"I must demand that you remove your mask!"

The young man did so, and Kate involuntarily uttered a low, suppressed scream of amazement.

CHAPTER XVII.

THE young man stood calmly before her, but it was evident that he was undergoing intense inward excitement.

"Are you acting?" he asked.

Kate laughed.

She had recovered command of herself, and she answered:

"Certainly."

"I do not believe it."

"What do you believe?"

"I believe that you have seen my face before."

"Never!"

The young man had resumed his mask.

"You think I have seen your face before?"

"I do."

"I never did."

"Then why were you so surprised and agitated when I first removed my mask?"

"I thought you were a ghost!"

"A ghost?"

"Yes."

Kate spoke in a perfectly natural and really girlish manner.

"Why did you think I was a ghost?"

"I can not tell."

"You must have had some reason."

"Let me see your face again."

The young man removed his mask.

"I know now!" cried Kate, quickly.

"You know what?"

"Why I thought when I saw your face I had seen a ghost!"

"Will you tell me why?"

"Certainly."

"Do so."

"You resemble the portrait of a man who has been dead a great many years—a hundred, for all I know!"

"Where did you see the portrait?"

"I once paid a visit to an old country mansion."

"Where?"

Kate named the Raymond house.

"And you saw a portrait there that I resemble?"

"I did."

"It's strange!"

"What is strange?"

"That I should resemble a man who has been dead a hundred years."

"It is strange. What is your name?"

"Arthur Everdell."

"That is your real name?"

"Certainly. What reason would I have for concealing my name?"

"I do not know."

"Shall we return and dance?"

"Yes."

Kate had made a wonderful discovery.

When Arthur Everdell had removed his mask he had revealed the same face she had seen reflected in the mirror at the Raymond mansion.

The mystery deepened.

How had the young man so changed his appearance? and why, when he was out on a burglarious errand, did he appear as Balfour Raymond?

Kate had assumed that he was upon a burglarious errand, and yet she had no proof that the young man really intended to steal.

They returned and danced, and afterward Kate's hand was claimed by another partner.

She saw the brigand no more during the continuance of the party.

She did not know whether he had left the house, or whether he remained. He did not come to look for her, she did not go to look for him.

Lady Kate had much food for thought.

The resemblance was established; the identity of Arthur Everdell and Randolph Cummings as the men who bore the resemblance was established; and now the question arose, was it an accidental resemblance? or was the burglar really Balfour Raymond?

If it was Balfour Raymond, circumstances pointed to him as the assassin. If he were the assassin, Kate had a duty to perform, and her horrid dream was called to her remembrance.

Here was another mystery.

Did the young man know of his relationship? If he had committed the murder, the chances were that he did; and if he did he held the will; and if he did hold the will he must know that he was the sole heir to the magnificent estate. If he knew that he was the heir, why did he not claim the estate?

Alas! in the latter fact lay the most convincing proof that Arthur Everdell was a cruel assassin.

As the murderer he did not dare claim the property, lest there might follow a renewed investigation into the circumstances of Mrs. Balfour Raymond's death.

Kate's reflections brought nothing but the keenest anguish to her soul.

She, of all the world, knew the identity of the true heir. She, of all the world, knew the identity of the cruel murderer, and the assassin was the savior of her life!

To perform her duty and denounce him, she would be compelled to hang the man who had imperiled his own life to save hers, and in daring the peril he had only been actuated by the most disinterested of motives.

"What shall I do—what shall I do?" was the thought that pierced her soul like a flame of living fire.

Mr. Dennison knew Kate's disguise, and late in the evening, just before the unmasking was to take place, he came to her and whispered:

"What have you discovered?"

"I fear my suspicions were true?"

"Is there a burglar among my guests?"

"I can not tell you now."

"Why not?"

"It is but a suspicion."

"Then why not send for the police and have the suspected party arrested?"

"And create an unnecessary scandal?"

"But we must not permit ourselves to be robbed!"

"You will not be robbed."

"How do you know?"

"The burglar has been frightened off."

"You should not have permitted him to escape."

"You forget I had no proofs; we can not arrest a man on an idea."

Poor Kate! ere morning dawned she almost wished she had made an arrest on suspicion.

CHAPTER XVIII.

ARTHUR EVERDELL had said, in a bantering tone, "The tragedy will come last," and it appeared as though his strange words were to be verified.

Kate retired to her room, and for a long time lay awake thinking over the strange incidents of the night.

In all her life she had never heard of a stranger mystery than the one in which she found herself involved.

She had come to the masked ball intending to bait a thief, but upon retiring to her room she gave up all idea that her little game would prove successful.

The lady detective fell into a doze. She had remained awake watching, but at length she dropped off into a light sleep.

Kate had not disrobed in going to bed, but had merely unloosed her hair as a blind, and had drawn a coverlet over her.

She had calculated, at the proper moment, to spring from her couch and confront the burglar, and was fully prepared for her experiment.

The time sped by, however, and no burglar came.

"Oh, Heaven!" involuntarily ejaculated Kate, "I would that proof would come that he were, after all, a true and honorable man!"

The wild longing wish betrayed to the beautiful woman herself how deep an interest she had taken in Arthur Everdell.

At length Lady Kate fell off into a doze.

She was awakened by a strange, oppressive feeling, and when she first unclosed her eyes, and before she was fully aroused, she believed that she had been the victim of some oppressive dream, but in an instant that impression was removed, and she awoke to the dreadful consciousness that the burglar and assassin was in the room.

The man had placed a bull's-eye light so that its sharp piercing ray was shed upon the dressing bureau.

Kate opened her eyes and gazed.

The figure of the burglar was fully revealed, and she recognized the form of the man with whom she had held the strange dialogue in the conservatory.

Terrible was the anguish and deep agony that filled her soul.

All hope had been banished from her heart.

The wretch stood before the glass, his back toward the bed.

Kate could just dimly discover his reflection in the mirror and saw that he wore a mask.

She was a brave woman, and made a movement to rise from the bed, but at the instant discovered that the burglar was turning round.

She settled back upon her pillow.

She knew that she had lost an advantage, but could not resist the desire to brave all chances and see what the man would do.

She feigned sleep, but kept her eyelids sufficiently parted to faintly perceive his movements.

The man turned toward the bed.

On tiptoe he crossed the room.

The brave woman lay like a person soundly sleeping.

The burglar came and stood over her. She was conscious that his face was bent down over her own.

Quick as a flash she reached forth a hand, tore aside his mask.

She felt herself equal to the occasion, though she was but a woman.

"Foolish man," she said, "what brought you here?"

"You are not frightened?"

"No."

"Yet, your life is at my mercy."

"You would not kill me!"

"You are cool."

"I am."

"Why should I spare you?"

"Why should you kill me?"

"If I spare your life I am at your mercy!"

"How so?"

"You have recognized me."

"I have."

"You could identify me?"

"I can. What brought you here?"

"I came for your jewels."

"You are a thief!"

"I am."

"You are frank."

The man laughed and answered:

"Why should I be otherwise? I am in your room at this hour. I am masked. I hold a dagger to your fair throat. Why should I deny that I was a thief?"

"I had hoped you were not."

Again the man laughed in a strange, weird manner, and said:

"I have been a thief all my life! I was born a thief!"

"Would to Heaven that one so generous, and so handsome and brilliant, were not a thief!"

"How is it you know anything about me?"

"I will tell you."

"Do."

"I recognize you as the guest of this house, as Mr. Arthur Everdell!"

A deep agitation was betrayed in the man's voice as, in a low, deep tone, he answered:

"You lie!"

Kate, on the instant, remembered that, to a certain extent, she had given her secret away. It was not the face of Arthur Everdell that had been revealed to her in the conservatory.

Kate laughed, as she added:

"I know now why you were so sensitive when I said your actions comported with your assumed character."

"You recognize me as your partner in the dance?"

"I do."

"And you call me Everdell?"

"Yes."

"Will you tell me why you call me Everdell?"

CHAPTER XIX.

KATE did not lose voice or courage as she answered:

"Certainly I will."

"Do."

"I had danced with you."

"Yes."

"A gentleman came to me afterward and asked me if I had recognized my partner. I replied he was a stranger, when the gentleman said: 'I will give you a little advantage. Your partner is Arthur Everdell, one of the handsomest and most brilliant men in New York.' You did not come to me again after our talk in the conservatory, and I had no opportunity of letting you know that I had been informed as to your identity."

The explanation was a natural and plausible one.

Arthur Everdell was led astray.

"You will denounce me!" he said.

"Certainly."

"Dare you tell me so?"

"Why not?"

"You hold me in your power."

"I do."

"You admit it?"

"Yes."

"But mark you, your life is at my mercy. I can not afford to let you live to denounce me."

"I am not afraid."

"Not afraid?"

"I am not."

"On what do you rest your assurance of safety?"

"Although you are a thief and burglar, you would not murder a helpless woman—not even to save your own life and liberty."

"You must swear, then, not to betray me."

"I will not swear."

"Then you are your own executioner. I offer you your life; you refuse to accept it."

"I dare you to kill me! I trust myself to your own manhood."

"Do you look for honor and manhood in a thief?"

"Not honor, but manhood; you are too generous a man to murder a helpless woman."

"You are a strange woman!"

"Am I?"

"You are. Most women under the circumstances, would plead and beg for their lives, and promise anything."

"I reckon I am not like other women."

"I will spare your life. You trust my mercy; I will trust your generosity. I came here to take your jewels; your life and property are both at my mercy. I go away empty-handed."

The young man turned as though to go away, when Kate said:

"Hold! you must not trust my generosity."

"And you will denounce me?"

"A sense of duty checks any leaning toward generosity. If I were generous to you I would be cruel to others."

"How so?"

"Duty compels me to avail myself of my discovery to bring the career of a criminal to a close."

"I repeat, you are a strange girl!"

"And I charge that you are a stranger man!"

"What is there strange about me?"

"You were born with splendid abilities; you could make a success in an honorable calling, and you have chosen the infamous career of a thief."

"Ah, you do not know my history!"

"Tell me your story."

"No. I have not a moment to spare; I must go."

"Listen," cried Kate, as an idea struck her. "I will promise not to denounce you until I have heard your story."

"We may never meet again!"

"But we can meet again."

"What do you mean?"

"I can arrange an appointment with you.'

"You arrange an appointment with me?"

"Yes."

"Never!"

"Why not?"

"You are a cunning woman!"

"What do you suspect?"

"You would arrange a meeting with me, but it would be but a trick to hand me over to the police. No, no; it is a clever game, but not to-night, some other time, ta, ta!"

The burglar had dropped his solemn tone, and spoke in a light, frivolous and sneering manner.

"I would not betray you in that way. I would not take advantage of your confidence to betray you!"

"Why should I believe you?"

"My previous frankness should win your confidence. I refused to promise not to betray you while you held your dagger at my throat; now I do promise."

"What do you promise?"

"I promise not to denounce you until after I have heard your story."

"And you, a high-born, cultured young lady, would make an appointment to meet a low, vulgar thief?"

"I will meet you!"

"You must have some motive?"

"I have a motive."

"What is your motive?"

"You are young."

"I am not old."

"You are talented."

"Thank you."

"The greater part of your life, in all probability, remains to be lived."

"Possibly so."

"I would save you."

"Save me?"

"Yes."

"How save me?"

"Save you from a criminal career; bring you to a condition of mind to resolve to live a nobler life!"

The man laughed a laugh that caused Kate's blood to run cold round her heart.

In all her life she had never heard a laugh so expressive of bitterness, scorn, and sarcasm.

"Your labor would be lost!"

"But let me try."

"And you would really meet me?"

"Yes."

"Arrange a tryst with a thief?"

"I would."

"I will never give you the opportunity."

"You will! you shall!"

CHAPTER XX.

KATE spoke in a determined tone, as she exclaimed: "You will! you shall!" and again the burglar uttered that soul-piercing laugh of bitter irony.

"Are you afraid to meet a young lady?"

"No; but I will not permit you to meet a burglar."

"You forget."

"What do I forget?"

"You have two characters."

"How do you know?" demanded the young man, in a quick tone.

"You have supported two characters in this house since sundown. I have seen you in both. I danced with a burglar, but I did not know who my partner was."

The young man made no reply.

"You can meet me as a gentleman. I will know you are a thief; no one else will."

The man winced when Kate, in so matter-of-fact a manner, said:

"I will know you are a thief!"

The burglar exclaimed involuntarily:

"I was never before ashamed to hear myself called a thief!"

"Then there is hope for you!"

"Hope for me?"

"Yes."

Again came that strange, weird, bitter laugh.

"There is no hope for me!"

"Will you meet me?"

"When?"

"To-morrow night."

"Where?"

"Anywhere you may name."

"I will meet you."

"At what hour?"

"Eight o'clock."

"Where?"

"On the street."

The burglar named a locality.

"You will not fail me?"

"I will not."

"Then go!"

At that moment the door of the bedroom opened.

The burglar had closed the door upon stealing into the room.

The light in the hall was at full blaze. A man stood across the threshold.

"Aha! you scoundrel!" he exclaimed. "I've run you down at last!"

The man leaped across the room.

Kate sprung up in bed with a shriek. For the moment she was a woman; a tragedy was imminent. She sat spell-bound. Having uttered the one shriek, she was powerless to move or speak.

There followed a struggle in the room, and in a moment the armed officer was disarmed and borne to the floor. The burglar had him at his mercy.

Kate would have spoken, but could not. Her tongue cleaved to the roof of her mouth, and a strange and remarkable incident followed.

Oh, that Kate could speak! but horror held her silent and rigid.

Suddenly the burglar in low tones muttered, speaking to himself:

"No, no; oh, God! I've never yet stained my hands!"

He sprung to his feet and darted away.

The detective, for such he subsequently proved to be, also sprung to his feet, and drawing another pistol, he aimed it at the form of the retreating burglar.

Still Kate remained spell-bound and speechless; she knew that the quality of mercy was not to be exercised by an officer in the discharge of his duty. Then came a flash and report, and Kate fell over and covered her face with the bed-quilt.

Report followed report; then all was still.

Kate felt thrice guilty.

She had screened a burglar. She had failed to save the life of the man who risked his life to save hers.

A moment later, and she rose from the bed and turned on the gas.

She heard voices in the lower hall, but dared not go and view the sight.

Ten minutes passed.

To the lady detective those ten minutes were so many hours. Then she heard steps on the stairs, and as she stood motionless and pale upon the center of the floor, she saw the detective coming through the hall toward the room.

The agony of that moment ever remained to her a terrible remembrance.

She felt that she was to be upbraided, but she cared not. She felt that she had failed in her duty.

The detective came into the room with the exclamation:

"Well, Lady Kate, I arrived just in time to save your life!"

An inward feeling of relief ran over Kate.

"Did you kill him?" she asked.

"I don't know. He got away, but I winged him."

"And he got away?"

"Yes; but, Kate, he had you dead, eh?"

The beautiful Lady Kate was quick enough to perceive that some strange chance had conveyed a certain impression to the detective and she answered:

"Yes, he held a dagger to my throat."

"If I'd been a moment later, Kate, you'd been a goner!"

"But he spared your life, Tom."

"That's so, he had me 'bedded' but let up."

The detective told his story.

A male servant had been aroused. The man had run down and aroused his employer, and Mr. Dennison had sent for a policeman. As it chanced, the detective was passing the house, saw that something was wrong, hailed the servant, learned that there was a thief in the house, announced himself as an officer, and the scenes followed as have been described.

The detective, who was only a local officer, gave to Kate the above explanation.

"I had three dead cracks at him," said the detective, "and I think I've 'downed' him."

The detective only remained a moment, and left.

Kate fell into a chair in a helpless condition as Mr. Dennison entered the room.

"Did he get away with anything?" came the inquiry.

CHAPTER XXI.

LADY KATE knew that it was necessary for her to dissemble and act a part, and she answered:

"He did not succeed in securing anything, the wretch!"

In her inmost heart she hoped and prayed he had got away with something—his life.

Mr. Dennison, seeing Kate was fully attired, entered the room.

"Well," he said, "you have escaped a great peril."

"Yes, sir."

"I put but little faith in your original suspicions, or I should have had several male detectives in the house, but you must have recognized him."

The new complication flashed across Kate's mind.

The question of Mr. Dennison warned her that she would be placed in a very equivocal position.

The remarkable woman had made one more discovery, which made the situation most strangely and wonderfully embarrassing.

"It would be hard to swear that I recognized him!" she said.

"Well, yes, in the excitement of the moment one would hardly note their assailant's features."

Kate knew that great publicity would be given to the case, that able detectives would be put on the burglar's track, and that she would be looked to as the main witness to identify him, and she was a professional detective.

"It is necessary, sir, to serve the ends of justice, that my own identity shall not be disclosed in the affair; it must be given to the public as though I were a guest of the house."

"Oh, certainly, certainly; I understand that."

Kate had previously so instructed the ward detective, the man who had fired the shots at the retreating burglar.

The detective had communicated with the sergeant on duty at the station-house, and a general search all over the ward had been instantly instituted.

It was known that the burglar had been wounded, and it was looked upon as a sure thing that he would be captured.

Kate, as a detective, knew just what steps would be taken, and she, too, feared that the unfortunate young man would be trailed and captured.

The few remaining hours of darkness was a season of great anxiety to her.

She hoped and prayed that Arthur Everdell would escape.

In all the strange complications, one fact shone out bright and clear:

Arthur Everdell was not a murderer. Kate, although powerless to interfere or make an out-cry at that critical moment, still retained all her other faculties. She had heard the burglar's low, muttered remark, and she felt assured that he was not a murderer.

She took in the full significance of his words: "*I never have* stained my hands with human blood!"

Whatever other crimes the strange young man might have been guilty of, he was not a murderer; never had taken human life; and if such were the fact, the blood of Mrs. Raymond must cry out against some other more soulless villain!

Upon the following day Kate was visited by several detectives. They had all been warned that her name as a detective was not to figure in the affair, and in all the accounts in the news-papers she was spoken of as a beautiful and in-nocent young lady, a guest at the house where the stirring incidents had occurred. Indeed, in the accounts it was stated that the beautiful young lady was confined to her bed in a condi-tion of extreme nervous prostration, as a result of her terrible experience.

Kate's most difficult task lay with the detect-ives.

She was unable to aid them in the least.

The officers were amazed; they had calculated upon having their man dead to rights, owing to the fact that Lady Kate, the cool, brave, profes-sional, had met him face to face in that fatal room.

The day passed and the burglar was not tracked. He had succeeded in covering his trail despite his wounds.

Kate wondered whether he were really badly hurt, and if not, whether or not he would keep his appointment with her.

There were reasons why she did not dare go to the hotel where Everdell resided.

She remembered she had an appointment with him in another rôle earlier in the evening.

She did not calculate that, under all the cir-cumstances, the young man would think of meeting the poor mendicant girl whose life he had saved. She determined, however, to get up in the beggar disguise and be on hand.

Kate got herself up and appeared at the ap-pointed place. She arrived just at the hour named, and to her joy and surprise saw Arthur Everdell walking down toward the trysting place as coolly and unconcernedly as though he had not been fired at a half dozen times the previous night.

Indeed, there was not a question but that he had been wounded. Kate with her own eyes had seen the stains upon the stairs and in the hall, and yet as the young man sauntered leisure-ly down the street toward the spot to where he was to meet her, he showed no sign of having been wounded.

CHAPTER XXII.

As Kate saw him approach she almost re-gretted that she had kept her appointment.

She felt herself becoming fearfully agitated, and was alarmed lest her agitation might betray her.

Arthur Everdell came along and, in a pleasant tone, said:

"Well, my poor girl, I see you are on hand."

"Yes; you told me to come."

Kate's emotion almost choked her utterance.

The young man observed her emotion, and said:

"There, there, you need not be afraid; it's all right!"

"I'm not afraid, but I weep with mortifica-tion at the thought that I should need charity."

"Poor girl! you are rich—rich, indeed, if all your life you have only taken that which was *given to you!*"

A thrill went through Kate. She saw that through some strange process the singular young man had come to despise himself.

One other fact she had observed, and that was that he presented the appearance of Arthur Everdell, and there was not in any particular a resemblance to the young man who in the brigand costume had removed his mask, and had shown his face in the conservatory.

Arthur Everdell was a decided brunette, while the man who resembled the portrait in the Raymond library was a decided blonde.

The contrast in the appearance of the two men was positive and striking.

Kate could readily discern how Arthur Ever-dell had escaped identification and capture.

He evidently possessed some deep secret whereby he was enabled to so wonderfully change his appearance.

That the man who resembled the portrait, and the man who passed as Everdell, were one and the same, there was no doubt in the mind of the lady detective.

She had succeeded in establishing the one fact beyond all dispute or question.

As stated, Kate was pleased to hear the strange words fall from his lips with such peculiar emphasis.

"It's terrible to be poor!" she said in answer.

"It's better to be poor than be a criminal."

"I'm not a criminal!" exclaimed Kate, hotly.

"I did not say you were."

The lady detective was misleading her man when she took him up so sharply.

"I am poor but honest," said Kate.

"I do not doubt, girl, but you came here ex-pecting to get something from me?"

"I came here because you bid me come."

"Yes; I promised you help, but the fact is, girl, I'm dead broke. I haven't made a raise yet; you come here to-morrow; no one knows what a night may bring forth."

"You need give yourself no uneasiness on my account, sir; you were very kind when you risked your life to save mine."

"Oh, that's nothing, girl. I've saved many a life in my time, and I'm not very old, either."

"I hope you will take good care of your own life, sir."

"Bah! my life is not of much account; and, to tell the truth, girl, I wish I had never been born!"

"Sir; what is that you say?"

"I say I wish I had never been born."

"What, a rich, handsome young man like you to wish that you had never been born?"

"It's little good I've done in the world. But good-day; come here to-morrow. I may do something for you."

With a polite bow, an obeisance as low as though the seeming mendicant girl had been of the blood royal, the young man sauntered away.

He was a thief, a common burglar, and yet one of the most fascinating men Kate had ever met in all her life.

"He is the son of Balfour Raymond!" she muttered, as she stole away.

He had been on hand to keep his appointment with her, despite the fact that he must have known that detectives were on his track.

The one side of his life was dark and disgrace-ful, the other side all bright and noble.

We are not attempting to prove, dear reader, that a thief is noble and generous because he is gallant and handsome.

When our strange narrative is concluded, our friends will know how and why we can use cer-tain expressions concerning the man whom Kate Edwards had been trailing.

Lady Kate hastened to her lodgings, changed her clothing, and once more appeared upon the street.

There was but a short interval of time be-tween the two appointments with the same man, under such different auspices.

Attired as an elegant young lady, with dia-monds and jewels, the beautiful Lady Kate started out to meet a common burglar.

Arthur Everdell was on hand to keep his tryst.

He did not dodge around or make any effort to conceal his presence in order to guard against a surprise.

He had promised to meet Kate, and he was on hand.

The novelty of meeting lay in the fact that he would be compelled to meet Kate in the guise that accorded with his strange resemblance to the portrait of Balfour Raymond.

It was dark when they met, but Kate, anx-ious to study well his real face, suggested that they should go to some public restaurant.

Arthur Everdell objected.

"You would not have me stand upon the street?"

"You are right!" he said. "We will go to some restaurant!"

They did go, and immediately upon entering, Kate, who was well prepared for her part, made a strange inquiry.

CHAPTER XXIII.

THEY had taken their seat at a table, were under the full glare of the gas-jets, when Kate suddenly exclaimed:

"What does this mean! Who are you, sir?"

A strange look came into the young man's eyes as he answered:

"I am the young man who played the rôle of burglar at your uncle's residence last night!"

"I beg your pardon, sir, there is some mis-take here!"

"Wherein lies the mistake?"

"The young gentleman who met me in the conservatory I recognized as the same man who held the knife to my throat!"

"I am the gentleman who met you in the con-servatory."

"The gentleman who danced with me?"

"Yes."

"Will you tell me what this means?"

"What would you have me explain?"

"The features of the gentleman I met in the conservatory were indelibly impressed upon my memory. I tell you that the burglar I recog-nized is the same man, and you do not bear the least resemblance to the man."

"It is easily explained."

"Please explain it."

"When I go out on a burglarious errand I assume a disguise."

"You are now your proper self?"

"I am."

"Who was your model when you practiced for a disguise?"

For the first time the young man really showed signs of being taken dead back; but in a mo-ment he recovered, and said:

"I had no particular model, merely sought to change my appearance."

"Do you remember that last night I told you that you resembled a portrait?"

"You did."

"Isn't it strange that you should have acci-dentally hit upon a disguise which accorded so remarkably with the appearance of another?"

"It is merely one of those strange coinci-dences that sometimes surprise us."

"Frankly, your explanation is not satisfac-tory."

"What do you suspect?"

"I suspect that the burglar, fearing a be-trayal, has sent one of his 'pals' to represent him."

"Yours is a shrewd suspicion, but I assure you that I am the burglar, the man whom the police are searching for at this moment. I am in your power; you can hand me over to the police if you choose."

"Your explanation is not satisfactory," said Kate.

"You are determined to doubt my word, I see."

"I have reason to doubt your word."

"Indeed!"

"You have not spoken the truth to me; *you are in disguise now!*"

The young man laughed, and answered:

"You are shrewd and sharp enough to be a detective."

Kate glanced at him keenly to learn if there was any meaning in his remark.

"My explanation is not satisfactory to you, and you do not believe I am the burglar?"

"No."

"I wish I could laugh in your face and say I've been fooling you. I am not a burglar, I am an honorable man! but I can not do so, alas! I am a thief, a professional thief, a life-long criminal!"

"I believe you are the burglar!"

"I will not thank you."

"It is not necessary, but why should you be a criminal?"

"I told you last night I was born a thief."

"You were to tell me your history?"

"I will."

"Do so."

"My story is a brief one. I found myself at an early age the companion of thieves. I was adopted by a man who was probably the most daring and expert thief who ever lived—a man whose real adventures were more wonderful than the recorded exploits of the great criminal, Claude Duval.''

"Do you mean to tell me that you were the associate of thieves all your life?''

"I was the associate of thieves all my life!''

"But you appear to be a man of superior education?''

"My adopted father was a man of education and culture, and he took great pains as my instructor to educate me.''

"Where were your own parents?''

"I never knew any. I have a faint remembrance of a miserable, pale-faced woman who, in the midst of squalor, I called mother. I do not know whether she was my mother or not; but her memory is preserved to me in my dreams, as even now at times she appears to come to me in my sleep, a pale, ghostly looking creature.''

The mystery deepened.

Kate listened to this strange story, and all the time was making running comments in her mind.

She did not believe the young man was telling her the truth. She believed the pale faced woman was a myth, and that he was telling a romance.

"How old are you?''

"I judge I am about twenty-five. I know I am no older.''

Balfour Raymond, the younger, if living, would be about twenty-nine. Kate was certain that the young man was deceiving her.

"Where is your adopted father?''

"I do not know whether he is dead or living.''

"Where was he when you last saw him?''

"In jail.''

"Have you ever been in jail?''

"Not as a prisoner.''

CHAPTER XXIV.

KATE could not conceive what purpose the young man had in manufacturing such a story, until the suspicion crossed her mind that she was being sadly fooled.

She remembered how Arthur Everdell had pierced her former disguise, and how in a remarkable manner he had identified her as the young lady whom he had met at the Raymond mansion.

"Have you no suspicion concerning your parentage?'' Kate asked.

"Yes, I have a suspicion.''

There was something frank in the young man's last answer.

"Who do you think your father was?''

"A man who was hung when I was about two years old.''

Kate was at length assured that the young man was making a fool of her. She would have liked to have told him all she knew and all she suspected, but did not consider the proper time had arrived.

She thought she would humor the romance, and learn how wild a tale he would tell about himself.

"What led you to think,'' she asked, "that you were the son of a man who was hung?''

"My adopted father told me I was the son of an executed felon.''

We have previously intimated that Arthur Everdell was a fascinating man, and Kate was absolutely charmed with him.

She could not realize that he was a burglar, a criminal, the life-inured wretch that he proclaimed himself.

They were still talking, when a man entered the restaurant.

The new-comer took a seat in an adjoining booth, and did not permit himself to be seen.

Even Kate was so engrossed with the story she was listening to that she had not noticed the man's entrance.

Had Kate seen the man enter, she might possibly have prevented the startling and almost tragic incident that followed.

"Why do you tell such a story concerning yourself?'' she at length said.

"I am telling you the truth; telling all that I know about myself. I stand before you a man who never received one moral lesson in his life. I was regularly trained to the profession of a thief, and yet I know that I am a man naturally of good impulses, and only since I met you have I realized what a wretch I really am; when I think how I was reared as a criminal my blood boils; but it is too late to indulge regret now.''

"You are mistaken! You can even now desert your evil ways, and become a bright and honorable man.''

"No. no; I would always be hounded as the ex-burglar.''

"No one will be able to identify you, when you resume your proper character and appearance.''

"It is too late now for me to think of changing my life; and between you and me, Miss Dennison, the shadow is deepening over me!''

At this moment Kate chanced to catch sight of a face in the glass that caused her to exclaim:

"Oh, heavens!''

The restaurant was a complete gallery of mirrors: almost every article in the room was duplicated by reflection, and the lady detective chancing to glance into one of the mirrors, saw the face of the man in the adjoining compartment reflected.

She recognized the man as a detective, an able officer, but a very stern and uncompromising man.

She recognized at a glance that Arthur Everdell had been "piped,'' that the detective had come there to arrest him.

It was the discovery that caused her to exclaim:

"Oh, heavens!''

At once the whole front of the situation was presented to her. Arthur Everdell would pronounce her guilty of treachery, despite her positive promise not to denounce him until after she had heard his story.

Kate determined to save him.

It was a novel position for her, a detective, to resolve to screen a villain, but, alas! she was urged by a strange motive which she had not as yet permitted to become well defined in her own mind.

Her companion had observed her sudden exhibition of emotion, and he said:

"What is the matter?''

"You will believe me if I make a declaration?''

"I may.''

"You have been 'piped' to this place, but all may not yet be lost!''

A hard, stern look overspread the young man's face as he said, without any show of fear or excitement:

"It is just as I anticipated.''

"What do you mean?''

"I have been betrayed.''

Kate had no opportunity to offer any explanation. It was a critical moment.

The detective had come from his place of concealment. He approached the young man, laid his hand upon his shoulder, and said:

"Randolph Cummings, I have got you at last!''

Arthur Everdell was prepared. He had seen the reflection in the glass. He had known the detective was there.

The officer was taken off his guard. He was usually a very careful man; but Everdell was so gentlemanly looking, he had not calculated upon what was to follow.

As the officer spoke, Everdell leaped to his feet, drew a club, which he had concealed on his person, and with it he dealt the officer a sudden blow that felled him to the ground.

Kate leaped to her feet and made an effort to clasp the burglar, but he eluded her grasp and darted away.

CHAPTER XXV.

The detective had been momentarily stunned by the blow that had brought him to the ground, but upon recovering from the effects of it, he leaped to his feet with the exclamation:

"Where is he?''

"You have spoiled all,'' replied Kate.

In the meantime the proprietor of the saloon and his assistants had crowded around, also a few customers who were in the place.

The proprietor was very indignant until informed as to the character of the parties who had raised the row.

Kate and the detective left the dining-room together.

And on the street Kate once more said:

"You spoiled it all.''

"Hush!'' cautioned the man.

"I had everything dead to rights; you should have waited for a signal. Now, the man will

know me, and we may never get hands on him again.''

"I'll catch him,'' came the reply, "if I follow him to the ends of the earth!''

"How did you chance to spot him?''

"I've been laying for him for weeks. To-day one of his pals gave him away. The fellow is the murderer of old Mrs. Raymond.''

Kate did not scream, but she felt a strong desire to do so.

What she had most dreaded had come upon her. She had feared lest Arthur were a murderer, and the charge was now made.

She did not betray herself. She was perfectly cool as she queried:

"How do you know he is the assassin?''

"Got it down fine.''

"I do not believe you are on the right lay there.''

"I am; his pal opened the whole thing to me.''

"What pal?''

"I can't give it out yet, Kate; but I tell you we must collar that fellow. He's the most desperate criminal in New York to-day!''

"I had things all fine to snap him, but you've spoiled it!''

"Good-day, Kate, I'm on his track and I am bound to nab him.''

Kate walked on alone. She returned to her lodgings and sat down to think matters over.

The charge against Arthur Everdell was a terrible blow to her.

She had been led to believe that he was not an assassin, and even in the face of the declarations of her comrade, she still doubted the truth of the allegation.

The detective had the word of a pal, a man who might make the charge in order to screen himself. No true man would give a companion away; and the very fact of the man's seeking to betray a pal was evidence that he was an untrustworthy sneak even for a thief.

Against the thief's confession Kate had the evidence that Arthur had shown himself to be a generous man. Twice she had heard him declare that his hands were clean of the stain of human blood; and once she had seen him spare a man's life when his own was in danger, when as a thief it was necessary for him to kill to save his own life; and yet he had spared his man and taken the chance of being shot down himself.

"No, no,'' she exclaimed to herself. "He is not an assassin! It is the false charge of a coward who would save himself!''

That same night Kate, closely veiled and outwardly disguised, went upon the street.

She had changed her apparel, but upon removing her veil could disclose her face for recognition. She was determined to get upon Arthur Everdell's track.

To herself she kept muttering: "He will think I betrayed him!''

It was strange that Kate Edwards, the great lady thief-taker, should fear the fact that a thief and a burglar might suspect her of having betrayed him.

Kate was on the lookout for Arthur. She had "piped'' him down to his usual haunts.

One fact she considered, and that was that he would go under a disguise after the startling incident that had occurred in the restaurant.

The lady detective met with a strange and remarkable adventure before she returned to her home.

She had sought in every direction for Arthur Everdell, but had failed to find him, and had at length started to return home, when on crossing the plaza on Fourteenth Street, she met a young man face to face under one of the lamps.

The young man was elegantly dressed, a perfect specimen of the "splendid'' young man about town.

A thrill shot through Kate as she saw him.

She had come upon her man.

He had changed from Arthur Everdell, and appeared in his original character.

As she glanced at him she realized that he was indeed changed.

She remembered the portrait, the lineaments of the painted face was indelibly impressed upon her mind; and as she gazed it struck her that the portrait might have been painted for the young man.

Kate was nervous and agitated, and after the young man had passed, she turned and followed him.

She did not like to speak to him in the open space, as detectives might be upon her track as well as his.

No one better understood the keen cunning of an experienced detective, and Kate recognized the possibility that she might be under suspicion, and if so she would not know it until some critical moment.

CHAPTER XXVI.

KATE followed Arthur until he had passed some way down a side street, when she came close to him, laid her hand on his shoulder, and said:

"Come with me!"

The young man turned and asked:

"Who are you?"

"Miss Dennison."

"I beg your pardon, Miss Dennison, but you have made a mistake."

Kate was amazed at the wonderful change Arthur had made, not only in his appearance, but in his voice and general demeanor.

"I know you," she said. "I have made no mistake."

"If you know me I must know you; but I do not recollect ever having met any lady of the name of Dennison."

"It is useless for you to attempt to deceive me, Arthur. You may think that I betrayed you earlier this evening, but on my life and soul and honor I did not!"

"Miss, I assure you that you have made a mistake! My name is not Arthur, and no one did anything to me earlier this evening that would lead me to believe I had been betrayed."

"Why persist? Your safety demands that you should come with me!"

"I am in no peril."

"I swear I did not betray you."

"I have not accused you of betraying me; you are crazy, or you are laboring under some strange hallucination."

"Will you not come?"

"You are veiled."

"For your sake."

"Veiled for my sake?"

"Yes."

"Miss, I am completely mystified; will you let me see your face?"

"Will you come with me?"

"If I recognize you as a friend, I will not object to going with you, provided I can be of any service."

"Come to the light."

The two, so strangely met, walked to a gas-lamp, when Kate drew aside her veil, and said:

"Look!"

The young man started on beholding so handsome a face, but no sign of recognition came to his countenance.

"I never saw you before!" he said, and he spoke in a tone of calm sincerity.

"If you will come with me, Arthur, I will save you!"

"I can not go with you!" And in a tone of contempt the young man added: "Miss, you must carry your fish to some other market!"

A flush of indignation reddened Kate's face as she turned away, and said:

"I trust you will never have occasion to regret your obstinacy."

The young man laughed, and Kate recognized the laugh. But one man whom she had ever met could laugh in that same irritating and sarcastic manner.

Kate walked away.

She was indignant and mortified, and felt something of the sensation that is said to agitate a woman scorned.

The lady detective was once more upon Broadway, and was crossing the plaza, and at about the same place where she had first met Arthur she encountered him again.

Upon the second occasion he appeared as Arthur Everdell as she *had known him.*

She was completely bewildered. She could not explain how the young man could have so suddenly changed his appearance and have got around so as to meet her again at that spot.

As he had failed to recognize her under his previous character, Kate determined not to recognize him after the transformation, and she kept upon her way without noticing him.

She had made up her mind that having changed his appearance he was prepared to remember that he had seen her before.

Our heroine had walked but a few steps when she became aware that she was being followed.

Upon the former occasion she had followed the young man, and he in turn was following her.

She determined to give him a tramp, and started to walk up Fifth Avenue toward the residence of Mr. Dennison.

She had gone but a short distance when the young man overtook her. He did not address her, but passed on ahead and only turned when at the corner, when suddenly he faced her, tore aside her veil, and in a matter-of-fact tone, said:

"I thought so!"

The movement had been so quick Kate could not guard against it.

"How dare you!" she said.

"I wished to make sure it was you."

"Well, sir, what have you to say?"

"I will first ask your pardon: what I did was very rude, but I did wish to speak to you."

"You did wish to speak to me?"

"Yes."

"A few moments ago you were not so anxious."

"I do not understand you."

"Oh, you are playing the know-nothing again; you play it well."

"You bewilder me!"

"Do I?"

"Yes."

"Well, you were bewildered a few moments ago; you denied knowing me."

"You are making sport of me."

Kate was getting somewhat bewildered herself.

When she had met Arthur before under a different guise, he had spoken in a sincere tone, and now again he spoke with seeming equal sincerity.

"You wished to speak to me?" she said.

"I do wish to speak to you; but on my honor I do not know what you were alluding to a moment ago!"

"Did you not meet me ten minutes ago?"

"I did not."

"Why deny it? Do you not know that I can identify you when disguised?"

"I swear you are talking to me in riddles; but I think now I can understand what it all means!"

"What does it all mean?"

"I did not believe, until this moment, that you were a false woman, and that my peril to-night was part of a game!"

CHAPTER XXVII.

"You would charge me with having attempted to betray you?"

"I did not mean to so charge you, but your attempt to prove that you saw me a few moments ago, convinces me that in some way you would make me a victim of your cunning."

"And you still proclaim you did not meet me?"

"I do."

"It's all very strange!"

"I solemnly declare I did not meet you!"

"And I as solemnly swear," said Kate, "that I did not betray you!"

"I know you did not. I was betrayed by one of my pals; but he will not betray me again."

There was a deep meaning in the young man's tone, and Kate exclaimed:

"You will not harm him!"

"No."

The lady detective felt that the mystery was becoming shrouded in deeper gloom every hour. Involuntarily she exclaimed:

"Oh, that you would forsake your present evil ways!"

"It's too late."

"Then why do you not fly from New York while you have a chance?"

"It's too late."

"Too late to fly?"

"Well, I may leave in a few days."

"But within that time you may be captured; your disguise has been penetrated."

"I can not help it; I can not 'flit' now."

"You can."

"Well, I will not."

"You are resolved to brave all chances?"

"I am."

"Suppose you are captured?"

"Then it's good-bye."

"What do you mean?"

"I never could live in prison."

"And yet you will brave arrest?"

"Yes."

"If captured, you intend **to commit suicide?**"

Kate spoke in a very anxious tone.

The wonderful woman, who had been counted one of the nerviest women on earth, had become as weak as a school-girl; some strange spell had come over her. She, a criminal-hunter, interesting herself in the safety of one of the most inveterate house-breakers in the country!

Ah, woman, thou art a strange compound! Sympathy in a woman's heart is a blinder to all sense of justice.

The strange, weird character, Arthur Everdell, had won the lady detective's deepest sympathy; and her sympathy once aroused, she forgot that he was a desperate character, an outlaw, a thief, and only remembered that he was generous and kind-hearted, and had risked his own life to save hers.

"You must make me one promise!" she said.

"What shall I promise?"

"You must promise me that under no circumstances, in case of arrest, will you take your own life until you have seen me?"

"That is a strange request."

"Will you promise?"

"Who are you—and why your sympathy for me?"

"You saved my life!" Kate involuntarily exclaimed.

"Eh?" ejaculated Arthur.

Kate had spoken unthinkingly, but she could not recall her words, and she repeated:

"You saved my life!"

"Your sense of gratitude is very keen. I *spared your life,* but I had no right in the first place to put your life in peril; you are under no obligations to me!"

Kate saw that he had mistaken her remark, and resolved to be more careful in future; the hour had not yet arrived for her to reveal her real identity.

"Will you promise me?"

"I may regret it, but I will make the promise."

Kate had observed a man dodging around and watching them, and she said:

"You are being 'piped.'"

"Good-night!" said Arthur, and he walked away.

Kate returned to her lodgings a bewildered woman.

She was satisfied that for some reason Arthur desired to preserve one of his incognitos inviolate; but she was still satisfied in her own mind that it was Arthur whom she had first met; indeed, it was an utter improbability that it could have been any one else.

Upon the following day Kate called upon Colonel Prang.

The colonel listened to her strange story and said:

"Well, you must go and solve the mystery."

"What is your opinion of the situation?"

"I have no opinion."

When Arthur Everdell left Kate, he proceeded along the street a careful and watchful man. He had seen the dodger even before Kate had espied him.

The young burglar had a special reason for not leaving New York.

He and several other expert cracksmen had laid out to rob a certain mansion. They had reason to believe that they would make a large haul.

Arthur Everdell was "dead broke," as the cant phrase goes, and he had no notion of leaving New York until he had "made a stake."

Since his meeting with Miss Dennison a great change had come over him. The idea of ever reforming had never entered his mind. He had led a wild, reckless life, and proposed to lead one to the end; his motto had been "a short life and a merry one;" but suddenly there had come over him a feeling of deep despair, and he cursed the fate that had made him a burglar and had prevented him from growing up an honest man.

It was one of those strange and unaccountable anomalies, but the burglar had learned to love the woman who had been hired to bring him to justice.

Her cool, calm courage, her instantaneous sympathy for him, had won his admiration from the very start; and later on he had conceived the most strange and wild yet pure love for the beautiful woman whom he had met under such singular circumstances.

CHAPTER XXVIII.

THE young man had never indulged the hope for one instant that his love would be returned. He did not indulge even a wish to declare it. He looked upon Kate as a brave, sympathetic young lady, whose sympathies had been aroused for a lost youth. He felt that she was a brave, romantic young lady, who believed herself performing a Christian duty in seeking to turn a terribly wicked man from the error of his ways.

He wanted to make one grand stake and he would leave New York, fly from the city that held the girl who had won his heart, but who, because of her purity, was removed from him as an angel in heaven would be removed from an imp of darkness.

Arthur kept upon his way, and was soon fully assured that the man whom he had seen was really following him.

It became necessary to throw his pursuer off his track. He was on his way to join his pals. He had but just escaped with his life from one attempted burglary, and was preparing to engage in another.

Everdell doubled on his tracks several times, but the man was always at his heels.

It was an awkward situation for a man prepared to engage in a criminal operation. The time had arrived when he was to meet his pals, and yet he could not go and lead a "shadow" to the rendezvous.

Arthur passed round and approached the vicinity of one of the parks, when he came to a halt and permitted the man to come upon him.

The "shadow" also came to a halt, when the burglar turned the tables and advanced upon his pursuer.

The latter maintained his ground.

"You are following me!" said Arthur.

"Am I?"

"You are!"

"What makes you think so?"

"I do not think so; I know it."

"Well, suppose I am following you?"

"You have no right to do so without offering an explanation."

"I am not giving out explanations to-night."

Arthur Everdell sprung upon the man, whom he supposed to be a detective.

A struggle followed, when our hero, through a certain exclamation that fell from the man's lips, discerned that he was wrestling with a highwayman.

It was a case of "Greek meet Greek."

Arthur gave a signal, when the man at once ceased struggling, and the two men stood apart.

"Well, this is a nice go, Johnny!"

"I'll be hanged if it ain't, 'pard!'"

"Good-night; I'm in a hurry!"

"Good-night, and blast my eyes, if it ain't a good 'un!"

Arthur started on his way, and the man with whom he had been struggling muttered:

"I've got him down fine now!"

Arthur had been deceived; the man really was a detective, and had misled the burglar.

The detective did not follow his man further. He had only laid in to establish a certain fact, and he had succeeded.

It was a success on both sides, as, detective or no detective, Everdell had thrown the man from his track.

The young man went down to the river.

It was after midnight. He passed out upon one of the piers, and at the same moment observed a figure sitting on the string-piece.

Everdell uttered a sharp signal whistle, which was immediately responded to, and he advanced upon the man.

"You're late, 'pard.'"

"Had a shadow over me."

"Did you drop it?"

"Yes."

"All right; the boys are in the boat."

It was a dark night; the stars were veiled behind heavy clouds.

There were four men in the party, including Everdell.

Two of the men took the oars, while Everdell commenced making a change in his apparel.

There was a bundle in the boat, from which he selected such articles as he wanted, and in a few moments he was as rough a looking man in appearance as any one of his companions.

Four more expert burglars never started together to crack a mansion.

Two of the men were strangers to Everdell; the third man was an old pal. The latter was also an intimate of the two other men.

They were all powerful fellows, and the two oarsmen sent the boat through the water at a rapid rate.

They pulled some six miles up the river, when the boat was run in shore.

But little talk had passed between them, but as they started to file away from the beach, one of the men remarked:

"There may be some trouble to-night, as there are three or four men in the house."

Another of the men remarked:

"Let's set in then for another 'bank.'"

"Why?" came the query.

"Another affair like the last and we'll be followed too close."

"No man must open fire unless it's to save his own life."

It was a strange phase of human nature that these villains, who were about to invade the peaceful residence of a citizen, should excuse to their own minds a possible murder on the plea of *saving their own lives.*

Were they lawfully engaged, their lives would not be endangered.

With silent steps they kept upon their way, under the lead of the man who had spotted the selected ranch.

A few moments and they had entered the grounds of a private residence, and having walked a few steps they came in sight of the house.

CHAPTER XXIX.

IT was an elegant villa, which lay somber and silent, its occupants evidently all asleep, dreaming themselves safe from every danger.

A robbery, looked at calmly and considerately, is a terrible incident, and the midnight burglar is beyond question one of the meanest wretches that walks the face of the earth.

Of all the horrors that can be conceived of, there are none more terrible than to be awakened at the dead of night, to discover a masked burglar at your bedside.

The men approached the house like so many evil shadows. They had brought implements with them, and soon managed to raise a window opening upon the broad veranda.

They all wore moccasins. One of their number was stationed outside to watch around the grounds; a second was detailed as a patrol in the house, and the other two were to go for the booty.

Before entering the house the men had made a perfect study of the interior arrangement.

They were all experts, and were able to approximate pretty accurately as to all the passages and modes of ingress and egress.

Arthur was detailed as the inside patrol.

It was his duty to be on the alert to discover should any of the occupants of the house become aroused, and he was to give an immediate alarm.

The men went into all the minor details of the business.

As stated, they forced an entrance and entered the house.

One of them started for the room where the silverware was supposed to be stored; and the other man went about above stairs to make a raid of the several bedrooms, and secure money, watches, diamonds, and jewels; indeed, anything that was portable.

A few moments passed; like so many masked devils the heartless villains went about their separate work.

Suddenly Arthur, who was in the hall of the second story, saw a gleam of light shoot through the crack of a partly opened door.

At once he knew that, despite their noiseless entrance and caution after entrance, some one had been aroused.

He could have slipped away and have saved himself. He could have run down the stairs and then have given the alarm.

The door-way through which the light flashed opened wider, and the burglar could see the forms of two men fully dressed, and in their hands they carried cocked revolvers.

The intended robbery must have been suspected.

There was not a moment to spare. One of his pals was one flight of stairs above the spot where Arthur stood.

He could have given the signal and have run, but even then the chances would be against the man on the upper floor.

To ascend the stairs and secretly warn him, it would be necessary for the young man to pass close to the partly opened door, and in so doing he ran the chance of being shot down like a dog, as he deserved.

He did not hesitate, however, as to his course. It was his own life or his pals'.

An alarm would cause his pal to run down the stairs, and at once he would have become the target of the two men.

Arthur moved forward, and thought he would successfully pass upstairs. He was half-way up when the door opened, and there came a flash and report. He had been discovered.

Up he dashed, and at the head of the stairs met his pal.

"Take to the window and out upon the veranda!"

"The game's up?"

"Yes."

In the meantime the two men had sprung from the room, and had started to follow the burglars up the stairs.

One of the burglars reached the window, but Arthur's progress was blocked by an armed man who came from one of the attic rooms.

A bright light flashed from the room, and Arthur's form was distinctly revealed to the marksman; indeed, he was between two fires.

His pal saw his peril, and from the window turned to fire, when Arthur sprung forward, and jerked the innocent man aside, and received his pal's shot in his own person.

He had saved the man's life.

It was a strange and remarkable fact that, even in such a moment of critical excitement, the man whose life had been saved recognized that one of the burglars had imperiled his own life for him.

The two other men, meantime, had come up the stairs; indeed, all the incidents we have described transpired in a few seconds.

Arthur gained the window and ran along the roof of the veranda, while his pal made an effort to descend one of the supporting columns.

Arthur reached the end of the veranda and let himself down to the ground.

He could not help his friends unless he returned to take life; and even then he would have but put his own life in jeopardy, and might have been of no assistance to them.

CHAPTER XXX.

As Arthur darted away he heard several shots behind him in the house, and at the same moment made the startling discovery that he was being pursued.

The catastrophe came. Arthur fell from loss of blood and exhaustion, and the pursuer sprung upon him.

The burglar had dropped his mask, and, at the moment he fell, the moon came out bright and clear.

The pursuer had a clear, full view of the burglar's face and handsome features, but ere he could fire, he was in turn knocked over.

The pal who had been left outside had seen Arthur dart away, and had also seen a man spring after him.

The pal became a double pursuer, and arrived just in time to save Arthur's life.

Arthur, by a superhuman effort, gained his feet, and seized his pal's arm.

"Don't shoot!"

"He would have sent you up!"

"Never mind! Don't shoot!"

The gentleman, who was a son of the owner of the mansion, knew that he was at the mercy of the burglars.

He did not dare call for help, as help could not arrive time enough to save him, and the attempt might only infuriate the burglars.

It was a terrible moment.

His life hung upon the decision of a man whom he would a moment previous have shot like a dog, and what was worse, the man knew it.

"Don't shoot!" again said Arthur.

In the meantime the fallen man had taken advantage of the situation, and had leaped to his feet and had darted away.

The two burglars were compelled to flee.

The pal was fresh, and got away easily, but Arthur had hard work to drag one foot after the other.

He would have been taken had not the man whose life he had saved been as generous as himself.

The gentleman purposely threw the pursuers off the track. He did not wish the man captured, who, beyond all question or doubt, had saved his life.

Arthur struggled on, and managed to reach the river.

His pal was already in the boat, but Arthur did not join him.

The young man felt that he had got his death-wound, and at that awful moment resolved to crawl off somewhere and die by himself.

He wandered up the beach, and came to a place where a row boat had been hauled ashore.

He entered the boat, and finding the oars, managed to launch it, when he paddled away.

The tide was running up and he let the boat drift.

He drifted until daylight, when he paddled the boat to the shore.

He landed at a rocky place, and managed to crawl to a sheltered nook, where he lay down.

He did not know how long he had slept, when he was aroused by hearing a voice, and upon looking up he saw a kindly faced man standing over him.

"Hello, young man! what are you doing here?"

Arthur was quick-witted, and answered:

"I am wounded, and drifted here in my boat."

"How did you get your wound?"

"I was trying to board a sloop, and was mistaken for a thief, and the man on deck shot me."

"Well, I live near here; can you walk?"

"I'll try."

Arthur was just able to walk, and the man, who was a fisherman, led him to his cottage.

That night a raging fever set in, and Arthur became a very sick man.

The fisherman did not believe the young man's story, but he had become interested in him, and resolved to save his life if possible.

The fisherman had no family; he lived alone. He had been in the war, and as a hospital sergeant had encountered considerable experience in the treatment of gun-shot wounds.

He made an examination of the burglar's hurt, and came to the conclusion that his life could be saved, and that it could be saved without the aid of a surgeon.

The burglar had been fortunate in falling into good hands.

CHAPTER XXXI.

THE fisherman succeeded in reducing the fever, and in an able manner dressed the wound.

The bullet had struck a place where it had gone clean through, and by careful nursing the fisherman hoped the wound would heal.

Ten days passed, and the wounded man had made great progress toward recovery, although the chances were that weeks, and possibly months, would intervene before he would be able to get about again.

The fisherman, whose name was Sturgis, had never asked the young man any questions, but one day he came in, and seating himself beside the bed, said:

"Well, my friend, how do you feel?"

"I feel that I am progressing well, owing all to your careful nursing; but, after all, it might have been better had I died."

"Why do you say that?"

"I sometimes feel so."

"Have you no friends who would miss you?"

"I do not know that I have a friend in the world."

"I have thought it strange you have not asked me to send for your friends."

"I have none."

"Will you tell me how you got your wound?"

"I told you once."

"Frankly, I did not believe your story then; I do not now."

"What do you suspect?"

"I suspect nothing; but at times it has crossed my mind that I might be nursing a viper back to life."

"Then you do suspect something?"

"I would prefer that you would tell the truth."

"You are a kind, good man. I will tell you the truth."

"Do so."

"I am a burglar. I was shot while attempting to rob a house."

The countenance of the fisherman fell as he said:

"I am sorry I came across you, young man."

"Why?"

"A disagreeable duty is imposed upon me."

"It is your duty to surrender me to the law?"

"Yes."

"Do not let me stand in the way of your duty."

"What would you advise me to do?"

"To do your duty."

"And surrender you?"

"Yes."

"You are a strange young man. I pity you; it may be this was your first attempt to commit a crime?"

"No, sir."

"You have attempted burglary before?"

"I am an old criminal."

"That can not be; you are young in years."

"I am young in years, but I am an old criminal all the same. I have been a thief all my life."

Sturgis looked at the young man in an incredulous manner, and said:

"I believe you are deceiving me."

"How so?"

"You are gratifying a whim."

"How so?"

"If you were really the criminal you claim to be, you would not be so ready to avow it."

"I am telling you the truth."

"And you advise me to surrender you?"

"I advise you to do your duty."

"If you are such a stickler for duty, how is it you are a criminal?"

"I was born a criminal."

"Oh, no, that can not be."

"It is true in my case."

"Tell me your story."

Arthur Everdell told the same story he had related to Kate.

When he had concluded, the fisherman said:

"Your frankness has saved you."

"How so?"

"You are more deserving of pity than censure if your story is true."

"My story is true."

"I will not surrender you. I have nursed you back to physical life. I will try and win you back to moral life!"

"I do not think you will succeed."

"Are you determined to remain a villain?"

"I don't see much chance for me to be anything else."

"Do you forget you have a soul?"

"I have not forgotten, simply because I have never thought on the subject at all."

"You are a handsome man."

The invalid made no reply.

"You are a smart man, and you are well educated. There is no reason why you should not be an honest man and a successful one."

"The cops are on my track for past crimes; sooner or later they will hunt me down!"

"You can go to some other land."

"I have no money."

"Ways can certainly be provided for you to go, if you really wish to become an honest man!"

"I do not wish to become an honest man!"

"Ephraim is wedded to his idols!" murmured the fisherman.

"I am wedded to a life of crime!"

"If you are so resolved, I am bound to do my duty. I can not let you go free, to become again a prey upon society."

"You had better do your duty!"

"I may yet persuade you. Listen: I have a little money; were you ever in California?"

"Never!"

"Suppose, when you are recovered, I loan you money enough to go to California to begin an honest life, will you go?"

"No, sir."

"You are determined to be a thief?"

"I was born one."

"That is no reason why you should remain one!"

"Yes, it is."

"We will talk this matter over again."

CHAPTER XXXII.

WHILE Arthur Everdell remained an invalid at the fisherman's house, strange and wonderful occurrences were happening in the great city of New York.

Upon the morning following the robbery, the city was startled with an account of the intended burglary.

It was not until noon that the account appeared in an extra.

Kate Edwards read of the bold attempt and tragic result, and her heart sunk within her.

The papers furnished an account of the personal appearance of the dead cracksmen, and the description of one of them tallied exactly with the personal appearance of Arthur Everdell.

We will here explain that the descriptions became mixed, and the measure of one of the living men was printed as the description of one of the burglars who had escaped.

"Just what I feared!" murmured Kate, and a hard, rigid look settled upon her face.

The bodies of the dead robbers had been brought to New York by night, an inquest having been held the same day.

The inquest was not a formal one, but merely an inaugural, which permitted the removal of the remains.

Kate, as an officer, had no difficulty in gaining admission to the Morgue to view the remains, and it was with a trembling heart that she cast the first glance upon the bodies of the victims of their own criminal intent.

One glance was sufficient, and her heart gave a great bound of joy. She did not recognize either of the corpses as the body of the handsome and elegant Arthur Everdell.

A hope arose in her heart that Arthur had not been with the cracksmen, but upon the following morning the hope was dispelled.

A more detailed account was furnished, and the statement was made that a third burglar had been mortally wounded, and had been carried away by a portion of the masked gang who had escaped.

The description of the wounded man proved to her that Arthur Everdell had really been with the gang, and had in all probability forfeited his life.

We will not attempt to describe Kate's feelings; but one thing was certain, her heart was filled with sorrow and regret.

That night, in a proper disguise, she went upon the street.

There was a faint chance that Arthur had not been wounded as badly as represented. She well knew the tendency to exaggerate, and made many allowances for the chance that the strange, weird young man had escaped.

One fact struck her as a convincing proof that Everdell was the wounded man—the description given of him accorded with his resemblance to the portrait in the Raymond mansion.

Kate had, as stated, indulged a hope that there might be a mistake as to his serious wounding.

She had started out early in the evening, and unexpectedly came upon Colonel Prang.

The colonel had never seen her under the disguise she was then wearing.

As upon a former occasion, she was veiled.

Kate glided up behind Colonel Prang and addressed him.

The gentleman turned, and, in a sharp, rebukeful voice, said:

"Well, what do you want?"

"You do not recognize me?"

"I do not wish to recognize you."

"I am in your employ."

"Ah! Lady Kate!"

"Yes."

"You took me unawares. I forgot that you detectives have a habit of coming upon us in questionable shape."

"I would speak with you."

"Well?"

"Have you read an account of the burglary?"

"I have."

"Did you read a description of the personal appearance of the burglars?"

"I did."

"Did you recognize one of them from the description?"

"I did."

"Arthur Everdell was with the gang."

"So much the worse for Everdell."

"But suppose—"

"I suppose nothing. Good-evening."

It was evident that for some reason Colonel Prang did not wish to hold any conversation concerning the young man whom Kate had time and again hinted she believed was the heir to the great Raymond estate.

Kate parted from Colonel Prang and was on her way to police head-quarters, when she saw a young man come staggering out of one of the magnificent drinking hells to be seen on Broadway.

The woman's agitation was intense.

At a glance, she recognized Arthur Everdell, but the young man was disguised, or rather was undisguised, and stood before her the perfect counterpart of the portrait. Indeed it was Balfour Raymond.

The young man was under the influence of liquor.

Kate did not speak to him at once; she feared to do so on the public thoroughfare, which even at that hour was crowded with a throng of pedestrians.

She followed him.

The young man walked up Broadway, and then turning off, came to a halt before a house, where resided one of the most wicked and dangerous women in New York.

The young man came to a halt before the door, as stated, and stood muttering to himself.

Kate advanced, and, laying her hand on his arm, said:

"Do not go in there!"

"Who tells me not to go in?"

Kate was dressed as she had been upon a former occasion when she met Arthur, as she supposed him to be, and she answered:

"I do."

"Who are you?"

The young man fixed his eyes upon her. He could not penetrate with his glance behind her veil, but he said:

"I think I have seen you before."

"Yes, you have seen me before. And now tell me why you do not fly from New York?"

"Why should I flee from New York?"

"You have been spotted. You will be surely arrested."

The young man came to the conclusion that his steps were being haunted by a crazy woman, and he said:

"Where is your keeper?"

Kate discerned what he meant, and involuntarily answered:

"Oh, Arthur! Arthur! for Heaven's sake flee, or you will be put in prison, and I will be compelled to testify against you!"

CHAPTER XXXIII.

"Look here, young lady, if I am ever arrested, I am perfectly willing that you should testify against me!"

"I will be compelled to do so."

"You are welcome. But please go off about your business, and do not come croaking around me, or I will be compelled to hand you over to the police!"

"Hand me over to the police?"

"Certainly, as a nuisance. You are following me around and dinning a mess of gibberish in my ear all the time!"

"Randolph Cummings, I warn you that the law is upon your track!"

"Oh, that's another name you have for me now. Which am I, Everdell or Cummings?"

"You are both. Let me ask you, have you read the papers of to-day?"

"I have."

"Did you observe how accurately your description is furnished as you appear now?"

The young man showed signs of agitation. The question appeared to sober him a bit, and he answered:

"Do you know a man who answers that description?"

"I do."

"Where is he?"

"He stands before me."

"Do you know another man?"

"No."

"The description in the paper described a burglar?"

"Yes."

"I'm not a burglar."

"What is your name?"

"George Gordon."

A strange, weird suspicion found lodgment at length in Kate's mind.

"Where were you last night?"

"I was around town."

"You swear you were not with the gang of masked burglars?"

"Miss, I did think you were crazy, but now I am led to believe that you are the victim of some strange mistake; you have been misled by some fatal resemblance."

"I begin to think I have been."

"You have called me Arthur Everdell, and Randolph Cummings, and I swear I have never been known by either name."

"Were you ever known by the name of Balfour Raymond?"

The young man's agitation became more apparent, as he said:

"What do you know about Balfour Raymond?"

"I know a great deal about Balfour Raymond."

"And I know very little," came the reply. "I should like to learn something about that man."

"You have heard of such a person?"

"I have."

"Will you tell me your history?"

"No."

"Why not?"

"There is no reason why I should."

Kate thought a moment.

It came over her that indeed the mystery was deepening.

"Will you meet me to-morrow?" she asked.

"Why should I meet you to-morrow?"

"You wish to learn something of Balfour Raymond?"

"I do."

"If you will meet me to-morrow, I will tell you a strange story."

"Why not to-night?"

"We have not time."

"I dare not meet you to-morrow."

"You dare not meet a lady?"

"I am not assured that you are a lady."

"And you refuse to meet me?"

"I do."

"Then you do not wish to learn the history of Balfour Raymond?"

"I do wish to learn the history of Balfour Raymond."

"Was your portrait ever painted?" asked Kate, abruptly.

"Why do you ask?"

"I have a reason—an important one."

"My portrait was never painted to my knowledge."

"Come and meet me to-morrow, and I will show you a portrait of yourself."

"What strange game is this you are playing?"

"I am playing no game; but I will explain to you why I have been misled by a fatal resemblance. There is a great mystery surrounds you."

"How do you know there is a mystery surrounding me?"

"The fact that I have, upon two occasions, addressed you as another man shows that there is a mystery somewhere."

"Will you answer me one question?"

"It depends upon the question."

"Do you know a man who resembles me, or whom I resemble?"

"I know of a portrait painted many years ago that you resemble."

"I wish I could believe you were not up to some game."

"I am not up to some game."

"All this is very strange."

"Yes; and you will not aid in unraveling the mystery."

"You wish me to meet you to-morrow?"

"Yes."

"Where?"

"At the Hudson River Railroad Depot."

"And if I meet you?"

"I will take you to a place where you will see your own face upon canvas."

"And then?"

"Together we will try and get at the bottom of the mystery. I pray you come and meet me, lest your fatal resemblance may lead you into a peril from which you can not extricate yourself."

"You are a strange young lady, and yet I will admit to you that I have been aware for some days that there was something wrong somewhere."

"Will you meet me?"

"I will."

CHAPTER XXXIV.

KATE was not satisfied by any means that there was not something wrong. She still in her heart believed that she had been talking to Arthur Everdell, and that the young man was taking advantage of a certain secret to befog and mislead her.

She knew that Everdell was smart and cunning enough to carry on a double game, and it did not seem possible to her that there were two persons living who bore such a wonderful resemblance to the portrait hanging on the wall of the library at the Raymond mansion.

It was much easier to believe that Arthur Everdell was seeking to deceive her.

She had made up her mind to escort him to the Raymond mansion, when she would reveal enough to gain his confidence

She still indulged a suspicion that Arthur might have discovered her identity, and might fear that she was really "piping" him, only to close in on him finally, in a most effective manner.

Upon the following morning, at the appointed time, she was at the depot, and a few moments later she was joined by the man who called himself George Gordon.

Kate could not but remark what a really handsome and engaging gentleman he was; and the fact that he came openly, without any attempt at disguise, was a staggering blow to her theory that he was really Arthur Everdell.

Later on, while en transit to the Raymond place, she failed to discover that brilliancy in his conversation that distinguished Arthur.

Indeed, she was compelled to admit that Arthur Everdell as Arthur Everdell was a much more fascinating man than Arthur Everdell as George Gordon.

The lady detective was in the midst of a maze of mystery, but she determined to get at the bottom of all the strange circumstances, come what may.

"You are on hand," she said.

"Yes, I am on hand. I have made up my mind to see this strange adventure through."

They boarded the train, when, to Kate's terror and annoyance, she discovered that a man was upon their track.

A fellow was on the train who was connected with a private bureau.

Our hero knew the man to be a bigger rascal than the criminals he was supposed to shadow.

He was a "divvy" man, a fellow who would run down a noted criminal, and then place him under a sort of tithing or blackmailing system.

He was a cunning fellow, very shrewd, possessed considerable political influence, and worked his profitable game very acutely.

The man did not know Kate as she was got up upon this occasion.

He knew her by sight, as she ordinarily appeared as Lady Kate, the detective.

There was as wide a difference between her different characters as there was in the changed appearances of Arthur Everdell.

Kate was not certain at first that the man was following them; but when the train reached the station where she proposed to debark, she was satisfied that he was really "piping" her companion.

Gordon had noticed the man, and addressing Kate, he said:

"Do you see that sharp-faced fellow?"

"I do."

"That man has been hovering on my track for three or four days. I believe he is following us now."

The young man made the remark just as they reached the station nearest to the Raymond mansion.

The young man's admission confused Kate; it was another evidence against her theory that Gordon and Everdell were one and the same person.

"That man has been following you?"

"Yes."

"Has he ever spoken to you?"

"Never."

"Do you know who he is?"

"I have been told he is a detective."

Kate was all adrift. Gordon was altogether too simple-minded for Arthur Everdell, as he was the smartest man she had ever met.

"You know I told you last night that your resemblance to a certain painting might lead you into a peril."

"I know you did, but I have no fear; my record is perfectly clear. No man can charge me with crime."

"You have no idea of the complications that may involve you; you may yet owe your life to me."

"I can not see how my life can be imperiled."

They proceeded toward the mansion, and were soon upon the grounds.

Kate had been on the lookout, and recognized that the man Sheehan was still upon their track.

She made up her mind in case of any interference on his part to adopt very decided measures.

Kate was ordinarily but a woman. But when once aroused she could perform feats that would well become a man. And any of our readers who have attended the circus know very well to what a wonderful degree a woman's muscle can be cultivated, while she still retains her delicate and lady-like appearance.

Kate had deliberately prepared herself for her profession, and she was a magnificent female athlete, and, like several other lady detectives who have been known in New York at different times, was an expert in the use of weapons.

Like a well-known noble lady in France, Kate, if so minded, could have gone into the field and have defended her own honor at the point of a sword or the muzzle of a pistol.

The Raymond mansion from the outside presented the appearance of a deserted house.

"Do you intend entering that house?" queried Gordon.

"I do."

"There does not appear to be any one at home."

"There is something in that house that will fill your soul with wonder!" was Kate's strange reply.

CHAPTER XXXV.

KATE went up to the grand door and rang the bell, and in a few moments the old man who had admitted her upon a former occasion answered the summons.

She presented an order which the man recognized, and she said to him:

"No one else is to be admitted while I am in the house."

"All right, miss."

Kate proceeded direct to the library, threw open the windows opening upon the veranda, as upon her former visit, and addressing Gordon, said:

"Now look around the room!"

The young man did look around the room, and in a moment his startled eyes rested upon the portrait.

A strange, startled cry fell from his lips, and a look of wild amazement settled upon his handsome face.

There was no "put on" about the expression upon his face, nor was there any dissimulation in the cry that fell from his lips.

"Oh, Heaven!" he exclaimed, "what does it all mean?"

"You never saw that picture before?"

"I never did."

"You never heard of it?"

"Never!"

"Look in the glass."

"It is not necessary; that portrait could have been painted for me."

"And you never saw any one who resembled that picture?"

"As I live, I never did."

"You had a father?"

"I never had a father to remember him."

"Where were you born?"

"In France, I have every reason to believe."

It was now Kate's turn to show signs of amazement; and indeed the strange mystery was growing more shrouded than ever.

"You were born in France?"

"I was."

"And where was your father born?"

"I do not know. I never remember seeing my own father."

"Will you tell me your history?"

"All I know about my history is that I was brought up in an English family living in the south of France. I believed them to be my

parents until I was fourteen years old, when one of my brothers in a fit of passion taunted me with the fact that I was not his brother, but a pauper whom his father had taken to educate!"

"Did you prove his story true?"

"I went to the lady whom I had always supposed to be my mother, and forced her to tell me the truth as far as she knew it; and all she did know was that I was left in care of her husband by a man named Balfour Raymond."

"Did she not tell you Balfour Raymond was your father?"

"She did not; indeed she and her husband both proclaimed that they did not know whether the man named was my father or not."

"They did know."

"They never told me."

"Were you kindly treated?"

"I was, and placed at the best schools until I was one-and-twenty, when my reputed father died, and in his will left me a sum of money."

"What was your after career?"

"I went to Australia, where I made some money."

"Why did you leave Australia?"

"I met a man there who told me he had once met an American to whom I bore such a remarkable resemblance, that he would believe the man was my father."

"Did he mention the American's name?"

"He did."

"And the name was—"

"Balfour Raymond."

"You have always led an honorable life?"

"Why do you ask that question?"

"A great deal depends upon your answer."

"I have always led an honorable life."

"Oh, heavens!" murmured Kate, "how strange this all is; the mystery grows deeper and deeper."

The young man laughed; his laugh was that strange, sarcastic expression of bitterness that had fallen from the lips of Arthur Everdell.

"Why do you laugh so bitterly?"

"I laugh that you should say there was any mystery about the matter."

"There is a deep mystery; what is your age?"

"I am about twenty-nine."

"And you say there is no mystery?"

"I do say there is no mystery, I can see through it all."

"What do you perceive?"

"My father could not give me his name. He must have given me my mother's name. I believe lads born as I must have been, are entitled to their mother's family name."

Kate discerned what the young man meant when uttering his ambiguous declarations.

"That portrait was painted many years ago," said Kate.

"So I should judge; the style of dress would so denote."

"One fact is settled," said Kate, "Balfour Raymond was your father."

"Yes, curse—"

"Hold, young man!"

"Why should I?"

"Listen to me. If Balfour Raymond was your father, you were honorably born."

The young man turned deathly pale.

"Say that again!" he exclaimed.

"I believe you are the son of Balfour Raymond; and if you are his son you are as honorably born as a prince of the blood royal!"

"You knew my father?"

"I never saw him in my life."

"Then on what grounds do you make the declaration?"

"I have heard your father's story."

"Will you tell me the tale?"

"I will."

At that moment a shadow was thrown across the room, the shadow of a man who must have been standing upon the veranda.

CHAPTER XXXVI.

"THAT man has followed me here!" said Gordon.

Kate advanced to the window, drew the shutters close and lowered the sash.

"Why should he follow me?" asked the young man.

"There are probably to-day a dozen men on your track."

"A dozen men on my track?"

"Yes."

"Why am I thus 'shadowed'?"

"I will tell you presently, but, in the mean-

time, let me tell you the story of Balfour Raymond."

Kate proceeded and told the story up to the point where Mrs. Raymond was murdered by the masked burglars; but said nothing about the will.

The young man listened with breathless interest, and when Kate had concluded, he exclaimed:

"If I am Balfour Raymond's son, the murdered woman was my mother!"

"She was your mother."

"And that is the portrait of my father?"

"That is the portrait of your father."

"Answer me; have I any brothers or sisters?"

"You have no own brothers or sisters."

"This is a strange story, and, indeed, there is a mystery surrounding me. But why am I pursued?"

"If I tell you, will you act under my advice?"

"I will."

"Do just as I say?"

"First tell me who you are."

"I am a detective."

"A lady a detective!"

"Yes; I am a lady detective."

"And why have you sought me out?"

"I have been employed to discover the murderer of your mother!"

"But upon one or two occasions when we met before you called me Arthur Everdell and once Randolph Cummings."

"I did."

"Why did you call me by those names?"

"Therein lies the mystery."

"Will you explain to me?"

"Not now. I must first solve the mystery myself. I could tell you nothing now."

"Why am I followed?"

"You are looked upon as the murderer of your mother. You are being shadowed because you are suspected."

"Oh, Heaven!"

"Such is the fact."

"Why am I thus shadowed as a criminal?"

"Therein, as I told you before, lies the mystery."

"And you will not explain the mystery to me?"

"Not now; but as I told you before, you are in great peril; you may be sent to prison for life, and naught on earth save you."

The young man turned deathly pale, his eyes assumed a wild, horror-stricken expression, and in low tones he murmured:

"I see it all! I see it all!"

Kate remained silent, when the young man proceeded, and said in tones of wild despairing anguish:

"My father is a criminal! My resemblance to my father is my danger!"

It was a most natural conclusion, and for purposes of her own, Kate determined not to undeceive him, but let him believe it was his father who was his fatal double, until such time as she had fully solved the mystery.

"Oh! would I were dead!" murmured the young man.

Kate's strange silence had confirmed him in the idea that he had fallen upon the correct solution of the mystery.

"Strange complications have arisen," said Kate.

"I will leave America," cried the young man.

"No; you must not."

"But this infamy!"

"Everything will come out all right in the end; listen, there is no proof that your mother was murdered by a Raymond; indeed, I am satisfied in my own mind that she was not."

"Then why am I pursued?"

"The mystery in the end will all be cleared up."

"Who will clear it up?"

"I will," said Kate, and she drew her really elegant figure to its full height.

"What would you advise me to do?"

"Return to New York and assume a disguise."

"I will go away."

"You must not."

"Why?"

"It would be a dangerous experiment; you are 'shadowed,' and should you attempt to go away the catastrophe would be hastened."

"How so?"

"You would be arrested."

"And what will be gained by time?"

"I will catch the real criminal."

"You will fail."

"I will not fail. I have found you. I have discovered much more which it is not prudent at present to reveal."

"I will do as you say."

"You promise to do so?"

"I will keep my promise, but my heart is breaking. Oh, Heaven! but this is terrible!"

"What is terrible?"

"My father."

"But I tell you there is no proof that your father is a criminal."

"You forget the burglary, the description in the paper."

Kate was silenced. She dared not speak lest she might be compelled to reveal more than she desired to at the moment.

"There is no proof, I tell you, that your father is a criminal!"

"I answer exactly to the description of the burglar."

"You recognized your own description?"

"I did."

"It may be an accidental resemblance; there is no proof that your father has been in this country for twenty years."

"There may be no proof, but a moral certainty."

"We must return to New York," said Kate.

"You remember we have been followed?"

"Yes."

"The man may arrest me when we go forth!"

"He shall not arrest you, I will take care of that; you can depend on me!"

CHAPTER XXXVII.

KATE, in her own mind, had concluded that there was a chance that the shadowing detective might attempt an arrest; and when she said he should not do so, she had come to a desperate resolution.

"I may be compelled to leave you at the depot, and ask you to return to New York alone."

"Why do you not accompany me?"

"I will if I can; but the detective who is lurking around here must be thrown off the track at any hazard; you must not be arrested."

Kate and Gordon left the house, and walked down toward the depot.

The man followed, and finally overtook them.

Advancing to Gordon, he said:

"Young man, I would like to speak to you a moment."

"You are a stranger to me, sir," was the reply.

"If you will step aside with me I can explain who I am."

"You need not mind my presence, sir," said Kate.

The lady detective had her veil drawn down over her face.

"My business is with the young man."

"The gentleman is in my company."

"You had better step aside with me, sir."

"No, sir, I decline."

The man brought a slip of newspaper from his pocket and handing it to Gordon, said:

"Will you read that?"

Gordon glanced over the printed slip and saw that it was a cutting from a newspaper containing a description of the missing burglar.

"What have I to do with that?"

"You ought to know."

"I do not."

"It's a pretty accurate description."

"That is nothing to me."

"Don't you know the man described?"

"No, sir."

"I reckon you have not looked in a glass lately."

"Will you explain your business with me?"

"I will."

"Do so."

"I am an officer."

"Very well, what is that to me?"

"I am on your track."

"I can not help that."

"You take matters very coolly."

"Do I?"

"You do."

"It's a way I've got."

"You are my prisoner!"

Kate spoke up and said:

"Have you a warrant?"

"I don't require a warrant, miss, under the circumstances."

"Oh yes, you do."

"Well, I will act on my own authority."

"You dare not make an arrest."

"Your friend is already under arrest, but he might go free."

"Ah, indeed!"

"Yes."

"On what terms?"

"A couple of thousand."

"Why should my friend pay a couple of thousand?"

"To 'keep down.'"

"You mean to keep out of jail?"

"Yes. It's a fifteen-year job, dead sure."

"And you will take a couple of thousand, and let him go?"

"Yes, that's my figure."

"But my friend is an innocent man."

"Oh, I know they're all innocent."

"You can not have the money."

"Eh? You mean to force an arrest!"

"We do not mean to pay a cent to keep an innocent man from arrest."

"Don't fly too high, miss."

"I mean what I say."

"You may come down with a run."

"You have no warrant; you dare not make an arrest."

"The young man, I tell you, is already under arrest."

"He will not go with you."

"Yes, he will."

"No, sir."

"We will see."

"He is safe if no resistance is offered."

"He will not resist you."

"He had better settle, and save trouble."

"He will not pay one cent!"

"You appear to be the boss, miss."

"I am."

"And you proclaim war?"

"I do."

The man drew a pair of handcuffs and seized hold of Gordon.

The next moment he lay in the road.

"We will go now," she said to Gordon.

The thing had been done so quickly Kate's companion hardly realized what had transpired.

The detective lay motionless in the road, and Kate and her companion hurried on to the depot.

The train was just coming in, and when it arrived, they got aboard.

The train only waited a moment, and sped on its way.

"You are safe for the present," said Kate.

"I am saved, through your quickness and address."

"That man is a rascal! He got his deserts!"

"Is he dead?"

"Oh, no. He will come round; indeed, there he is."

As Kate spoke, she pointed to a man running down the road, waving his hat.

He appeared to think the train would stop.

Kate laughed in a merry way, and said:

"He is too late."

"I should say so," came the remark, and the conductor, who was passing through the car, was the speaker.

At the next station, Kate said to her companion:

"We must get off here."

"But we are not in the city."

"I know it, but a telegram is, and somebody we do not wish to see may be waiting for us at the depot in New York."

———

CHAPTER XXXVIII.

KATE and her companion finally, after several minor adventures, made their way to the city.

Kate led the young man to her own home; she was an adept at disguises, and had in her possession all the paraphernalia for the purpose.

Lady Kate had not fully explained to young Gordon the nature of the danger which threatened him.

As intimated in previous paragraphs, she had come to the conclusion that Arthur Everdell and Gordon were two different individuals. There was a mystery which she had not fathomed, but in her own mind she had partly discerned the probable solution.

There was a distinct and positive contrast in the characteristics of the two young men, and yet both bore a striking resemblance to the portrait of Balfour Raymond.

The lady detective succeeded in changing young Gordon's appearance, and when the young man first looked in the mirror, after the transformation, an exclamation of amazement fell from his lips.

To Kate he remarked:

"I would not know myself!"

"I trust no one will penetrate your disguise!" was the reply.

"It is a mystery to me that a disguise should be necessary; indeed, I am in a maze of mystery."

"I will in time solve the mystery, but in the meantime you must be very careful; on no account put aside your present disguise, or the consequences may be fatal!"

A suspicion flashed momentarily across the young man's mind.

To him it appeared strangely improbable that peril could menace him; and with the suspicion came an idea that he was being made the victim of a designing enchantress.

There was but one fact that led him to follow the directions of the strange and mysterious woman who had come across his path in such a singular manner.

She had shown him the portrait of a man who must have been his father. The wonderful fact was undeniably proclaimed by his extraordinary resemblance to the portrait. He knew it could be no chance resemblance. As he had gazed upon the picture, and then upon his own features as reflected in the mirror, he could have been easily persuaded that some weirdly skilled artist had painted his own face from remembrance.

Kate arranged a subsequent meeting with the young man; she had promised to tell him the story of the portrait.

When alone after the departure of young Gordon, Kate sat down and thought over all the strange incidents that had been encountered by her.

There was a difference between the ages of the two young men according to their own statement of their birth dates, and as Kate studied over the matter a glimmer of light as to the true facts was let in upon her mind.

Of one fact Lady Kate was assured—the two young men were not twins.

After busying her mind for a long time, and after arriving at certain conclusions which were to be the guiding lines of her future movements, her thoughts turned upon Arthur Everdell.

A shadow seemed to fall over her as her thoughts centered upon the strange, reckless, generous youth to whom she owed her life.

Kate feared, indeed felt assured, that Arthur Everdell was dead, that he had met a felon's fate.

Believing him dead she permitted her eyes to open to a fact that would otherwise have remained hidden.

Tears filled her eyes, and a great sob of sorrow struggled up from her inmost heart.

She blushed as the consciousness settled upon her mind that she had conceived much more than an ordinary interest in whom? a criminal!

Now that he was dead, she forgot that he was an outlaw, a fugitive from justice, and only remembered that he was handsome, brave and generous. She had come to believe his story, and fully considered the incidents of his early youth: remembered that he had been born among criminals, had been reared as a criminal, in fact, had been, like Oliver Twist, trained to grow up a thief and law-breaker.

It was night when Kate passed forth from her lodgings to the street.

She was to meet young Gordon. The latter appeared to her as an ordinarily bright young man, good-natured and kindly, but he was not Arthur Everdell, that strange, fearless, reckless fellow, who, although reared in the midst of the vilest influences, retained flashes of a glorious nature, which under other circumstances would have made him a very prince among men.

Young Gordon was at the appointed place, and the two proceeded to one of the public parks, where, seating themselves upon one of the benches, they could discuss the situation.

Kate told the story of the elder Balfour Raymond, the wayward, passionate man whose portrait hung in the library at the Raymond mansion.

Young Gordon listened with breathless interest, and when Kate had concluded he exclaimed:

"I am the heir to that estate!"

"The chances are that you are the heir to the estate."

"Then I should put in my claim at once!"

"You can if you choose, but it is my advice that you wait."

Kate had not mentioned to young Gordon the fact of the existence of Arthur Everdell.

"Why should I wait?"

"There are many reasons."

"I know of no reason why I should not present myself as the heir."

"How will you prove that you are Mrs. Raymond's son?"

"My resemblance to the portrait is sufficient—that man was my father!"

"I so believe, but your resemblance to a portrait would not be evidence sufficient by itself in a probate court."

CHAPTER XXXIX.

LADY KATE was not pleased with the spirit displayed by young Gordon. The youth's mind appeared to be fixed upon receiving the estate. The fact of his mother's terrible " taking off " did not appear to excite his attention.

He said:

" I must make the claim, and then proceed to establish my identity."

" It might be fatal to you to succeed," said Kate.

" Fatal to me to succeed?"

" Yes."

" How so?"

" There are many mysteries involved."

" And we must solve those mysteries?"

" Yes."

" We can do so more easily after I have put in a claim for the estate."

" But I tell you success might prove fatal."

" Will you explain how?"

" I would prefer that you would place confidence in me, and wait until I have had an opportunity to work up the case secretly."

" I do not approve of secret measures."

" And you will—"

" Proceed at once to announce myself as Balfour Raymond!"

" And the moment you do you will be arrested."

" Arrested?"

" On what charge?"

" Murder."

The young man leaped to his feet, and, in an excited tone, demanded:

" What do you mean?"

" It is suspected that Mrs. Balfour Raymond's son was her murderer."

" I my mother's murderer!"

" I said that circumstances pointed to her son as the assassin."

" But I can prove my innocence!"

" The chances would be against you.'

" The chances against me?"

" Yes."

" This is horrible."

" Do you not remember that we have but just escaped from a man who was upon your trail? I rescued you; had I not done so, at this moment you would be in prison on the charge of murder!"

" But why as her son am I suspected?"

" That is a question I can not answer at present; but I will say that, owing to a strange and wonderful combination of incidents, circumstances point to Mrs. Raymond's son as her murderer, and your resemblance to the portrait of your father points to you as the son and assassin."

" I tell you I can prove my innocence!"

" I am a detective."

" So you informed me."

" I have had a great deal of experience."

" That may be true."

" I know many circumstances in connection with this case that are unknown to you."

" That also may be true."

" I warn you that at present it would be utterly impossible for you to prove your innocence; for all I know, you may be guilty!"

The young man turned pale, and in an angry tone demanded:

" Do you dare call me an assassin?"

" No; I only said for all I know you may be one; indeed, did I only possess the facts as they appear, I might believe you a murderer, but I am possessed of facts that are known to me only, and I am as fully convinced of your innocence as you are yourself; but even with all the facts in my possession, I could not prove your innocence, and others might most successfully prove your guilt!"

" All this is very strange to me."

" Remember, your whole life has been a succession of strange incidents; you were left by a stranger in care of a strange family, by whom you were reared; you come to a strange coun-

try, and a strange woman, in a strange manner, shows you a portrait to which you bear a most strange and extraordinary resemblance."

" That is all so."

" There are still stranger incidents that shadow over you which have not yet been revealed."

" And you possess the facts?"

" I do."

" Why not reveal them to me?"

" The time has not yet arrived for the revelation; but I am your friend."

" Your friendship for a total stranger is a singular fact in itself."

" I can readily explain my interest in you."

" Please do so."

" I was employed to investigate the mystery of the murder of Mrs. Raymond, and in studying events I was forced to the conclusion that the assassin was a relative—indeed, the murdered lady's son."

" Then you still believe me a guilty man?"

" I do not; and that is why I am interested in your affairs, knowing facts that satisfy me that the murderer was a stranger, and, urged by a common feeling of humanity and professional pride, I have determined to save the innocent from suffering for the guilty."

" Why can you not proclaim my innocence?"

" The mere declaration of your innocence on my part would not save you, as against the singular chain of incidents that point toward the son of the murdered woman as the murderer!"

" What are the incidents?"

" In a legal sense the murdered woman's son is the only person who would have a motive for committing the murder!"

" Is that the only evidence pointing toward the son as the assassin?"

" No."

" What are the other facts?"

" You bear a resemblance to a man against whom all the evidence as uncovered points."

Young Gordon turned pale, and in a tremulous tone exclaimed:

" My father?"

" I can not tell you, but one thing is certain, you are not safe until the real assassin is discovered."

" Tell me, do you suspect my mother's husband?"

" He may have been the murderer!"

" Then, for Heaven's sake, woman, proceed no further in your investigation. I will leave this land; I will never claim the estate. I will not be the means of condemning my own father!"

CHAPTER XL.

" YOU forget that I said I was satisfied that the murder was perpetrated by a stranger."

" You said it might be my father."

" I said it might be your father toward whom the evidence pointed. I admitted that he might be the other man, but I do not believe he was the assassin; indeed, I know he was not."

" And do you propose to run down the real murderer?"

" I do."

" And you will succeed?"

" I will."

" Suppose in the end it should prove that my father is guilty?"

" I know he is not; but I tell you a most strange and extraordinary chain of incidents entangle you. Trust me, and I will establish your innocence, disentangle the skein, and in the end place you in possession of your rights."

" I will trust you."

The words had but just fallen from the young man's lips when two men suddenly leaped forward and seized hold of Gordon.

The first act of one of the men was to tear off the wig that covered the young man's head, revealing the fact that he was in disguise.

Gordon was cool and showed no signs of fear. Kate also was cool and showed no signs of excitement, although it was a critical moment.

The lady detective was in disguise, a " cover " that even hid her identity from the members of the regular detective force.

At a glance she recognized that her companion was under arrest, that his captors were members of the regular force; they were keen men, and had gone under Gordon's skillful disguise.

Kate was a quick thinker, and an emergency had arisen when quick thought was required.

As the men seized George Gordon, one of them exclaimed, " Nab the woman!"

Kate moved a step back, and, as the man reached forth to seize her, she suddenly dealt him a blow that sent him reeling to the ground,

and quick as a flash she darted away in the fast deepening twilight.

One of the men started in pursuit, but Kate had sped like the wind, and, once behind a clump of foliage, a startling transformation occurred.

The woman disappeared, vanished like a puff of smoke in a brisk gale of wind, and a man appeared in the pathway.

The change had taken place in a few brief seconds. The secret of her sudden change was one of the mysteries of Lady Kate's wonderful art as a detective.

The man who was pursuing the woman came upon a man.

" Did you see a female pass here?" came the inquiry.

" Yes."

" Which way did she go?"

" Through the narrow path."

The detective darted away, and Kate leisurely returned to the spot where the original arrest had been made.

It is not a necessary part of our duty to detail how the detectives so successfully trailed down George Gordon. It is sufficient to state that a description had been left at head-quarters of the appearance of the robbers who had made the daring attempt to commit the burglary in the mansion, as described in a former chapter.

The detectives had trailed one man answering the description as having left the train at the Grand Central Depot, and like sleuth-hounds they had trailed him down to his disguise, and had come upon him in the manner narrated.

The detectives were just leading Gordon away, when Kate, in her disguise as a man, came back to the spot.

There was no one around save the actors in the exciting incident.

Kate walked forward and managed to attract Gordon's attention, and sought to signal to him, but he failed to discern her signal.

At the gate leading from the park, the captors were joined by their companion, who had started after Kate.

" Did she give you the slip?"

" She did; it's the most mysterious set-back I ever got. I was close upon her, when suddenly she vanished as though she had ' lit out ' with wings."

Gordon was led away to head-quarters, taken before the chief and questioned.

Kate had given the young man his cue upon a former occasion, and he declined to answer any questions.

The evidence was dead against the prisoner. His disguise was removed, and he stood revealed as answering the description of the burglar to a " clear bill."

The chief said to him:

" You may as well make a clean breast of it, my man, as we've got things dead on you!"

" I am an innocent man," came the reply.

" Oh, yes; you chaps are always innocent when you've the nippers on you; but if you are innocent, how is it you found it necessary to go under a cover?"

Gordon made no reply, but a cold chill passed over him as he fully realized how damning was the fact in favor of guilt.

A suspicion crossed his mind that after all it might in the end prove possible that he had been made the victim of the strange, fascinating woman who had pretended to have such an interest in his welfare.

Bitter thoughts arose in his mind, and he was on the point of breaking through his barrier of imposed silence, when an incident occurred that restrained him.

The chief handed him a daily paper, and pointed to the date, and then to a marked column.

The young man read the matter inclosed in inked brackets, and a look of amazement overspread his face.

The reading was an account of the burglary, and in the description of the escaped burglar he read an exact portraiture in print of himself.

CHAPTER XLI.

THE chief of the detectives sat with his keen eyes fixed upon the prisoner as he read the account, and at the conclusion of the reading said:

" Well, young man, how's that?"

" I am mystified," was the reply.

" Oh, you are mystified, eh?"

" I am."

" Well, now listen to me; it will go easier with you to confess and save us trouble."

" What shall I confess?"

"We want a give-away."

"I do not understand."

"Oh, you are mighty innocent!"

"I am, in two senses."

"Very well, you will have plenty of time to reflect."

The chief gave an order to one of his aids, and George Gordon was led away and locked up in a cell.

Once alone, and indeed he did have time to reflect; but the reflection did not result in furnishing him with a key to the mystery.

He was keen enough to suspect one fact. He was the victim of some mysterious double; but who could the double be? Who was the man who was a criminal and who bore such a resemblance as to lead to the series of strange and humiliating adventures in which he was in the midst?

"Who can he be? Who can he be?" was the inquiry which continually ran through his mind.

After having read the description which had led to his own arrest, he knew that the mysterious double who had involved him in such dire trouble could not be his own father.

Founding a conviction on his resemblance that he was the son of the original of the portrait he had seen, he was satisfied that it was a physical impossibility that the real criminal could be his father.

Knowing his own age, by an easy method of reasoning he was able to conclude that his father could not be less than upward of fifty years, and the description was positively that of a *young man;* and the question arose, who could that *young man*—a criminal and an outlaw—be?

George Gordon was forced to the conclusion that his arrest had been in good faith, that robbery had really been committed by a professional burglar, to whom he unfortunately bore a fatal resemblance.

The young man was still revolving the matter in his mind, when his cell door opened, and a veiled female was ushered into his cell.

"*Speak low!*" came the caution from under the veil.

"Who are you?"

The visitor removed the veil and exhibited a face that, by the dim light, the young man failed to recognize.

"Who are you?" he asked.

The visitor stepped close to the light so that it shone fully upon her features, but the young man could not remember that he had ever seen tne woman before.

"Your 'jig is up,' Arthur Everdell," came tae strange remark.

Young Gordon felt a strange thrill upon hearing the name. He remembered that upon a former occasion he had been persistently addressed by the name of Arthur Everdell. He made no reply.

"You are in a nice predicament," came the additional information.

"If you have merely come here to tell me that, you may consider your visit at an end," said the prisoner.

"Why do you not confess and claim all the advantages that would follow such a course?"

"I have nothing to confess."

"Randolph Cummings, you are unmasked!"

"Go ahead, madame, and call me General Grant if you choose, since you have already applied to me two false and lesser appellations!"

"Do you attempt to deny your several *aliases?*"

"I deny nothing; I admit nothing!"

"Who are you?"

"Politeness requires that I should first know who you are. I first demand an answer."

"Are you really George Gordon?"

"Will you believe me if I answer your question truthfully?"

"I will."

"To the best of my knowledge and belief I am George Gordon."

"And you were not engaged in the burglary?"

"I was not engaged in any burglary."

"Where is the lady who assisted you to assume a disguise?"

"I do not know; it may be you are the person. Indeed I am prepared for all manner of surprises."

"The fact of your being found in a disguise is fatal, when combined with other facts that are known to the police."

"Will you tell me who you are?"

"You have already guessed."

"Is it possible you are—"

"Hush! speak low! Yes; I am the friend who unwittingly led you to 'go under cover.'"

"And you have come to confess to me that I am the victim of a very neat piece of detective strategy?"

"I have come for no such purpose."

"If you are——, you have succeeded in changing your own appearance."

"I have."

"What is the object of your visit?"

"I am here to save you."

"To save me?"

"Yes."

"From what peril?"

"Prison—for a term of years."

"Let me tell you that I have no fear but that I will be perfectly able to establish my innocence."

"Never! You will be railroaded."

"I do not understand."

"You will be tried, convicted, and sentenced in forty-eight hours."

"That is most cheering news."

"I will save you."

"I am in your hands, it's all one to me; in fact I know not what to think, what to say, what to do."

"I came here to ask if you will still trust me?"

"I will trust any one who professes to be a friend; it is evident that I can do nothing for myself."

———

CHAPTER XLII.

"In the end," said Kate, "all shall be made plain to you. At present you must consent to be led blindly along"

"I am being led blindly along without any chance to choose. But tell me why you come to me in a form that I failed to recognize. How do I know that you are the mysterious lady who heretofore has shown such an interest in my affairs?"

"It is a part of my trade to appear under many disguises; you will recognize me when I repeat parts of previous conversations."

Lady Kate did repeat parts of conversations she had held with Gordon, and the young man said:

"I am satisfied."

"Fully?"

"Yes, fully."

"Then I have a revelation to make. A man will be brought here who will positively identify you as a burglar."

"He will perjure himself."

"No; the man, to the best of his knowledge and belief, will swear to the truth."

"Will you not fully explain everything to me?"

"Not now."

"I have already guessed that there is a criminal whom I resemble personally."

"It is possible that you have discerned the truth."

"Who is the man?"

"I can not tell you."

"You have seen him?"

"Possibly."

"Why not be frank with me? you will remember when you first met me you addressed me as Arthur Everdell?"

"I did."

"Who is Arthur Everdell?"

"That is the mystery I am trying to solve."

"At the time you first met me you appeared to think I was this Arthur Everdell?"

"I did."

"You thought I was denying my identity?"

"I did."

"The resemblance must be very remarkable."

"If you are not Arthur Everdell, the resemblance is certainly very remarkable."

"Your equivocal answer would indicate that you are not yet satisfied that you have not been deceived. I swear I am not Everdell. I swear I never heard the name until you addressed me."

"It is all very mysterious. I believe your word, but the circumstances beyond the resemblance are very remarkable. I will yet solve the mystery."

"What relation does this Everdell bear to me?"

"I do not know."

"You suspect?"

"I do."

"What do you suspect?"

"Detectives never tell to others what they suspect. They first solve the mystery and state facts."

"My double has been engaged in a burglary?"

"Yes."

"He murdered my mother?"

"I do not believe he did, but circumstances point to him as the murderer, and your resemblance to him has involved you in your present difficulties."

"Unless he is found I will suffer for him?"

"Cruel as the fact may be, I do not see how under heaven you can escape, unless the real culprit is found."

"If he resembles me he must resemble the portrait."

"Certainly."

"He would have as reasonable a claim to the estate as I?"

"Certainly."

"Oh, Heaven! what a terrible contingency is presented. He must be my brother, and my brother is a criminal. Possibly my father is a criminal?"

Lady Kate remained silent. The young man had certainly presented the probable facts.

"You are silent?"

"I can not say that your suspicion is true. I can not say it is false."

A strange, determined look came to the face of George Gordon, as he remarked in a low tone:

"I see but one way for me to escape from my present position."

Lady Kate read his purpose, and said:

"You must have courage. I am satisfied the mystery will be all cleared up."

"The clearing up may result in disgrace and humiliation."

"Not to you."

"Yes; to me."

"No; listen."

A shadow came over the face of Lady Kate, and there was sadness in her tones, as she said:

"I have every reason to believe that your double is dead. I am satisfied that the fact can be established, also your innocence. If your double be dead, it will never be known that you were in any way connected with him; the wonderful resemblance can be made to appear as merely a case of extraordinary coincidence; under any circumstances, you shall come forth from this trial fully cleared and exonerated from even the shadow of a disgrace."

"The mystery will overshadow me."

"What mystery?"

"The mystery as to the identity of the man whom I resemble."

"That mystery shall all be cleared up."

"But you say my double is dead."

"Never mind; I still hold facts sufficient to solve the mystery."

"Why not reveal them to me?"

"I must first satisfy myself that Arthur Everdell is dead."

"There is a chance that he lives?"

"Yes."

"Then it is better I were dead."

"No. Listen; I will speak plainly. I do believe Arthur Everdell is your brother; and should it prove that he lives, I will have some remarkable disclosures to make. There is a strange and wonderful mystery shadowing both your lives; and although Arthur Everdell may be technically a criminal, he is one of the noblest and most generous and worthy men that ever lived."

"A criminal noble, worthy, and generous?"

"Yes."

"Impossible!"

"What I say is true; and herein lies another mystery."

Further talk was at this moment interrupted.

———

CHAPTER XLIII.

An officer came to the cell and ordered George Gordon to come forth.

Kate at once discerned that he was being summoned for identification.

She managed to whisper to him:

"*Be silent* and brave, neither admit nor deny anything; and remember it will all come out right in the end."

Kate's suspicions proved correct.

George Gordon was led into a room and placed in the midst of at least a dozen other men, the latter representing as many different types of humanity. A few moments passed and a young man entered.

The party who was shown in ran his eye over the group of men until his glance rested upon George Gordon. At once a shadow overspread his kindly face, as, advancing to the prisoner, he placed his hand on his shoulder and whispered:

"I can not help it; I pity you!"

Several detectives stepped forward, and one of them asked:

"Is that your man?"

"That is the man."

"You have seen him before?"

"Yes."

"Under what circumstances?"

The young man, who was the party whose life Arthur Everdell had saved upon the night of the attempted robbery, detailed a portion of the incidents, all of which are well known to our readers.

"You are sure that is the man?"

"I am sure," was the reply, and again the young man turned to George Gordon and said:

"I pity you, but I can not help it."

A proud flash came into the prisoner's eyes as he said:

"Do you denounce me as a criminal?"

The young man stepped close to the prisoner, and, in a low tone, remarked:

"I am your friend. I will do all I can for you, but I can not deny that you are the man."

"I never saw you before in all my life!" said Gordon, in an indignant and positive tone.

The young man was silent, when Gordon started to say more. But at the moment he caught a warning glance: a pair of handsome eyes were fixed meaningly upon him, and he restrained his speech.

Lady Kate had entered the room. She had anticipated what the young man had determined to say, and she managed to warn, him in due time. Under no circumstances did she wish that the idea should be suggested that the prisoner had a double.

The fates were against the young man, and a great bitterness pervaded his heart as he was led back to his cell.

Upon the day following the incidents we have described, George Gordon was taken before a judge, and a regular preliminary examination was held.

The charge against him was attempted burglary and murder; the penalty upon conviction not less than ten, and permissibly, according to the option of the judge, twenty years imprisonment in state-prison.

Kate had managed to gain access to the prisoner in the morning, previous to his removal to the court-room.

Young Gordon had announced his intention of declaring his identity, when Kate urged him not to do so; she even urged him not to employ a lawyer.

"What shall I do?" was the question the young man asked.

"Nothing."

"If I do nothing I shall be convicted."

"There is nothing that you can do that will save you from conviction. If the Queen of England were to come over and testify in your behalf as to your previous good character and all, it would not save you in the face of the positive evidence of the young man who identified you last night as one of the burglars."

A fresh suspicion appeared to enter the young man's mind, and he said:

"How do I know that the identification is not all part of a conspiracy?"

"If there is a conspiracy against you, I must be at the bottom of it."

"How do I know that you are not? All your advice to me is very strange, and all these troubles have come upon me since *my first meeting* with you!"

"The latter fact is merely coincidental," said Kate; "but mark me, I do not propose to aid you any more if you are determined to look upon me as an enemy. If you desire to throw me over, secure a lawyer and do the best you can; but I warn you that you will go to jail for the better part of your life!"

Kate spoke in an excited and earnest manner, and the young man was deeply impressed. He said:

"I do not wish to throw you over."

"Then you must follow my advice implicitly. I can prove to you that I am a female detective officer; that I have no interest in sending you to jail: indeed, professionally, I have accidentally learned that you are innocent, and although convinced of your innocence, I can not prove it now; in the end I may be able to do so. As the matter stands, the evidence is dead against you, and it all comes of your fatal resemblance to a criminal, and unless that criminal can be produced dead or alive, neither now nor later on can you be saved!"

"It must have been a most wonderful combination of circumstances that brought you and me together," remarked Gordon.

"All the incidents in which you are involved are the most remarkable in criminal history. I tell you, as the facts stand, the fates are dead against you. Remember, you would have been arrested if you had not met me. The only really fortunate turn of affairs in your behalf is your meeting with me; and if you follow my advice, in the end you will be so convinced."

"I will follow your advice."

"You will not again have a suspicion of my motives?"

"I will not."

"Remember, the most startling developments may come out during the examination that is to take place."

"I am now fully resolved to leave my fate in your hands."

"Adhere to your resolution, and all will be well."

CHAPTER XLIV.

KATE had told the young man that he might expect the most startling developments, but she herself little dreamed how startling those developments would prove.

Additional witnesses came forward and positively identified George Gordon as one of the burglars. They were respectable men, and swore against him in the most positive manner.

Kate had managed to secure a seat in the court-room beside the prisoner, and during the fearful ordeal whispered words of encouragement and advice.

The young man had studied the face of his lady friend, and at length had come to place implicit confidence in her.

Having recovered from the original bewilderment attending his first arrest, he had been able to perceive how a strange and fatal resemblance could involve him as it had.

In the midst of the examination a witness was introduced who made the most startling revelations.

The witness was a man who had served Mrs. Raymond as a coachman, and he positively swore that he had seen the prisoner lurking around the grounds of the Raymond mansion upon the night preceding the murder.

The man was past middle life, evidently an honest and respectable fellow, and his evidence was as clear and positive as that of the other witnesses.

The testimony of the last witness put a new face on the whole proceedings.

The prisoner had previously been identified as a robber and attempted murderer, and at the last he was implicated as an actual assassin.

Poor Kate! her blood ran cold; and iron-nerved as she was, it required the utmost resolution to keep herself from making an outcry.

George Gordon remained calm under the later developments, but he saw the look of convulsive agony that came over the face of the lady detective, and at once a fresh suspicion took possession of his mind.

He still believed Kate to be his friend, but he thought he discerned the motive for her friendship. She would save him because she knew he was innocent, and Gordon decided that her knowledge of his innocence came of a previous knowledge of the guilt of another man—the man to whom he bore such a strange resemblance.

The suspicion that entered the young man's mind was that Kate was interested in his double, and hence her anxiety to have him keep silent on the subject of a mistake through a fatal resemblance.

She would save him, but she would save her friend—save the latter, in the end, at *his expense*, if necessary.

It will not interest our readers to have us record all the proceedings; it is sufficient to state that the charge of attempted murder was supplemented by a charge of actual murder, and the prisoner was held on the latter charge to await the action of the grand jury.

We have no interest in our story in the newspaper comments which followed the strange developments of the regular investigation.

George Gordon was led to prison as an accused murderer.

It was not until the day following the examination that Kate visited him.

The young man had resolutely adhered to his promise to remain silent before the public, but when Kate entered his cell he spoke out his suspicions.

To his visitor the young man said, abruptly:

"I see all; you are a friend of the real criminal; you are taking advantage of circumstances to *save him* at all hazards! You will save me if *you can!*"

"Listen to me, George Gordon," said Kate. "This is the last time that I shall seek to defend myself against your suspicions; they are all false! This moment, rather than see you suffer, I would surrender the real criminal were it in my power to do so, to save you. I do not know whether the really guilty man be alive or dead. I fear he is dead, or at least dangerously wounded. I again swear to you that I will do all in my power to rescue you from your present position. I would surrender my own brother were he guilty rather than that an innocent man should suffer!"

"I recall my words. You will never again be called upon to defend yourself against any charge from me!"

Kate had endured a continued agony of thought ever since the moment the coachman had made the terrible declaration.

Despite all Arthur Everdell's protestations to the contrary as to his blood-guiltiness, despite his seeming nobility and generosity, the conviction was forced upon her mind that he was an assassin—a cool, deliberate murderer—the slayer of *his father's wife!*

Bitterness and mortification filled her soul; she despised herself for her weakness; she could not deny to herself the truth; and it was a terrible thought, the realization of the interest she had taken—a woman's heart-interest—in a criminal!

As intimated in our opening chapters, Kate herself had been a waif; she had won her way to her position in the face of many difficulties; and it was because of the latter fact that she had been prepared to become interested in Arthur Everdell upon listening to his strange tale of his early life.

To George Gordon Kate said:

"You may not see me for a number of days. I will go to seek your double; but under any circumstances, follow out the instructions I have given you. I have engaged a lawyer, he will only act as a shield against the importunities of other counselors who will offer services; but mark my words, under no circumstances shall you suffer beyond what you have suffered!"

Kate left the prison.

That night the lady detective met with a startling adventure.

END OF FIRST HALF.

THE IRISH DETECTIVE.

By OLD SLEUTH.

Old Sleuth Library

Lady Kate, the Dashing Female Detective.—Second half.
By OLD SLEUTH.

This Number contains a Complete Story, Unchanged and Unabridged.

No. 30   { SINGLE }   { NUMBER. }   GEORGE MUNRO, PUBLISHER,   Nos. 17 to 27 Vandewater Street, New York.   { PRICE }   { 10 CENTS. }   Vol. II.

Old Sleuth Library, Issued Monthly. By Subscription, $2 per annum.
Copyrighted 1886, by George Munro.—Entered at the Post Office at New York at Second Class Rates.—September 1, 1886
Copyrighted 1882 and 1886, by George Munro.

LADY KATE,

THE DASHING FEMALE DETECTIVE.

By OLD SLEUTH.

SECOND HALF.

CHAPTER XLV.

LADY KATE was fully set upon discovering the fate or whereabouts of Arthur Everdell. She had fully determined to hand him over to justice.

To herself she muttered:

"I will do it and die. I will not survive the discovery of my own mortifying weakness."

Kate was going about in the disguise she had worn when present at head-quarters at the time young Gordon was first positively identified as one of the robbers.

She had just passed from the prison, and was walking down the street, when a pleasant-faced young gentleman accosted her.

The lady detective recognized the young man as the gentleman who had first identified Gordon.

"I would speak with you a few moments," he said.

"Proceed," came the abrupt response.

"You are a friend of the burglar against whom I testified?"

"Who told you I was his friend?"

"I assumed you were his friend."

"How did you chance to assume that I was his friend?"

The young man was a keen fellow, and at once answered:

"Possibly I was mistaken?"

"Possibly you were not."

"I did not think I was."

"We will assume that I am his friend."

"I owe my life to that young man."

"I thought he attempted to take your life?"

"I did not so testify. I only testified to the fact as to his being one of the gang who broke into my father's house."

"You now say he saved your life?"

"I do."

"In what manner?"

The young man related the circumstances as detailed to our readers in a former chapter.

"Great Heaven!" ejaculated Kate, "this man accused of murder, and yet on every hand he is saving life!"

The mystery was sinking into a deeper shadow.

Kate knew of generous and noble actions, she had heard of others, and here again came the testimony to Arthur Everdell's nobility, under the most peculiar circumstances.

The murder of Mrs. Raymond had been a horrible deed—an atrocious massacre of a helpless old lady. The indications were that the assassin had been a heartless and blood-thirsty brute. How could it be that Everdell was that assassin? All the testimony went to prove that he was a man who would rather lose his own life than take the life of another.

Kate inquired particularly into all the circumstances, and finally remarked:

"Why did you not give the prisoner the benefit of what you are telling me?"

"It would have done him no good before the court; but I wish you to understand that I am his friend."

"You the friend of a murderer?"

"I do not believe he is a murderer."

"You heard the testimony?"

"Yes; I heard the testimony; the witness only testified to seeing the prisoner around the evening preceding the murder."

"Why should he be there?"

"You must have a suspicion?"

"I have not."

"I have made some inquiries, and I am convinced that as far as the murder of Mrs. Raymond is concerned, the young man Gordon is merely the victim of an unfortunate incident."

"What have you learned?"

"All the facts that are already known to you."

"What facts?"

"That the accused is the son of the woman who was murdered?"

"From what quarter did you get your information?"

"I am a junior in the law firm that does business for Mr. Augustus Prang."

"And he told you the story?"

"No; but I learned the facts of the strange romance from papers on file in our office."

"Do the other members of your firm know the facts?"

"Not as connecting them with the prisoner."

"How is it that you have been able to connect the tale with the prisoner?"

"I was acquainted with Mrs. Raymond; there is a portrait of the lady's husband hanging in the library of the Raymond mansion."

"Well?" ejaculated Kate, interrogatively.

"The accused resembles the portrait in such an extraordinary manner that I am convinced he is the son of Balfour Raymond."

"How do you explain the fact that you are aware of my knowledge of all these details?"

"I saw you when you first visited the Raymond mansion. I thought nothing of the incident at the time; but, having since seen you interested in the prisoner, I am led to believe that you know all concerning him."

"And do you know who I am?"

"I do."

"Who am I?"

"Lady Kate, the great female detective."

"And now what do you propose?"

"I propose to save that young man if we can."

"Why are you so anxious to save him?"

"He saved my life, and besides, his has been a strange career. He merits sympathy from those who know all the circumstances of his life."

"I have a great mind to intrust you with a secret," said Kate.

"If you have a secret, the revelation of which would present the prisoner in a more favorable light, I pray you open it up to me."

"If I were assured that I could trust you?"

"You can trust me."

"What is your name?"

"My name is Edward Bayne."

Kate was thoughtful for a moment, when the young man said:

"You need not fear to trust me, and I may be of great service to you."

"You are the principal witness against Gordon?"

"I know it, but if you and I work right I will never be called upon to testify against him!"

CHAPTER XLVI.

LADY KATE did not fully catch the intent of the young man's declaration, and she said:

"What would you propose?"

"I would propose to get him out of the country!"

"Aid him to escape?"

"Yes."

"Do you remember I am a detective?"

"I do."

"And you propose to me to become a law-breaker?"

"Yes; circumstances alter cases."

"How did you come to learn that I was Lady Kate, the female detective?"

"That is my secret."

Kate had just come to appreciate that the young man really had a secret; indeed her suspicions were fully aroused to a belief that he had obtained information from some other source than the law papers in the hands of his reputed seniors.

"You keep your secret and I will keep mine!" said Kate.

"But you will assist in the rescue of Balfour Raymond?"

"I can not join any scheme with a party who keeps a secret from me."

"But you have a secret?"

"Yes; and I am willing to exchange secrets with you."

"I am not at liberty to accept your proposition."

"Aha! I see!" exclaimed Kate.

The young man's declaration, "I am not at liberty to exchange secrets," was a partial betrayal, and a full confirmation of Kate's suspicions. He was *acting under instructions*, and Kate concluded that it was Mr. Prang who was the instructor.

To Edward Bayne Kate said:

"Go and tell Mr. Prang that if he wishes me to co-operate with you, he must give you permission to reveal all secrets."

"I have had no talk with Mr. Prang over this matter."

"And you wish to aid the prisoner to escape?"

"I do."

"How would you proceed?"

"Any amount of money is at your command; the matter will be trusted to your ingenuity."

"I must have time to think the matter over."

"When will you meet me?"

"To-night."

"Where?"

Kate named the place of meeting, and they separated.

When once more alone the faculties of the lady detective were tested to the utmost to divine the meaning of the last development.

She had revealed nothing to Edward Bayne, and had only permitted him to believe that she was interested in the accused.

Edward Bayne had revealed nothing to her beyond the fact of a personal obligation, which, to say the least, was a questionable one.

The new mystery lay in the fact of Bayne's desire to aid Gordon to escape at all hazards, and in the fact, also, that he knew much of the history of Gordon, suspected his real identity, and knew of his being heir to a large estate.

It was still further a mystery to her how he chanced to have had her own identity down so fine, and a positive knowledge of her interest in the case.

Kate had been somewhat bewildered by the many incidents that had come so thick and fast; but she was becoming inured to surprises, and was about ready to settle down to earnest detective work.

She had a plain duty before her: at all hazards she must learn the fate of Arthur Everdell.

Edward Bayne's story of Arthur's nobility and daring generosity when it came to a question of life and death, aroused the hope once more in her bosom that Arthur was guiltless of the death of Mrs. Raymond.

That same night Kate got herself up in a disguise, the nature of which it is not necessary for us to record. It is sufficient to say that it was intended to enable her to traverse in safety, at any hour of the night, the worst quarters of the city.

Kate desired to go to places where the lowest class of burglars and thieves were wont to assemble.

Late upon the evening of the day when the incidents occurred which we have described, a rough, half-drunken sailor entered a low drinking-place.

Probably but one woman ever lived who was fully capable of assuming the rôle that Kate had chosen. Her early life had furnished her with an experience which enabled her to hide her beauty, harden the tones of her voice, and actually make perfect her metamorphose.

The sailor passed to the bar and called for a drink.

At once several sinister glances were fixed upon the new-comer.

The place was the resort of all manner of criminals. They hung around like so many birds ready to pounce down on a victim at a moment's notice.

A couple of the sharps set their "beaks" for the sailor, and when an opportunity offered, one of them stepped forward, and in a familiar tone said:

"Hello, Johnny!"

The sailor turned from the bar, faced the man who had addressed him, and said a few words that caused the man to fall back with a broad grin upon his face; at the same time he remarked:

"You work it well, 'cocky.'"

"I was in on the last 'skylark.'"

"A bad 'dip in' for the lads that?"

"Yes."

"Chances were dead agin' the boys."

"Dead agin' us; but tell me, has Cummings 'bobbed'?"

"Ain't seen nothing of him since the night afore the close play up the river."

"I'm afeared he crawled off like a wounded crow, and 'died on a branch.'"

"Can't tell; was he badly spoiled?"

"Can't tell, we all 'split' when the drum beat, and I haven't seen a familiar face since; have you seen Dandy Jim?"

"Yes."

"Had he no news?"

"He didn't 'puff' anything."

Kate's heart sunk within her; fate pointed as though Everdell were a corpse.

CHAPTER XLVII.

As our readers may not understand the thieves' *patois* used at the close of the preceding chapter, we will briefly explain the questions and answers.

Kate, when first addressed, had used some thieves' talk, and had put out two or three signals, intimating that she was under cover, hiding from the detectives who were, as she intimated, close upon her trail.

The remark "you do it well, 'cocky,'" was intended to convey the idea that her disguise and "get up" were perfect.

The remark that she was in the last "skylark," conveyed the information that she was one of the masked burglars for whom the police were looking.

The expression "a bad dip in," meant the attempted burglary had turned out a disastrous failure; and the inquiry "has Cummings 'bobbed'?" was asking had he been seen since the night of the attempted robbery.

The inquiry "was he badly 'spoiled'?" meant badly wounded; and the term all "split," meant separated; while the remark "died on a branch," meant by the road side like a bird wounded which could not find its nest and died on the branch of a foreign tree.

"He didn't 'puff' anything," meant he didn't tell anything.

As stated, the total result of the lady detective's inquiries pointed to the fact that Arthur Everdell was dead, had died in some strange place of the wounds he had received.

It is customary among thieves when wounded or in trouble of any kind to convey word concerning their situation to some of their friends, and the fact that Arthur had not sent any such word or communicated with his pals in any way looked bad.

Kate left the place, and was proceeding along the street, one of the worst and most dangerous streets in New York to travel after nightfall, when she was accosted by a man.

The man was roughly dressed, but his voice was pleasant as he said in a warning tone:

"*You are in danger!*"

Kate was not at all alarmed, but she was surprised; still in a careless tone, she answered:

"I reckon you're signaling the wrong craft, cap."

"You are down here for *news?*"

Kate did give a start upon being thus addressed, and at once said:

"Who are you?"

"I have the advantage of you, my land-lubber."

The man made the last remark in a semi-sarcastic tone.

"What advantage have you over me?"

"I know who you are: you do not know me."

"You know me, eh?"

"Yes."

"Mebbe you sailed with me, cap?"

The man laughed, but there was no roughness in his quiet hilarity.

"Heave along, cap," said Kate, "I've laid my course, and I don't wish to lose the fair wind."

"Suppose I take you under convoy?" said the man.

"Thank you. I'll make port well enough."

"Listen, *my lady*, I've something to say to you, and you might as well come along with me."

Kate was more than surprised. She was absolutely amazed that this man should have penetrated her disguise.

She was a bold woman, and having a certain purpose in view, she was prepared to take many risks.

"You have something to say to me?"

"Yes."

"You are a stranger?"

"I propose to remain a stranger."

"And you ask me to accompany you?"

"Yes."

"You have considerable 'cheek.'"

Again the man laughed in a quiet way, and answered:

"I will do you no harm, and I can impart some very valuable information to you."

"What right have I to accept your word for what you promise?"

"You have no right to accept my word; you must take chances. I can give you some strange and important information."

"On what subject?"

"You can guess."

"I am not guessing to-night."

"I can tell you about George Gordon."

Kate had anticipated that the man was in some mysterious manner connected with the purpose of her visit to that place, but it was still a matter of amazement to her the extraordinary manner in which she had been recognized.

"What can you tell me about George Gordon?"

"More than he can tell you himself."

A strange suspicion crossed Kate's mind, and she determined to brave all chances and accompany the man who had accosted her in such a strange place and manner.

"Where would you lead me?"

"Lady Kate, the wonderful female detective, does not care where I lead her; she can take care of herself anywhere."

"Lead on, I will follow you."

The man led the way along the street until he came to a sort of alley-way, a narrow street, the stench from which was horrible.

"We will go this way."

"One moment, my friend," said Kate.

"Well?" came the interrogative exclamation.

"You recognize me?"

"Yes."

"You may be an enemy."

"No."

"I would have you remember one fact; my colleagues will know where to look for me."

"That's all right!"

"If you mean treachery, you run a risk."

"You will learn that I do not mean treachery."

"You can make your revelations here."

"No."

"Why not?"

"We must be where there is no chance of listeners."

"I have warned you, my friend, and my warning was no idle boast; lead on!"

CHAPTER XLVIII.

SOME inexperienced detectives would have hesitated before following a man under all the circumstances, in such a place, but Lady Kate was too earnest in her purpose to let any chance slip by, no matter what risk might attend her adventure.

Kate had bidden the man lead on, and he obeyed.

The brave little woman felt her courage fail just a little, when the man stopped before a low door, and said:

"We enter here."

"Lead on!" came the response, and the lady detective spoke in a firm tone.

The man stepped beneath the door-way, and Kate followed. It was indeed a horrible and noisome place. The detective's strange conductor was fain to say:

"It is not a pleasant place to bring a lady."

"Never mind; proceed!"

The man led the way up a rickety and noisome staircase, and at length opened the door of a room on the top floor.

An exclamation of surprise burst from the lips of the disguised lady detective as she entered the room.

A light was burning in the apartment, which was neatly, even luxuriously furnished; and every article was the selection of a cultivated taste.

The man observed Kate's exclamation of surprise, and said:

"You are amazed?"

"I am."

"All is cleanly and pleasant here; we are at the top of the house, and I have pure air conducted into this room through the roof; you need have no fear now, although the approach to these rooms was through noisome passages."

"Are these your apartments?"

"Yes."

"You are evidently a man of taste."

"Well?"

"Why should you select such a place as an abode?"

"You see how I dress?"

"I do."

"You are a detective?"

"I am."

"Can you not discern?"

"You are in hiding?"

"I am in hiding."

"But I should say that the contrast between the *situation* and your apartments was a circumstance liable to attract attention and arouse suspicion?"

"No one comes into my apartments."

"Have you no neighbors in adjoining rooms?"

"None on this floor, and my outer rooms are a blind; you are now in the inner sanctuary."

"I am here, and now will you tell me how it is you chance to know me so well that you can even detect my identity under my present disguise?"

"I am an outlaw. I have been playing hide-and-seek with detectives for many years."

"Why should you admit to me that you are a criminal and in hiding?"

"I have nothing to fear from you."

"How do you know?"

"Well, I do know, and that is sufficient; and let me tell you that as it is your business to shadow people, so it has been my business to shadow you."

"Why have you shadowed me?"

"Some day you shall know."

"You had a purpose in bringing me here?"

"I did."

"Will you proceed and open up your business?"

"George Gordon is in jail?"

"He is."

"And he is an innocent man?"

"He *is* an innocent man!"

"You know that?"

"I do."

"The charge against him is murder?"

"Yes."

"Is it not strange that an innocent man should be arrested for murder?"

"You said you would tell me strange facts. You are merely asking questions."

"And you shall answer my questions."

For the first time the man used a threatening tone when he used the word *shall*.

"I will not answer your questions unless you tell me who you are."

"I will tell you nothing, and you *will* answer my questions."

"We will see!"

Kate began to feel that she had been inveigled into the den of a dangerous man, an enemy.

"We may as well understand each other, fellow!"

As Kate spoke she drew a revolver, covered the man, and said:

"Open that door, I will not remain here!"

"Ah! you are armed!"

"I am armed!"

The man showed no signs of fear as he remarked:

"I must take that weapon from you."

The fellow sprung toward her, but in an instant rolled over upon the floor, and lay still.

Kate had not fired her weapon; she had fallen back upon a more deadly article of defense, when used in the hands of an experienced and daring person.

The man lay upon the floor, and Kate stepped over his body to go from the room.

The man called.

"Do not go!"

"You scoundrel, you have shown your hand!"

"Do not go!" he repeated, and partly rose up.

"Your purpose is evil," said Kate.

"On my soul, no! I did mean to intimidate. I would not have harmed you."

"Why should you have intimidated me?"

"I wished to obtain certain information from you."

"And you would have scared me into telling all you wished to know?"

"That was my purpose."

"You are frank."

"Do not go; you have conquered me."

"Will you tell me who you are?"

"Before we separate I will. Do not go!"

"I will remain," said Kate.

CHAPTER XLIX.

As the man rose to his feet, Kate observed that he was a much older man than she had at first supposed.

Indeed, since her meeting with him, several suspicions as to his identity had crossed her mind. But the discovery of his advanced age had dispelled them all.

The man had risen and taken his seat, and Kate also resumed her chair.

"You are a wonderful woman," said the man.

"I did not come here to listen to compliments."

"As a favor, you will answer a few questions?"

"Not until you tell me how you chanced to know of my connection with this case."

"I have been shadowing you ever since your first visit to the Raymond mansion."

"What relation do you bear to the young man Gordon?"

"None whatever."

"Why are you so deeply interested in his fate?"

"I am not at liberty to tell you now."

"Then our interview is at an end."

"We may come to an understanding."

"How?"

"If you will answer a few questions for me."

"Why should I answer your questions when you refuse to answer mine?"

"It may be that before we part, if you will answer my questions, I will be at liberty to answer yours."

Kate thought a moment, and concluded that she could discern the old man's purpose, and she said:

"I may answer your questions—proceed."

"I once before remarked that it was strange that Gordon should be arrested."

"You did."

"There must be some secret reason why he was arrested."

"There is secret reason why he was arrested."

"You know that reason?"

"I do."

In an eager tone the old man said:

"Reveal it to me!"

"Since you know so much of my late plans and purposes, how is it that you are compelled to ask the question?"

"That is the one mystery I have failed to fathom."

"You do not know why Gordon was arrested?"

"I do not."

"I can tell you."

"I know you can."

"I will not until you tell me who you are."

"I am a friend of Gordon's father."

"Why not admit the truth? Why not admit that you are *Balfour Raymond, the murderer of your wife?*"

Kate had expected to behold the old man start and quake, but he only laughed in a quiet way, and said:

"You are wrong. I am not Balfour Raymond."

"Of course you would deny your identity."

"Can you not see I am an old man?"

"Ha! ha!" laughed Kate, "I am a woman, but do I look like one?"

"You would charge that I am in disguise?"

"You may be."

"I am not. Come, make an examination and satisfy yourself."

Kate did make an examination, and did satisfy herself that the man was not disguised as far as his age was concerned.

"You are satisfied?"

"I am."

"You will answer my question?"

"I will presently; but first tell me, where is Balfour Raymond?"

"In jail."

"You mean Gordon?"

"Yes."

"He is the son of Balfour Raymond. Where is Balfour Raymond, senior?"

"I do not know."

"He fled after the murder."

"Balfour Raymond is guiltless of the blood of his wife."

"Have you any suspicion as to who the real murderer is?"

The old man was silent.

"Come, answer my question!"

"I have no suspicion now."

"You say you are not interested in young Gordon particularly, and yet you admit that you are a friend of his father?"

"I am interested in him, but my interest extends beyond him. I said I was a friend of his father."

"You are anxious that Gordon should escape from prison?"

"I am."

"Why?"

"Because he is innocent."

"You have a reason back of that."

"I may have."

"What is it?"

"I can not tell you until you have given me greater information."

"Tell me why you are so anxious that Gordon should escape?"

"As matters stand he will be convicted."

"Yes."

"Nothing on earth can save him but one recourse."

"And what is that one recourse?"

"There must be a *double*; there must be a guilty man to whom George Gordon bears a most extraordinary resemblance."

The old man displayed a great deal of emotion as he uttered the words above written.

"Yes; there must be a *double*, a guilty man to whom Gordon bears an extraordinary resemblance!" repeated Kate.

"And herein lies the mystery of Gordon's arrest!" continued the old man.

"Herein lies the mystery of Gordon's arrest!" repeated Kate.

"To save Gordon the guilty man, his mysterious double, must be produced."

"You are right."

"And it is your purpose to hunt up the guilty man and produce him; that is your purpose as a detective?"

"Yes; that is my purpose as a detective."

The old man had spoken in a strange, wild tone, and there was a frenzy in his voice as he declared:

"You shall *never carry out your purpose!*"

CHAPTER L.

Kate sat silent; a new and startling mystery had come shadowing down upon all the others. She was perfectly cool, but at the same time she discerned that she had been deceived, and that the old man was "playing her" from first to last as the phrase goes. She discerned that she had been deliberately inveigled to that apartment, so that as a detective she could not clear George Gordon the innocent, by producing before the court Arthur Everdell, the really guilty man!

"You have opened up your game?" said Kate.

"Yes, I have opened up my game, but you can save your life."

"Thank you."

"You would defy me?"

"Certainly."

"You think because you knocked me over that you are my master?"

"I have not said so, but I think so."

"You think because I begged of you to remain that I am at your mercy?"

Kate remained silent.

"I was at your mercy then, I was ahead of time. I am not at your mercy now, you are at mine!"

Kate plainly read just what the man would imply and answered carelessly:

"I do not scare."

"I have not been alone shadowing you."

"Was it all the purpose of your shadowing?"

"Will you answer one plain question?"

"If I choose I will."

"Have you ever met George Gordon's double?"

"Possibly I have."

"You have penetrated his disguise—you can identify him?"

"I can."

"Would you save your life?"

"My life is not in peril."

"Would you earn a large sum of money?"

"You would buy me off from my duty?"

"Yes, I would buy you off—buy you only to save your life."

"I think it is about time for me to go."

"No, no; do not go now; it is death! I would save you. I told you when I first met you to-night that you were in peril. I brought you here to save your life."

"What do you desire at my hands?"

"I wish your aid to discover the man for whom Gordon is suffering."

"Why do you wish to find him?"

"To save him."

"And you would let the innocent suffer for the guilty?"

"No; Gordon shall escape."

"But the guilty must escape, at all hazards. I recognize your programme."

"Both must escape, at all hazards. Gordon is heir to a large estate."

"Such is the fact."

"So is his half-brother!" came the startling declaration.

"But you would save one brother by sacrificing the other—the innocent for the guilty?"

"No, no; both are innocent!"

"Where is their father?"

"Dead!"

"Was he guilty?"

"No: what object would he have in murdering the woman who was once his wife? But he was in his grave long before her murder took place."

"Are you not aware that all the evidence, then, points to George Gordon's half-brother as the murderer?"

"I tell you both are innocent!"

"The younger brother is a self-admitted thief."

The old man groaned in agony as he murmured:

"I know that! I know that!"

"Then why should he not be the assassin? A robbery was committed at the time of the murder, and Gordon's brother was seen near the place the evening preceding the tragedy."

"But he had no hand in the deed."

"Will you tell me who you are, and just the relation you bear to both these young men?"

"Not now; not now!"

"If you will, I can impart certain facts to you."

"I can not tell you who I am."

"You admitted you were an outlaw."

"It was a false admission."

"You are not a criminal?"

"I am not a criminal."

"Why did you proclaim yourself one?"

"I wished to impress you, but your brave demeanor has changed the whole tenor of my plans."

"But you said my life was in peril?"

"It was; I saved you."

"By whom was my life threatened?"

"By those who would prefer to have George Gordon die."

"Heavens!" thought Kate; "here is another mystery! Indeed, what a labyrinth of strange purposes and incidents environ these two young men!" was her conclusion.

"George Gordon has enemies?" said Kate.

"He has bitter enemies!"

"And they are on my track?"

"They are on your track."

"How did they learn that I was interested in saving his life?"

"From a detective who pointed you out to them."

"And they were following me to-night?"

"They were on the lookout for you."

"Is what you are telling me the truth?"

"It is the truth."

"Your first interest is in the real culprit?"

"If I admit so much you may use the admission."

"I will not."

"My interest is in the real culprit; if you knew all the circumstances of his life, your interest would be in him also."

"Possibly I do know the incidents of his life."

"Then you have met?"

"We will see; listen, he was born amidst poverty, reared to crime?"

"Yes, yes, that is true; and Heaven forgive me, it is all my fault."

The old man bowed his head and wept.

CHAPTER LI.

KATE began to feel that she was on the point of hearing strange revelations; why should the old man weep? Who was he? Why should he exclaim, "It is all my fault"?

As Kate knew the circumstances, there was but one man upon whose head would rest the blame of Arthur Everdell's misdirected career.

The old man had denied that he was Balfour Raymond, but he had made other misstatements.

Again, who but Balfour Raymond could cry out in agony, "it is all my fault"?

"It is all your fault?" queried Kate.

"Yes; it is all my fault!"

"And you are his father?"

"No."

"The young man's father is alone to blame for his wicked education."

"His father is to blame! his father was a scoundrel! his mother an angel!"

New light began to break in upon our heroine's mind.

"His mother was your daughter?"

"Yes."

"Tell me all about it?"

"There is no need."

"More need than you dream."

"You shall hear my story. Balfour Raymond married my only daughter."

"But he had a wife?"

"He had a divorce from his first wife—or at least pretended to have one."

"You did not approve of the marriage?"

"I cast my daughter off. It was a clandestine marriage. I am a rich English merchant. I have great wealth. I had a son—my son died—my grandson, the young man who should be legally in George Gordon's place, is my only living relative."

"When did you see your grandson last?"

"When an infant he was brought to my door in his mother's arms. I spurned her as though she were a common tramp. I never saw her again. When my son died I began to search for my grandson. I traced him up to the time he sailed for America."

"His was a life of crime in England?"

"A life of crime? Yes. I found the man who had adopted him, and who had trained him to become a thief!"

"How did you chance to come upon George Gordon?"

"I knew Balfour Raymond. He was my reputed son-in-law. I sought him out. He placed in my hands certain papers and proofs which would establish his son's right to the Raymond estate. He had always supposed that his second son was dead."

"Why did he desert your daughter?"

"He did not desert her. He was driven from England suddenly, and before it was safe for him to return my daughter was dead, and at the same time proofs were furnished him of the death of her child."

"He is not then directly responsible for his son's after career?"

"He believed him dead."

"Balfour Raymond must be a bad man!"

"He was a strange man."

"He is dead?"

"I have reason to believe that he is dead!"

"Who are the parties who are the enemies of George Gordon?"

"Balfour Raymond accumulated a large estate. He made a will in favor of his son, who is known as George Gordon; in case of the young man's death, the money was to go to strangers; the latter are the enemies who would destroy him."

"It is all a strange, weird tale."

"It is even so."

"But tell me how you recognized George Gordon?"

"I met him accidentally, and recognized him by his resemblance to his father. It was about the same time that you met him. I placed detectives on his and your track, and by degrees learned all the facts that are now in my possession concerning you and him."

"But your own grandson?"

"Your conversations with Gordon in the prison were overheard; a spy was on your track all the time, and I learned that you were cognizant of the existence of the double and real criminal, and I knew at once that the man you were seeking was my grandson."

"And you inveigled me here to kill me, so that I could not produce him in court?"

"No; I brought you here to assure myself of the truth of all I had heard."

"Why did you threaten me?"

"I wished to force the truth from you."

"I do know your grandson."

"You will not run him down and produce him to the officers of the law?"

"The innocent must not suffer for the guilty."

"No; but both can be saved. I have money; you have courage, knowledge, and cunning."

"But supposing your grandson is a murderer?"

"He is not a murderer."

"How do you know?"

"All accounts that I have obtained of him tend to prove that, although he was trained a thief's life, he possesses the noblest impulses, and is incapable of taking the life of a human being."

A thrill shot through Kate's heart as she said:

"I have reason to believe that your confidence in his innocence of murder is not misplaced; but he is a thief."

"We can rescue and save him from such a life; but if he is handed over to the police, Heaven help us! He will be lost to us forever."

Kate did not have the heart to tell the old man that she believed his grandson was dead.

"What is your name?"

"I will not tell my name."

"Listen. You are not a better friend to your grandson than I; you may rely upon my word that I will do all in my power to save him. I will aid you in every way. I will clear up the mystery of the murder. I will clear him before the law of all other crimes. But you must tell me your name, and look upon me as a friend."

"My name is Joseph Everdell."

"Heavens!" was the ejaculation that fell from Kate's lips.

CHAPTER LII.

STRANGE incidents had involved her in the midst of one of the most remarkable life-histories that had ever been called to her attention, either in real life or the picturings of fiction.

"Your name is Everdell?"

"Yes."

Kate could see how Arthur had taken his mother's name.

"I have seen your grandson."

"And you know where he can be found?"

"I do not know now, but I am hunting for him."

"You are hunting for him to surrender him to the law?"

"I am his friend. your friend, and I will aid you in effecting the release of George Gordon."

"And if George Gordon is released?"

"Your grandson will never take his place through my agency."

"Those are great words."

"Do you know a man named Edward Bayne?"

"I do."

"How did you become acquainted with him?"

"I only recognized him as the witness against George Gordon."

"He does not know of a double?"

"No."

"You did not tell him?"

"I did not. I merely utilized him to effect the escape of Gordon, in order to remove the necessity of producing my grandson."

"You have not made a full statement to him?"

"I have told him nothing. I have only taken

advantage of his desire to help Gordon, because of some fancied service.''

" But he knows that Gordon is the Raymond heir?''

" Yes; he obtained that information from some other source.''

" He made allusions as though he knew something of the career of your grandson.''

" In what manner?''

" Spoke of the sympathy that the prisoner was deserving of in case all the truth were known.''

" I led him to that belief while permitting him to think that Gordon was the real criminal.''

" And he knows nothing of your grandson's existence?''

" Nothing.''

" I will find your grandson, and you can rely upon me as your friend.''

" You will find him?''

" I hope to find him.''

" When?''

" I was ' piping ' to find him this very night. I will meet you to-morrow, and I may have something definite to report; but tell me, how shall I recognize the parties whom you say are seeking my life?''

" I will point them out to you.''

" And you have the papers establishing George Gordon's identity?''

" I have.''

" Will you meet me to-morrow?''

" I will.''

Kate named a place, and rose to go.

" I will escort you from this place.''

" I can go alone.''

" Are you afraid to trust me?''

" No; nor am I afraid to trust myself.''

Kate left the comparatively pleasant apartment and passed alone down the rickety noisome stairs, and along the reeking passages and lanes until she had reached the street.

The lady detective had made wonderful discoveries that night, and strange thoughts and wild hopes and fears were surging through her brain.

In all her life she had never read or heard of such an extraordinary combination of incidents.

" Oh, that he were still alive!'' was the one uppermost thought amidst the many that engaged her attention.

The brave little woman passed upon her way, and was just emerging to a more respectable quarter of the city, when she was met by a man, who, without an instant's warning, clapped a hand over her mouth.

The next moment the wretch lay upon the ground insensible.

The lady detective had held her *reliable* weapon of defense in her hand; its use required dexterity more than strength, and Kate possessed all the requisite dexterity.

As the man fell she sped forward upon her way.

During the brief encounter she had recognized her assailant, but wondered how her enemies so readily penetrated her own disguise.

Later on the mystery was explained. She was shadowed every hour and minute of the day, and she was located by place rather than by condition.

Two weeks passed.

George Gordon was indicted by the grand jury for murder, a most singular chain of circumstantial evidence was established.

Every incident of the evidence went to prove that Arthur Everdell was an assassin.

Kate spent her days and her nights seeking to solve the mystery of Arthur's death or whereabouts.

Several times she had met old Mr. Everdell, and perfect confidence had been established between the two.

Kate called daily upon George Gordon, and encouraged him in every way.

The lady detective had " tumbled '' (to use a detective phrase) to the mystery of her constant recognition, and she had studied to play a rôle that would baffle both friends and foes, until she chose to come from under cover.

She visited young Gordon in her ordinary disguise, but when away from the prison she successfully assumed a safe " blind.''

There was one man who was her most persistent " shadow,'' the fellow Sheehan.

It was Sheehan who had come suddenly upon her upon the night when she was passing from her remarkable interview with Mr. Everdell.

Twice she had got the better of the man.

Sheehan was a cunning fellow. He had managed to pick up considerable information, and could he get Kate out of the way he could play a game to his own profit. Kate, however, in the end was an overmatch for him.

CHAPTER LIII.

LADY KATE, during her investigations, was the victim of many changing intimations. Sometimes she would gather evidence that would indicate that Arthur still lived; and then again she would pick up some little scrap of information pointing toward his possible death.

As stated, two weeks passed and she was no nearer a solution of the mystery attending his fate than when she first started out.

At length she determined to attempt a very difficult feat.

She induced Edward Bayne to point out to her the last spot where Arthur had stood just previous to his disappearance upon the fatal night of the attempted robbery.

Lady Kate set out to work one of the most remarkable detective feats ever attempted.

Various were the motives that urged her on; but above all other incentives was a moving force which could only have found rise in a woman's brain.

She had not betrayed to Edward Bayne her purpose; the young man was still ignorant of the fact that George Gordon had a double, that the real culprit was still without the meshes of the law.

It was early morning, one bright, clear day, when Lady Kate appeared upon the scene of the desperate struggle between Arthur and his pursuers, and it was just there that she commenced the working up of her great detective feat.

Arthur had been wounded. He had crawled away from the scene of the encounter a wounded man.

Kate wondered that the latter fact had never caused a suspicion to arise in the mind of Bayne.

He must have known that the thief who had saved his life was badly wounded; and he must have known that George Gordon was not wounded. He was a bright young man, and, as stated, Kate wondered that he had not noted the strange fact indicated.

Kate had marked well the spot, when it was pointed out to her, and upon the morning when she appeared there alone, she was in a very peculiar disguise.

She was prepared for active service.

Her first movement was to assure herself that she was not being followed. She had noticed that young Bayne had shown considerable curiosity as to her purpose, and she feared lest he might attempt to secretly watch her.

Kate knew well how to draw a watcher under the circumstances from his cover.

She uttered a wild, piercing scream, a frantic cry like a woman in distress; as she uttered the cry she darted to a cover which she had selected before attempting her experiment.

Her cunning ruse brought no result, and she was satisfied that she had the field to herself.

Had young Bayne been " piping '' her, the cry would have drawn him from his cover. He came not, and she felt assured the coast was clear.

Kate settled down to a regular Indian trail; indeed, her disguise was such that she might have been mistaken for an Indian or a gypsy girl.

She found the first blood-marks, and the blood around her heart ran cold. Poor, brave woman! her imagination at once presented a most vivid picture, and she beheld the end of her trail as she pictured herself standing over the ghastly corpse of the once elegant Arthur Everdell, that strange, weird, wayward man who in all his existence was a living mystery.

Step by step Kate followed the trail. Over a month had passed since the fatal night of the tragedy, and yet she believed she was tracing the steps of the wounded burglar.

Kate was six hours going over a space that she could have traversed ordinarily in twenty minutes, and at length she reached the river bank.

Up to a certain point the trail was clear and distinct. She found the bowlder whereon the wounded man had sat while attending to his wound.

The indices were perfect and well marked.

The stains had become well fixed before the rains had descended, and the waters failed afterward to wash away the tragic traces.

Beyond this point the brave woman could not find a single mark, and she was left to conjecture.

A less expert and experienced person would have given up the search, but Lady Kate had set out to solve a mystery, and was not to be set back by any ordinary difficulty.

She sat for a long time pondering over the situation. She was studying to hit upon some plan for a renewal of her investigation.

At length an idea struck her. She had failed to discover the faintest sign of a trail beyond the rock smeared with the blood-stains, and the suggestion came to her that possibly the fugitive had found a boat at that point.

She walked along the beach, and at length met a boy.

The lad gazed at her in a serious manner, for Kate was a curious-looking person in her disguise.

She addressed the lad, who at first appeared reluctant to speak with her.

" Do you live around here, boy?''

The boy looked, but made no answer.

" Are you deaf and dumb?''

Still the boy gazed, but made no reply.

Kate took a silver quarter from her pocket, tossed it toward the lad, and said:

" That's for holding your tongue! I'll give you another the moment you answer my questions.''

The lad had never before owned a silver quarter, and the sight of the money made him bold, and at once he answered:

" Yes, I live around here.''

" How far from here do you live?''

The lady detective's questions in the end led to a remarkable discovery.

CHAPTER LIV.

KATE having once gained the lad's confidence, he talked fluently enough, and in answer to her question as recorded at the close of our preceding chapter, he said:

" I live just over the hill there; my father is a fisherman, and I help him haul the nets.''

" Your father is a fisherman, eh?''

" Yes.''

" *How many boats has your father got?*''

" Two; we did have three, but *one boat was stolen.*''

" Why, who would steal a boat?''

" Why, we don't know, missus; if we did, my dad would go for 'em.''

" You had a boat stolen, eh?''

" Yes.''

" How long ago?''

" Oh, nearly two months ago!''

Kate's heart pulsated with increased vigor; once again she had struck the trail.

" Where was the boat moored that you lost?''

" Down the shore a piece.''

" Come and show me.''

" Oh, it was down near the place where the blood-stains are on the rock.''

Kate trembled all over.

" Is there a place where there are blood-stains?''

" Yes.''

" How long have those blood-stains been there?''

" Don't know; we only saw them the morning after the boat was stolen.''

How straight and unerringly had the brave little lady detective traced the course of the wounded burglar.

The boat was taken just about the time of the robbery, and it had been moored opposite the rock on which the blood-stains had been discovered upon the morning following the theft.

There was no question as to the fact that the wounded man had taken the boat, and Kate only blamed herself that she had not sooner started upon the trail.

Over a month had elapsed, and the course of the fugitive would be hard to trace, but had she started upon the track the morning following the tragedy, she could have been assured of success.

Kate calculated the time of the robbery, and was able to approximate the time the boat had been taken.

Her following questions proved how cunning and long-headed she was for a woman.

It was her point to learn which way the boat had been propelled. She calculated that a wounded man would not be likely to attempt to pull a boat *against the tide.*

Addressing the lad, she asked:

"Were you fishing the morning the boat was taken?"

"Yes, miss."

"On a flood or ebb tide?"

The boy laughed, and asked:

"What do you know about a flood or ebb tide?"

"I guess I know something if I am a woman."

"I don't see why a woman would ask that question?"

"I'll tell you. I was thinking that your boat may have *drifted away*."

"No, it didn't, because that night the tide was a flood."

"Flowing up the river?"

"Yes."

"How do you come to remember?"

"Oh, easy enough."

"Well, tell me."

"Dad looked for the boat up stream. He thought that she might have drifted; and if she had drifted up stream he would have found her. No; she was stolen, and he was sure when he found the blood-stains."

"And he never had any idea who stole his boat?"

"Oh, yes, he did."

"He suspected some one?"

"Yes."

"Who?"

"One of the burglars who was in the robbery over at the Bayne place."

"And your father never got any clew to the thief?"

"Well, yes; he got the *value of the boat in money*."

"Got the value of the boat in money!" ejaculated Kate, in a tone of unrestrained amazement.

"Yes."

"How?"

"In a letter."

Strange were the suggestions that came with the fisher-boy's announcement.

"Where did the letter come from?"

"Don't know."

"Your father knows?"

"No; he don't know anything about it; a letter came with no name signed, saying, 'Here is the price of your boat.'"

"How long after the disappearance of the boat was it before the letter came?"

"About two weeks."

"Where is the letter?"

"I don't know."

"Has your father got the letter?"

"Guess not."

"Where is your father?"

"I reckon he's up to the tavern at the railroad station."

"What's your father's name, lad?"

"Golly, missus, you're asking a great many questions."

"Yes, I'm curious about your boat."

"My father's name is Bendergood, Hank Bendergood."

"Here's your other quarter, sonny."

"Thank you, missus; and if you'll come along with me I'll show you the rock with the blood-stains."

"Never mind; I do not wish to look at anything so horrid."

"Oh, it's all dried up now."

"Never mind, I will go down and look at it some other time."

Kate had spent a good day. It was late in the afternoon when she went to a solitary point on the shore and made a complete change in her appearance.

The noble girl was greatly excited; the news she had received, as stated, carried wonderful suggestions.

The fact that the man who had stolen the boat had returned its value was an evidence that he *was alive at the time the money was sent ;* and the fisherman had received his pay for his boat about two weeks subsequent to its disappearance.

There was but one thief whom Kate knew, or ever had known, who would be so considerate as to return to its owner, a poor man, the price of his boat.

The fact that Arthur Everdell lived appeared to be established; and the fact that he had returned the value of the boat two weeks after its theft would indicate that he had recovered from his wound, and if he had recovered from his wound, the question arose, where had he been during all the intervening time?"

One fact was certain; he had not returned to New York, or Kate would have got upon his track.

As the fair girl weighed all the evidence, she once more experienced a sense of regret that she had not sooner started upon the trail.

The gypsy girl had been transformed into a man, and late in the afternoon the young man appeared at the tavern where old Hank Bendergood was wont to loiter away the interval between the tides.

CHAPTER LV.

HANK BENDERGOOD was not around the tavern when our bright lady heroine, disguised as a man, appeared there, but about an hour later he put in an appearance.

Kate had spent the waiting moments conjuring upon a plan to draw out the information she desired from the honest fisherman, without arousing his suspicions.

When Bendergood came up, Kate managed to get into conversation with him.

She pretended to be an amateur fisherman, and soon succeeded in getting the old waterman to take a glass of beer with her.

As we wish to present Kate's skill, we will record the conversation that passed, showing the adroit manner in which she went to work to secure her information, and at the same time avoid arousing the old man's suspicions.

"I would like to go net-hauling with you some day," said Kate.

The old fisherman laughed, and replied:

"I reckon you wouldn't go more than once."

"Why not?"

"Well, you'd get wet from your feet to your waist, and if the weather was a little fresh you'd get wet through and through."

"I'd like it all the same; but tell me, don't you ever have your nets robbed?"

"Not often up this way; but they tell me that down near York they do get robbed sometimes."

"Then you never lost *anything* ?"

"Oh, yes; I lost a boat a spell back."

"Lost a boat?"

"Yes."

"Sunk?"

"No; it was stolen."

"A boat stolen!"

"Yes."

Our readers will remember that Kate accompanied all her questions and replies with gestures and intonations of voice that accorded most superbly with her rôle of an innocent young amateur fisherman.

"Well, that is a strange thing to have a boat stolen!"

"The first one I ever lost."

"You recovered it?"

"Never."

"Well, I can't see how a man could have a boat stolen and not recover it?"

"Well, I reckon I would have recovered it; but, you see, I got pay for it."

"Got pay for a stolen boat?"

"Yes."

"Who paid you?"

"The thief, I reckon."

"See here, old man, you are making sport of me."

"No, I am not, young man. It was a strange thing; but my boat was stolen, and about two weeks afterward I received its value—its full value."

"Well, that is the funniest thing I ever heard of, old man."

"It was funny; but then I've heard that sometimes regular thieves will never do a harm to a poor man."

"What makes you think it was the thief who paid you for the boat?"

"Well, who else would pay me?"

"You have rich neighbors around here."

"Yes; but what have the rich men around here to do with the loss of my boat?"

"You said you received the money in a letter?"

"Yes."

"No name signed?"

"No name signed."

"Well, that settles it; you see, some rich man has heard of the loss of your boat, and knowing you to be a poor man, unable to stand the loss, he has sent you its value."

"Well, I never thought of that."

"*I'll bet you the letter came from some where in the vicinity ?*"

"Can't tell where it came from."

"Ah, yes, you can."

"No, sir; there was no date or heading."

"That don't make any difference; you can tell where it came from easy enough."

"How?"

"Why, by the post-mark."

"Well, hang me, if I ever thought about that."

"Have you got the letter? and we can see, *just for fun !*"

"I don't know whether I've got the letter or not; it may be in my coat."

"Well, now, just look, just for fun, and don't give any credit to a thief unless you are compelled to do so."

The old man hunted through his oil-stained coat, and at length brought forth a soiled and ragged envelope.

Kate took the envelope, deftly managed to tear off and secrete the corner which bore the post-office stamp mark, and then pretended to look for what she had stolen.

"The post-office stamp is torn off," she said.

"Well, that's so," said the old man; and he added: "Darn it, I wish now I had kept the thing!"

Lady Kate had carried her point, and after a bit she stole silently away.

Once alone she produced a glass and examined the post-mark.

"Thank Heaven!" she exclaimed; "it is a precious guide!"

Within an hour Kate was on the railroad cars, and night found her in the village from where the letter had been posted.

Upon the following morning Lady Kate commenced her investigation.

She had once more assumed the garb of the gypsy girl. She had a method of her own for changing her appearance.

It is an easy matter for any one to change their complexion; there is a simple preparation known to almost every one that will produce the dark color in such a natural manner that it is impossible to detect it; but Kate's great secret was the method to remove the dark color almost instantaneously, and the latter method is known to but a few persons.

As the gypsy girl Kate started out to investigate; she had an idea that Arthur Everdell might be in that town, rusticating until the excitement attending the tragedy should blow over.

Her object in disguising herself so effectually was designed to hide her identity from Arthur, in case she should be so fortunate as to discover him.

Kate, in assuming the disguise, had gone the whole figure. She had provided herself with a guitar, so that at a moment she could play the character to perfection.

She wandered from place to place, and even in her disguise she preserved some of her beauty and attracted considerable attention as she moved about the village.

She desired to attract attention, thereby at some fortunate moment hoping to attract to her gaze the object of her studied search.

Kate went all around the village, and at one place before a tavern some of the loungers insisted upon a tune.

The detective was an excellent singer, and a good performer, and, besides, she could sing and talk both French and Italian.

Half the day passed, and she had made no progress, had not gained the slightest clew; and in the afternoon she wandered down along the shore, hoping to discover the boat, a description of which she had received from its original owner.

CHAPTER LVI.

IT had been Kate's intention to change her appearance when an opportunity offered, and pursue her continued investigations as a man.

She had just reached the shore when she made a startling discovery. She observed that she was being followed by a man. The discovery annoyed her, but did not alarm her, as she well knew that if worst came to worst it would be bad for—the man.

The discovery, however, as stated, annoyed her, as it soon became evident that the man was close upon her track, and was watching her every movement.

The lady detective had made one other discovery; the man who was following her was a foreigner—either a Frenchman or a Spaniard.

Kate made up her mind that it was necessary to send the fellow off about his business, and, selecting a secluded spot, she sat down.

A moment later and the man approached, and the moment he spoke Kate detected that he was a Frenchman.

In answer to his address, she demanded, in Italian:

"Well. what do you want?"

The man was a bold fellow, and indicated by gestures that he was going to kiss her.

Kate was glad that he had no other design, as at first she had feared he might be a detective, like herself, in disguise; and as to the kiss part of it, well, she was just able to take care of herself.

She did not disguise the fact but that she understood the meaning of his pantomime, and rising to her feet she walked away. The man followed her. By gesture, Kate warned him back, when he caught hold of her. The next instant he fell to the sand as though he had been shot, and, with a merry laugh, Kate walked away.

The Frenchman was only momentarily stunned, and springing to his feet, he ran after Kate.

He was brought to a sudden halt, as Kate presented a weapon at him.

The Frenchman took to his heels.

Kate wandered on a short distance, and finding a proper place, worked the change in her appearance.

As a young man, she wandered along the shore, and had walked fully three miles, when she came to a place where a fisherman was seated on the beach mending a net.

There were two boats moored near by to stakes driven in the sand, and Kate, with a thrill, observed the fact that one of the boats had been but *recently painted over*.

Kate had said nothing to the fisherman, but stood studying the appearance of the boat.

The fisherman eyed her suspiciously, and at length addressed her.

"Good-afternoon," he said.

"Good-afternoon," replied Kate.

The lady detective knew she had a keen part to play; the fact that the boat had been painted over suggested a desire to cover its identity.

Kate was not assured that she had found the missing boat, as it is not an unusual incident for a fisherman to paint his boat over, but there were little facts that led her to believe that there was a possibility that she had come upon the stolen skiff.

The newly painted boat, in all respects save its color, answered the description she had received from old Bendergood.

The skiff was about the size of the stolen one. It had been, as stated, but recently painted over, and it was found near to the village from where the letter had been posted containing the pay for the boat to old Bendergood.

"It's a nice afternoon," said the fisherman.

"Yes; it's a nice afternoon."

"Are you from the village?"

"I'm from York."

"Ah, a stranger round here?"

"Yes."

"Upon a fishing excursion?"

"No; I am seeking to buy a boat."

"This is a poor place to come to buy a boat. You can buy all you want up to Newburg."

"I did not start out with the intention of buying a boat; but, since I've been standing here, I've taken a fancy to that boat out there."

Kate pointed to the newly painted skiff.

"That boat ain't for sale."

"You own it?"

"Yes."

"How long ago did you paint it over?"

"What difference is it to you?"

"I'll be frank with you: I lost a boat about the size of that one."

"Well, what is that to me?"

"Nothing, I hope; but it seems strange that you should be afraid to tell me when *your* boat was painted over."

"I would just as soon tell you as not."

"I'd like to know."

"Why do you think it is your boat?"

"To tell the truth, I've a suspicion that it is my boat."

"I came honestly by that boat."

"Did you?"

"I said so."

"Who said you didn't?"

"Look here, young man, I think you're getting impertinent. I'll tell you nothing."

"I may compel you to tell where you got that boat."

"All right; go ahead and compel. Good-evening."

"Good-evening," retorted Kate.

The fisherman had made to go away, but in a moment he returned. The fact was, he had met his match, and there were reasons why he was rather uneasy.

"If you think that is your boat, I'll haul it in and let you examine it."

"Please do."

The fisherman hauled the boat in, and dragged it up on the sand.

With a trembling heart Kate stood beside the boat, and carefully examined it on the inside.

"Are you looking for a private mark?"

"Yes."

"I may aid you; tell me where the mark was. I've no desire to avoid a fair examination."

"You are willing to point out a private mark?"

"I am willing to aid you. I said *I came honestly by this boat, but it may* have been stolen all the same."

"Ah! you admit the boat may have been stolen?"

"It may have been."

"How long have you owned the boat?"

"About two months."

"Why did you paint it over?"

"Because it needed painting."

"You say you will aid me to find a private mark?"

"I will."

"You appear like an honest man."

"I am an honest man."

"Did you discover no marks when the boat came into your possession?"

"None."

"What became of the blood-stains?" demanded Kate, suddenly.

CHAPTER LVII.

THE man recoiled as though some horrid object had suddenly appeared before him. He turned pale and trembled like an aspen leaf.

Kate was cool as a cucumber, as she said:

"It is no use for you to deny the fact that you discovered blood-stains; your agitation speaks for itself."

"Who are you?"

"It makes no difference who I am; what did you find in this boat?"

The fisherman was thoroughly alarmed.

There were good reasons why he should feel alarmed, as it might in the end come out that he had been harboring a man for whose recovery the State had offered a reward.

The fisherman knew but little about law, and feared lest he might in some way make himself liable to punishment.

It was Kate's purpose to frighten the man.

It is a fact well known to experienced persons who have to deal with wrong-doers, that the moment you get them really scared you have them at your mercy.

"I did not find the boat. I purchased it."

"Yours was a *one-sided* purchase. You took the boat and fixed the price."

"It's false!"

"Never mind what is false or true. What did you find in this boat?"

"Nothing."

"You swear you found nothing in the boat?"

"I am not compelled to answer your questions, young man."

"You may find it to your advantage in the end to answer my questions."

"Tell me who you are, and I will answer your questions."

"I told you once it makes no difference who I am."

"If you are seeking information, you will find it to your advantage to tell me who you are."

"I will go and bring some one who will have a right to insist upon an answer."

The fisherman remained thoughtful a moment, but at length said:

"Well, go; and then I will know to whom I am giving answers."

Kate walked away. She was thinking that it would be a wise plan to pretend to go away.

She soon discovered, however, that she had a more cunning person to deal with than she had supposed.

She had gone but a few steps, when the fisherman jumped into his boat, and seized the oars preparatory to pulling away.

The latter was a contingency Kate had not calculated for, and she ran to the water's edge and called:

"Hold! come back!"

"I'll be back by the time you bring the squire down here."

"Come back, I say!"

The fisherman made no reply, but dipped his oars, when Kate drew a weapon and commanded him to come back.

"Eh! what do you mean?"

"Come back, I say!"

As our readers have been previously informed, Sturgis, the fisherman, was an old soldier. He did not scare at the sight of a weapon, and in a calm tone, he said:

"If I were on shore, young man, I'd lay you flat with one of my oars!"

"If you do not come ashore, I will lay you flat in the boat."

"Blaze away, if you dare, but make sure to hit me first time or down goes your shebang!"

As the fisherman spoke he lay-to heartily on his oars and pulled away.

Kate was baffled; she did not dare fire; indeed, she had no right to fire; she had intended to scare the man, and he wouldn't "scare worth a cent."

The lady detective stood on the shore and saw the man row away in the very boat she had taken so much trouble to trace.

She called to him in a coaxing tone to return, but the man paid no attention to her.

Kate was a woman, but she used a genuine masculine phrase, when she exclaimed:

"Well, I'll be hanged if I have not beaten myself!"

The man Sturgis was scared, but it was not the pistol that had scared him; it was the fact that some one had come to inquire about the boat and its freight as he found it upon the morning succeeding the robbery.

The detective's game had been to frighten the man into some sort of admission, and as she had failed, nothing remained for her but to seek to discover his abode.

Of one fact she felt assured: the man did not live far from the place where the boats were moored.

She commenced her search, but night was fast coming on and she hardly knew what to do.

Had it been a clear night it would have been all right, but since her meeting with the fisherman the sky had become clouded, and there were evidences of a furious storm.

Kate walked along the shore, but could not discover a location where it would seem probable a house would be placed.

She was loath, however, to give up the search. The manner of the fisherman had convinced her that his terror had not arisen from the mere finding of the boat in his possession; indeed, she felt assured that, could she find the fisherman's hut, she would also find the wounded burglar, Arthur Everdell.

Kate climbed the cliff, but found no road, and in the meantime the sky had become darker and darker; quick flashes of lightning played over the trees on the cliffs, and heavy peals of thunder reverberated overhead. Her position was indeed a dangerous one; should darkness settle down over her the chances were that at any moment she might go plunging over some cliff or whirling down some crevice in the rocks.

She started to go down once more to the river-shore, but, in the thick brush, was unable to find her way.

Once more she used a masculine phrase, by exclaiming:

"Well, this *is* a nice pickle I've got myself into, I must say!"

The storm burst upon the brave girl in all its fury, and she was compelled to take shelter under a thick clump of trees.

Kate had beheld many a furious summer storm, but it appeared to her at the moment as though she were in the most fearful tempest she had ever witnessed.

The elements appeared to have gone mad; the very woods appeared alive with flame; the lightning flash was continuous; the thunder rolled with one unceasing roar, and the rain fell in torrents.

Several trees near to where she stood were struck by the lightning, and one of them came crashing down just where she was crouching.

In a few moments she was drenched to the skin. Her shelter had proved but a momentary protection, and as she heard the tree crashing down overhead, she exclaimed, in a mournful tone:

"I'm gone!"

CHAPTER LVIII.

THE storm lasted for over an hour, and when its fury was spent, a drizzling rain followed, and the night set in dark and chilly.

Kate was uninjured, but wet through to the skin; still her spirit was irrepressible. She determined to look for the fisherman's hut: indeed, despite the peril, she said to herself, "The light in his window will serve as a guide."

Lady Kate emerged from under the shelter of the clump of trees where she had remained during the storm, and cautiously moved through the darkness.

She had gone but a few steps, when suddenly the catastrophe she had feared occurred: she felt herself thrown forward, and an instant later be came conscious that she was falling.

One prayer escaped her lips as she threw her hands out frantically, and instinctively she seized hold of something that struck against her hands.

She had caught a bush, and for a moment life was preserved to her.

Kate was strong for a female, very strong, and she held on a moment to consider what she should do.

She was quick to make a decision. She had an idea of the actual height of the cliff, and determined to lower herself from brush to brush rather than attempt to climb up to its verge.

She had let herself down carefully some distance, when her feet touched a projecting rock, on which she rested.

Fortunately, she had her dark-lantern. She had forgotten the fact when she had first started to find her way along the cliff. As she had a good footing she succeeded in igniting a match, and soon the clear flame from her lantern illuminated the darkness for a space around her.

A feeling of satisfaction thrilled through her as she discovered that she was not more than ten feet above the sandy shore of the river.

She ventured a leap, and landed on the ground without harm.

For the third time she used a very masculine expression, as, upon reaching the ground, she ejaculated:

"That's bully for me!"

Kate started to walk along the beach. There was little danger attending the march in the darkness, she having once got down from the cliff.

She was persistent, and kept upon her way, and at length her perseverance was rewarded, as she saw the glimmer of a light.

Excuse us and our heroine, dear reader, but once more Kate fired off a man's declaration, by exclaiming:

"Well, I'll be blamed!"

The exclamation was born of the fact that he had passed and repassed the house half a dozen times, and it was located less than a hundred feet from the spot where she had first discovered the fisherman.

She would not have discovered the house had it not been betrayed by the glimmer of light, as it was situated in a sort of natural court, an inclosed space in the side of the cliff, the entrance to which was through a narrow crevice.

Fisherman Sturgis had chosen a remarkable location for the building of his little hut.

Kate was tired and weary, and having found the object of her long and perilous search, she sat down awhile on the bowlder to consider her course.

Her emotion and agitation was great. Now that she had discovered the burglar in his lair, her heart relented.

She had been urged on by a sense of duty, but, alas! at the moment when she had achieved success, she had not the heart to proceed.

If she discovered Arthur Everdell it would be her duty to surrender him to the law; no other course lay open to her. An innocent man lay in prison, enduring confinement and ignominy in his place.

Could she surrender Arthur—that handsome but bad man—that child of a weird destiny, so noble and generous at heart, so bright and so brilliant, and to whom she owed her own life?

"What shall I do? what shall I do?" were the words that fell from her lips.

She did not appear to dream for one moment but that she should find Arthur in the cottage.

One other fact was presented to her: it was evident that the fascinating but wayward youth had won the heart of the honest old fisherman.

As Kate recalled the conversation she had held with the fisherman, she more fully considered the meaning of the good man's words.

It was apparent to her that he was an honest man. She knew that he had not stolen the boat, and the mystery of the money inclosure was explained. The fisherman had recognized the boat, and, rather than expose his charge, had sent the money to pay for it.

There was another significance in the whole action of the fisherman: it was evident that he knew something of the career of the man to

whom he had given shelter, else why would he have shown such terror?

The man had proved, as intimated, that he was no coward.

Talking to herself, Kate said:

"I've a mind to go away. Why should I prove the Nemesis of the man who saved my life?"

There she sat in her wet male attire, the rain pouring down on her, irresolute as to her course.

At length, however, she settled to a purpose; she remembered that George Gordon was innocent, that he was suffering from the sins of another.

Kate did not admire Gordon as she did admire Arthur Everdell, although one was an honorable man and the other a thief.

There was no need for Kate to be sparing as to terms. Arthur Everdell, handsome and generous and brave as he undoubtedly was, after all was in fact a professional thief, a common burglar.

Kate determined to secure her man, and rising to her feet she made one step toward the cottage, but suddenly came to a halt and her blood ran cold.

The question arose: suppose Arthur Everdell should offer resistance, what should she do? She could not shoot him down. She would rather have turned the muzzle of the pistol to her own temple; and then again came the consciousness that to surrender him to the authorities was but handing him over to a possible cruel death; and once more she murmured:

"What shall I do? what shall I do?"

CHAPTER LIX.

WHEN Sturgis, the fisherman, pulled away from Kate, he was laboring under great excitement.

The good fisherman had come to love the strange young man whom he had nursed back to life.

As recorded in a previous chapter, he had held a conversation with Arthur, during which the latter had frankly admitted his position.

The fisherman had closed the conversation with the remark, "We will talk matters over again at some future time."

As our readers will remember, during the interview alluded to, Arthur had refused to promise to reform. He had fallen back on his old-time remark, "I was born a thief." He had told Sturgis to do his duty; the strange young man had not pleaded for mercy or sympathy, but stood upon the stern phase of his remarkable character.

Sturgis was in a quandary as to his duty in the matter. He was an honest man. He did not feel that it would be right to turn a bold thief loose again upon the public, and yet he could not steel his heart so as to act as duty commanded.

He had said he would talk the matter over again with the young man, but he had let the days slip by, and had never again alluded to the subject.

In the meantime Arthur had made wonderful progress toward recovery. He possessed a naturally strong, healthy constitution, and had so far improved in health that had he chosen he could have decamped.

Sturgis was all the time hoping that the young man would run away. He was excusing himself from the performance of his duty, on the plea that his guest was still too sick to make it necessary to surrender him.

One day the fisherman had remarked as a hint to our hero:

"It strikes me, if I were in your position, I would take all the advantages that circumstances offered me."

Arthur understood the hint, and answered:

"I will not leave you until I am compelled to do so. This is a new life for me. I am doing no harm to any one here, but I suppose some day I must go; and mark me, good friend, I shall remunerate you fully for all your trouble in my behalf."

A smile crept over the face of the honest fisherman, as he answered:

"I never could receive money that was not honestly earned!"

"I never earned an honest penny in my life, but in order to pay you I'll try to earn some money honestly. I'll work in a bank digging with a shovel. I am strong, or will be when I am fully recovered, and after I have paid you, well, then I will—"

"You will what?" demanded the fisherman.

"Return to my old life!" was the frank reply.

"I begin to believe that there is no good in you at all, Arthur."

"Well, there is no good in me. I have never claimed to be good."

"There is a virtue in your frankness; and let me tell you that, with your talents and rare magnetism, you would make a grand success in any honest calling."

"But I do not know how to be honest. I was not trained to be honest."

"You can become honest."

"No, no, no; the shadow of my past career would always overhang me."

"Did you ever read the Bible, Arthur?"

"Never!"

"Were you never in a church?"

"Yes, once."

"Only once in all your life?"

"Only once."

"Well, how did you like it?"

"How did I like it?"

"Yes."

A strange look came into the young man's face as he answered:

"I was very much interested."

"Why did you not go again?"

"I had no right there."

"Yes; you had a right there."

"Oh, no."

"Why not?"

"Because I am a thief!"

Sturgis was a good man, and he told the story of Christ—told it in a straightforward simple manner, as a Christian missionary would tell it to a poor, ignorant heathen.

The young man listened respectfully, and when Sturgis concluded, Arthur remarked:

"That is a wonderful story."

"It is a true story, my dear young friend."

"Well, I don't know why it should not be true; it is good enough to be true."

"Well, if it is true, does it not apply to you?"

"How does it apply to me?"

"Though your sins are as scarlet, I will make them white as wool!"

"Who will?" came the abrupt question.

"Christ will."

"I'd like to read about all that myself," said Arthur.

"You shall!" was the reply.

Sturgis took down a large Bible from a shelf, and said:

"Here, the whole story is here; will you read it?"

"Yes, I will."

"Take my advice and read the Book from beginning to end."

Sturgis, the fisherman, every day received a daily paper from New York. He did not take the papers to his home, as he did not wish Arthur to read the news.

At length there appeared in one of the papers an account of the arrest of George Gordon as the robber who had escaped. There also appeared a description of the prisoner, and Mr. Sturgis had become greatly mystified.

When he had first found Arthur Everdell, the young man's hair was shaved close to his head, so close that it looked like a bald head, but during his illness his hair had grown out full and luxuriant, and he was about as handsome a young man as the poor fisherman had ever beheld.

The fisherman followed closely all the evidence as recorded against Gordon and printed in the daily papers.

At length he felt bound to make some inquiries of his guest. There was a mystery in the whole affair that he could not explain.

CHAPTER LX.

ONE day the fisherman came into the room where Arthur sat reading the Bible, and said to him abruptly:

"Arthur, if I ask you some questions, will you answer me truthfully?"

"Have you ever found me a liar?"

"Never."

"Have you ever noted an inclination on my part to practice any sort of deception?"

"Never."

"Then listen to me: I will answer you truthfully, though the truth condemn me to the gallows!"

"I believe you, my lad, and I trust that your answers will not cause me grief."

"Though the truth shall grieve you, I will still speak it."

"Did you ever commit a murder?"

"You have a reason for asking that question—a special reason?"

"Listen! You are a confessed burglar; it is but natural for me to seek to know whether or not you are an assassin as well as a housebreaker?"

"I am not an assassin!"

The good fisherman looked Arthur straight in the face and asked.

"Did you ever slay a fellow-being in self-defense?"

"Never!"

"You are absolutely blood-guiltless?"

"I am absolutely blood-guiltless!"

"Thank Heaven!" ejaculated Sturgis.

"And so do I thank Heaven since I've read this book!" came the startling response. "Do you know," added the young man, "I would not kill a man now, not even to save my own life!"

Sturgis was delighted, and believed the young fellow had told him the truth.

"Have you any relatives?" asked the fisherman.

"I have no relatives."

"Have you a brother?"

"I said I have no relatives."

"Is it not possible that you may have a brother?"

"Will you tell me why you ask?"

"First answer my question."

"I do not believe it possible that I have a brother."

"Suppose it were to be discovered that there was a young man who resembled you so closely that he might be called a twin?"

The young man laughed and remarked:

"It would be strange; and yet—"

Arthur stopped short.

"And yet what?" demanded Sturgis.

"I do not know as I ought to tell."

"Yes, tell me all."

"First tell me why you question me as you do?"

"I will tell you later on; but you tell me what you were about to tell."

"There is a mystery associated with me which concerns a resemblance."

"Ah! you have seen a man who resembles you?"

"Never."

"Then what do you mean?"

"I have seen a picture which I resemble."

"A picture which you resemble?"

"Yes."

"Where?"

"In a house."

"What sort of a picture?"

"A portrait."

"When did you see this portrait?"

"Some months ago."

"And it is the portrait of whom?"

"I do not know"

"Who showed you the portrait?"

"I discovered it accidentally."

"Where?"

"In a mansion some miles from New York."

"The Raymond mansion?"

"Yes."

Sturgis turned pale.

"Do you know of a tragedy connected with that mansion?"

"I do."

"A murder?"

"Yes."

"An old lady murdered?"

"Yes."

Sturgis had read all the testimony as adduced against George Gordon, and had made a memorandum of day and dates. Our readers are requested to pay particular attention to the continued conversation between Arthur and Sturgis, as a certain mystery will be opened up, or rather a certain remarkable coincidence will be explained.

It will be remembered that a witness had testified to seeing George Gordon on the grounds of the Raymond mansion on the evening preceding the horrid murder.

The witness was a respectable man, and his testimony was the strongest point in the evidence upon which the prosecution relied.

"*How did you come to discover the portrait?*"

"I was 'taking points' on the house."

"Taking points on the house?"

"Yes."

"What do you mean by that?"

"We had set to rob the house, and I was studying the lay of the rooms, the general features of the mansion, and the habits of the inmates."

"For the purposes of robbery?"

"Yes."

"You were on the grounds?"

"Yes."

"And you got into the house?"

"No; I was on the piazza, and got a glimpse of a picture hanging on the wall."

"The portrait to which you bear a resemblance?"

"Yes."

"Do you remember the exact date of the adventure?"

"I do; it is fixed in my memory, because of the date set for the robbery."

"What date was it?"

"The 19th of ——."

"The night preceding the murder?"

"Yes."

"Arthur Everdell," demanded Sturgis, in a solemn tone, "were you engaged in the robbery?"

"No."

A light broke over the face of the fisherman.

"You did not go with your pals to commit the robbery?"

"I did not."

"You were not in the house when the murder was committed?"

"I was not."

"You swear it?"

"I do."

"Do you know who the murderer was?"

"I do."

"Who was the assassin?"

"He is dead."

"Dead?"

"Yes."

"When did he die?"

"He was one of the men who was shot the night we attempted to rob the Bayne mansion."

"If you knew the murderer, why did you not denounce him?"

"I did not know he was the murderer until the night when we went to rob the Bayne house; but I would not have given him away even if I had known it."

"What would you have done?"

"I would have refused ever again to have gone on an expedition with him."

"Why did you leave the party after getting the points on the Raymond mansion?"

"I did not join the party, because I had seen the portrait."

———

CHAPTER LXI.

"You have an idea as to the identity of the original of the portrait, have you not?" asked Sturgis.

"I have not."

"Have you sought to solve the mystery?"

"Yes."

"And you have made no discoveries?"

"I have made no discoveries; it is still a mystery to me. One day, some time after the murder, I paid a visit to the house. I was upon the balcony, looking into the room, when I was discovered."

"By whom?"

"A young lady."

"Who was the young lady?"

"She is as great a mystery to me as the portrait."

"Tell me about the meeting with the young lady."

"If I do, I will be compelled to tell you all."

"Tell me all."

"You remember that when you found me wounded on the river shore my head was shaved close to the skull?"

"Yes."

"As a burglar, I had a method for changing my appearance."

"And that was why your head was shaved close?"

"Yes."

"Tell me all about it, please."

"I had a wig made of *my own hair* by one of the best *coiffeurs* in the world; and then I had a second wig made of dark hair, as perfect as the one made from my own hair. I possess a secret for changing the color of my skin, and also I am able to make certain other changes so that I can alter my appearance in such a wonderful manner that even you would not recognize me five minutes from now."

"You chose to act as a burglar when wearing the wig made of your own hair?"

"Yes."

"That was a strange idea?"

"No."

"Why not?"

"I had become marked as a thief by the police in London before I had learned to change my appearance. I adopted the new disguise as a matter of safety, and ever after committed my robberies in the character of my proper self, and I was thus enabled to go under a safe cover in another rôle."

"Yours is a remarkable story; proceed and tell me about your visit to the Raymond mansion after the night of the murder, and of your meeting with the young lady who you say is the great mystery to you."

"Well, I succeeded in mystifying the young lady also; indeed, it has been a deep game all round."

"Tell me about it, please; I am greatly interested in your wonderful tale."

"I went to the house, and as I said I was once more on the piazza, when I saw a young lady enter the room and stand studying the portrait; she at length discovered me and I ran away."

"Why did you run away?"

Arthur laughed, and answered: "The wicked flee when no man pursueth."

His answer showed that he had read well the good book that had been put in his hands by the fisherman.

"Yes, I ran away," continued Arthur, "and changed my appearance."

"Why did you change your appearance?"

"I had gone on the piazza in my thief's rôle. I wished to compare myself to the portrait."

"The lady pursued you?"

"Yes."

"Did she discover you?"

"Yes."

"And what followed?"

"Well, she was put to her wits' end; she had seen a man resembling the portrait on the piazza, but when she found the man he did not look like the portrait at all; but she was a wonderfully keen woman."

"Did she suspect?"

"I think she did."

"Have you seen her since?"

"I have."

"Have you discovered who she really is?"

"I have not, but I have a suspicion."

"But you do not know of a man living who resembles you?"

"I do not. Will you tell me now why you have asked me all these questions?"

"Not just at this moment; but I will."

"When?"

"I wish to think over all you have told me a bit."

The above conversation had occurred between the fisherman and his strange guest a week previous to the meeting of the former with Kate on the shore.

Sturgis had taken the whole week to think over Arthur's strange story. He was awaiting developments.

Arthur had once or twice asked for an explanation, but each time had been put off.

When the fisherman heard Kate's strange inquiries he was greatly alarmed. As stated, he had come to love the young man, thief as he was, and he had resolved to save one who, naturally so noble, had become the victim of an adverse fate.

Sturgis mistook Kate for a foe—a detective, who, like a Nemesis, was on the track of Arthur—and he resolved to aid in the young man's ultimate escape.

All sense of duty had departed from the mind of Sturgis, as far as the surrender of Arthur to the authorities was concerned. He had come to feel that he could serve God and the people better by recovering the young man to an honorable life than by surrendering him to punishment as a criminal.

Had Arthur been an assassin, Sturgis would not have dared to stand between him and the law; but as he was merely a thief, under such wonderful and extraordinarily extenuating circumstances, he felt that he had a right to extend to him his aid and sympathy with his recognized purpose in view.

Sturgis pulled across the river merely as a blind, as certain birds will run chattering away from bush to bush to allure an intruder from the vicinity where its nest is hidden.

As soon as darkness fell, the good fisherman pulled back to the shore, on which his humble hut stood.

He got to his little cabin ahead of the storm, and found Arthur seated with the great Book upon his knees.

The good fisherman was greatly excited, and Arthur, observing his agitation, asked:

"What is the matter?" and the fisherman answered, "Young man, God help you!"

CHAPTER LXII.

ARTHUR turned slightly pale, but was as cool as a cucumber. He was no coward; he was one of those men who could have walked to the gallows, guilty or innocent, without the tremor of a single muscle.

"What is the matter?" he asked, in a calm voice.

"You have been tracked to your lair!"

"Tracked by whom?"

"A detective."

"All right, I am ready!"

"Ready for what?"

"Punishment."

"Why should you surrender?"

"Why should I not?"

"Answer me; why should you surrender?"

"Shall I tell you why?"

"Yes."

"I am a guilty man."

"Well, hang it, lad, guilty men don't always surrender!"

"Possibly guilty men have not learned what it is to be as guilty as I have from this grand Book."

Sturgis started back in blank amazement, and yet his honest face was ablaze with delight.

"What is that you say?"

"I have come to a certain resolution."

"What have you resolved?"

"To be a thief no longer! Come starvation, come infamy, come death, I'll steal no more!"

"Heaven bless you, boy! I'm glad to hear you say so; but I'll rot if you shall surrender yourself to go to jail, just as you have learned to become an honest man!"

There was something wondrously grand in the tone and manner of Arthur Everdell. His language appeared simple, but he was no simpleton. He was a man possessed of a Napoleonic will and determination. It was this extraordinary strength of character which made him resolve in such a seemingly simple manner to become a reformed man.

There was no display about his sudden resolution. He was as calm in resolving to be an honest man as he had been quiet and determined at a former period to remain a thief.

"You shall not surrender, boy!"

"What shall I do?"

"Escape."

"But you say I have been traced to my lair."

"But mark me, that door is open and it is night; go forth in the darkness! fly to another land and become an honest man."

"No; I will not fly."

"You shall! Do you suppose I'm going to stand by and see you led off to prison? Never! No, by thunder! not if I have to knock flinters out of that pesky detective!"

Arthur laughed in a quiet way, and said:

"So you would have me 'flit'?"

"What's 'flit'?"

"Run away."

"I would, of course. Hang me! if it's any fault of yours that you were a thief. And now that you have resolved to become an honest man you are entitled to a chance, and you shall have it, boy, if I have to chuck the detective into the river."

"I reckon you have not read this book," said Arthur, as he laid his hand on the Bible.

"I stand rebuked, lad; yes, I stand rebuked. But listen: if you are set to surrender yourself, get the credit of it. Don't be captured. No, no, don't be captured by a pesky detective. Listen! I've something to tell you."

"Go on and tell me something."

"You remember the talk we had a week ago?"

"Yes."

"You suspected I had a reason for asking you certain questions?"

"I did."

"Well, so I had, and I am going to tell you my reasons for asking you all those questions."

"Please do."

Sturgis proceeded, and told Arthur all the circumstances attending the arrest and indictment of George Gordon.

Everdell was usually one of the coolest men, but when he heard the strange story, he displayed the most extraordinary excitement and agitation.

Sturgis went into all the particulars, and told a clear story, and when he had concluded, Arthur asked, in a trembling voice:

"Who is this young man, Gordon?"

"I do not know."

Arthur was silent and thoughtful for a few moments, but suddenly rising to his feet, he said:

"I will not surrender to the detective!"

"What will you do?"

"I do not know exactly, but one thing I will do."

"What will you do?"

"Escape for the present."

"That's it, my lad, hang the pesky detective. I do not see why he should have come 'mousing' around here."

"I am glad he came," said Arthur.

"Why are you glad?"

"It has led you to reveal to me the facts concerning the innocent man who is in jail in my place."

Sturgis had an idea as to what the young man had resolved to do, but he said nothing as to his suspicions.

Arthur extended his hand to the fisherman, and said:

"You have been a good friend to me."

"I love you, my boy, love you as though you were my own son; you a thief, eh? Why, hang it, you are one of nature's noblemen!"

"Wait till I prove myself an honest man; and in the meantime listen."

"Well?"

"I am in your debt."

"Hang the debt!"

"It may be many years before I can pay you with honestly earned money."

"Shoot the pay."

"You must be paid."

"Why, boy, I'm paid a thousand times already; and if it were not for the *fool* in jail in York, I'd help you myself to leave this country."

"You are a noble man."

"Never mind, no 'taffy,' lad."

"I am going to bid you good bye."

"Heaven bless you, boy."

A strange look came into Arthur's eyes, as he said:

"The day may come when even I may look for Heaven's blessing."

"Indeed you may. You're a jewel!"

"No 'taffy,'" retorted Arthur, with a quaint laugh, and suddenly he turned upon his heel, darted through the open door and disappeared in the darkness and in the midst of the tempest.

CHAPTER LXIII.

"WELL, I'll be hanged!" was the ejaculation that fell from the lips of old Sturgis as Arthur so suddenly darted away.

The fisherman had intended to give the young man some money, as he had reason to believe that Arthur was penniless. It was too late, however; the weird youth had fled, gone forth amidst the lightning's flashes and torrents of rain.

Sturgis had an idea that he had discerned the youth's purpose.

As a man he would have advised him against his course, but as a conscientious Christian, he could not so advise him.

In the meantime the storm raged without, and the fisherman sat thinking over the singular events that had followed his first discovery of the fugitive.

At length the storm abated, and still there sat the good fisherman thinking over the strange events, when suddenly he was aroused by hearing a voice, and looking up, he beheld like an apparition, a man standing across his threshold.

Sturgis was taken at a disadvantage, taken by surprise, and instinctively he leaped from his seat, and sprung across the room to secure a double-barreled gun hanging upon the wall of his cabin.

"Hold on, my good man!" exclaimed the stranger, "I do not come here as a robber or hostile intruder."

Sturgis recognized the party standing in his door-way as the man whom he had met down on the beach.

"What do you want here?" he demanded.

"Shelter."

"Well, hang it, if that is all you want you are welcome. I'll not shut my door in any man's face."

"I may come in?"

"Yes."

Kate advanced in the room, and taking a seat, said:

"You appear to be all alone here?"

"I am."

"Have you no family?"

"I have no family."

"*Where is your lodger?*"

"I have no lodger."

"Ah! how long since your boarder left you?"

"You're too smart altogether!" exclaimed Sturgis.

"How too smart?"

"Well, you think to take me by surprise."

"How take you by surprise?"

"Force me into some sort of admission."

"What sort of an admission could you make if you chose?"

"I could admit that I did have a lodger."

"That is an admission."

"Is it?"

"Yes."

"Then you have caught me, after all," remarked Sturgis, with a merry twinkle in his eye.

"You did not try very hard to evade me."

"Ah, thank you!"

"You did have a lodger here?"

"Yes, I did."

"For how long?"

"About two months."

"Where is your lodger now?"

"One moment, stranger; I wish you to understand that I am no fool!"

"No one here called you a fool."

"I know who you are."

"Do you?"

"I do."

"Who am I?"

"A detective from York."

"You are pretty good at guessing."

"I am; and now listen. I've known who you were from the first, and I would not answer you one word unless I had a mind to do so."

"I am glad you have a mind to do so."

"That's all right; but let me tell you that you have come too late."

"Too late for what?"

"To catch Arthur Everdell, the burglar."

Lady Kate was taken all aback, and a horror filled her soul as she realized the terrible suggestion contained in the fisherman's words.

Why should old Sturgis be so bold in announcing Arthur's escape, unless the young man had escaped beyond all chance of ever being produced before an earthly tribunal? Indeed, the old man's frankness indicated that Arthur Everdell, the strange, wayward, elegant youth, was *dead!*

There was a tremor in Kate's voice, as she said:

"He has escaped?"

"Yes; he has escaped."

"Where has he gone?"

The old fisherman laughed, and answered.

"I would be a fool to tell you."

"Then you admit that you could tell me?"

"I've admitted nothing of the kind."

"Do you know I could arrest you?"

"What for?"

"Harboring a criminal."

"You had better not try it on."

There was a world of threat in the old man's voice.

"I do not wish to arrest you."

"Oh, thank you."

"I would rather be your friend."

The fisherman had evidently at one time in his life peeped into the classics, as he answered with aggravating coolness:

"I fear the Greeks when they come with presents in their hands."

"You were evidently a friend of Arthur Everdell?"

"Yes; I *was* his friend."

"You *were* his friend?"

"Yes."

Kate at length managed to put the fated question:

"Is he dead?"

"Well, I hope not."

"I will tell you something, old man."

"Do."

"I also am a friend of Arthur Everdell."

"Ah, give us a rest, Mr. Detective."

"I speak truly."

"You are his friend?"

"I am."

"And you have come to run him down?"

"I have come, as a friend, to find him."

"Why did you wish to find him?"

"Because I am his friend."

"You claim to be a friend of a burglar; oh, no, that will not do. I'm old now, Mr. Detective, but I was young once, and I am not taking soft-soap for that kind of a wash."

"Still, I swear to you that I am Arthur Everdell's friend."

"Then will you tell me frankly why you wished to discover him?"

The consciousness flashed upon Kate that, even as a friend, her purpose had been to trail Arthur, to hand him over to justice.

She was silent.

"Come," said the fisherman, "tell me why you wished to find him?"

"I will tell Arthur my reason."

"Very well; go and find your man and tell him."

"My man is here."

"You think so?"

"I do."

"Well, find him here. I will not put a pin in the way of a most thorough search; you certainly are entitled to find your *friend*."

CHAPTER LXIV.

THE fisherman spoke in a very satirical tone. Kate was satisfied that Arthur was not in the cabin, and that a search would only prove a waste of time.

A moment the two sat in silence eying each other, when the fisherman at length broke the silence with the remark:

"You have been out in the storm?"

"I have."

"You are wet through to the skin?"

"I am."

"I can give you some dry clothes; they may not fit you, and they are rough, but they are better than your wet duds."

"I am much obliged to you; I will not change my clothes."

Kate was compelled to blush at the suggestion of changing her clothes in the presence of that rough old fisherman; the latter, however, did not observe the blush, as he was totally unsuspicious of the real facts.

"You want to sit there in drenched clothes?"

"Yes."

"Well, go it, old man; but if you don't have a high old cold in the morning you're lucky."

"I trust I will be lucky."

"You'll stay all night here?"

"No."

"It's three miles to the village."

"I can not help it."

"Oh, that's all nonsense; stay here to-night."

Kate began to wish herself on the road to the village. The good fisherman was getting too hospitable altogether, under the circumstances.

"Never mind about me," said Kate, in a shaky voice.

"Oh, all right; but I tell you that you can stay with me just as well as not."

"No, no; I wish to ask you about the young man who was lodging here with you."

"Well, what about him?"

"How did he happen to be here?"

"I reckon there's no reason why I should not tell you all the facts."

"Please do."

"Well, one morning about two months ago I went to where I keep my nets, when I saw a strange boat rocking on the beach, and soon after I found a handsome young man lying on the rocks."

"It was Arthur?"

"Yes, and he was in a sorry plight: it was the morning after the attempted burglary at the Bayne place. He had received a bad wound."

"How did you know he was a burglar?"

"He told me himself."

"It's strange he would confess he was a burglar."

"Well, it was sort of strange; but, mister, that young man is a strange sort of a burglar; indeed, he is the strangest chap I ever met, and I've met some strange ones in my time."

"Did he confess to the doctor what he confessed to you?"

"Yes."

"It is strange he was not surrendered."

"Well, the doctor was a pretty good sort of a fellow."

"Who was the doctor?"

"I was the doctor."

"You?"

"Yes."

Kate was amazed.

"You nursed him back to life?"

"I did."

"You appear to have formed a strong friendship for a common burglar—for an assassin?"

A wicked light shone in the old fisherman's eyes, and there was anger in his voice, as he said:

"Don't repeat those words!"

"Why not?"

"It might be dangerous; you are an officer, but you must not call Arthur Everdell an assassin!"

"How do you know that he is not an assassin?"

"I do know that he is not an assassin!"

Kate's heart thrilled; she was rejoiced to hear the old fisherman speak in his earnest manner, and she kept addressing him in a manner to compel him to keep repeating his denial.

"Old man, on my honor, I assure you I am a friend of Everdell, and I am rejoiced to hear you so positively assert that he is not an assassin."

"He is not."

"Will you tell me why you are so assured?"

"I questioned him."

"And his bare word of denial is enough?"

"Yes; enough for me. I believe that young man is incapable of telling a falsehood. Why, he could have deceived me, but he made no attempt to do so; and when he confessed, I said to him it was my duty to hand him over to the police, and what do you think he said?"

"What did he say?"

"He said ' *Do your duty* '!"

"And why did you not do your duty?"

"I will tell you why. I do not consider that young man responsible for his career. He has told me his whole story, and I believe his tale."

"There is a mystery connected with his life."

"There is. I suppose you know there is a man in jail in New York who bears a remarkable personal resemblance to Arthur Everdell?"

"I do."

"Have you seen this other man?"

"Yes."

"Is the resemblance really so remarkable?"

"It is."

"How do you explain the mystery?"

"The time has not come for explanations."

"Ah, I see. I reckon you could explain the mystery."

"Answer me one question," said Kate. "Does Arthur know of the young man in jail in New York?"

"He does."

"What does he say about an innocent man suffering in his stead?"

"He did not know of it until about two hours ago."

"Two hours ago!"

"Yes."

"Where was he two hours ago?"

"Here."

"Where is he now?"

"Heaven knows!"

"You warned him?"

"I did."

"You urged him to escape?"

"I did."

"Why?"

"I did not want him to fall into your hands; that's frank!"

"Yes; what did he say when you told him of the young man in New York?"

"Nothing."

"See here, old man, Arthur Everdell is not far from here."

"No; he could not have gone so very far in such a tempest."

"You know where he is?"

"I do not."

"You swear?"

"I only swear when I break a net."

Kate smiled, but said:

"You are evading me. Listen, it is better for Arthur Everdell that he should see me; I can do him good."

"What good can you do him?"

"I can afford him a chance to begin an honest life."

The fisherman sprung from his seat, seized Kate by the hand, and exclaimed:

"What is that you say?"

"I can afford him a chance to lead an honest life."

"You can rescue him from the penalty of his past crimes?"

"I can."

"I wish I could believe what you promise!"

"Why?"

"Arthur Everdell has become an honest man. He would die before he would ever steal

again. He is the victim of an adverse fate, and did he have the chance he would become a great and good man!"

"Tell me where I can find him, and I promise you that, if he is not a murderer, he shall have the chance!"

CHAPTER LXV.

"I WISH I could tell you where he is, but I can not."

"He has fled?"

"Yes; he has fled."

"Then I must go seek him."

"Go!" said the fisherman.

"Has he gone to New York?"

"On my honor, I do not know where he has gone; I did not wish to ask him. *I desire to be able to say to any one, ' I do not know where he has gone.'* I do not know."

Kate remained and had some further conversation with the fisherman, and then announced her intention to return to the village.

"Why should you return to-night? You can not accomplish anything; remain here until morning."

"No; I will go to-night."

"Oh, go 'long. I shall insist upon you remaining. I wouldn't let a dog return to the village at such an hour with the roads in their present condition."

"I shall go to-night, good friend."

"Then you have a reason?"

"Yes," answered Kate, "I have a reason for going to-night."

Kate bid the man adieu; she stepped across his threshold into the darkness; the fisherman followed her to the door, and standing there and presenting at the moment a weird picture, he said:

"I do not know whether you are really a friend or foe of Arthur Everdell."

"I am his friend."

"Then listen: I charge you, as a friend, not to interfere with him in any way; do not follow upon his track; do not seek him; leave him to himself."

"Why are you so particular in this respect?"

"I am satisfied he has a purpose, and I wish him to have a clear opportunity to carry out his purpose."

"You may depend I will not interfere with him in any way, nor place any obstacles in his way, provided his purposes are honorable and worthy."

Kate stepped from the door, and, a moment later, was on the beach.

The storm had all cleared away, and the stars had come out bright and serene, and, as she gazed heavenward, there recurred to her memory the weird words of Byron:

"The night hath been to me a more familiar face than that of man, and in its solitary loveliness I have learned the language of another world."

Strange thoughts floated through the mind of the lady detective. She was at sea as to her future movements.

One fact came with pressing weight to her memory, and it was a recollection of the magnetism of Arthur Everdell's presence.

The strange young man had been the associate of thieves and criminals all his life; his mentor in his early boyhood had been a noted criminal—a man who had died upon the gallows or in prison—and yet he charmed every one with whom he came in contact.

Kate met the honest fisherman, a man who it was evident detested crime and criminals, and yet knowing Arthur to be a criminal, he had formed an extraordinary affection for the youth.

A certain truth known to Kate had always brought the flush of shame to her cheek every time the consciousness crossed her mind, and yet she was under the spell of the willful criminal's fascination.

As she walked along, but one thought filled her mind, and there came to her the constant query: "What shall I do? what shall I do?"

She imagined that she understood Arthur's character well. The latter was striking and well defined in its peculiar characteristics.

Again and again, in the most feeling and eloquent manner, she had urged upon the young man to reform, and attempt a new career in life, but always her pleadings had been met with the one answer, delivered in a tone of heart-piercing sadness:

"No, no; I was born a thief. I was trained to a criminal life! I will always be a rascal!"

The fisherman had made a new revelation to

her. He had related in a dramatic manner the story of Arthur's gradual awakening to the fact that there was hope for him! that there was a chance for him to commence a new career. Sturgis had concluded his narrative with an account of Arthur's last words, "I will die, but never again as long as I live will I be a thief!"

If Arthur really uttered the words credited to him, Kate could perceive their full significance and importance; such language falling from the lips of a man of Arthur's marked and decided characteristics, could only come of the most set determination. Arthur was a determined man.

Kate believed in her heart that he had made the declaration, and having made it, she knew he would abide by his words; and thus was presented her dilemma: should she surrender Arthur to the authorities, it would be tantamount to turning the key of the prison doors upon him for fifteen or twenty years; should she fail to surrender him and aid him to escape, it would be turning the key upon an *innocent man* for the same length of time.

Kate well knew that no earthly power could save George Gordon from conviction but the production of the real criminal. His fatal resemblance to the real burglar shadowed down upon the innocent man all the fatal evidence that tended toward a certain conviction and sentence.

As stated, the query constantly arose in her mind, What shall I do? what shall I do?

Our readers must surely appreciate her dramatic position.

Back of all was the consciousness that, when she surrendered Arthur Everdell to punishment, she handed over to a living death her heart's idol.

It is useless for us to attempt to conceal the fact—Kate had learned to love the weird criminal as only a strong-willed, strong-hearted woman can love.

She had struggled against the passion, had sought to crush out the new love, but alas! the love of woman is uncontrollable, even as the driftwood on the surface of the flooded river is borne resistlessly down to the sea.

It was a struggle between a sense of duty and a wild, passionate love; and the aggravating element was the consciousness that were Arthur spared he would become in deportment what he was by inherent nature, a noble and exemplary man. To surrender him to the authorities was to blast his life; to shield him was to blast the life of an innocent man.

CHAPTER LXVI.

THE agony of her thoughts caused great beads of sweat to burst out upon the lady detective's fair forehead, and yet the night was cool, and the season pressed onward to the period when the nights were really cold.

Again and again in the anguish of the moment she wailed out in audible tones:

"What shall I do? what shall I do?"

Kate had walked along the beach, and was at the moment passing under a cliff, whose sides were covered with a dense growth of brush.

As she wailed forth the words there suddenly fell upon her ears the distinctly pronounced admonition:

"*Do your duty! do your duty!*"

Kate came to a halt and glanced around. Nowhere could she see any one, and a strange, superstitious feeling crept over her.

She was no coward, although but a delicate woman. Night had no terrors for her. She was inured to peril and danger, and yet as the strange response had fallen upon her ears, her heart had momentarily ceased to beat.

Kate stood rooted to the spot: fully three minutes passed, and under the circumstances three minutes are quite a length of time.

At length, she again in a clear, distinct voice wailed forth:

"Oh, what shall I do? what shall I do?"

A minute passed, and then there fell upon her ear with wonderful distinctness the response:

"Do your duty! do your duty!"

"Who speaks?" demanded Kate.

There came no response.

Again she demanded:

"Who speaks?" and as she made the demand, she closed her grasp upon her pistol, as there was a possibility that the words came from human lips, and it was prudent to be upon her guard.

Again Kate pronounced the words, "What shall I do? what shall I do?" and once more, and almost immediately, came the response:

"Do your duty! do your duty!"

The superstitious spell at once passed away, and Kate became convinced that some one was concealed in the bushes, and a suspicion crossed her mind that the refrain had been spoken in jest.

She started to go upon her way, but an influence urged her to remain and make an investigation.

It was a plucky performance for a woman under all the circumstances, but Kate was a plucky woman.

"Who speaks?" she demanded.

There came an immediate and direct response to her question.

"Take the advice you have received, and go follow it!"

"I would like to stand face to face with the adviser."

The bushes were pushed aside, and a man stepped from their cover.

Kate felt an inclination to scream. Arthur Everdell stood before her.

His face, pale and thin, was clearly revealed under the moonlight; for a half-moon had risen, and was casting its radiance upon the water and on the shore.

Arthur stood revealed as the exact counterpart of the portrait, and again the almost exact image of the young man George Gordon, who at that moment languished in prison, enduring the penalty of another's crimes.

Kate's disguise was perfect; it would have been impossible for any one to have discovered her real identity.

The lady detective had also made it a study to so modulate her voice as to make it accord with her character as a male.

In order to more easily do so, she always adopted a sort of broken English, and when in male attire never failed to preserve her incognito in voice and manner.

Her agitation upon beholding Arthur was great, and for a moment she merely stood and gazed in blank amazement.

Her agitation could not have excited suspicion, as, under the circumstances, considering the singular appearance of the intruder, any one would have shown signs of surprise.

In a strangely satirical tone and with semi-dramatic emphasis Arthur said:

"You have sent for me, and I am come!"

"Who are you?" demanded Kate.

"Well, it matters not who I am, as probably you and I will never meet again."

"It was you, however, who ventured to give me advice."

"Yes. The advice was good, was it not?"

Both had adopted a sort of bantering tone.

"The advice was really conventionally good."

"It was really conventionally given."

"How did you come to give it?"

"I'll tell you: I was seated under the cliff. I heard approaching footsteps, and I crawled under the cover of the brush. The party whom I heard approaches and repeats the query in audible tones, 'What shall I do? what shall I do?' and, as a good Samaritan, I respond, 'Do your duty! do your duty'!"

The situation was an odd one, and the query now pressed upon Kate with enhanced significance, and to herself she mentally questioned:

"What shall I do? what *shall* I do?"

"You pronounced the advice in an earnest manner," said Kate.

"Well, we can well be earnest when delivering good advice."

"You know the advice to be good?"

"I do."

"You propose to take the precept to your soul?"

"I do."

It was hard for Kate to keep the tremor from being betrayed in her voice.

"May I ask you a question?"

"You may."

"What were you doing on the beach at this hour?"

"I will answer your question Yankee fashion. What were you doing on the beach at this hour?"

"I am entitled to a first answer, but I will waive my right; I was looking for some one."

"Well, as you are so frank, I will be equally so. I was seeking to avoid some one."

"Whom were you seeking to avoid?"

Arthur laughed, and answered:

"*The party who was searching for me.*"

"Possibly we are well met," said Kate.

"Possibly we are."

Kate, looking straight at the young man, in a stern voice declared:

"Arthur Everdell! Randolph Cummings! you are my prisoner!"

CHAPTER LXVII.

ARTHUR did not wince or betray the least fear or excitement, but, in a calm, determined voice, answered:

"I am not your prisoner!"

"Will you resist?"

"I will not become your prisoner."

"Will you compel me to resort to violence to secure you?"

The young man was silent a moment, but at length replied, in a strange, sad voice:

"You could perform for me no kinder act. Fire—and may Heaven bless you!"

Kate, had she followed a womanly impulse, would have cast aside her weapon, and have thrown herself upon Arthur's bosom, with the words, "My love, your life is more precious than mine own!" She could not do it, however, as in her ears constantly rang the weird admonition, "Do your duty! do your duty!" and before her imagination was presented the picture of an innocent man enduring ignominy and pain for the crime of the criminal who stood before her.

Kate felt bound to insist upon a surrender; but shoot him—never! Her hand would have become palsied as her finger pressed upon the trigger of her weapon.

"Arthur Everdell, you bid me do my duty!"

"I did."

"I now bid you do your duty."

"Point out my duty."

"Surrender."

Arthur laughed, and it was that strange, peculiar laugh that Kate had listened to upon one or two other occasions.

"You must take me."

"You will resist?"

"I will never become your prisoner."

But one course lay open to Kate; should she persist she knew well that, previous to his illness, Arthur had been a young man of extraordinary strength and agility; in a struggle with him she would have no chance unless she did as she threatened.

It had never been a part of Kate's professional duty to make an arrest. Her duty consisted in ferreting out information, and on her information many an arrest had been made.

At this moment the words of Sturgis, the old fisherman, came to her recollection, "Do not stand in the way of Arthur Everdell," and she had promised conditionally that she would not.

"Do you deny your identity?"

"I do not."

"Do you recognize me?"

"I suppose you are a detective officer."

"Then you must know that in case of resistance I shall be justified in taking you prisoner at any cost."

"I will not become your prisoner; do as you please!"

"Good-night, Arthur Everdell," said Kate, "we may meet again."

The lady detective had suddenly come to a resolution as to her line of action. As she exclaimed, "good-night, Arthur Everdell, we may meet again," she had started to walk away.

"Hold!" called Arthur.

"Well?"

"Why do you not do your duty?" came the query.

"It is not my duty to arrest you. I have been trifling with you. We are square on the admonition you gave me from the bush."

"You know me?"

"I've called you by name."

"Who are you?"

"Never mind."

"You amaze me."

"Do I?"

"Yes; you declare yourself a detective; you know there is a reward offered for my apprehension, and yet having trailed me, walk away with a sweet good night."

Kate laughed, and said:

"Why, young man, it's all a good joke; you are the coolest joker I ever met."

"I do not know what you mean."

"You are not Arthur Everdell!"

"I am not Arthur Everdell?"

"No."

"Then why did you address me as Arthur Everdell?"

" Because you look like the real Arthur; you can not fool me. Do you suppose that if you had really been that notorious criminal, you would have acknowledged your identity so readily? No, no, young man, you can not get the laugh on me, not to-night—ta, ta!'

"Hold!"

"Well?"

"I am Arthur Everdell."

"Nonsense! Arthur Everdell was arrested and put in prison two months ago. He will be tried for his life in a few days. He has been fully identified; indeed, does not deny his identity, and the evidence is dead against him. You are a good joker, but mark me! I was only joking with you, so you have not got the laugh on me as sweet as you think you have!"

Arthur Everdell listened with a peculiar expression upon his handsome face.

"Good-night!" said Kate.

Arthur made no response, but stood gazing like one suddenly stricken dumb.

Kate walked away. Arthur did not call her back.

The lady detective walked some distance up the beach, and upon turning around, saw Arthur standing motionless on the same spot.

Once more, in low tones, she moaned out: "What shall I do? what shall I do?"

There was a far different significance, however, attached to her words than when she first wailed them forth.

Her womanly nature was fast asserting itself, and she longed to return, proclaim her identity, and advise Arthur as a friend; but she dared not do so. It would have been her proper course, but she could not trust herself; had she once spoken, she would have betrayed herself, and her advice would not have fallen from the lips of a mere friend; she would have spoken as a madly loving woman. She would have urged him to fly, to leave his fated counterpart to his fate.

Kate stood but a moment, then resolutely faced about with the remark, "Let matters take their course; the drift of events is beyond my control now!"

It was far into morning when Kate reached the village. She did not go to a hotel, but went down to the wharf. She knew that one of the river freight boats touched at the pier, and that she would have a chance to return to New York

An hour passed, when the lady detective discovered the lights of the boat as she came steaming down stream.

CHAPTER LXVIII.

THE lady detective was sad indeed as she stood upon the pier in the early morning watching the lights of the approaching boat.

The dock watchman came down and prepared for the landing, and in time the boat was made fast, and the deck hands began putting aboard the small pile of freight.

Kate had gone aboard and taken a position on the promenade-deck, and, while seated there, she beheld Arthur Everdell walk down the pier and step aboard.

Kate did not wish to be seen by him, and sought a part of the boat where she would be most likely to escape observation.

The lady detective congratulated herself upon following the advice of the old fisherman Sturgis.

The freight was soon put aboard, and the boat steamed on its way down stream, and about eight o'clock in the morning ran alongside the dock at the great city.

Kate watched to see the passengers go ashore; but when all had departed she had not seen Arthur among them.

A terrible suspicion crossed her mind, and she searched the boat through and through, but failed to find him.

Addressing one of the men, she asked if they had noticed Arthur come aboard.

The answer was:

"Yes, sir."

"Where did he get off?"

"I have not seen him, sir, since he came aboard."

"Oh, heavens!" murmured Kate, "can it be possible he has escaped all by throwing himself into the river?"

She remembered how he had invited her to shoot, and had said death would prove his sweetest boon.

Kate lingered around the boat for two hours, but saw nothing of the strange young man.

She made inquiries in every direction of the officers of the boat, but not one of them could remember having seen the stranger after his entrance upon the boat.

The conviction was forced upon the mind of Kate that indeed the young man had thrown himself from the boat into the river.

It was with a heavy heart that she sought her lodgings and prepared for a visit to the cell where George Gordon was confined.

At the door of her abode she met old Mr. Everdell.

"I have hunted for you high and low," said the old man.

Kate had been absent two days and nights.

"I am here; what do you wish?"

"I came to inquire whether or not you had made any discoveries?"

Kate was in a quandary as to how to answer the old man.

"I have made no discoveries that it is necessary to reveal at present."

"You have discovered something?"

"I have answered you."

"Do you know that George Gordon's trial is set down for next week?"

"I did not know it."

"Yes, he is to be tried next week."

"Well?"—the well was spoken interrogatively.

"Something must be done."

"What can we do?"

"That young man must be rescued!"

"You recognize the fact?"

"I do."

"Will you tell me how he can be rescued?"

"Money ought to do the thing."

"Why do you not try money?"

"I will furnish you the money."

"We will talk this matter over at some future time."

"Tell me that my boy is dead!" said the old man, suddenly.

"I can not say that Arthur is dead."

"You believe so?"

The fact was, Kate did fear that indeed Arthur was dead, but she indulged one hope—he might have left the boat at some of the landings below the one where he had gone aboard.

"I am tired," said Kate. "I can not talk to you now. I will see you this evening."

"Where?"

"I will come to your rooms."

The lady detective desired time to think over matters; and besides, she wished to wait and learn whether or not Arthur would appear in life.

While Kate was talking with old Everdell, a strange, ay, indeed, a most wonderful scene, was in progress at the jail where George Gordon was confined.

Arthur Everdell, at the time Kate had left him standing upon the beach, had received a terrible shock.

He knew that when Kate so suddenly announced herself as the champion jokist, she was not joking at all, and he knew that her revelation was part of a design.

He stood for a long time like one suddenly paralyzed or turned to stone.

A man resembled him! Who could the man be? And this strange counterpart was in jail, had been arrested as Arthur Everdell, and as Arthur Everdell was to be tried for his life!

The above were the thoughts that crowded through the stricken man's mind.

At length he moved and started to walk slowly toward the village.

As he walked along he muttered to himself:

"I know my duty now. Well, what matters it? Mine is a blasted life; it were well brought to a close. What care I how I may be removed? I am innocent of murder, but as a murderer I will be tried, as a murderer convicted, and as a murderer executed! Well, so be it! I can not overrule fate!"

Arthur reached the landing, and discovered Kate sitting on the string-piece waiting for the boat.

A sight of the self-declared detective set the young man to studying as to who the officer could be.

As stated, he knew that the mysterious detective was not joking when she had denounced Arthur Everdell; and it was a mystery that the young man could not solve—the singular conduct of the officer.

A day came when the mystery was explained; and indeed it was a dark day for all concerned.

Arthur did not wish to be seen by the detective, and waited until the latter went aboard.

Upon going aboard himself, he learned that

he had been discovered, and he did just what Kate had sought to do—avoided observation.

Arthur did not remain in the boat until it reached its dock, but had left at the last landing before New York was reached.

The young man went to the railroad station, and secured passage on a train which arrived at New York some two hours ahead of the boat.

CHAPTER LXIX.

UPON reaching the city, Arthur at once set about the performance of his duty.

The young man had a trunk in the possession of one of his former pals, and he proceeded to the "hanging-out place" of his former comrade.

He was fortunate in finding his man, and an hour afterward appeared upon the street so thoroughly disguised that even Lady Kate would have failed to discover his identity.

Arthur had an acquaintance a gambler, a man who possessed greater influence than a person of his character deserved.

From the party named, our hero secured a special pass to the jail where George Gordon was confined.

As young Gordon had not been tried, the special watch which is usually set over condemned homicides, had not yet been placed.

The turnkey who attended upon Arthur, asked:

"What is your business?"

"Counsel," came the equivocal answer.

"Will you remain some time with the prisoner?"

"An hour at least, with your permission."

It was with a heart almost bursting with emotion that Arthur Everdell was led to the cell.

As he approached the iron door he feared that he should faint. Usually he was a man of iron; but the circumstances were so extraordinary that even Arthur's iron will seemed ready to succumb.

The keeper opened the door. Arthur entered, and, as his glance fell upon the prisoner, a wild cry fell from his lips. It was not a loud ejaculation, but full of agony, long drawn, and freighted with singular significance.

George Gordon gazed in amazement. He could not interpret why a stranger had been thrust in upon him.

Arthur stood and gazed with starting eyes. It was as though he were gazing upon himself, so wonderful and striking was the resemblance.

Our readers will please remember that Arthur was in disguise, and that Gordon had no cause for astonishment, beyond the fact of a stranger's having been thrust in upon him.

The prisoner demanded:

"Who are you?"

Arthur made no reply, but stood and gazed with starting eyeballs.

Again Gordon demanded:

"Who are you?"

Arthur, in a trembling voice, responded:

"Indeed, I may ask who you are?"

In a low tone the prisoner remarked:

"They have thrust in upon me some lunatic!"

"You think I am mad?"

"Yes."

"I'm not mad!"

"Why did you come here?"

"You ask me why I came here?"

"I do."

Arthur suddenly drew aside his wig and other articles of disguise, and stood revealed as his proper self, and at the same moment he exclaimed:

"I came to have this mystery solved; can you solve it?"

It was Gordon's turn to start back and gaze with starting eyeballs, while a startled ejaculation fell from his lips.

"Do you ask me now why I came?"

Gordon was speechless.

"Have I a right now to demand," said Arthur, "who are you?"

Still Gordon remained speechless. He had detected what Arthur had previously noted, the wonderful resemblance.

"I'll tell you now," said Arthur, "why I came here. I came to take your place. I am guilty! you are innocent!"

"My double!" ejaculated Gordon.

"Yes; your double!"

"You have come here to take my place?"

"Yes."

"Why?"

"Because you are innocent!"

"And you?"

"I am guilty."

"A murderer?"

"No."

"You are blood-guiltless?"

"I am, as Heaven hears!"

"Thank Heaven, *my brother!*"

"Hold! What did you call me?"

"Brother!"

"Never do so again."

"I will, before all the world! Nature proclaims you my brother. This wonderful resemblance between you and me could never come unless the same blood ran in our veins!"

"But you must not call me your brother."

"Why not?"

"I am a thief!"

"And I am indicted as a murderer!"

"Because of your fatal resemblance to a scoundrel like me. But your sufferings are over; I will take your place; I came here to release you—to suffer as I deserve."

"Who sent you here, my brother?"

"No one; my own sense of honor bid me come."

"How did you learn of me?"

"Through accident, and at once I came to release you."

"There is good in you, brother."

"I am a thief!"

"A thief?"

"Yes."

"Why are you a thief?"

"I was born a thief."

"Your hand, brother!" exclaimed Gordon, extending his own hand.

"I can not take it."

"You refuse the hand of a brother?"

"I do."

"And yet you have come here to suffer in my place?"

"I have."

"Do you know what you brave?"

"I do."

"You may be convicted as a murderer."

"I know that well."

"The penalty is death."

"I am no coward."

"You swear you are innocent?"

"I swear I am blood-guiltless!"

"Then why proclaim yourself a criminal?"

"I have been a criminal all my life."

"Listen, brother. I fear you and I are the victims of a greater criminal. Tell me your story."

Arthur told his tale going into details that he had never mentioned to any one else. When his strange tale was concluded, George Gordon exclaimed:

"Poor boy! how you have been sinned against; indeed, more sinned against than sinning. Listen, I will tell my tale."

George Gordon related the early incidents of his life, and when he had concluded, asked:

"How old are you?"

Arthur gave a date, which would indicate his age at five-and-twenty.

"I am four years your senior, boy; but we are brothers all the same. I think I pierce the mystery. Would to Heaven we had met sooner; it's too late now; *death overshadows one of us!*"

CHAPTER LXX.

IT was a strange scene presented at that moment, as the two brothers stood face to face, the striking likeness between them so wonderfully apparent.

They were both handsome men, but as they stood together it was apparent that George Gordon was a shade the taller of the two, a shade stouter in build, and his face showed the difference in their years.

The difference was so slight that it would only have been noted when, as stated, they stood side by side.

George Gordon betrayed the fact that under his seemingly cold manner there dwelt a noble nature.

The brothers frankly discussed possibilities, and arrived at the conclusion which has already been reached by our readers, they were brothers born of different mothers.

After a long discussion, George Gordon said:

"And now what shall we do?"

Arthur spoke at last with his old-time firmness:

"There remains but one thing to be done—you must leave this place. Our fatal resemblance that has served to place you here shall also serve to release you. Brother, if you will permit a man like me to so address you, go! I will remain and meet all consequences!"

"It is easy to say go, but how shall I go?"

"Put on the disguise which I wore here purposely, and go forth when the turnkey comes. He will not know, nor will the world know, neither lawyers, judge, nor jury, that there has been an exchange of prisoners."

"You bid me go?"

"I do."

"Listen; I will not go—I'll remain!"

"You remain! Why, man, you are innocent! I am guilty!"

"I will remain to atone for my father's sin; it is not your fault that you are a thief, it is only my good fortune that I am not worse than you."

It was a strange scene and a peculiar situation.

As intimated, the brothers had come to a clear understanding as to their relationship.

They had no positive evidence to confirm their conclusions, but the evidence was at least satisfactory to them.

Arthur Everdell was the stronger of the two in will and determination of character, and he said:

"You *shall* go hence!"

"I will not."

"Listen to me. I can compel you to go. I can proclaim myself the guilty man!"

"You will not."

"I will."

"This is terrible, brother. No more horrible alternative was ever presented to two mortals."

"I can clear myself of the charge of murder. For the attempted burglary I must suffer—I am guilty!"

"You can clear yourself of the charge of murder?"

"I can."

"And you bid me go?"

"You must go! Why should you remain here? I positively assure you that I am determined to proclaim myself the guilty man. And now, hark you! we have not a moment to spare. The guard will be here in a moment, and it will be too late. If discovered as we are, we would both be held as confederates."

"I will go!"

George Gordon had formed a certain resolution, or he would never have consented to leave Arthur to his fate.

The brothers changed clothes, and Gordon was arrayed in the disguise that Arthur had worn upon entering the cell.

Steps were heard.

"The guard comes!" said Arthur.

Gordon grasped his brother's hand, and said, in a tone of deep feeling:

"Innocent or guilty, you shall not suffer!"

The keeper came to the grated door, opened it, and said:

"Time is up!"

George Gordon passed out.

Arthur was alone, and a feeling of satisfaction came to his mind.

A wonderful change had come over the strange young man.

Some hours passed, and his cell-door opened. A lady was shown into the cell.

It was Lady Kate, the female detective.

The moment she entered the room and fixed her eyes upon Arthur, an exclamation of astonishment fell from her lips.

Lady Kate had seen so much of George Gordon, and was of such an observant character, she at a glance discerned that something extraordinary had occurred.

The guard locked the door and went away, when Kate said:

"Well, what does this mean?"

"Madame, I do not understand your question."

"Where is the real prisoner?"

"You talk in riddles."

"Do I?"

"Yes."

"You are surprised at my question?"

"I am."

Arthur was surprised. He wondered how this female visitor should have at a glance detected the truth.

"I will surprise you still more, Arthur Everdell. Where did you leave the '——'?" Kate named the steamer upon which she and Arthur had embarked the previous night.

Arthur was indeed surprised, and he showed his perfect amazement in his face.

"How could a prisoner have been upon any boat last night?"

Kate laughed in a strange manner, and said:

"The guilty man is here! where is the innocent man?"

Arthur Everdell was more and more amazed, but he was no fool. He began to perceive the

truth, and in a calm, matter-of-fact tone, he said:

"It's time you and I came to a clear explanation."

"Yes; it is time we came to a clear explanation, Arthur Everdell."

"Who are you?" demanded Arthur.

"You shall know; but first answer me a few questions."

"I am ready."

"Where is George Gordon?"

"Gone."

"Where?"

"He is free!"

"How comes it he is free?"

"He is innocent."

"I know that; but how is it the innocent man is free, and the really guilty man in his place?"

"The guilty man came and set the innocent man free!"

"Who knows of the change?"

"Evidently three persons."

"Who are the three persons?"

"An inquisitive lady, Arthur Everdell, and George Gordon!"

"No one else is in the secret?"

"No one."

CHAPTER LXXI.

"ARTHUR EVERDELL, did you come here voluntarily?"

"Before I answer any questions, I should know my questioner."

"You shall, but you need not fear to answer my questions. I am your friend."

"Thank you; I need a friend."

"You will find me a true friend."

"Again, thank you!"

"Answer my question; did you come here voluntarily?"

"I did."

"What induced you to put yourself in such peril?"

"Could a guilty brother stand and see his innocent brother suffer in his stead?"

"Brother! Is George Gordon your brother?" demanded Kate, in a tone of surprise.

"You have seen George?"

"Yes."

"You behold me!"

"Yes."

"Could we be aught else but brothers?"

"Had you ever met before?"

"Never!"

"It was your first meeting in this cell?"

"Yes."

"Did you know it was your brother before you came here?"

"I did not."

"Then your former answer to my question was an evasion?"

"How so?"

"You said you came to release an innocent brother. How could you come to release a brother when you did not know you had a brother?"

"I will tell you. I first heard that there was a man in jail who had been arrested in mistake for me; later on I was informed that the man bore a wonderful resemblance to me."

"But you previously resolved to take his place?"

"Yes."

"Before you heard of the wonderful resemblance?"

"Yes."

"Who told you first of the resemblance?"

"You did."

"I did?"

"Yes."

Kate started back in amazement.

"I told you?" she repeated.

"Yes."

"When?"

"Last night."

"I told you last night?"

"I repeat, yes."

"Where did you see me last night?"

Arthur laughed in that peculiar manner we have formerly noted, and answered:

"I saw you last night on the shore, near the village of ——."

"How do you know you saw me?"

"Well, I do know it."

"Then, if you know who I am, why did you inquire as to my identity?"

"I did not know that it was you I met in the disguise of a male until you revealed the fact."

"How did I reveal the fact?"

"By asking me where I left the boat. You

must remember, I am posted as concerns disguises and the like."

"You believe George Gordon to be your brother?"

"I do."

"Have you any proofs of the fact?"

"None."

"Whereon is your belief founded?"

"Our resemblance and our strange histories."

"You *are* brothers!"

"You know us to be so?"

"I do."

"Will you tell me who you are?"

"Have you not placed me?"

"I suspect."

"Who do you suspect I am?"

"*Lady Kate, the female detective.*"

A chill shot through Kate's heart.

"How many times have we met?"

"Several times."

"Admitting I am Lady Kate, the female detective, I must have appeared to you under many disguises."

"That is true."

"In how many of those disguises have you recognized me?"

"All."

"Enumerate them."

"Why should I?"

"I desire that you should."

"If I do, will you tell me how it is that you chance to be upon my track?"

"I will."

"I met you first at the house where the tragedy occurred."

Kate winced.

"When did you meet me again?"

"Upon the cars. You were disguised as an old lady."

"Did you identify me at that time?"

"I did."

"How?"

"Your inquiries betrayed you. You attempted to draw me out to commit me."

"Did you recognize me at that moment as Lady Kate?"

"I did."

"When did you identify me as the detective?"

"Within the last ten minutes."

"When next did you meet me?"

Arthur laughed and answered:

"The next time we met was under peculiar circumstances. You will remember I called you *Sis*, and warned you?"

"When next did we meet?"

"*At the masked ball!* Not between times, that I remember."

"Then I deceived you once."

"You did?"

"I did."

"When?"

"Do you remember the beggar whose life you saved?"

"And were you that beggar?" ejaculated Arthur, betraying genuine astonishment.

"I was."

"Then you are indeed a wonderful woman!"

"When next did we meet?"

"When you were trying to bait the burglar with your display of jewels. The mystery of your coolness upon that occasion of the burglary after the ball is explained; but why you did not surrender me to the police after you had so positively identified me, I can not understand."

"I will explain in due time why I did not hand you over to the police. But tell me when next we met?"

"When I told you the story of my life."

"And you told me the truth then?"

"I did."

"It was when you told me your history that I decided not to hand you over to the police."

"Why did you come to that decision?"

"Because I considered you more sinned against than sinning."

"You were very charitable."

Kate could have added another reason, and as the remembrance flashed across her mind a blush mantled her cheek.

"When did we meet again?" asked Kate.

"Last night."

"And it was not until now that you really identified me as Lady Kate?"

"I had my suspicions, but it was not until a few moments ago that I absolutely joined all the incidents attending our several meetings."

CHAPTER LXXII.

KATE felt strange indeed while thus holding a confidential conversation with Arthur.

She was proud that he had taken his brother's place; the act showed him to be a sincere man, and confirmed her previous conception concerning his innate nobility of character.

It was indeed a strange and weird phase of life, a most extraordinary combination of incidents that should make a man a criminal, and still permit him to preserve the noblest qualities of heart.

The two held a long explanatory conversation, and in the end all the strange incidents in which they had been intermixed were explained.

Kate told the story of Balfour Raymond, and explained to Arthur who his mother really was, and filled the young man's soul with joy by telling him that his mother was pure and good, the victim of circumstances. The stain which the young man had supposed rested upon his fair fame was removed, and he was made to understand that barring his career as a criminal he could look any man squarely in the face.

The relationship existing between Arthur and George Gordon was fully confirmed.

"I knew he was my brother," said Arthur.

"Yes, he is your brother, and I am proud to say, as far as I know, a true and noble man."

"He is a true and noble man!" exclaimed Arthur, with deep feeling; and he proceeded and related all that had occurred between him and his new-found brother.

Kate was delighted to hear Arthur's story, as she had come to think that George Gordon was cold-hearted and selfish.

"How did you learn all the facts concerning my brother and myself?" asked Arthur.

Kate had not told of her meeting with the young man's grandfather.

There was one strange circumstance Kate had been unable to explain.

To the public. Colonel Prang had stated that the missing heir to the Raymond estate was a girl; and yet, to our hero, he had always spoken of the heir as a son.

"The time has not come for me to tell you where I got my information; it is sufficient for you to know that it is authentic. And now tell me, were you free to-day what would you do?"

"I do not understand what you mean."

"You remember you once told me you were born a thief—you would always remain one?"

"I told you that?"

"You did."

"I have learned something since then. Were I free to-day, I would lead an honorable life."

"But do you know it would prove a hard task for you to lead an honorable life now?"

"Why?"

"The shadow of your past life would always hang over you; no honorable employment would be open to you?"

A strange look passed over Arthur's handsome face as he replied:

"I once determined to be a criminal against all perils; the same determined will aids me to become an honest man—no, I have done with criminal life forever."

"I am rejoiced to hear you speak so!"

"I owe much to you. It was your admonitions that first set me to thinking. And I owe much to that good old fisherman, Sturgis. He was indeed as a father to me, and I may clearly say led me to recognize the possibility of my becoming an honest man."

Arthur did not speak in a canting and overdevout manner, but in a calm and determined spirit, like a man who had really discovered the advantage of living an honorable and Christian life.

As Kate listened to his words, a new hope rose in her heart. She could not help it. Her heart was agitated with a sentiment which found a growth there independent of her mind and judgment.

With the hope, however, there came a bitter recognition. Arthur was a criminal, under indictment for a capital crime, and the evidence was clear and positive against him.

Kate was fully capable of weighing all the evidence, and could not discover how it were possible to establish the innocence which he asserted.

A shadow came over her beautiful face, and there was deep sorrow in her voice as she said:

"Arthur, do you fully realize your present position?"

"I do."

"Do you realize that you have voluntarily put yourself in the place of a man who was under an indictment for murder?"

The young man spoke in a perfectly calm voice. as he answered:

"I do."

"Tell me truthfully, are you innocent?"

"I am innocent—as innocent as yourself!"

"Do you know how terrible is the array of evidence against you?"

"I do."

"And what do you propose to do?"

"What can I do?"

Kate was silent.

"Come," said Arthur, "what can I do?"

"I feel certain if you stand trial you will be convicted."

"And if convicted, hung?"

"Yes."

"Well, what shall I do?"

"You have sworn to your innocence?"

"I have."

"You are certainly the victim of a strangely adverse fate."

"I am."

"I have been thinking."

"Well, what is the result of all your thinking?"

"An innocent man must not be convicted and hung."

"It would be hard."

Arthur spoke in a calm tone.

"It can not be," said Kate.

"But how are we to prevent it if the evidence is so dead against me? How shall I meet it?"

Kate's voice was low and firm as she answered:

"You must not meet it."

"I do not understand you."

"My suggestion is plain."

"Make it plainer in words."

"You must escape."

"How can I escape?"

"I will aid you."

"You will aid me?"

"I will. You are innocent and yet you may be convicted. Circumstances are dead against you."

"Could you consistently aid a criminal to escape?"

"I can not consistently see an innocent man executed."

"How comes it that you will peril so much for me?" asked the young man abruptly.

Kate was taken off her guard, but by a mighty effort she hid her inward agitation and answered:

"I will tell you."

CHAPTER LXXIII.

THERE was a curious look upon Arthur's face as he listened to Kate's explanation.

"I was employed," said Kate, "in this case, to run down a criminal. I studied well upon the case, and trailed you down. I started upon your track, to gather evidence establishing your guilt. While so doing I discovered qualities in your character which made it appear to me as an utter impossibility that you could be an assassin."

"What did you discover?"

"I discovered that you were willing to peril your own life to save the life of another, and that is not a quality that distinguishes an assassin."

"I will frankly say for myself that I am incapable of murder."

"I believe you; and still further, I discovered that you were the victim of a weird destiny, and at once I set about discovering facts that would establish your innocence; my warmest sympathies were aroused in your behalf."

"And your sympathy for me impels you to suggest that I escape?"

"Yes."

"I will not attempt to escape," answered Arthur, in a decided tone.

"What will you do?"

"Remain and stand my trial."

"But conviction is sure to follow."

"No."

"What do you mean?"

"I do not fear the charge of murder."

"You do not fear the charge of murder?"

"I do not."

"Why not?"

"I can establish my innocence."

"Establish your innocence?"

"I can."

"You may think so."

"I am sure of it."

"How will you do it?"

"I will establish the most perfect *alibi* ever presented to a court and jury."

"Thank Heaven, if what you say is true!" exclaimed Kate, as the tears of joy came welling to her eyes. "Are you sure?" she said, her voice tremulous with emotion.

"I am sure. There is no question of my ability to establish my innocence. Had I been arrested originally, I could have established my innocence at the preliminary examination."

"Will you tell me the facts?"

"I will. You have told me the chief evidence is the fact that I was seen on the grounds the night preceding the murder, and that it will be proved that I am a professional burglar."

"There is other evidence of a most damaging character; but it is all built upon the incident you have mentioned."

"If I prove my whereabouts upon the night of the murder, the evidence will fail?"

"Yes; if the proof comes from parties whose standing in society entitles them to belief."

"Then it is all right; you need have no fear."

"Will you tell me more?"

"Not now; all I ask of you is to deliver a note for me."

"I will." Arthur wrote a note and handed it to Kate.

The note was addressed to one of the best known physicians in New York.

"Is this gentleman your witness?"

"Ask me no questions now, but I tell you it will all be right."

"If you are cleared of the charge of murder, you will be held on the burglary charge."

"All right; I will then possess a burglar's privilege, but 'sufficient unto the day is the evil thereof.'"

Kate's time had expired, and at the moment the keeper appeared at the door.

Lady Kate left the prison with a light heart. She proceeded direct to the office of Mr. Prang.

The gentleman had not seen the lady detective for a number of days.

Kate was shown into his private office.

"Well, what have you to communicate?"

"I have important news."

"What is your news?"

"The time fast approaches when you can proclaim the heir to the Raymond property."

"I fear not."

"What do you mean?"

"Without the will, we can not establish the young man's claim."

"The will shall be produced—or at least, evidence so positive as to the heir's identity that the will can be dispensed with."

"We can not announce the heir without the will."

"Tell me why you first announced the heir as a girl."

A pallor overspread the face of Mr. Prang, and for the first time a suspicion flashed across Kate's mind that there was a possibility that the man, after all, was not the disinterested gentleman he had appeared.

"If there is a will, it shall be found!" said Kate, in a decided tone.

"There was a will."

"Where is it now?"

"It is lost."

"Is it destroyed?"

"I do not know."

"Answer me frankly, sir. Will you refuse to acknowledge the heir should we fail to produce the will?"

"Undoubtedly."

"If no will is produced, who becomes the heir?"

"If no heir is produced within a given time, the property reverts."

"That is an absolute provision?"

"An absolute provision."

"But how can that provision be established without the will?"

"That is a question that remains to be answered," was the evasive reply.

Kate did not press the subject any further; a suspicion had taken possession of her mind, and she determined to remain quiet until the proper time should arrive for her to act.

Kate left the office of Mr. Prang and was proceeding along the street, when a hand was laid upon her shoulder. She turned and recognized that a man had touched her.

"Well, what do you wish, sir?"

The man spoke and Kate laughed outright. She had recognized George Gordon.

The young man was still arrayed in the disguise under which he had left the jail.

"Do you recognize me?"

"Certainly."

"You see, I have escaped."

"Your brother is in your place, though."

"Wonderful woman. You appear to know everything!"

"I have just come from the prison. Remember, I knew your double before I met you."

"Yes, I remember."

"What do you think of the present aspect of affairs?"

"It's all right."

"Are you an enemy or a friend of my brother?"

"A friend."

"Enough. Come with me. I've a proposition to make."

CHAPTER LXXIV.

KATE thought a moment, and then said:

"We must be very careful for the present."

"How do you mean?"

"You must not be recognized."

"Why not?"

"Your recognition would positively result in the hanging of your brother, Balfour Raymond. We must now be more careful than ever before, you must go away until—"

"When?"

"Your brother is acquitted."

"My brother is not to stand his trial?"

"He will."

"Never!"

"What would you propose?"

"He must escape."

"And be a fugitive the remainder of his life?"

"He can go to some other land."

"Alone?"

"I will go with him."

"They would find him, though he fled to the ends of the earth; besides, it would be absolutely impossible to effect his escape."

"Then I shall go and put myself in his place."

"You will do nothing of the kind."

"Who made you the dictator?"

"Your brother."

A troubled look settled upon the face of George Gordon, and he said:

"You have something to reveal?"

"Your brother will not be convicted."

"How can he escape?"

"He can prove an alibi."

"Can he?"

"He can."

"Thank Heaven!"

"He will then be held on the charge of burglary."

"We can buy him off."

"Where will the money come from?"

"I will surrender all I am worth in the world to effect my brother's freedom! I am rich!"

"How rich are you?"

"I have money of my own."

"You are far richer than you suppose."

"The Raymond estate is mine?"

"You are heir to more than the Raymond estate."

"I am?"

"You are."

"You mystify me."

"The career of yourself and brother has been a mystery from the start; you are heir to a large estate left by your father."

"My father?"

"Yes."

"What do you know about my father?"

"We will go to some public park, where we can sit down and talk matters over."

"To Central Park?"

"No."

"Where?"

"We will take a carriage, cross the river and go to a park in Brooklyn."

"I am at your command."

George Gordon called a carriage, and entering the two were driven to the Fulton Ferry; at the ferry-house they left the cab and crossed to Brooklyn, where they entered a car of the Flatbush Line, and proceeded to Prospect Park.

There is no finer place in the world for a private confab than Prospect Park, Brooklyn.

One can find a hundred places where a conversation can be held without the least fear of being overheard.

Kate and her companion proceeded to a grove commanding a view of the great common, where they seated themselves upon a bench under a thickly overhanging tree.

The lady detective had a particular reason for taking George Gordon to Brooklyn; she intended that he should not return to New York until the trial of Arthur Everdell was concluded.

Kate had told the young man that should he be discovered, such discovery would result in his brother's conviction. She was a sharp and far-seeing woman. She knew that both the young men had secret enemies, and any one of them would take any advantage to bring trouble upon the brothers.

Were George Gordon discovered, and the fatal resemblance established, Arthur Everdell's alibi would be made null and void, as it would be contended that the brothers were in collusion, and that the alibi was only a cunning trick, made possible by the fact of their wonderful personal likeness to each other.

We will here explain that the several enemies of the young men had no knowledge of the two identities.

Seated on the bench beneath the trees, Kate related to George Gordon all the strange facts she had previously revealed to Arthur. When her tale was concluded, Gordon said:

"Your revelation agrees with the theory I had formed, save that I fear there was a stain upon my brother's birth."

"He was honorably born."

"And I thank Heaven! But tell me, how did you become posted concerning all the facts?"

Kate had not revealed to young Gordon the fact of her acquaintance with Joseph Everdell, and she made the same reply to him that she had made to Arthur.

"The time has not arrived when I shall reveal the source of my information, but it is true, all true, this that I have told you."

"You said I was heir to an estate other than the Raymond property?"

"You are."

"What estate is it?"

"Your father's estate."

"My father left an estate?"

"He left a large property by will to his elder son. He supposed his younger son to be dead."

"The younger son shall have the estate."

"He does not need it."

"He does not need it?"

"He does not."

"I do not understand."

"He also is heir to a large estate independent of the money that will come to you through your father and mother."

"This is wonderful!"

"Yes it is wonderful; but Arthur Everdell is the heir of his mother's family, and he will have a large estate."

"My father is dead?"

"Your father is supposed to be dead."

"Supposed to be dead?"

"Yes."

"Why do you merely suppose his death?"

"Your father left in the hands of a friend the proofs that will establish your claim to the Raymond estate, and made his own will in your favor; but not being assured that you were living, he made provision for contingent legatees; and I have proofs that the contingent legatees are on your track as enemies. You dead, the property would revert to them."

"Strange woman! I must say that the story of my own and my brother's life is not more wonderful than the fact of your extraordinary faculty for trailing down facts."

Kate chanced to glance across the common, and she beheld the figure of a man whose presence caused her to exclaim:

"An enemy is approaching!"

CHAPTER LXXV.

OUR readers will remember that Kate had adopted an entirely new disguise, in order to baffle the constant "piping" of a certain man; but upon the occasion of her last visit to the prison she had assumed an old "cover," and the presence of the man whose approach she had so abruptly announced went to prove that an enemy was once more upon her trail, and that in returning to an old disguise she had been very indiscreet.

Kate pointed out the figure of the man to Gordon, when the latter exclaimed:

"That is the fellow whom we met up at the Raymond mansion!"

Sheehan had adopted a disguise, and Kate said:

"How did you chance to recognize him?"

"By his walk."

"Good! you would make a good detective that man is on your track!"

"What shall we do?"

"Drown him!" replied Kate, with a laugh.

"That is just what I should like to do."

"His presence is very awkward."

"Why should we fear him?"

"Of all the men in the world, that is the last man who should discover that there are two Arthur Everdells."

"What must I do?"

"You were reared in France?"

"I was."

"You speak French?"

"I do."

"So do I."

"Well?"

"You must play off as a monsieur: we will let that fellow come upon us; we will give him every opportunity to *listen to what we say, but you must speak every word in French.*"

"That is a capital idea."

"He has recognized me. He must not recognize you."

"Can I chastise him as a Frenchman?"

"If an opportunity offers, yes."

"I trust the opportunity will offer."

George Gordon was a powerfully built young man, and when he asked for the privilege of chastising the man who was on his track, it was a favor of which he could avail himself should the opportunity offer.

The two young people kept their seat, and continued their conversation in French.

We have upon a former occasion informed our readers that Kate was an ambitious young lady, and among other accomplishments she had acquired, could be numbered a knowledge of the French language.

As also intimated, Sheehan was in disguise, and Kate made up her mind to pretend that she had not fallen to the fellow's identity.

Sheehan's later actions indicated that he relied upon his "cover," and acted like a man who believed he was playing a *safe game.*

George Gordon came the Frenchman to perfection. He accompanied his words with the traditional shoulder-shrugs and other gesticulations so peculiar to the French; and here, dear reader, forgive us for saying frankly, that in our opinion there are the meanest people on the face of the earth, and their reputed politeness one of the veriest shams; as a people they do not know what true politeness means; they are boors of the worst sort at home; in fact, as Americans say, they are too previous altogether, and as false and treacherous as old Satan himself.

Sheehan worked his little plan very neatly, and his game might have been all right had it been played against a less shrewd person than Lady Kate, the wonderful female detective.

George Gordon jabbered away to Kate, and the lady detective jabbered in return, and in the meantime Sheehan, the detective, strolled over near to where they were, and in an off-hand manner threw himself upon the grass. It was his purpose to make it appear that he was merely an afternoon lounger idly passing away the time.

Kate and her companion continued to talk, speaking in a loud tone, and had they been talking English Sheehan could have understood every word that was said.

At length Kate and Gordon rose and walked away. They passed beyond the common over to an unfinished portion of the Park, where laborers had dug out several great holes; into the latter there had accumulated considerable water.

The two Frenchies sat down on a bank overlooking the largest of the holes.

It was a descent of at least a hundred feet down a steep embankment to the verge of the excavation.

A few moments passed, and the "sneyd" detective Sheehan came strolling along.

Still speaking in French, Kate said, suggestively:

"That fellow would look nice floundering in the water down there."

"That's so!" was the ready response.

"Oh, don't throw him there!" said Kate.

"Certainly not," came the reply, in a bantering tone.

Sheehan had grown bolder. He approached quite near to the couple, when Kate remarked:

"Be on your guard; that fellow is up to some mischief!"

A moment later the lady detective remarked:

"The scamp suspects you; be guarded."

"What will he attempt?"

"Some sudden movement to uncover your disguise. He is a shrewd rascal, and has discerned that you are under cover."

"Let him keep his distance, or he will go swimming!"

"Where?"

"Down in yonder hole."

"He would look real funny down there!" remarked Kate, in a girlish manner.

"It would amuse you?"

"It would amuse me very much."

"You shall be amused."

George Gordon had just uttered the words when Sheehan sprung forward.

George Gordon was an athlete; Sheehan had intended to take him by surprise, but he was met, and in most lovely broken English, Gordon exclaimed as the two men clinched:

"Eh! vat you means?"

The next moment Sheehan went swimming. He was hurled with great force down the embankment.

Kate laughed merrily as she saw the fellow give one final turn and go splashing into the yellow water.

The water was just about up to his waist, but the sides of the excavation were perpendicular, and it was impossible for the fellow to get out without assistance.

Kate and her companion remained a few moments to watch his frantic efforts to extricate himself, and then coolly walked away.

George Gordon was led to a small private residence, in the vicinity of one of the Greenwood Cemetery entrances, and then the lady detective resorted to one of her cunning tricks so as to effectually throw the fellow Sheehan off the trail.

CHAPTER LXXVI.

AT the house where Kate had taken Gordon for refuge was a young man who, in height and general build, was a counterpart of her *protégé.*

At Kate's command, this young man, who was also a powerful fellow, assumed the disguise that had been worn by Gordon.

As soon as the change had been effected, Kate hurried back to the Park, and reached there just in time to see some laborers assist Sheehan from his unpleasant position in the excavation.

Sheehan discovered Kate also, and the lady detective intended that he should.

As soon as she was satisfied that the detective had seen her, she strolled away with her new companion.

The latter had his instructions, and was a man fully capable for the performance of the part that had been assigned to him.

Kate and the substitute for Gordon found their way to the ferry, which they crossed, and when on the New York side they separated.

Sheehan did not follow the female, but started to trail the man.

The lady detective had timed her movements, so as to afford her pursuer an easy chance to "pipe" her route

As stated, Sheehan followed the man, and the result was that in the end he discovered that he had been outrageously fooled.

He had started out with the idea that he had struck a dead lead, and wound up with the knowledge that the lady detective had been too much for him.

That evening Kate met Joseph Everdell.

The old man was becoming uneasy and impatient.

He had informed Kate in the morning that the trial of Gordon was to come on within a few days.

Upon meeting Kate in the evening, he exclaimed, as he had in the morning:

"Something must be done!"

"Something has been done," replied Kate.

"Has he escaped?"

"Who, Gordon?"

"Yes."

"He has escaped."

"Thank Heaven! Now you can tell me about my boy!"

"Arthur Everdell?"

"Yes, yes."

"He is in jail."

The old man recoiled—a wild glare shone in his eyes, and his features became convulsed; for a moment he could not speak; but when he did find utterance, there was a terrible display of agitation in his tones.

"You have succeeded! You have saved Gordon! you have betrayed my boy!"

"No, no, old man, you are mistaken!"

"Did I hear you aright? Did you not tell me my boy was in jail?"

"You heard me aright; your boy is in jail."

"Then who could have betrayed him but you?"

"I did not."

"You can not deceive me."

"Arthur Everdell is a noble young man. Strange revelations have taken place within a few hours. The brothers have met."

"Who brought about the meeting?"

"Arthur Everdell."

"Tell me all."

"Your grandson was desperately wounded the night the attempt was made to rob the Bayne mansion. He escaped, and lay for a long time hovering between life and death. His life was spared, and it was then for the first time he learned that an innocent man was in jail suffering in his stead. At once he came to the city, went voluntarily to the jail, recognized his brother, and released him by taking his place!"

"And my boy is now in jail?"

"Yes."

"He will be tried and convicted?"

"He will be tried, but not convicted."

"He is innocent?"

"He is innocent of the murder."

"But he is a burglar?"

"Yes."

"They will send him to prison for life?"

"No."

"How will he escape?"

"Let him stand his trial for the murder, and be honorably acquitted, and then—"

"Well, what then?"

"He shall escape; they will not hunt a mere burglar as they would hunt an assassin."

"You are right; but is it certain he will be acquitted of the charge of murder?"

"He will assuredly be acquitted, but it is necessary that he should stand his trial so that his innocence can be positively established to the world; it will lift the shadow from over his future life."

"If what you say is true, it is better he should stand his trial; but I must see my boy."

"You are a stranger to him."

"I know it."

"He is not even aware of your existence."

"Have you not told him concerning my relationship to him?"

"I have not."

"Will you take me to him?"

"In good time, not now. I must prepare him to meet you."

"When will you do so?"

"At once."

"Where is Gordon?"

"You must not mention to a living soul the existence of Gordon."

"Why not?"

"It would result in the hanging of your grandson should Gordon be produced in court."

Upon the day following the scenes recorded, Kate called once more at the prison. She found Arthur in a cheerful frame of mind. His first inquiry was concerning his brother.

"Your brother is all right."

"He must not come to the jail under any circumstances."

"He will not come."

"Should he be recognized it would go hard with me."

"Who told you?"

"My counsel."

"You have counsel?"

"I have; and I have put my whole case in his hands. He says it will prove an easy matter to achieve my acquittal."

"Have you seen your witness?"

"My counsel has seen him."

"And it is all right?"

"Yes."

"Arthur, I have some strange and startling news to impart."

The young man's face showed a shade of anxiety.

"You have a warm friend in New York."

"Yes, my brother."

"A stronger friend even than your brother."

"I do not catch your meaning."

"You have a relative."

"Who can it be?" and there was a tremulousness in the young man's tone.

"Your mother's father."

"My mother's father?"

"Yes."

"My grandfather? Oh, Heaven! What is to come?"

CHAPTER LXXVII.

"You need fear nothing; your grandfather is a kind, honorable, and noble old man."

"How did he come to learn of the fact of my existence, and our relationship?"

Kate told the story.

"My poor, poor mother!" were the words that fell from Arthur's lips.

"Your grandfather is rich, very rich; you are his heir!"

"I care not for wealth; it is enough that I have a name."

"Your real name is Raymond."

"I shall never assume it."

"Would you see your grandfather?"

"Yes."

That same day grandson and grandfather were brought together. We will not attempt to describe the scene that followed the meeting.

Kate introduced them and went forth, but when the old man joined her outside the prison walls some hours later, his face was beaming with joy and happiness.

Grasping Kate by the hand, he said:

"You are a noble woman! You have made your fortune! You have no idea of my wealth; my grandson will be one of the richest commoners in England!"

Upon the week following the trial of Arthur Everdell commenced.

The testimony against him was overwhelming, and there was not an auditor present listening to the trial who did not believe that he would be convicted. Indeed, it was believed that the verdict would be rendered upon the first ballot of the jury.

The defense had not opened, but the evidence for the prosecution was so strong it did not appear possible that the defense could overcome it.

Arthur was defended by one of the ablest criminal lawyers in New York.

The latter did not cross-examine the witnesses for the prosecution to any great extent, and the State looked upon the omission as a virtual giving over of the case.

Our hero's lawyer, however, knew his ground. He was a man who delighted in dramatic effects, and he was determined at the proper time to, allegorically speaking, explode a bombshell in that court-room.

The evidence of the prosecution was all in and the evidence for the defense commenced.

Arthur's counsel called the name of a well-known merchant in New York.

The character of the witness was above possible question. He was a man of wealth and high standing.

Arthur's counsel said to the witness:

"Will you please look at the prisoner at the bar?"

The witness did so.

"Did you ever see the prisoner before?"

"Yes."

"Upon what occasion?"

"The evening of the —."

The date named corresponded with the date of the night of the murder.

"Where did you see the prisoner on that date?"

"At the railroad station at ——."

The station named was the railroad station nearest to the Raymond estate.

"You saw the prisoner upon that occasion?"

"Yes."

"You are sure?"

"Yes, sir."

"Sure as to date?"

"Yes, sir."

"Why are you sure as to date?"

"Upon that evening I went to Philadelphia in answer to a telegram."

"There is no possible mistake?"

"No, sir."

Some moments were spent in absolutely fixing the date, when the counsel said:

"And upon that evening you saw the prisoner?"

"Yes, sir."

"Did you speak to him?"

"I did."

"What led you to speak to him?"

"I was a visitor at the Raymond mansion, and I was struck by the prisoner's wonderful resemblance to a certain portrait I had seen in the library."

"You addressed him?"

"I did."

"You held quite an extended conversation with him?"

"I did."

"There can be no possible mistake as to his identity?"

"None whatever."

"Did you see the prisoner again upon that date?"

"I did."

"Where?"

"In Philadelphia."

"The bombshell had been exploded. If the witness saw the prisoner in Philadelphia, he could not have been present to commit the murder.

"You saw him in Philadelphia?"

"Yes."

"At what hour?"

"Fifteen minutes past eleven o'clock."

"You saw the prisoner in Philadelphia on the night of the —?"

"I did."

"You so swear?"

"I do."

"Where did you see him?"

"At the Continental Hotel."

"When you left the station at ——, you were on your way to Philadelphia?"

"I was."

"Did you see the prisoner on the train?"

"I saw him at Jersey City going aboard the train, and I saw him in Philadelphia."

"When next did you see him?"

"At twelve fifty."

"Where?"

"Going into the room adjoining mine at the hotel."

"When next did you see him?"

"At six o'clock upon the following morning."

"Where?"

"In the hallway adjoining his room and mine."

"Were you alone all this time?"

"No, sir."

"Who was with you?"

"Dr. ——."

"Dr. —— was with you?"

"Yes, sir."

"Was he with you when you first met the prisoner at the railroad station, at ——?"

"Yes, sir."

"And again when you saw the prisoner in Philadelphia?"

"The doctor was with me when I saw the prisoner at eleven fifteen, but he did not see him at six o'clock the next morning; I did."

"That will do, sir! Is Dr. —— in court?" demanded the counsel.

Dr. —— was in court, and took the stand.

The doctor's evidence in every particular was confirmatory of the testimony of the witness who had preceded him.

There were many side incidents, which it is not necessary to the purpose of our story to relate, but one fact we will state, the jury did bring in a verdict, and the verdict was reached upon the first ballot; and when they returned into court, in answer to the judge's demand, there came the response, "*Not guilty!*"

CHAPTER LXXVIII.

ARTHUR EVERDELL was congratulated on every hand; even strangers came forward to sympathize with him; a more perfect *alibi* was never established in a court of justice.

Sheehan the detective was present, and a scowl rested upon his ugly face.

The fellow knew that there was a mystery somewhere, but it was beyond his ken. He believed there was a large "divvy" that could have been picked up, but he had not managed to strike the cupboard in which the "pie" was hidden.

Lady Kate the detective was present in a close disguise, and a happier woman lived not in New York upon that auspicious day when Arthur's innocence was pronounced by a body of twelve honorable men.

The murder charge was disposed of, but Arthur was immediately rearrested on the charge of attempted burglary.

The prosecuting officer exhibited an unwonted zeal in his endeavor to convict the accused, and there was a malignant satisfaction expressed upon his face when he demanded the warrant on the second charge.

Kate felt assured that some powerful enemy was behind the district attorney, as there was no reason for his unwonted zeal, otherwise than as a public officer, he would naturally desire to secure a conviction, but his feeling went beyond the mere professional ambition of a county official.

Arthur was remanded to prison on the latter charge, or rather on the original charge which had led to the first arrest

Immediately upon the rendition of the verdict, Kate had left the court-room.

Joseph Everdell, the grandfather of the accused, followed her out; the old man was in high glee.

"What shall we do now?" he asked.

"Oh, we have plenty of time to consider our next move; the real danger is past."

"But my boy will be convicted on the latter charge and sent to prison for a long term."

"Not if we know ourselves, and we think we do!" was the confident reply.

Kate hastened to Brooklyn and held a long consultation with George Gordon. The lady detective had made up her mind to have a little fun. Sheehan had annoyed her. He had caused her more trouble than we have deemed it necessary to present; she knew that the man was constantly on her track, and she determined to take advantage of the wonderful resemblance between the two brothers to play a trick on him. She had a deep purpose, however, under her design.

Kate knew well that there was no living show for the accomplishment of the acquittal of Arthur Everdell on the charge of burglary.

She had come to suspect that Colonel Prang was not the honorable and disinterested man he had pretended to be. She had come to learn that if he were a villain, or even a dishonorable man, he was one of the deepest plotters she had ever met.

As Kate had thought over the man's many statements, she became more and more of the opinion that he had some deep design.

Colonel Prang had first given out that the heir to the Raymond estate *was a daughter;* but to Kate, from the very first, he had admitted that the heir was a son. He had sought to explain away this discrepancy, but, under the light of later developments, Kate did not accept his explanations as altogether satisfactory.

It was because of the above facts that she set to fool Sheehan, and at the same time legally establish a certain remarkable fact which would serve well when she should come to make her grand move on the property held in trust by Augustus Prang.

The lady detective had spent some hours "piping" Colonel Prang, and had made the startling discovery that the quiet and seemingly wonderfully correct man was an inveterate gambler.

Kate had studied on his purpose, and the result of her studies was the subjoined theory:

Colonel Prang had originally started out to secure the property to himself. He was the thief who had stolen the will, and at the proper time, when its provisions would accrue to his benefit only, he would suddenly discover the mislaid document. He had given out that the real heir was a daughter, intending, as a *dernier resort*, to fight a male heir in the courts, or, at least, force him to a profitable compromise; later on, he had come to believe that the assassin was the heir, and then he had employed a detective; and, still later on, he had decided that the heir was not the assassin, and he had since been secretly plotting against the very detective who was in his employ.

He did not dare discharge Kate. He had originally confided too much to her, and she had subsequently learned enough to make her dangerous to his interests.

Colonel Prang had come to hate the lady detective, and he would have given a large sum of money could she have been bribed and bought off.

We have merely indicated Kate's theory; in her own mind she had worked out the full details of his supposed plans.

Colonel Prang had been in court during the trial, and to Kate had taken occasion to express his hope that her *protégé* would be acquitted. He had not spoken of the young man as Balfour Raymond, nor had he made any allusion to the young man's extraordinary resemblance to the portrait at the Raymond mansion.

Colonel Prang did not know of the existence of the *double*.

In court Kate had secretly watched the varying expressions upon his face. She had seen a satisfied look while the evidence against Arthur was being delivered, and she observed a look of dismay when Arthur's counsel exploded his bombshell.

As stated, Kate proceeded to Brooklyn after the rendering of the verdict, and had a long interview with George Gordon.

The young man was jubilant upon hearing the result of the trial, and at once proclaimed that in some way his brother must be gotten out of the prison and sent to some other land a free man.

"Leave it all to me," returned Kate.

"Indeed, we can leave it all to you, most wonderful of women!"

Kate explained her plan to young Gordon, and the young man at once entered into the spirit of the game.

Upon returning to New York the lady detective called upon Colonel Prang, and in a lively manner pulled off that gentleman's mask.

CHAPTER LXXIX.

COLONEL PRANG received the lady detective in a very courtly manner, but there was an iciness in his demeanor that Kate was very quick to perceive.

"I suppose," said the colonel, in a cold tone, "you have come to discharge yourself from my service?"

The intent of the remark was to convey a hint that the colonel wished to discharge Kate.

He had his match, however, as Kate demanded, in a curt tone:

"Have you ever paid me any money, sir?"

"I have not."

"Have I ever demanded any pay?"

"I am prepared to respond to your demand at any moment."

"Thank you, sir; but I have no bill to present. But tell me, what do you think of the result of the trial?"

"Your *protégé* was very lucky. He had a good lawyer, who worked up his case well "

"Did you recognize the young man whom you call my *protégé?*"

"*I did not.*"

"You certainly must have been struck with his wonderful resemblance to the portrait of Balfour Raymond?"

"Yes; he does bear an extraordinary resemblance to *his father.*"

"Then you admit that he is a son of Balfour Raymond?"

"I neither admit nor deny; but it strikes me as quite possible that he is a son of Raymond; that Raymond was a wild fellow. He may have *other sons,* but I doubt if any of them bear such a striking resemblance to their father as your *protégé.*"

"You do not believe he is the son of the lady who was murdered?"

"Certainly not."

"It is strange that he should bear such a wonderful resemblance to his father, is it not?"

"Oh, no; I've known of hundreds of such resemblances. It was said that some of Napoleon's sons bore a greater resemblance to their father *than did the prince!*"

"You do not believe my *protégé,* as you call him, is *the prince!*"

"I know he is not."

"Who is he?"

"You must ask himself."

"But why are you so sure he is not the heir?"

"He is too young by a number of years."

"How old is he?"

"Twenty-five."

"How do you know?"

"He swore to his age in the court-room."

Kate smiled as grimly as it is possible for a woman to smile, and answered:

"That is his age."

"The heir would be about twenty-nine, were *he* living?" said Colonel Prang.

"As Arthur Everdell is undoubtedly the son of Balfour Raymond, would it not be a just thing to surrender the estate to him in case it is established that the real heir is dead?"

Colonel Prang laughed in a satirical manner, and answered:

"You are disposed to be very liberal with other people's money."

"Oh, no; I merely asked the question, because I know the real heir is living."

"You know the real heir is living?" almost screamed Colonel Prang.

The man was thrown completely off his guard by Kate's abrupt announcement.

"Certainly, the real heir is living!"

"Where?"

"Here in New York."

"It's false!"

"I beg your pardon, it is not false."

"I will prove it false, and I will tell you in the outset that you had better abstain from entering into any conspiracy to get my property."

"Your property?"

"Yes; my property!"

"When did it become your property?"

"That's my business!"

"Well, it will cease to be your property the moment the young man is produced—the real heir!"

"*A young man* is not the real heir."

"You told me he was."

"I had a purpose. The real heir is a young lady, and I am on her track, and she will claim the property, and I will surrender it to her!"

"She is one of Balfour Raymond's daughters, I suppose?"

Colonel Prang turned red in the face, and answered:

"She is his daughter."

"All right, colonel; you produce the daughter and I will produce the son!"

With the latter startling announcement Kate departed.

Colonel Prang walked his office floor in an excited manner.

"Hang that woman!" he said to himself. "Why was I fool enough ever to employ her? She is deeper than any man in New York. I employed a woman 'to do the piping' for my own purposes, and I am beaten at my own game."

The fact was, Colonel Prang was a bankrupt, and he was indebted to the estate for which he had been acting as trustee.

He had been anxious to find the heir, that he might destroy him, as admitted by his involuntary exclamations. He had employed a woman only that he might use her as a blind when his real purpose became revealed.

The woman, as he had also involuntarily admitted, had proved too much for him.

Her statement that the real heir was in New York he did not believe, and he honestly did think that a conspiracy was on foot to take advantage of Arthur Everdell's resemblance to secure the property.

The trustee was still walking his floor, when a visitor was announced.

Sheehan the detective had worked his game close enough to have learned that Colonel Prang had some interest in the lady detective. He had called upon the colonel, and had been taken into his service.

The sneyd detective cared not whom he served, so long as he gathered in the shekels.

Upon entering Colonel Prang's presence the detective said:

"Well, sir, the game is against you as it stands!"

"What do you mean, fellow?"

The colonel had not made a confidant of Sheehan, but the latter had learned a great deal, and had suspected and discerned much more, and he was trying to force the colonel into making a confidant of him.

"Oh, it's no use, colonel; I know the game, and you may as well make a friend of me. I'm the only man in New York who can get away with that woman, Lady Kate!"

"So far she has got away with you."

"Oh, I've only been giving her rope."

"Why, man, she snaps her fingers at you; does not consider you worth a moment's thought."

"I'll teach her to fear me in a few days."

"You will?"

"I will."

"Then come to me and your fortune is made."

CHAPTER LXXX.

SHEEHAN had struck bottom at last. It was the first time he had succeeded in forcing the colonel to admit that he feared Lady Kate, and it was a part of the sneyd detective's game to work upon the fears of the victims he set out to pluck.

"I'll attend to her case. I could have 'closed in' on her a long time ago, only it had not been made an object for me to do so," said Sheehan, in answer to the declaration of Colonel Prang, as recorded at the close of our preceding chapter.

Colonel Prang was a deep and cunning man, and he pondered well before he made a reply. He had set in originally for the playing of a very intricate game; indeed, all his moves had been merely preliminary. In the end his scheme was to have developed as a Machiavellian plot. He had made one false play, and all the complicated webs of his game were broken.

Augustus Prang understood Sheehan fully, and appreciated the man's aims and motives. He had been using Sheehan while permitting the detective to think otherwise.

The colonel was by far the abler man of the two. It had been all his life one of his strong points to appear simple, innocent, and off-hand, when, in fact, he was just the contrary.

He had at length reached a point where Sheehan held the advantage. The detective was necessary to his scheme. He felt assured that the fellow could be of great service to him, but he hesitated before placing himself absolutely in the man's power. He determined to skirmish a bit, hoping to gain a service and still hold his advantage.

"You have a hold on the woman?" he remarked.

"I have a hold on the whole gang!"

"There is a gang?"

"Yes; there is a gang."

"Who are in the gang?"

"I could give you a great deal more information if you would open up a bit yourself."

"I have nothing to state. I have no interest in the gang."

"Well, I can tell you one thing, they have great interest in you; and they are hatching a scheme to get possession of all the property."

Sheehan's last remark was based upon a suspicion merely, but the man's shot went right home to the bull's-eye.

Sheehan had studied all the points well and knew his premises.

"What are you driving at?" inquired Colonel Prang.

"Well, you ought to understand by this time. I know that at present this Lady Kate has got the 'bulge' on you, and I want to make some money out of my power to 'tip her off the line.'"

"Can you 'tip her off the line'?" asked Prang, in a cautious manner.

"I can, and I can upset the schemes of the whole gang."

"I have no instructions to give, Sheehan," said the colonel.

"You play very cautious."

"I've no game."

"Then I'm out of the boat. I don't pull an oar where there's no game or gain."

"There might be some gain."

"Ah, now you talk."

"But I've no instructions."

"What would please you, should something happen?"

"I am easily pleased."

"What would please you most?"

"I don't like Lady Kate."

"You gave her too much of your confidence in the go off, and she's turned on you, eh?"

"She can't turn on me."

"Mebbe you have not discovered it yet, but she's dead set against you."

The colonel turned pale. Sheehan was forcing him closer and closer to a revelation.

"What game can she play against me?"

"She has the son of the man whose portrait hangs in the parlor at the Raymond mansion, and she has with her an old coon who was a friend or relative of the original of that mysterious picture, and he's got some 'paper,' and I tell you there's a big game on foot."

"And the object of the game, Sheehan?"

"Their game is to get possession of the murdered woman's estate. Arthur Everdell may not have murdered the old woman, but he was in with the gang, you may bet safe; and if there were any papers taken he has them, and they are in the hands of a gang who knows just how to make the most of any sort of a deal."

Colonel Prang was beginning to weaken. He began to perceive that Sheehan held too many cards for him.

"Who is at the bottom of the game?"

"Lady Kate is to the front; but it's my idea that there is some mysterious *man,* who is behind every move she makes."

"Who is this mysterious man?"

"That I have not been able to discover yet."

"There is our starting-point, Sheehan."

"Where?"

"This mysterious man, find out who he is."

"I can."

"Do so."

"But I have no interest in the man."

"I have."

"What's your interest?"

"Two hundred and fifty dollars."

"Two hundred and fifty to learn who he is?"

"Yes."

"Well, that will do for a start, but I would have you know that I am a player for larger stakes."

"This may lead to a larger game."

"All right, colonel. And now let me tell you I could be of much greater service to you if you would open up."

"Go first and find out who this man is!"

"I will."

Sheehan and Colonel Prang separated. The former was well satisfied with the progress he had made, and to himself he muttered, when alone:

"I'll make a cool fifty thousand out of him. He's my bird now."

Sheehan set out to strike the trail of Lady Kate, and the lady detective set out to have the sneyd detective fall on her trail. It was a part of her game to have him do so.

Kate saw Sheehan enter the office of Colonel Prang, and she was not far off when the man came forth after the interview.

Sheehan soon discovered Kate. The latter pretended to be seeking to avoid observation, but her disguise was a very flimsy one.

"Fortune favors me," was the remark that fell from the male detective's lips as he started to "pipe" Kate; and "Fortune favors me!" was the idea that floated through Kate's mind as she .ed off to be piped.

It was a neat game all round, but the woman proved the better *man* of the two in the end.

CHAPTER LXXXI.

SHEEHAN was in high glee the moment he started in pursuit. He had been beaten by Lady Kate so many times, he had come to hate the lively lady with a bitter hatred.

"I'm just on my guard against her this time!" he muttered to himself; "and if I don't get the best of her just once I'll sell out, and let some other man take the job!"

Kate, in the meantime, kept upon her way; she had arranged all her plans for a master stroke.

The pursuit and retreat was continued for some time. Kate went up one street and down another, and finally took her stand on a certain corner; a few moments passed, and a man, evidently disguised, appeared upon the scene Kate held a few moments' conversation with the man, and they separated.

Upon starting once more upon a tramp, Kate learned that Sheehan continued upon her trail. She finally entered a restaurant, and remained some time, leisurely consuming a very elaborate dinner she had ordered.

When Kate issued from the restaurant it was night, and almost the first person whom she saw upon coming forth was Sheehan.

The man had patiently waited. The lady detective walked down toward the jail where Arthur Everdell was confined. Around the corner from the jail stood a close carriage, which Kate entered.

Sheehan was close upon her track, and the man was amazed at what he witnessed.

A few moments passed, and a man, muffled in a slouch hat and heavy coat, came from toward the prison entrance and entered the carriage, and upon the instant the vehicle was driven away.

"Great Heaven!" ejaculated Sheehan, "I see it all! My fortune and reputation are made—it's an escape!" The man followed the vehicle, which was not driven at a rapid rate.

Some dozen squares from the jail the coach was stopped, and Kate and the disguised man alighted and entered a restaurant.

A few moments passed, and Sheehan, accompanied by half a dozen men, entered the place.

Kate and her companion were seated at a table; the men approached and seized hold of the latter.

Sheehan actually shouted with delight as he tore off the stranger's hat and wig, and disclosed the handsome face of Arthur Everdell.

"Aha! aha!" he shouted. "It was a nice game, but I was too much for you this time, my smart Lady Kate!"

Kate was cool as a cucumber, and so also was Arthur Everdell, who had been thus cleverly caught in an attempt to escape.

"Be careful what you do, Sheehan."

"Oh, I'll be careful! No fear, I made for a dead set on you this time, my smart lady, and I've got you!"

"All right; as a friend, I've warned you, and now you can work your own passage!"

Arthur Everdell was led out and put into the carriage; two of the men accompanied Sheehan, and the driver was ordered directly to the jail.

The sneyd detective was just wild with delight and excitement; it was the most eventful feat of his whole life. He would be heralded in the morning as the smartest detective in New York, and he would have a grand grip on all the parties with whom he had been trying to deal.

The prisoner was left in the coach with the two men, and Sheehan, in grand style, entered the office of the keeper of the jail.

"I've a present for you, warden," he said.

The warden of the jail did not like Sheehan; the two men belonged to opposing political factions.

"A present for me?"

"You bet."

"Well, trot it out"

The warden felt very uneasy. He knew that Sheehan had some game on hand, or had secured some advantage over him.

For months efforts had been made to remove the warden.

"Come down with me," said Sheehan.

"If you have a present, bring it here."

"I have a prisoner whom I wish to *restore* to your custody."

"A prisoner to restore to my custody?"

"Yes, old man; you are a good official, you are, to let an important prisoner slip out right under your nose."

"Talk just what you mean, Sheehan."

"Come down to the door, and get your man. *I've brought him here* for you."

"What man is it?"

"Come and see."

"You're crazy, Sheehan."

"Am I?"

"Yes."

"Well, come down and see."

"There is no need; you've been fooled, man; all my prisoners are present and accounted for."

"They are, eh?"

"Yes, sir."

"Well, come down and see."

The warden was irritated, but followed the man down to the carriage, when Sheehan said, as he opened the coach door:

"You've always pulled against me, old man, but I've proved myself your friend. I could have had your head in the basket in about four minutes, but I wanted to give you a show; look there."

The two men inside the coach had slipped forth with the prisoner, and the moment the keeper's eyes fell on the latter, he uttered a low cry like an enraged bull!

"Aha! old man, how is that?"

So bitter was the rage and disappointment of the keeper he could make no reply.

Arthur was led into the office, and all the under-wardens were summoned.

As one after the other entered the office, they uttered an exclamation of amazement as their eyes fell on the prisoner.

"A nice lot of jail officials you fellows are!" exclaimed Sheehan in a taunting manner.

The keeper who had charge of the corridor where Arthur Everdell was confined was the last to enter the office, and as he did so he exclaimed:

"Well, I'll be blowed! What does this mean?"

"That's just what we want to find out!" said Sheehan, who was blustering around, the hero of the hour.

The warden had recovered his voice and composure; and demanded of the keeper:

"How did your man get away, Martin?"

"How did my man get away, sir? I don't understand you! *My man is all right in his cell!*"

CHAPTER LXXXII.

WELL, there was a buzz of excitement in that jail office for about one minute.

"Your prisoner is all right?" at length demanded Sheehan.

"Yes; he's all right. I don't understand this."

"Well, you can thank me that he is all right."

"He's all right, and no thanks to you, either!"

"I've just brought your man back, you fool! If it had not been for me he would have been out of the city an hour ago!"

"Explain this, Martin!" said the warden.

"I've nothing to explain, sir. It's a mystery that gets me; I don't know who that chap is."

As the keeper spoke he pointed to Sheehan's prisoner.

"You don't know who the prisoner is?"

"No, sir."

"Wasn't he under your charge?"

"Not that man."

"Not that man?"

"No, sir."

"What are you giving us?" demanded Sheehan.

Addressing the warden, the under-keeper said:

"My prisoner, sir, is in his cell all right at this moment!"

"Your prisoner in his cell?"

"Yes, sir."

"This prisoner?"

"That man was never under my charge."

"What do you mean? Are you trying to face the matter out in this cheeky manner?"

"I've nothing to face out; bring Sheehan's man along, and I'll show you mine all right!"

"Go and bring your prisoner here!" said Sheehan, in a jeering tone.

"I don't take orders from a duffer like you!"

"Oh, you don't, eh?"

"No."

"Well, you'll be looking for a job to-morrow, my Jersey blue."

"I'll turn the key on you first, and if you had your deserts, I'd have done it long ago!"

"Is your prisoner in his cell?" demanded the warden.

"He is, sir."

"Go and bring him down here."

"All right, sir."

The under-keeper started to leave the office, when Sheehan said:

"Send an officer with him, warden, or he'll 'flit' on you; this is serious business!"

During all this time the prisoner had stood listening to the talk with a quiet smile upon his face.

"Martin knows his business, Sheehan," said the warden, in answer to the sneyd detective's caution.

"Yes; you all appear to know your business around here pretty well."

The under-keeper departed, and in a few moments returned to the office, bringing his prisoner with him.

Sheehan uttered a yell, and gazed as though a corpse had leaped from a coffin and had confronted him.

All hands stared in amazement, but the warden was jubilant.

Sheehan was about the most abashed man who was ever suddenly cut down in the midst of a grand flourish of airs.

"Take your prisoner back," said the warden.

Sheehan was silent, while his companions who had aided him in making the arrest, shrunk away.

Addressing the prisoner who had been brought in by Sheehan, the warden asked:

"Young man, what is your name?"

"Monsieur Gordon."

"Where do you belong?"

"I was born in France."

"How long have you been in New York?"

George Gordon mentioned the time and also stated that he had been a passenger on a steamer which had reached San Francisco from Australia upon the very day following the murder of old Mrs. Renton.

It was still early in the evening. The warden sent for the district attorney, and upon the arrival of the latter official, explained to him the singular circumstances.

George Gordon was subjected to a critical cross-examination, and gave answers that caused considerable amazement.

He told his story, announced himself as the son of the murdered woman, the heir to the estate, and went into details that were extraordinary.

Sheehan was present and heard the whole story; the sneyd detective gnashed his teeth in rage. He realized that the game was all out of his hands. Kate, after all, had proved too many for him.

George Gordon was asked why he had gone under cover—assumed a disguise—and his answer was, that after his arrival in New York he had learned that he bore a fatal resemblance to some man who had been guilty of numerous crimes, and that he had gone under cover to avoid disagreeable complications. He went into full details in the most satisfactory manner, and at the close of the examination, the district attorney told him he was at liberty to go, and at the same time assured him that there was no more need for the cover of a disguise, as the real culprit had been taken into custody.

George Gordon had been questioned as to the mystery of the fatal resemblance, but to all questions he had refused to answer.

The young man left the prison. He was followed by Sheehan who would have addressed him, but George gave the man to understand that he would hold no conversation with him.

A few squares from the jail George met Lady Kate. Sheehan was at hand.

To the sneyd detective, Kate said:

"Well, Sheehan, how did you work it out?"

"I'll tell you to-morrow."

"You thought you had a big thing, eh?"

' So I have; I've a card to play yet.''

'' Oh, have you?''

'' Yes, I have.''

'' Well, play it before to morrow's sunset, or you may be where the dogs can't bite you! I've a little budget to open on you!''

Sheehan went his way gnashing his teeth.

The man proceeded direct to the house of Colonel Prang. He had promised the colonel some startling news, and he certainly had some very startling facts to detail.

Colonel Prang was not at home. Sheehan had piped his man, and knew where to go to look for him.

The colonel was found in a first-class club-room, where a nice little game could be had, and he was in just a good humor to listen to the good cheer of Sheehan.

CHAPTER LXXXIII.

The colonel was looking to hear good news, but the expression on Sheehan's face when the two men met did not promise well.

'' Colonel, your game is up.''

'' I've no game, you fool! What do you mean?''

'' Oh, you're mighty innocent! But the real heir is in New York!''

The colonel turned slightly pale, but answered, coolly:

'' That's no news to me.''

'' But how are your chances?''

'' I've no chance in the matter. I shall surrender property to the heir the moment the will is produced.''

'' Make a friend of me, Colonel Prang, and the will shall never be produced.''

'' First tell me your story.''

Sheehan did proceed and tell his story, and when he had concluded the colonel said:

'' So you advise me to make a friend of you?''

'' I do.''

'' What advantage will it be for me to have any dealings with a villain of your stamp?''

Sheehan recoiled, and ejaculated:

'' Eh? What's that you say?''

'' My words were plain.''

'' You dare call me a villain!''

'' What else are you?''

'' And what are you?''

'' Be careful, you scoundrel! Do not use any impudence to me, or I will knock you down! I've been using you as a scoundrel in the interest of the true heir. I've no need to hold the property that belongs to another. You have mistaken me all the time. I'm an honorable man, who needed the services of a rogue and a fool, and you have well served me in both capacities; so good-evening.''

Sheehan did go. The man was completely upset; the tide had set in against him.

Colonel Prang was a shrewd, cunning man. He was a wonderfully smart man—just smart enough to know when he had lost the game.

There are a great many men who are smart enough to scheme, but there are few men who are smart enough to know when they are beaten, and make the discovery in time to save themselves from impending consequences.

He had come to the conclusion that he had lost in the game. He had set out to play a very able one, but he had made one false move where he had calculated he was playing his best card, and having lost, he did not propose to involve himself legally. He had come to hold Lady Kate in high reverence, as one of the smartest women, in a quiet way, he had ever met, and he decided to give up the game.

He was not a man to resort to murder and forgery and kindred crimes. He relied upon his fine play, and again, as stated, having lost, he was prepared to give up the game.

The colonel felt very happy over one fact. He had not committed himself to Sheehan, and had been prepared to treat that sneaking scoundrel as he deserved.

As our readers have discerned, Kate had reached a point where she had determined to play out her full hand; she had permitted George Gordon to be arrested. Her motive had been to have his identity established by a legal officer; she had instructed him just how much to tell and how to tell it. She had anticipated just what had subsequently happened.

Having carried out her purpose, she was prepared to go on and proclaim George Gordon as Balfour Raymond.

Upon the morning following the incidents detailed Kate called upon Colonel Prang.

The colonel received her in his usual icy man-

ner. He admired the wonderful woman's wit and keenness, but he did not forget that she had beaten him out of a large fortune.

'' Good day, Colonel Prang,'' said Kate.

'' Good day, Miss Edwards,'' came the cold response.

'' I have called to see you upon important business.''

'' My time is at your disposal.''

'' The real heir has turned up.''

'' What real heir?''

'' The heir to the Raymond estate—the son of Balfour Raymond and Grace Renton.''

Kate had expected to see the colonel turn pale and ejaculate and declaim, but on the contrary he said, in the calmest tones:

'' I am very glad.''

'' You, of course, will dispute his claim?''

'' I dispute his claim? Why. certainly not. Did I not employ you to find both the murderer and the heir?''

'' But the heir is not a murderer.''

'' I am satisfied of that.''

'' I do not know how to take you, colonel.''

'' Well, I am certain I am talking in plain terms. You say the heir is found, let him prove himself the heir and I will surrender my trust gladly.''

'' You talk fair enough seemingly, but there is a reservation in all your remarks.''

'' I am not conscious of any reservation.''

'' Why do you not proclaim at once that you will dispute the identity of the heir?''

'' Simply because I have no such intention; on the other hand I will co-operate with you in the establishment of the identity of the heir.''

Kate was all adrift. She did not understand the colonel at all.

'' You will aid me to establish the heir's identity?''

'' I will.''

'' I am very much obliged for your proffered assistance, but his identity is established.''

'' So much the better.''

'' And you will put him in possession of his property?''

'' Certainly, as soon as I can legally do so.''

'' What is to prevent? He is the heir.''

'' But where is the will?''

'' Ah, that is your game!''

'' I beg your pardon, I have no game. I am a trustee; there was a will; it is missing.''

'' It may never be found.''

'' Then I will do all in my power to establish the heir's rights as heir-at-law.''

'' Are you in earnest, Colonel Prang?''

'' Certainly I am in earnest.''

'' Then permit me to say that I have done you great injustice.''

'' How so?''

'' I did think you were disposed to keep the heir out of his rights, as you were the residuary legatee.''

'' I had no such idea; you certainly did me an injustice; and now listen—I would be delighted to meet young Balfour Raymond, and we will see what can be done.''

CHAPTER LXXXIV.

'' Balfour Raymond is here.'' said Kate, and at that moment the young man whose name had been mentioned entered the room.

Kate introduced the two gentlemen. Colonel Prang from the first addressed George Gordon as Mr. Raymond, betraying on his part a willingness to recognize the young man as the heir.

Explanations followed; all the facts known to our readers were fully laid before Colonel Prang.

The gentleman listened patiently and in the end said:

'' I have no doubt in my mind as to your identity, young sir, and I shall do all in my power to establish your claim, but I fear that without the will we can not turn the property over to you.''

Balfour Raymond said:

'' The signers of the will as witnesses would most likely remember the provisions of the paper they signed.''

'' Hardly.''

'' Mr. James Throckmorton and Mr. Andrew Ballantine will certainly recognize their own signatures.''

Colonel Prang gazed in amazement, and so also did Lady Kate.

'' You know the gentlemen?''

'' I know that they were the subscribing witnesses to the will.''

'' How did you learn that fact, young man?''

'' I have the will!''

Kate could not restrain an exclamation of amazement.

'' You have the will?'' she said.

'' I have.''

'' How came it into your possession?''

'' It is enough that I have it in my possession.''

Kate understood that the refusal to explain was intended for Colonel Prang, and she did not press her inquiry.

'' If you have the original will,'' said the colonel, '' all is well; you come into possession of your estate.''

Such proved to be the case.

At the proper time the will was duly presented.

Kate, in the meantime, had learned the circumstances under which the will had been procured.

Arthur Everdell had given the valuable document to his brother.

Arthur had not been with the thieves who committed the robbery, but having heard that some papers had been taken, he had managed to secure possession of them; the young man had an idea that in some way any private papers from that particular house might some day have an interest for him.

Colonel Prang fulfilled his promise, and George Gordon was put in possession of his property.

The papers contained a passing allusion to a romance in real life, but no allusion was made to the lucky heir's equivocal connection with the young burglar who awaited trial in the Tombs.

When the lucky man is wealthy, the daily papers have a kindly way of omitting names, and special facts that might prove disagreeable, if printed, to the parties concerned.

Some days had passed.

Kate wondered that she had not seen old Mr. Everdell, but that gentleman appeared to purposely avoid a meeting with her.

One day George Gordon visited the prison where his brother was incarcerated.

The two young men had a long talk together, and during the interview Gordon, or rather Balfour Raymond, said:

'' Arthur, something must be done for your escape.''

'' I will escape in good time,'' came the reply.

Arthur Everdell had suddenly assumed a sort of reserve toward his brother.

Balfour Raymond, upon a previous visit, had dropped a certain remark, and from that moment the seeming reserve on Arthur's part had been apparent.

'' I have a confession to make to you, Arthur,'' said Balfour, upon the occasion of his last visit.

Arthur asked no questions, but waited for his brother to proceed.

'' What is your opinion of Miss Kate Edwards, Arthur?''

'' You ask my opinion of Miss Edwards?''

'' Yes.''

'' Why do you ask?''

'' I will tell you after you have answered my question.''

'' I consider her the most beautiful, the most brilliant, and the most lovable woman on the face of the earth!''

'' I am glad to hear you say so, Arthur.''

'' Why?''

'' I love Kate Edwards, despite the fact of her being engaged in the unwomanly profession of a detective!''

A singular look came into Arthur's face, but he was silent, while his brother went on and said:

'' I have reason to know that Miss Edwards loves me. I have had the most satisfactory and unequivocal testimony to that effect, and I love her; indeed, I conceived a violent affection for her the first moment I saw her. She is a sweet and fascinating woman, brave, generous, and cultured—and I shall make her my wife as soon as you are out of prison and safely away to some foreign land—of course it would not be safe for you to remain in America.''

'' And you?''

'' I like America; I shall make it my home.''

George Gordon proceeded and revealed all his plans to Arthur, and throughout exhibited the most brotherly feeling.

Arthur said but little. He spoke in terms of the warmest admiration of Lady Kate, and congratulated his brother upon having won the love of so true and noble a woman.

Half an hour after the departure of Balfour Raymond, Lady Kate appeared at the prison.

Arthur received her in his usual calm and pleasant manner.

"What has become of your grandfather?" asked Kate.

"He comes he. every day."

"Was he to see you to-day?"

"He was."

"I have not seen him for several days. I should like to see him."

"You know where he lodges?"

"I have been there, but have never found him at home of late."

"I will tell him you wish to see him."

"Please do."

"Miss Edwards," said Arthur, after a moment's silence, "you have been a warm friend to me."

There was something peculiar in Arthur's tone, and the lady detective acted just *like a woman* and placed a barrier between herself and her own happiness.

CHAPTER LXXXV.

THE secret is out, Kate loved the burglar, the strange, fascinating, and singular man, Arthur Everdell.

Arthur had said, "Miss Edwards, you have been a warm friend to me!" and fearing the conversation might take a certain direction, Kate answered in a cold tone:

"I have been the friend to you that I would have been to *any young man under the same circumstances.*"

Kate spoke in a cold and indifferent tone.

"I know you would," returned Arthur. "Still I am none the less grateful for your interest in my behalf. I know that I am an unworthy man, and it was kind and noble in you as a *detective* to seek to save me from crime, rather than pursue me for the purposes of visiting upon me its consequences."

"We will not talk of that now; the question to be considered is, how shall you escape?"

"Are *you* interested in my escape?"

"Certainly, I wish you to have an opportunity to lead a better life; you certainly were the victim of the sins of others during your early years, and now that you are disposed to become a better man, you should have the chance."

"Do you think it would be right for me to escape, in the face of the fact that I am really guilty?"

"Under all circumstances, I feel that I would be justified in aiding you to escape."

"And should I escape, what would you advise me to do?"

"You will have to fly from this land, or you would always be a fugitive."

"And you are willing to aid me to escape?"

"I am."

"I thank you; and now, Miss Edwards, I will a k you to remember the brief conversation that has passed between us."

"Why are you particular about my remembering the talk of to-day?"

"Circumstances may occur that may make it desirable."

Kate felt a cold chill; it was evident to her that there was a hidden meaning under the strange young man's words.

"Arthur," she said, "I trust you do not contemplate some rash act?"

"Why should I contemplate some rash act?"

"I do not know, but your words are strange."

"I am a strange man, and I sometimes indulge strange fancies."

"Will you answer me one question fairly?"

"I will."

"Do you really wish to escape from this prison?"

"I do, and I am determined to escape."

"And I will aid you."

"Thank you."

There came at the moment an interruption to the conversation, and a few moments later Kate left the cell.

That same afternoon the lady detective held an interview with Balfour Raymond.

"I fear," she said, "your brother contemplates some rash act."

"What rash act could he contemplate?"

"You forget he is a very strange young man."

"What do you fear?"

"I saw him to-day."

"Well?"

"He talked in a very strange and weird manner."

"He is low-spirited, possibly, at being confined."

"That is what I fear."

"And what else do you fear?"

"He may contemplate taking his own life."

"Nonsense!"

"Remember, I know your brother's disposition much better than yourself."

"Why should he contemplate taking his own life?"

"He is a young man of fine feelings, although he has been a burglar."

"He is."

"He has come to a condition of mind where he fully realizes his position, and he considers his life blasted."

"We must get him out of prison."

"The sooner the better."

"How shall we proceed? What will bribery do?"

"We must concoct some other plan."

"Are you willing to aid us?"

"I am."

"What would you suggest?"

"I will think the matter over, and report a plan to-morrow."

"Do so."

Kate went down to the place where old Joseph Everdell resided. The old man was not at home, but in coming from the house Lady Kate met him.

"I have been looking for you."

"Have you?"

"I have."

"Well, what is your business with me?"

The old gentleman spoke in a cold and very indifferent manner.

"The trial of your grandson on the charge of burglary is set down for next Monday."

"So soon?"

"Yes."

"Well?"

"We must do something at once. He must never come to trial."

"No; he must never come to trial."

"Will you meet me to-morrow?"

"For what purpose?"

"I will have a plan matured for effecting his escape."

"You are very kind and thoughtful."

Kate did not like the manner in which the old man spoke.

"Will you meet me?"

"Where?"

Kate named a place.

"I *may* be there, but possibly I may have another engagement."

"Can any other engagement interfere with your interest in your grandson?"

"No."

"Then will you meet me?"

"I may; but in the meantime I am in your debt."

"In my debt?"

"Yes."

"I am happy to have you under an obligation to me."

"I wish to discharge it."

"How can you?"

"Here is a check for five thousand dollars!"

"I will not receive the money."

"Why not?"

"I will present my bill after your grandson is free."

"Very well, we will talk the matter over at some future time."

Kate, as she walked away, felt very uncomfortable. Arthur had spoken to her in a strange and ambiguous manner, and now his grandfather, who heretofore had been so simple and straightforward, adopted the same tone. Upon the following morning all was explained.

CHAPTER LXXXVI.

KATE was at her home when George Gordon, or rather Balfour Raymond, was announced as a visitor.

The detective received her guest in the parlor of her residence, and the moment her eyes fell upon him she knew that something extraordinary had occurred.

Balfour Raymond was usually an undemonstrative man. Upon the occasion named he betrayed a decided excitement.

"What has happened?" demanded Kate.

"Something extraordinary."

Kate turned pale, and in a tremulous tone asked:

"What has happened?"

"Can you not guess?"

"I can not guess."

"Arthur has escaped!"

"Escaped!"

"Yes."

"When did he escape?"

"Last night."

"How?"

"No one knows. All that is known is, that this morning his cell was found vacant, the prisoner had mysteriously disappeared."

A deathly pallor settled upon the face of Lady Kate.

"Are you telling me the whole truth?" she demanded.

"What object would I have in deceiving you?"

"None."

"My brother has certainly escaped. And now the only question is, Will he be recaptured?"

Kate remained silent.

"You do not appear pleased."

"I am glad, of course."

"You are deathly pale."

"Am I?"

"Yes."

"Well, your news came upon me very suddenly. If you will excuse me, I will get ready and go to the prison."

"I have already been there; you can learn nothing more."

"I will try," said Kate.

"I only trust my brother will not be retaken."

"You may rest assured he will not be retaken."

"Why are you so certain?"

"Your brother is a smart man. He was smart in escaping, and you may rest as I told you, he will not be retaken."

Kate dismissed young Balfour Raymond and retired to her room. It was a strange fact that our heroine had conceived a positive dislike for the brother of Arthur.

Once in her room the woman in her nature asserted itself, and, throwing herself upon a sofa, she buried her face in her hands and wailed out.

"It's all over! My dream is past! I will never again see Arthur Everdell in life! It is evident he did not care for me as I cared for him!"

Kate reasoned as a woman in love usually reasons; there was no sense in her conclusions.

Our readers must not set her down as a silly girl, simply because of her love. She acted in a silly manner; love is a terrible foe to dignity, and it has made simpletons of some of the greatest men and women the world has ever known.

We do not assert that Kate was mistaken, but we do say that there were no grounds for her conclusions upon the basis of the single fact that Arthur Everdell had escaped from his prison cell.

Kate had said she would go straight to the prison, but she had no heart to do so, and it was late in the day when she did finally muster sufficient courage to go.

One thing was assured, the conduct of both Arthur and his grandfather was fully explained; at the very moment when both had been talking to her, their plans for escape had been matured, and they had not seen fit to make a confidante of her.

Their failure to do so was suggestive, but did not in any measure warrant Kate's conclusions.

When Kate reached the prison, she was met by the warden.

"So your prisoner has escaped?"

"Yes, but we will have him back in his cell again before night."

"You are on his track?"

"We are."

"How did he get away?"

"I fear that is a mystery that will never be explained unless the prisoner when recaptured chooses to tell."

"Who was the under-keeper on duty?"

"The under-keeper is exonerated from all blame; it was a marvelous escape, and there was a *woman concerned* in it, and I am satisfied that the woman is the fellow's wife."

"A woman concerned in the escape?"

"Yes."

"How did you come to discover that much?"

"He was visited by a young woman just before sundown yesterday."

"Well?"

"The woman must have managed to smuggle several instruments into the prisoner's cell."

"Where is the woman?"

"Heaven knows, I don't."

"Did the woman get away?"

"Yes."

"Did no one recognize her?"

"She was veiled; and she is the last veiled visitor who will ever enter a cell while I am in charge of this jail."

" You have no clew to the woman then?"

" None whatever."

Kate left the prison and returned to her home, where she met with a genuine surprise.

There were two letters awaiting her, and her heart fluttered as she tore the seal of the first one and glanced over the contents.

The letter was from Joseph Everdell, and as Kate opened the envelope, a check fell upon the floor.

She did not stop to examine the check, but ran her eyes over the contents of the letter.

The latter read as follows:

" Miss Edwards,—Inclosed please find check for five thousand dollars, which I consider fair payment for all services rendered to myself and son; before finally sending the amount, I consulted with Arthur, and we decided that it was fair remuneration. Of course there is now no need for my keeping my appointment with you, as the object for which we were to meet, you will have learned ere this, has been accomplished.

" We send our united thanks along with the check, and although we may never meet again in this world, we shall always hold you in grateful remembrance, and trust you may do the same as concerns your friend and well-wisher,
" Joseph Everdell."

" And this is the end?" murmured Kate, as the ——welled into her eyes.

She still held the second letter in her hand, and after a moment broke the seal.

CHAPTER LXXXVII.

Kate trembled as she glanced down at the signature affixed to the second letter.

It was signed " Arthur Everdell," and it ran as follows:—

" Miss Edwards,—I should never have taken the liberty to write the words contained in this letter, had I ever expected to meet you again on earth. We will never meet again, and before going into the subject that is on my heart, let me wish you for the remainder of your life all joy and happiness. I know that you will be happy with my brother. He is a noble fellow, and I think fully worthy of the great prize he has won—your love!"

Kate stopped short in the reading of the letter, and gave utterance to a very manly expression.

" Great thunder!" she ejaculated, " what does he mean?"

She recommenced the perusal of the letter.

" We met, most beautiful and noble of women, under the strangest circumstances, and still stranger incidents attended our continued intercourse; and yet, I, the burglar, the man of sin and crime, dare confess that no man ever loved woman as I loved you, from the moment when, upon the night after the masked ball, I entered your chamber to rob you of your diamonds. A strange time to fall in love indeed, but such is the fact. Do not consider me bold; as I stated in the opening paragraph of my letter, I should not have confessed all this did I not know that we will never meet again; and besides, as you are about to become my sister-in-law, I can take a brother's liberty in revealing my secret. I would not do so did I not know how heartily you despise me, and possibly your abhorrence will be greater after this reading; but I am selfish enough to write these lines as a relief to my own pent-up feelings. Remember, I never indulged the hope that one as pure as yourself would ever return the love of a criminal like Arthur Everdell; and did I dream that circumstances would ever throw us again into each other's company, I should not write this confession now.

" We will never meet again on earth, and all I ask is, that in your prayers you will not forget to ask too for me sufficient strength to live an honorable life. I do not know what my plans will be; of course you know that as far as money is concerned, I shall never need to take again what does not rightfully belong to me. I have been a thief, but I will steal no more!

" I will not tire you with a repetition of my thankfulness for all that you have done for me and yet, as I now feel. I would that we had never met; but enough, tear up this letter when

you have read it, and let your indignation be lessened by the remembrance that to write this much has been a comfort to one whose life was blasted at his birth.
" Yours,
" Arthur Everdell."

When Kate had read the letter a second time, she sat down and cried outright.

She did not cry because of her own disappointment, but because her sympathetic heart was wrung with sorrow for the strange, weird young man who had penned the epistle.

There was one part of the letter Kate could not understand, the allusion to the worthiness of his brother, and the announcement that she was to become his sister-in-law.

" The silly fool!" she muttered; " whatever could have put that idea into his head? Certainly not anything that I have ever done or said, for in truth, I know not why, but I really detest young Balfour Raymond!"

The time came when Kate fully understood the meaning of Arthur's allusions.

Talking to herself, Kate said:

" Well, so he has decided that we shall never meet again on earth! Now, we will see about that. He is not going to confess his love and run away from me in this manner!"

A week passed, and despite the warden's confident boast, Arthur Everdell was not retaken.

It was a mystery to the lady detective who the woman could be who had figured in the case. Kate envied the strange female the privilege of having assisted Arthur to escape from the jail.

Kate, for reasons of her own, gave up her position as a private detective. Indeed, ever since her meeting with Arthur, she had paid but little attention to her regular duties as a detective.

Lady Kate was not poor by any means. She possessed no great fortune, but she had accumulated quite a sum of money, and could afford to give up business at least for a season. She had come to a determination which necessitated her retirement. In fact, she had determined to do a little detective work on her own account.

Kate was at home one evening, dressed as became her sex and condition, after her retirement from the detective service.

It was still early in the evening when a visitor was announced.

" Pshaw! it's that Balfour Raymond. I can not see what that man means calling upon me evening after evening!" exclaimed Kate, with a very lady-like shake of the shoulders.

Balfour was shown in and the two had the drawing-room to themselves.

" Well," said Balfour, " I reckon the authorities have given up all idea of ever catching the escaped prisoner."

" Yes; it is certain that Arthur has made good his escape."

" I should think, Miss Edwards, that you could now afford to retire from the detective business."

" Why should I retire?"

" It is such an unlady-like profession."

" But I am well adapted to it. I am sure I have met with phenomenal success."

" Yes; you are a wonderful woman, and you would attain success at whatever you might undertake!"

" Thank you, sir, you are very complimentary."

" Indeed, I intend to be complimentary."

" Well, sir, I have already resigned my position as a private detective."

" You have already resigned your position?"

" I have."

" Well, I am glad of that."

" You are glad?"

" Yes."

" Why are you so glad, Mr. Raymond? What interest can you have in my decisions?"

" I will tell you, Kate, I've a secret which I have at last decided to reveal."

CHAPTER LXXXVIII.

Kate had an idea as to what was to follow, and a strange look came into her eyes; had Balfour Raymond been as observant as his brother, he would have left unspoken the words that subsequently were spoken by him.

" You have a secret to reveal to me?" said Kate.

" Yes."

" Well, out with it. I love to listen to secrets."

" Have you no idea as to the nature of my secret?"

" How should I? No, I've not the least idea."

" Can you not guess?"

" I am not good at guessing."

" You are good at forming theories."

" I used to be, but you must remember I am not a detective now."

" And I am glad."

" Well, so am I, since you are so well pleased."

" I am glad to hear you say that!"

" Why?"

" It encourages me to tell my secret, when you confess that it gives you pleasure to please me."

" Well, tell me your secret, you have me certainly sufficiently prepared."

" Kate, I love you!"

Kate did not start or blush or throw herself into the young man's arms; but, with the unlady-like expression, " Well, I'll be blamed if that don't explain the mystery!" greeted the young man's declaration.

Balfour Raymond was prepared to throw his arms around Kate, but he didn't. He merely rose to his feet, and, after gazing at her a moment with a perplexed look upon his face, said:

" Kate, did you fully understand what I just said?"

" Fully."

" And what have you to say?"

" I say it fully explains the mystery."

" May I inquire the meaning of your language?"

" You must excuse me, Mr. Raymond. I have been very rude, but you took me very much by surprise. I was not as well prepared as I thought I was."

" And what have you to say in answer to my confession?"

" Only that I am very sorry that you have been so foolish as to fall in love with me."

" I am to understand that my love is not returned?"

" Certainly. I do not understand how it is you did not perceive it before."

" Kate!"

" Well, sir?"

" Is my honest confession of love to be treated in this rude manner?"

" We will see, Balfour Raymond. I wish to ask you a few questions."

" A dozen, if you choose."

" Did you ever tell your brother Arthur what you have just told me?"

" I did."

" Did you tell him more?"

" What more was there to tell him?"

" Did you give him to understand that you had ever received any encouragement from me?"

" What difference does it make?"

" A great deal of difference. I have an important reason for asking the question."

" If my memory serves me right, I did give my brother to understand that I had every reason to believe that my love for you was reciprocated."

" I thank you for your frankness, but must add that you certainly took a great liberty."

" How so?"

" You must know yourself, since you know as well that I never did give you any reason to believe that I loved you!"

" You forget your interest in my behalf."

" But did I not have a greater interest in your brother?"

" Do you confess to me that you love a criminal?"

" I will confess to you that I never could love a man who, under all the circumstances, could use the word criminal in the relation that you have just now."

Balfour Raymond colored to the temples, while a singular remembrance flashed over Kate's mind.

She recalled the story of the incident that had occurred in France many years ago, and the consciousness came over her mind that there was something of the character of the mother in Balfour Raymond, after all.

" I am to understand that my love is rejected?"

" You are to understand that your love is rejected!" answered Kate, coldly. She could not lessen the full mortification of her refusal after the unkind allusion to her possible love for a criminal.

" You will not consider my offer?"

"I will not."

"Your refusal is absolute?"

"It is absolute!"

Balfour Raymond's pride was severely injured.

"Am I to understand that you love my brother?"

"You are to understand that it is none of your business whom I love, it being plainly understood that I do not love you!"

Balfour Raymond rose to go.

"Miss Edwards," he said, "I trust you and I will not become enemies."

Kate did not understand the sense in which the young man spoke, and answered, hotly:

"It's a matter of indifference to me whether we do or not!"

"Then the enmity must all be on your side, as I shall never forget the obligation under which you have placed me!"

Kate was ashamed of herself on the instant, and hastened to say:

"You must forgive me! I received your former remark in the sense of a threat!"

"It was not so intended, as I am anxious to remain your friend, and have you remain mine."

"Here is my hand, Balfour. We met under strange circumstances, and there certainly should be no enmity between us."

"There shall be none; and now let me say, since I have failed in winning your love, I am rejoiced that *my brother* has proved himself so much more fortunate than myself!"

Kate blushed as she answered:

"I did not say I loved your brother; I merely resented the allusion to him as a criminal!"

"There, again you misunderstood the sense of my remark."

"I am glad that I did."

Balfour Raymond took his departure, and after he had gone, Kate muttered:

"I am trying hard to hate that young man, but I can not. He is a noble young fellow, after all!"

CHAPTER LXXXIX.

The letter Kate had read, as stated, caused her to resign her position, and come to a certain determination.

A month passed, and the lady detective was a passenger on a steamer sailing for Europe.

As the great vessel moved from the New York pier, she muttered:

"I'll find him, or I will never return to New York, and as a city, to me it is the dearest spot on earth!"

We will here ask our reader's permission to state that it is only necessary for one to leave old New York for a season, in order to fully realize what a glorious old city it is, and what a grand, noble people reside within its vast limits.

Kate arrived in London, and had no difficulty in learning the location of the home of Joseph Everdell.

The gentleman had an estate near the border line between England and Scotland, and the lady detective took an afternoon train to proceed to the distant town.

Kate reached the town where Joseph Everdell resided, and once more resorted to one of her old tricks. She disguised herself.

She had been in the town two days, and had gathered all the information she desired.

Upon the third day, in a disguise, Kate entered the grounds surrounding the house in which Joseph Everdell resided. It was a magnificent park, and she had been in the grounds but a few minutes when her eyes rested upon the form she had crossed the ocean to behold.

Arthur Everdell was at home, adorning the social position in life for which he was intended.

Kate approached near to him and studied his appearance.

He was a remarkably handsome man—as Kate stood there and gazed at him she so thought.

Kate loved to perpetrate surprises, and she suddenly appeared in front of Arthur Everdell. Her disguise was perfect, and he did not recognize her.

"Well, madame," said the young man, as Kate was presented before him, "what can I do for you?"

Kate returned answer in a joke, without any idea as to the result that was to follow her simple words.

"What can you do for me?"

The lady detective had adopted the Irish brogue.

"Yes; what can I do for you?"

"Well, ye can tell me what ye are doin' here, *Arthur Everdell*, in thim foine clothes an' the airs of a lord!"

A spasm passed over Arthur's face, a look of agony convulsed his handsome features. his eyes started with terror, and in an instant he was transformed from a fine, handsome man into a terrified, cowering wretch.

"Hush! hush! woman!" he almost wailed, "hush! hush!" and to himself, in accents of the most concentrated agony, he murmured: "Alas! I knew it! I knew it! How could I hide? My sins have found me out! Would that I could call upon the sea to swallow me, or the mountains to cover me over!"

Kate discerned the situation at once; she was one of the quickest-minded women on earth.

Dropping her brogue, in her own familiar voice she exclaimed:

"Heaven forgive me, Arthur; no harm shall come to you!"

"*Kate!*" cried Arthur.

"Yes, Kate!"

A complete change had come over the young man's face, his features became illumined with delight, as he exclaimed:

"You here!"

"Yes, I am here."

"Why did you come?"

Kate was a straightforward person, and she answered frankly, and in a clear, firm voice:

"I came to tell you that your letter filled my heart with gladness."

"What do you mean?"

"I mean as you love me, so I love you!"

"Love me! the criminal! the burglar! the fugitive!"

"Yes; I love you for what you are, not what you were!"

"Oh, Kate!" cried Arthur, and in a wild delirium of passion he clasped the disguised beauty to his arms.

Explanations followed, and the mystery of Arthur's agitation was explained.

He had been introduced in the neighborhood as Arthur Raymond, the grandson of old Joseph Everdell.

The fact of his mother's marriage had been established, and he had a right to his father's name.

Kate was led to the house, even in her disguise, and introduced once more to the old man whom she had met in the New World under such strange circumstances.

Reader, our tale is ended.

THE END.

OLD SLEUTH WEEKLY

A Series of

THE MOST THRILLING DETECTIVE STORIES EVER PUBLISHED

| No. 9. | THE ARTHUR WESTBROOK COMPANY, CLEVELAND, U. S. A.
AUGUST 7th, 1908. | Vol. I. |

THE GREAT BOND ROBBERY

------OR------

TRACKED BY A FEMALE DETECTIVE.

By "OLD SLEUTH."

CHAPTER I.

THE CHIEF DETECTIVE'S STORY.

CAPTAIN J. S. YOUNG, once chief of the New York detective force, and, at the time we write, head of a private detective agency, sat in his private office, thinking over the various aspects of a case that had just been presented to him, when there came a low rap at his office door.

As a rule, the great detective was as inaccessible to ordinary visitors as the Emperor of all the Russias; but the rap for admittance mentioned was accompanied by a little private signal that caused him to exclaim:

"Come in!"

The door opened, and a woman, closely veiled and of most graceful figure, glided into the great thief-taker's presence.

"Thank Heaven! Miss Kate, of all people on the face of the earth, you are the one I was the most anxious to see!"

"I am here, chief, and at your service," came the reply, in a sweet, pleasant voice.

As the woman spoke she cast aside her veil, and disclosed a face of rare beauty and intelligence.

One would have expected to have met such a lovely being under the glare of gas-jets, glittering in silks and jewels, rather than in a detective office, at night, plainly clad.

She was not more than three-and-twenty, and nothing in her beautiful countenance seemed to indicate that she possessed the courage, cunning, patience, endurance and sagacity of the most experienced officer on the whole detective force.

Kate Goelet's life had been a romance from the hour that she was born until the moment when, as described, in a quiet manner she glided into the presence of the great detective chief.

"Are you engaged at present, Miss Kate?" asked the detective.

"I am not; I dropped in to see if you had anything on hand."

"I have; and I was thinking of you in connection with the affair when, like an apparition, you came gliding into my presence."

"What is it—a murder?"

"No."

"I am glad of that! I have just been working up a murder case, and I am soul-sick with horrors."

"All your sympathies have been enlisted, as usual, for some poor devil, I suppose?"

"No; my sympathies this time were aroused for the innocent victim of a most dreadful crime. But enough; it is over, as far as I am concerned, and I am glad that you have a job for me on another lay."

"Well, Kate, you always said that your profession was distasteful to you; that you would like to make a big stake and quit it?"

"Your memory serves you correctly; it's strange that a person of my organization should have drifted into my present employment, but I have been a woman of such strange fortunes that I am prepared for anything that may come; but to business."

"All I was going to say was that if you succeed in the business in hand you will make a stake that will enable you to pull out."

"I hope I may succeed!" murmured the woman as a sigh issued from her lips and a shadow fell upon her beautiful face.

"One of the richest banking-houses in New York has fallen victim to a defaulter; the amount stolen is nearly a million."

"A large haul."

"Indeed it is; and the peculiarity of the case consists in the fact that the company have discovered their loss unbeknown to the defaulter, who is still in their employ."

"What do they want of a detective then? Why don't they close in on the thief?"

"They want their bonds and money back; that's why they don't close in on the thief."

"How do they expect to get them?"

"I'll tell you.   There is a woman in the case, a cunning she-devil who has led the young man to his ruin; they want to run her close in shore, and drop to the hiding-place of the bonds; it's a case where a naturally noble young man has been beguiled and ruined by a beautiful fraud."

Kate Goelet was thoughtful a moment, and then in a sad tone, she murmured:

"It's going to be a trying case, I see."

"You will receive ten per cent. of every dollar you recover. Go it, you can win. I have thought the case over well. What do you say?"

"I am at your service, and ready for orders."

"Good! I know that when once you start you'll go through, and your first point will be to ring in an acquaintance with Henry Wilbur."

"Henry Wilbur is the thief?"

"Yes."

"Have you seen him?"

"Here is his picture!" and the chief handed a *carte-de-visite* to the lady detective.

The latter glanced at the pictured face, and a sad look glimmered into her beautiful blue eyes as she murmured: "What a handsome man! what an honest, open face! I tell you, chief, there is a mistake here; no woman in the world could allure the original of that picture to crime!"

"You will learn differently when you have worked awhile on the case."

"The directors think they have this young man 'dead to rights,' eh?"

"They have evidence that would convict an angel!"

"Mark my words, chief, I have an inspiration in this matter; that young man is not a criminal! remember my words!"

"You're wrong once, Miss Kate. I've studied this case, but I see, as usual, your sympathies are aroused. and now let me tell you something. The directors believe that Henry Wilbur is but the victim of a siren; recover the money, and you save him from punishment; fail, and they will be compelled to close in on him!"

The strange, beautiful woman was silent a moment, but at length she said, after having studied the picture awhile:

"I'll recover the bonds, or at least trace them up; and I'll not only save that young man from prison, but I'll prove him as innocent as you or I. Mark my words, chief!"

Although Captain Young was, at the time we write, only the head of a private detective agency, he was always addressed as chief, from the fact of his long service as chief of the New York police under the Metropolitan Board, where he had obtained the reputation of being a second Fouché.

Kate Goelet remained an hour in conversation with the chief, during which time she learned all the details of the great defalcation.

There was one great mystery in the whole affair—although it was known that a *woman was in the case*, no one had been able to find out who she was.

Henry Wilbur had been "piped" day in and day out, and yet had never been tracked to the lair of the siren who had wrought his ruin, and led him to steal from the bank a million in bonds.

The stolen bonds were not the property of the bank, but were owned by a depositor, who was not at the time aware of his loss, the officials being determined to keep the terrible truth from him until every effort had been exhausted to recover them.

When Kate Goelet, the lady detective, left the presence of Captain Young, she carried with her the photograph of Henry Wilbur.

It was after midnight, and only a woman of her profession and experience would have dared to pass through the streets at such an hour.

She, however, was perfectly capable of taking care of herself, and she had not been half an hour from the presence of the chief when she was put to the test.

For reasons of her own, she had determined to walk instead of taking a conveyance to her lodgings.

She had a little business on hand that carried her up Broadway.

Kate Goelet had reached the corner of Broadway and Howard Street, and was proceeding rapidly along, with her veil drawn down, when she passed a company of young men standing upon the sidewalk in front of a place which she recognized as a famous resort for gamblers and fast men about town.

The men were standing directly under a gas-light, and as the lady detective passed them, her glances fell upon one of their number.

Her heart stood still.

Her last words to Chief Young had been:

"I will prove that Henry Wilbur is not the thief!" and there, within the first half hour, a little incident had occurred that went far to prove all her confidence in the accused man's innocence misplaced.

Standing in the midst of the young men, and evidently a boon companion with them, was Henry Wilbur.

At a glance she saw that the young man was under the influence of wine, a bad omen where innocence is looked for.

She recognized him as the original of the photograph she carried.

"Heavens!" she murmured under her veil, as she hurried by, "my confidence was misplaced; the company he is in would proclaim his guilt; and yet how handsome he is," she added.

Kate had just passed the young men, and was hurrying on, when she heard one of them exclaim:

"By heavens! boys, there goes a woman fair with her *visor down!* I am going to rudely rend that veil aside, and gaze upon the lovely face it must conceal!"

Kate did not tremble; she did not fear the rending aside of her veil; she was perfectly ready to deal with a whole squad of audacious young scamps.

She still kept upon her way, however, and had proceeded but a few steps, when she became aware that she was being followed.

CHAPTER II.

THE STRANGE OLD WOMAN.

THE lady detective turned her head, and a smile crossed her face as she discovered that the young man who had so rashly volunteered to rend aside her veil was Henry Wilbur.

At once she resolved to play the fearful young miss, and increased her pace, as though greatly alarmed, although, in reality, the young man had undertaken to accomplish just what she wished.

Immediately upon finding that she was being followed, she turned down the first side street.

She had not gone far, when she heard rapid but unsteady steps following close behind her.

She increased her speed, and had traversed one block, when she heard her pursuer mutter:

"By thunder! that veiled angel is traveling as fast as a gazelle!"

Again Kate made a turn, and passed up a street where they were most unlikely to meet with pedestrians.

The man started upon a run, reached her side, and placed his hand upon her shoulder.

The lady detective did not scream, but, coming to a halt, asked in a stern voice:

"What do you want, sir?"

"I want just one glimpse at your face, my sweet angel, and then you shall go upon your way rejoicing."

"What right have you to address me?"

"Oh, nonsense!" exclaimed Henry Wilbur; and he boldly reached forth his hand to tear aside her veil.

Kate Goelet stepped back, raised her hand, and said:

"Be careful, sir! What do you want to see my face for?"

"Well, I have an idea that it must be very beautiful."

"And you have made a wager with some of your companions that you will find out, eh?"

"Not exactly; but I'm bound to see it, nevertheless!"

"What is your name, young man?"

"Well, you are turning the tables on me!"

"What is your name?"

"They call me Tom Paine."

"And you want to see my face?"

"I do."

"Have you any money?"

"I have plenty of it."

"Well, hire a carriage and go home; it's late for a boy of your age to be out."

"Now I swear I'll see your face!" And as the young man spoke he sprung forward and sought to seize hold of Kate.

Her veil was torn aside and her lovely face revealed.

"I beg pardon!" exclaimed the man.

It was evident he had expected to behold the face of some brazen creature, and when he beheld the countenance

58

of a lady, and a beautiful one at that, a feeling of shame came over him.

"Are you satisfied?" asked the lady detective who could have prevented him from tearing aside her veil if she had wished.

Again the young man said:

"I beg your pardon!"

The lady detective drew back her veil, and turned to go home, when the young man, who had thus grossly insulted her, said:

"On my honor, I will escort you in safety to your home if you will permit."

"I certainly ought to feel safe under your protection after your rudeness."

"Let me atone for my rudeness."

"No, no; I need no escort," said Kate, and she resumed her way.

The man at first appeared inclined to follow her, but a second thought restrained him.

The next morning Kate Goelet, in the disguise of an old woman, issued from her lodgings.

She felt assured that, after all, it was possible that Henry Wilbur might be innocent, despite the fact that she had seen him in such questionable company.

He had shown that he had the instincts of a gentleman, even during the adventure of the previous night; as the moment he discovered that she was not what he had first supposed, he had ceased to molest her, and had apologized for his first rudeness.

The private banking-house of Attry, Comstock & Co., had been opened for several hours, and business had been proceeding in the ordinary manner, when an old lady, dressed in the most grotesque manner and looking exactly like some old farmer's wife, came bustling into the counting-room.

In a loud, screechy sort of voice she exclaimed:

"Is this Attry, Comstock & Co.'s money-house?"

The porter, who was standing near, answered:

"This is the banking-house of Attry, Comstock & Co., old lady."

"Indeed! And who be you?" asked the old woman, glancing through her spectacles at the porter.

"I am connected with this house."

"Oh, you are, eh? A cousin, I suppose? Well, I thought they were Americans: but if you are connected with them, they must be furriners, arter all!"

The old lady spoke in such a loud tone that all the clerks overheard the singular conversation, and a suppressed laugh followed the funny dialogue.

"Who do you wish to see, old woman?" asked the porter.

"Old woman, eh! Well, you are werry perlite, if you are a connection of the firm."

"Well, madame, who do you wish to see?"

"One of the firm."

"What is your business?"

"I reckon I'll tell my business to the one I want to see."

"Do you wish to see Mr. Attry or Mr. Comstock?"

"Either one of 'em will do."

"What shall I say your business is?"

"Well, may be I want to borrer some money to raise a mortgage."

The porter passed into the private office of the firm, and after a few moments returned and said:

"The members of the firm are both busy; you will have to come some other time, Mrs. —— what's your name?"

"My name is Rebecca Brown. I am from the Forge, Greene County, New York State; and I've come a long distance to see one of this 'ere firm, and I ain't going away until I see 'em!"

"You will have to come again."

"I will, eh?"

"Yes, madame."

"Well, I guess not; I ain't comin' trudging way down here to be put off in that way. You just go and tell the gentlemen my name, and let 'em know my business is important, and that I must see 'em right off the reel, will you?"

The porter was considerably put about. He did not exactly know what to do under the circumstances.

Again he entered the private office, and once more came forth and said that the members of the firm were all too busy to see her at that time.

"Well, now, I've jest got a letter of introduction to this 'ere firm from the bank up our way, and if you will just take it in, I reckon they'll conclude to see Rebecca Brown this morning, although she hain't come down in a kerridge covered with silks and feathers."

The porter took the note, and handed it to Mr. Comstock, the second member of the firm. The banker glanced at the note, which read as follows:

"The bearer of this note, no matter under what guise she may present herself, must be seen at all times. If it is possible to accomplish your business, the party who bears this will succeed. YOUNG."

"Ah!" said Mr. Comstock, who was a shrewd man, "you say this is an old lady?"

"Yes, sir,"

"Well, I suppose I must see her. Please show her in."

The old lady was ushered into the private banking-office. As she entered she said:

"Well, one would think that you fellers were President and Vice President of the United States the way you make people hop around to get in to see you!"

"We have a great deal to do, Mrs. ——. I beg pardon, what's the name?"

"Well you have got a bad memory, when your relative there just told you what my name was. My name is Rebecca Brown.

"Well, Mrs. Brown, what can I do for you?"

"You have a mortgage on our farm?"

"I beg pardon!" exclaimed Mr. Comstock, for the moment forgetting, when he was recalled to himself by a little gesture conveyed to him unobserved by any one else.

"Come to think, I believe one of our customers has deposited a mortgage with us."

"Well, I've just come down to see about that 'ere mortgage."

The banker had got his cue, and fell into the conversation with the strange woman.

All the time the talk was going on, the old lady was glancing from behind her spectacles at different objects around the room.

She was seated in such a position that she could see the clerks in the outer office, and, at the same time, she could catch just a glimpse of a man, seated at a desk in an office adjoining the one occupied by Mr. Comstock.

While carrying on her talk she fidgeted around, pretending to be very uneasy, but a keen observer would have noticed that she appeared to be very desirous of watching the face of the man in the inner office.

After awhile she lowered her voice, although still talking business concerning a supposed mortgage on a farm.

Suddenly she slipped a paper before Mr. Comstock, on which was written the question: "Who is the man in the next office?"

The banker wrote upon the card: "Our junior partner, Mr. Cameron."

There was a looking-glass in the room, and, going to it, the old lady said:

"Well, I declare! traveling in them boats has made me look quite a fright!"

While pretending to look at her strange face in the glass, and while still talking, the old lady placed the glass in such a position that she could watch the movements of the man in the inner office while sitting with her back toward him.

CHAPTER III.

ON THE TRAIL.

THE glass was skillfully adjusted by a practical and cunning hand.

Still talking about her appearance, the old lady resumed her seat and watched the man in the adjoining room.

He had clean-cut, shrewd features. Once or twice he turned his head, so that the old woman got a full view of his whole face.

Mr. Cameron, to an ordinary observer, was a very ordinary-looking man; but a pair of keen eyes, hidden behind a pair of blue-glass spectacles, read other indices in his face, although only rewarded with an occasional glimpse of his features.

There this observer read cruelty and cunning, deceit and avariciousness.

The same observer saw that she was gazing upon a man

capable of assuming the rôle of a very virtuous person while acting the part of a rascal.

The old lady seemingly had about completed her business with Mr. Comstock, and rose to go.

The banker whispered to her:

"What hope have you?"

"I will recover the bonds!"

"You really think so?"

"I will not fail; I know I will recover them."

"You knew who the suspected man was before you came here?"

"Yes."

Mr. Comstock said:

"Come this way, Mrs. Brown and I will see if your recollection of the date of the last payment on the mortgage is correct."

The banker led the old lady into a small side office, and closed the door behind him.

"You are the detective?" he said.

"I am."

"Excuse me, but am I addressing a man or a woman?"

The old woman smiled behind her specs as she answered:

"Don't I look like a woman?"

"Yes; but you know we can never tell about detectives."

"Neither will I tell you any more than is necessary."

"You feel confident of recovering the stolen property?"

"I do."

"Do you think we have taken the right course in tracing the bonds before letting our loss be known?"

"I do."

"You know you will have to follow Mr. Wilbur closer than he has ever been followed, as he is a most cunning rascal, and has covered his tracks so well that it will be hard to run him to his lair—or rather the woman's lair."

"Why do you think there is a woman in the case?"

"Did not the chief give you all the facts?"

"He claimed to have done so."

"Well, then, you know why we are sure there is a woman at the bottom of the robbery."

"I do not believe a woman has had anything to do with it."

"You astonish me."

"I will astonish you still more within a few weeks."

"You have a theory?"

"I have."

"You do not appear to have more than glanced at Mr. Wilbur."

"I have taken a good many glances, more than you think," answered the detective, in a significant tone.

The old woman and the banker came from the office again, talking about that imaginary mortgage in the most business-like manner.

As they came out, an elegantly dressed woman of about thirty entered the office and passed through to the room where Mr. Cameron was seated.

"Who is that woman?" asked the lady detective.

"A cousin of our partner, Mr. Cameron," answered Mr. Comstock, in a tone calculated to imply, "Oh, she is all right; she has had nothing to do with the thief, Wilbur."

The old lady bundled together her traps and prepared to leave the office. As she reached the door, she said, in a loud tone:

"I am going to stay a few days in the city, and will drop in again, when possibly we may come to some settlement about that ere mortgage!"

Once in the outer office, she took a good look at Henry Wilbur.

He was dressed entirely different from what he had been the previous night, and looked very little like a man who had been upon an all night's spree.

Besides, he looked so frank and handsome, that it appeared astonishing that any one could ever have suspected him of being a thief.

The old woman passed from the bank, and, when once without, murmured:

"There is some strange mystery there; that young man is an extraordinary individual, or else one of the most accomplished scoundrels in the States. How innocent he looks," she added, "compared to his appearance last night when he was determined to catch a view of my face. What a demure puss he is just now!"

The old lady stopped at a pie-stand and bought some cakes and managed to linger around for some time.

In fact, an hour passed, when the lady who had gone in to see Mr. Cameron, the junior member of the firm, came forth.

The old woman hobbled after the elegantly dressed lady, muttering to herself, "There may be a woman in the case, after all!"

Henry Wilbur had entered the banking-house in which he was employed at the time our story opens when but a boy.

He was the son of a widow, came of a good family, but had no means save what he earned at the banking-house, just sufficient to support himself and his mother comfortably.

On the evening of the same day that the strange-looking old woman had visited the banking-house, Henry returned to his home—a modest two story building situated in the outskirts of Brooklyn.

He looked calm and serene when at the banking-office, and very little like one who was the bearer of some terrible secret—like a man who had stolen one million dollars.

Once away from the bank, however, and a look of keen anxiety came over his handsome face.

He looked like one who had suddenly, through some mysterious influence, grown old in looks, while still young in years.

Upon reaching home, his mother met him at the door.

The latter was a handsome woman, and it was evident that all her hope in life lay in her handsome son.

A mother's eye had long ago detected that her son was the bearer of some secret sorrow or care.

Upon the afternoon in question he looked more careworn than usual.

Heretofore his mother had forborne to speak to him, hoping that in due time the cause of his trouble would pass away, or that he would conclude to take her into his confidence.

Upon the evening in question she determined to speak to him.

"Henry," she said, as he entered the sitting-room and threw himself upon a lounge with a weary sigh, "what is it that troubles you?"

"Nothing, mother."

"Are you sick?"

"No."

"Then certainly you have something on your mind. Why have a secret from me?"

"You are mistaken, mother. We are very busy over at the office, and I get very tired lately."

Mrs. Wilbur glanced at the large form and muscular limbs of her handsome son, and a look of incredulity came over her face at the idea of that strong, handsome man becoming tired.

"Henry, you can not deceive a mother's love. I have watched you closely lately. Whatever your trouble is, confide in me."

"Oh, mother!" burst out the young man, involuntarily, "I can not tell you my trouble!"

"Ah! then there is a trouble, Henry?"

"Mother, you have forced me to so much of an admission."

"Having admitted so much, my son, tell me all."

As the mother spoke she went and folded her son's head in her arms, kissed and caressed him as she had when but a boy that she could clasp upon her lap.

The strong man could stand no more.

His great broad chest began to heave, and an instant later a sob burst from his lips.

A mother's love had pierced the steel casing that hid the secret, and at last Henry Wilbur had determined to disclose his fearful tale.

CHAPTER IV.

PIPING DOWN FOR FACTS.

THE words were upon his lips, but he caught a glimpse of a look of expectant agony upon his beautiful mother's face, when down fell the gates over the coming flow of disclosure, and he was silent.

"My son, my son, you must unburden your heart to me!"

"Mother, you shall know the truth!" exclaimed Henry. "I have borne the tortures of hell for the last three months!"

"I have suspected as much, my dear boy; and now tell me all!"

"Business is bad in our office. I have long known that there were more clerks than needed; some must be discharged; the junior partner is prejudiced against me; lately he has shown his dislike more and more. When the discharge takes place I will be the first to go."

Henry Wilbur had told the truth, but, alas! not all the truth.

His mother believed it to be all the truth, and considered the disclosure sufficient to account for her son's evident long mental distress.

The news was bad, but, being so far less distressing than what she had expected, she breathed a sigh of relief; a smile broke over her face, and in a cheerful and reassuring voice, she exclaimed:

"Well, my son, is that all the bad news you have for me? and has such a commonplace incident been the cause of all your late anxiety?"

"Yes, mother."

"You can be happy, then, for it is not worth all the misery you have caused yourself."

"But, mother, what shall we do? I have saved nothing from my small salary."

Over the mantel in the parlor was hung one of those fancy needle-worked mottoes, "The Lord will provide."

Mrs. Wilbur pointed to the scriptural legend, and said, cheerfully:

"My son, there is truth in that promise. Do your duty, sin not, and go forth boldly, and all will be well in the end."

Until lately Henry Wilbur had always been regular in his habits, home early, cheerful and kind in his demeanor, and in every way had shown the possession of a contented mind.

Just previous, however, to the scene above described, a complete change had come over him.

He had remained out late at night; he had risen in the morning, after a short sleep, moody and cross.

His mother upon two occasions had thought she had detected signs of liquor upon him, and she had feared in her heart that when the truth became known some terrible disclosure would be made.

When her son told her his trouble, it made her comparatively happy, since she had dreaded admissions much more fateful.

Upon the following morning Henry told his mother that he would not be home that night until very late.

At the front door he kissed her good-bye, and seemingly was more cheerful than he had been for months.

Little did that fond and loving mother dream that at the moment he kissed her good-bye, he carried a loaded revolver in his pocket, ready, upon certain contingencies, to blow his brains out.

Henry Wilbur had a secret on his conscience yet untold, and, although he appeared calm and cheerful, a fearful tumult was raging in his mind.

He went to the corner of the street, hailed a passing car, and took passage to the ferry.

At the corner below where he had entered the car, it stopped again, and a lady entered.

The latter was a strange-looking person.

She had lovely blue eyes, but, singularly enough, a very dark complexion, a contrast seldom seen in womanhood.

She was exceedingly handsome, however, and, despite the sorrow at his heart, our hero could not avoid an occasional glance over his paper at her.

At length an undefined impression crept over him that he had seen her before somewhere; yet, rack his memory as he might, he could not recall when and where.

Owing to the peculiarity of her appearance, it struck him that if he had once seen her he must certainly identify her, and at length concluded that he must be mistaken.

He reached the ferry, passed upon the boat, and seated himself in the cabin, where, upon raising his eyes, after a moment, he saw that strangely beautiful woman sitting directly opposite to him; and it was not long before he discovered, also, that he was the subject of her observation.

He left the boat and proceeded to his office; and as he passed through the door-way leading to the banking-house, he saw the same strange lady passing along on the opposite side of the street.

"Hang that pretty creature! I wonder if I have ever seen her before?"

Then a certain thought appeared to flash over his mind, a pallor overspread his face, and in a low, terrified tone, he muttered:

"Heavens! can it be possible that I am being spotted?"

As the suspicion flashed through his mind instinctively his hand rested on the spot over the pocket where the loaded pistol lay concealed, ready at any moment for its deadly suicidal purpose.

Henry Wilbur was not deceived by his memory.

The lady who sat opposite to him in the cars and ferry-boat, and who passed on the opposite side of the street when he entered his office, was Kate Goelet, the lady detective.

She had seen him when he parted from his mother; she had overheard even their parting words; and she had been "shadowing" him as surely as though she believed in his guilt.

Had she overheard what had passed between the young man and his mother the previous evening, she might have been somewhat staggered in her belief in his innocence.

The mere fear of a discharge from a situation does not usually lead a young man to meditate a violent death at his own hands.

Henry Wilbur was the victim of conscious guilt.

Every sense of suspicion was on the alert, every movement of every clerk and each member of the firm was watched with cat-like patience.

Any moment he feared a terrible discovery and an awful scene—ay, a tragedy!

He was living a life that can only be termed a "living hell." Conscience-seared, he stood day after day at his desk, and, being naturally a keen, nervous, observant man, his suspicions were aroused at the slightest incident.

In fact he led what may be termed a suspected life. He felt that his crime was known, and that the members of the firm were only waiting a fitting moment to brand him as a thief.

He felt that he was being shadowed. And when he met the strange-looking woman upon the car and ferry, and saw her pass his office, he at once, with guilty terror, conceived that he was being "piped" by one of those terrible scourges to the guilty—a detective.

The fact that the "shadow" appeared in the form of a woman was no relief to him. He knew that there were skillful detectives who could assume the guise of womanhood; and, besides, he knew that when necessity required, there was a corps of lady detectives on hand to "pipe" and prepare the way for more able-bodied officers.

During the course of the day Henry Wilbur was standing unintentionally close to the partition that separated the private offices of the firm from the main office.

His quick ear detected a conversation between the junior member of the firm and the second partner.

The words caused his blood to run cold and his heart to stand still.

It was the junior member of the firm, Mr. Cameron, who spoke, and his words carried an awful suggestion.

"What has been done regarding Mr. Wilbur?" was the question.

"The matter is in progress," answered Mr. Comstock.

"I fear you are making a mistake," said Cameron, in a cold tone.

"How?"

"Your bird will take flight."

"No, sir; he does not dream that he has been discovered, or even suspected."

"He is a cunning and deep rascal; I have been watching him closely, lately; he suspects more than you have any idea of, and you will learn, when too late, that I am right."

"The matter, Mr. Cameron, is in skillful hands, and in a few days Mr. Wilbur will be in jail, from whence he can not escape."

Had any of the other clerks observed the expression upon Henry Wilbur's face, as he staggered across that counting-room, they would have thought that a ghost was walking in their midst.

Henry Wilbur, however, was a man of iron nerve.

Within a few moments a desperate purpose had entered his heart.

His resolution caused him to become perfectly calm.

The color returned to his cheeks and the brightness to his eyes, and he went about his duties as calmly as though it were not to be his last day on earth.

How little did that young man dream how, having plotted against himself, a higher fate had ordained that out of his contemplated death should blossom life! That same night told a thrilling tale.

CHAPTER V.

ON THE BRINK OF PERIL.

HENRY remained at his office until the hour came for the bank to close.

Not a soul of all those with whom he exchanged the friendly good-night dreamed of the fearful purpose that he had formed.

He went to a restaurant, sat down, and partook of a hearty dinner.

Opposite to him sat a young, boyish-looking man.

Henry was so absorbed in his own dark thoughts that he failed to notice a pair of handsome blue eyes fastened upon him.

The young man thought that all his dark purposes were concealed in his own brain; but, strangely enough, a magnetic nature sitting near him, by some weird influence, had half read his purpose upon his calm brow.

Not the details of all his plan, but enough to create a desire to watch him.

Henry eat, drank, and left the restaurant, proceeding up town to a billiard-room.

Had he noticed the young man in the restaurant, he would have been startled to see him in the billiard-room; but not having noticed the " shadow " in the first instance, his attention was not attracted in the second.

Night fell, and Henry Wilbur came forth and sauntered down Broadway.

It was after ten o'clock.

He strolled into Union Square Park.

Throwing himself upon a rustic seat, he removed his hat, and a long-drawn sigh fell from his lips.

He looked around him, and seemed to be alone.

He did not observe a lithe, graceful form stretched upon the grass along the shadow of the trunk of a giant tree.

His overcharged heart could not restrain the audible words that struggled to his lips.

"Heavens!" he muttered, " what a hell is my life, and what a hell am I preparing for my poor mother! Oh! my God!" he sobbed, " my mother, my poor, poor mother! but it will be better, ay, far better. For sorrow must come! Did I do different, it would be the longer drawn out; now, one agony, one sharp scream of terrible misery, and then God will send her peace! But were it otherwise, alas! the disgrace would cling forever."

A moment the young man sat silent, then again he spoke. The second time his voice was hard and resolute—the tenderness and pathos had vanished.

"It is the cast of the last die," he said. "I have played a deep game; I must play it once more—to win or to lose! If I lose, all is lost! And then—well, well, no danger—I'll not fail myself."

Henry Wilbur rose from his seat, clapped his hat upon his head, and walked toward the north-west exit from the park.

His shadow still close behind him.

Every word that he had uttered was overheard by a pair of sharp ears, and the heart that responded to the knowledge was sad and heavy.

Kate Goelet had experienced strange emotions since first her eyes had rested upon the handsome face of Henry Wilbur.

The latter was beyond question one of the handsomest men in New York.

He combined great beauty with that appearance of decisive manliness which has such a charm for the female heart.

Henry had drunk considerable, both in the restaurant and during the time he had been in the billiard-room.

At length he stopped in front of a famous gambling " hell."

Once he passed up the stoop of the brown-stone gambling-palace, his hand was upon the bell knob, but it was withdrawn, and he descended the stoop.

At the bottom he met a slender-framed young man.

The latter addressed him, and his words showed that he had been a witness of Henry's movements.

"Young man, follow the good impulse: do not enter that place."

Harry was excited with wine, and asked, in a harsh, fierce voice:

"Who the devil are you?"

"A stranger who would urge you to refrain from entering that place."

"What do you know about that place?"

"I've been there."

"Oh! you have? Well, there's one place it's evident you have not been."

"Where is that?"

"Where you were taught to mind your own business," was the savage retort.

"I have intended no offense."

"And you will give none if you go on about your business."

"One word, young man, remember your mother."

Henry Wilbur was half crazed; in his state of mind, filled with the terrible purpose he had determined upon, he did not stop to consider right nor wrong, nor motive, good or bad.

The stranger's words stung him, and at the moment sounded to his ears as a sort of taunt; his great, strong arm was upraised quickly and the well-advising stranger went reeling into the street.

Up the stoop Henry leaped, and rang the bell.

The rude act he had just performed appeared to have excited all the demon in his nature.

The violence of his passion appeared an instant later to have subsided, and he realized that his conduct had been very brutal.

His naturally good heart caused him to regret his ill-judged temper, and, running down the steps, he advanced to assist his victim to his feet.

His services were not needed, however, as the stranger leaped to his feet without assistance.

Again Henry returned to the gambling-saloon, and, without further ado, passed the fatal portals.

He had determined to take his last chance—to cast the last die—and, in case of failure, resort to that last refuge so often sought by maddened and desperate men.

In the meantime, the victim of Henry's brutal rudeness had risen to his feet, and, as he rubbed the side of his head, muttered:

"My lucky face!—had that blow taken me squarely, the long-dreaded catastrophe would have come, and I should have been doomed to be a thief-taker all my life."

Thus muttering, the stranger passed up the street, when a most singular transformation scene occurred.

The light wig was removed, and one as black as a raven's wing substituted. A mustache suddenly appeared where the lip had been smooth; as quickly and as completely a change of dress followed, and the puny-faced little gent of the restaurant and billiard-room was transformed into quite a dashing-looking man of very Frenchified appearance.

It was evident that the transformed eccentricity had not been discouraged by the treatment he had received.

He advanced to the gambling-saloon, rang the bell, and was admitted.

What passed beneath that roof it is not for us to record.

The strange being who had been watching every movement of Henry Wilbur, remained at his side like a shadow until, in a fit of desperation, the young man, after having cast the last die and lost, hastened from the place.

The stranger, on the alert, followed, and was close upon the young man's track ready to intervene in case some rash deed were attempted.

Once in the street Henry passed toward the river.

With noiseless step the stranger followed.

Straight toward the river glided the pursued and the pursuer.

As though the desperate youth's purpose had been revealed to him, the stranger appeared to understand it.

The river was reached.

The night was dark and Henry seemed hardly to know for a moment what course to take.

At length, after waiting the passage of a policeman, he stole across the street and started out toward the end of the pier.

The stranger followed, uttering no cry for help nor signal for assistance.

At the extreme end of the pier he saw Henry mounted upon the string-piece—one plunge and he would be in the river.

With a noiseless tread, and as swiftly as the tiger springs upon his prey, the stranger leaped forward.

With a savage cry, Henry turned upon the man whose meddling hand had averted the wild, mad act.

The young man evidently had run stark mad.

"Fiend!" he hissed, "you would save me, and, by the gods! now shall you go first, and then I'll follow you!"

He caught the light form of the stranger in his firm grasp, and madly he rushed toward the string-piece.

The latter was but a feather in his clutch.

"Henry Wilbur, what would you do?"

The young man stopped; he set the stranger upon his feet. Reason for a moment appeared to have returned.

The mention of his name seemed to recall him to reason.

"You know me?" he said.

"I do."

"Who are you?"

"You would not know me."

"Ah, ha!" almost screamed the young man, as a fit of madness appeared once more to come upon him; "I see: you have been tracking me! Ha, ha! you would save me only to hand me over to the law! No, no! you have put yourself in the clutches of the lion! By heavens! nothing shall save you! Together we will take the mad leap! You shall not escape! In my grasp I'll hold you beneath the waters! Come, quick—say a prayer!"

"My only prayer, Henry Wilbur, is for you. Calm yourself; consider what you are doing."

"No, no! the hour for consideration on my part has passed. I did not bid you follow me. No living person must know my fate! You should not have followed me—you have come to your doom!"

"You must listen to me. Remember your mother!"

"Now, surely you shall die!" and with the glare of madness blazing in his eyes, Henry seized the stranger in his arms.

He had rushed toward the string-piece A moment and all would have been over.

"Mercy!" pleaded the stranger.

"Ha! ha! ha!" laughed the madman.

"Mercy!" again pleaded the stranger.

"You die!"

"Spare me—I am a woman!"

Henry Wilbur stepped back. Once more he stood the stranger down, and said, now in perfectly calm and reasonable tones:

"You are a woman?"

"Yes."

"What brought you here?"

"To save you."

"To save me?"

"Yes."

"What interest have you in me?"

"I can not tell you now, even to save my life."

"A woman! I can not take revenge upon a woman! my mother is a woman! But one thing you must promise me, woman."

"I will promise you anything."

"I spare you on one condition."

"Name it."

"The waters call for me; I go to them. On your knees swear that you will never disclose the fate of Henry Wilbur."

"Are you still determined to die?"

"I am."

"Then I die with you. My promise shall be kept in that way."

Henry was astounded. Had one of the firm come to him at that moment and told him all was right, he could not have been more astonished.

A moment he stood silent and irresolute, when his companion advanced and laid her hand upon his arm.

CHAPTER VI.

THE LADY DETECTIVE AS A SAVING ANGEL.

"HENRY WILBUR," said the party who had so strangely proclaimed herself a woman, "there is no need for you to destroy yourself. I know your secret!"

"You know my secret?"

"Yes."

"To what secret do you allude?"

"The secret that has caused you to seek to take your own life."

"If you speak truly, woman, you must know that you can not save me."

"I know that I can!"

"How came you to be the possessor of my secret?"

"At some future time I will tell you; but now let it suffice that I will prove your innocence."

"Prove my innocence?"

"Yes."

"Pray, woman, who are you?"

"It matters not; I would save not only your life, but your honor."

"You are certainly a mysterious person: pray how came you to be interested in my affairs?"

"That too shall be explained at some future time; but now promise me to be a man, and come away from that horrid water! Ugh! it makes me shudder—the thought of what might have occurred."

"If you are a female, why are you dressed in male attire?"

"You must wait for an explanation of that also."

"And you say you will prove me innocent?"

"I will."

"Then you do not know my secret."

At that moment a step was heard walking toward them along the pier.

Both turned, and two officers—ordinary policemen in full uniform—approached.

"What are you two doing on this pier at this hour?" came the question.

"We are just going home," answered Kate Goelet.

"I reckon it's to the station-house you will go and give an account of yourselves."

Henry Wilbur felt very blue just at that moment, and in his heart cursed the luck that had brought that mysterious *woman*, as she called herself, to interfere with him.

He knew what New York policemen were, and expected, as a matter of course, they would both be taken to the station.

Another idea flashed over his mind.

If his companion was really a woman, was not her sex likely to be discovered? and then what a nice position he would be in!

He was saved from any such dilemma, however, in a most extraordinary manner.

The woman advanced to the policemen, whispered a few words to them, and both departed as quietly as though the command had come from the chief of police.

"Now come with me," said our hero's companion.

The curiosity of the latter was aroused, and he concluded to follow her.

It was certainly a most extraordinary adventure, and had given, for the time being, a more normal turn to the drift of his thoughts.

The lady detective had formed a desperate resolution, and she was determined to carry it out that very night.

Disguised as she was, she was known at a certain public-house as the little Frenchman, and no one in the hotel had ever suspected or questioned her sex.

It chanced that the house in question was but twenty minutes' walk from the pier where a terrible tragedy had almost occurred.

Henry Wilbur followed the strange party at his side, determined to see the adventure through without asking any questions.

His companion did not appear disposed to talk, and they walked along in silence.

At length they arrived in front of a hotel, which Henry recognized as a great resort for sporting characters.

"We will enter here," said his strange companion.

A suspicion flashed over Henry's mind, and he was constrained to exclaim:

"Hold on! What is your purpose in entering this place?"

"I must see you alone."

"Do you know the character of this place?"

"I do; it is the resort of sporting men and 'knucks.'"

"And you, a woman, would enter such a place?"

"Oh, I am a man now, you know; and I know of no other place where we can gain entrance at this hour."

"All right; if you are not afraid, I do not know why I should be," answered Henry.

"I am not afraid. Come along: no one will have anything to say to us."

The lady detective had spent many an hour in that same house, laying for points for male detectives, and so cunningly had she performed her part that her real purpose had never been suspected.

Followed by Henry Wilbur, she passed through the barroom, which was occupied by quite a number of hard-looking men.

With some she exchanged greetings, and others she passed with merely a nod.

Henry followed his strange conductress out into a lighted hallway, up a pair of stairs, and along a second hall, until she stopped in front of a door on which was a number.

She placed her hand upon the knob as though to enter, when a certain recollection flashed over Henry's mind.

"Is it best for me to enter that room?" he asked.

"Desperate cases require desperate remedies. I must have a few words with you; one place is as fitting as another!" and with an impatient gesture the lady detective turned the knob, pushed the door open, and entered the room.

Without further dissent, Henry followed.

There was no furniture in the room, save a table and two chairs.

Our hero's companion pointed to a chair, and said: "Sit down!"

The light from the hall illuminated the room; but the strange woman struck a match, lit the gas, and pushed to the door, when she seated herself in the other chair directly opposite Henry.

Fixing her eyes upon him, she asked, sharply:
"What led you to attempt to take your life to-night?"
"You said you knew my secret."
"I do."
"Then you know why I attempted to take my life."
"But why should you seek to take your life, when you are really innocent; why should the innocent fear?"
"I thought you knew my secret?"
"I do, I repeat."
"Then you must know that I am not innocent."

The lady detective gave a start, and a frightened look overspread her face, as she exclaimed, interrogatively:
"You are not innocent?"
"See here, strange woman, who are you? and what interest have you in my fate?"
"There is no reason why I should not tell you. I am a detective. I have been 'piping' you for some days. I am employed to recover the bonds that were stolen from the firm of Attry, Comstock & Co."
"The bonds stolen from Attry, Comstock & Co.?"
"Yes."
"Great heavens! has a robbery been committed on that firm?"
"Yes."
"Strange I should know nothing about it," exclaimed the young man, in the most innocent manner possible.

A smile played over the lady detective's face.

The keen eyes had been fixed upon her companion, and she knew now that her first confidence was not misplaced, but at the same time another suspicion flashed over her mind.

"Yes," she said, "bonds to the value of one million dollars were stolen from the safe of the firm you serve, and you have been dogged and 'piped' for weeks as the thief."
"Great heavens! can this be true?"
"It is true; and now let me tell you that I know you are a defaulter, but you did not steal those bonds."

Henry Wilbur gazed in amazement, but at length he said: "Tell me all about this matter."

"No, no; first tell me how you came to appropriate the firm's money, how you became a defaulter, and then you shall hear what I have to say."

Henry gazed like one dazed at the extraordinary being sitting opposite him. He could hardly realize but what he was the victim of some strange delusion.

"Come," said his companion, "I am your friend! You will find me your rescuer: and you shall know in time why I have made your cause mine."

Henry Wilbur was a strong-nerved, self-willed man, and yet he was strangely under the influence of the magnetic little creature who sat opposite to him with her keen blue eyes fixed upon his face.

Again, in an impatient tone, Kate Goelet said:
"Come, come, tell me how you came to fall! Tell me the whole truth. You shall be saved, your honor saved; but tell me the whole truth."

After a moment's hesitation, Henry Wilbur said:
"It's the old, old story!"
"Well, let me hear the old, old story, and it may prove your salvation—yours and your mother's!"

CHAPTER VII.
THE OLD, OLD STORY.

THE allusion to our hero's mother touched a chord that no other appeal could have reached, and he said:
"A dear friend of mine came to me one day in dire distress, and wanted the loan of two hundred and fifty dollars. I did not have the money, and told him so."
"Ah! I see it is the old, old story," commented our hero's companion.
"My friend was engaged to be married; I knew well the lady, and I loved both of them as I would have loved a brother and sister, if I had had them."
"You yielded to your friend by lending what did not belong to you."
"Listen! I did not yield until he assured me that he only wanted the money for twenty-four hours. He told me that he needed it to save both life and honor. I knew that I had money in my possession that I could use without its loss being missed for weeks, if necessary, and, after much persuasion, I did yield, and let my friend have the money fully believing that within twenty-four hours I could return it from whence I took it."
"Your friend failed you?"
"He did; before twenty-four hours had passed my friend was dead. The money had come too late to save him, and he shot himself!"
"Then you are a defaulter to the amount of two hundred and fifty dollars?"
"Oh! would that it were only two hundred and fifty dollars!" moaned Henry.
"How much do you owe the firm?"
"Nearly three thousand dollars."
"How came the amount so large, when the original amount was only two hundred and fifty?"
"A week passed after my friend's death: my salary was already overdrawn, and I was almost frantic, fearing discovery."
"Go on; tell me all!"
"I had never been in the habit of staying out late nights, but I was too restless to remain home, and I wandered out nights; one night, with a chance acquaintance, I entered a faro-room."
"Ah! go on, I see," muttered the lady detective.
"I saw men winning large sums of money; in a few seconds a mad thought seized me. I thought that I might win enough to restore the money I had appropriated."
"Yes, yes, the same old, old story!" muttered the lady detective, meditatively.
"You know what followed. I need not say more. I lost, and lost, and lost; to-night you saw me make my last venture; again I was the loser, and then madly I resolved to die!"
"And I saved you!"
"You saved me from death, but can you save me from disgrace?"
"I can."
"Again, who are you?"
"Oh! my story is a commonplace one. I am but a plain woman, compelled like many other women to earn her own living, and I became an aid to a detective; there are some things in our profession that a woman can better perform than a man; you know all the great thieves are not men?"

Henry felt constrained to say:
"You must run great risk in your profession; you are weak in body, and you may be killed."
"Oh! I can take care of myself!" answered Kate Goelet, in a confident tone.
"How could you have taken care of yourself to-night, when I caught you in my arms and was rushing with you toward the docks?"
"Ah! had you been a thief with whom I was struggling,

and had it been only a question of saving my own life, I could have freed myself in an instant!"

"What, from me?"

"Yes."

"Pray, teach me how?"

The disguised woman raised her hands, and by some secret movement that Henry could not detect, she touched a spring that caused two slender stilettos, fully six inches in length, to shoot out from under her sleeve.

In a quaint, determined manner she said:

"I could have sent this through your heart. I do not fear men when they are foes, and bad."

"I would like to see you when not in disguise!" exclaimed Henry, involuntarily.

"I do not suppose you ever will. But now listen "—and the lady detective proceeded, and told our hero all about the stolen bonds; how he was suspected as the thief; and it was believed that there was a woman in the case, the latter fact leading to her own employment in tracing the stolen property.

Henry was amazed, and, in a reflective tone, said:

"This accounts for Mr. Cameron's strange watchfulness."

"Has Mr. Cameron watched you lately?"

"He has. And I have always suspected that he knew of my defalcation. I knew nothing of the stolen bonds."

The lady detective was silent and thoughtful for a few moments; but at length, in a business-like tone, she asked:

"Henry Wilbur, are you a man of nerve?"

"Well, I used to think I was, but my nerve appears to have failed me lately."

"If the money you have used from the bank were restored, do you think you could, as an innocent man, go through a very trying ordeal for a good purpose and a rich reward?"

"I do not understand you."

The lady detective repeated her words.

"As an innocent man I could go through anything!"

"Could you stand to appear guilty for awhile, knowing that in the end your innocence would be established?"

"I could!"

"If you can, you and I together can run down the real robber of the million dollars in bonds!"

"Then you suspect some one?"

"I do."

"Who?"

"In our business we make no confidants until our work is accomplished; it is enough for you to know that the real robber has skillfully cast a most damning net-work of circumstantial evidence about you; and, although I am but a woman, I do say, had I not come into the case, you would have been convicted as the thief!"

"No; I would have been lying at the bottom of the Hudson!"

"Your memory would have been damned! And your mother?"

"Oh, hush! do not mention my poor mother! I shudder when I think of the fearful calamity that came so near to her but for you!"

"Meet me to-morrow; go to the office—act as usual—meet me at noon, and you shall be a free, honest man once more!"

Henry Wilbur parted from the remarkable woman who had so strangely become mingled in his concerns.

The lady detective accompanied him to the door and parted from him.

As Henry walked down toward the ferry on his way to Brooklyn, his thoughts were strange indeed.

He was like one in a dream!

There were a thousand questions he would like to have put to the woman who had saved him against himself, but a sense of delicacy restrained him.

Some people are peculiarly and sensitively conscious to certain impressions.

Henry had sat directly opposite to that disguised woman, with her blue eyes fixed upon his, and at moments when she addressed him a certain expression beamed in her orbs, the memory of which caused a strange flutter at his heart.

His thoughts found utterance in mutterings. "Some raw-featured, homely, cunning woman, I suppose, smart as a steel trap; and yet those women are sometimes capable of an intense passion. Why should she be so interested in my fate? Toward what am I rushing, should she free

me to-morrow? She can command my gratitude, but, by Heaven, what more may she expect?"

Henry Wilbur could not fail to recognize the importance and value, in one respect, of his personal advantages; and vanity and self-conceit are not confined altogether to the bosom of females.

Upon the following morning Henry was at his desk, when the same strange old woman, Rebecca Brown, called at the banking-office.

The porter announced her presence to Mr. Comstock, and she was admitted.

It chanced that upon the occasion of her second visit, Mr. Comstock was alone in the private offices.

The doors communicating with the outer offices were closed.

"Well?" exclaimed Mr. Comstock, interrogatively.

"It is well so far, and I have discovered that your original suspicions were correct, there is a woman in the case."

"Have you discovered her?"

"I think I have."

"Is she young?"

"No; not very."

"Who is she?"

"I can not tell until I get through, but of one thing be assured, the bonds are held intact, not one of them has been negotiated."

"You amaze me!"

"You will be still more amazed; but I have an order to present," and the lady detective handed the banker a written note.

The latter glanced at it, and assumed a thoughtful attitude.

The note was an order for three thousand dollars, an installment on the eventual reward; the chief, who was a man of large means, offered to consider the amount a loan if the bonds were not recovered.

After a moment's thought, in a very solemn manner, peculiar to moneyed men when giving out checks, Mr. Comstock said:

"This is all I shall advance."

CHAPTER VIII.
CLOSING IN ON CLEWS.

AT the appointed hour, Henry Wilbur was at the corner named for his appointment with the lady detective.

He was anxious and expectant, and was pacing the sidewalk in an abstracted manner, when a hand was suddenly laid upon his arm.

He looked up, and encountered the old woman who had been in the banking-house upon two occasions.

In a shrill voice, she exclaimed:

"Young man, you seem to be in a bad way! What's the matter? Have you a headache, or troubled with dyspepsia? 'Cause if you are, I kin jest recommend something that will do you a world of good."

Our hero was taken clean aback, and, in an impatient tone, answered:

"When I want medical advice, old lady, I'll let you know!"

"Well, now, I didn't mean no offense, only I saw you tramping up and down the sidewalk, and I thought you might be ailing. You should never git mad at people whose intentions are good!"

Henry regretted his impatient manner, and said:

"You must excuse me, old lady; I did not mean to be cross; but, really, there is nothing the matter with me, and I have no need for your good offices."

"Well, I have for yours. I am a stranger, and an old woman, and I want you to just come and show me where Exchange Place may be."

"On right down this street, cross two others and you are in Exchange Place."

"Come along and show me, may be my eyesight ain't good."

"I have not the time."

"Ah, you are ashamed to be seen walking with an old woman! Well, well, I'll go, and if I find it, not much thanks to you!"

Henry was really a noble-hearted fellow, and glancing at his watch, he saw that he was a little ahead of time, and he started in pursuit of the old lady, and upon overtaking her, said, in a kindly voice:

"I have a moment to spare. I will walk with you to Exchange Place, and hurry back to keep my appointment."

"Well, now, see here, young man, may be you can save me the trouble of going to Exchange Place?"

Henry stood aghast, but was a hundred times more astonished when the strange old lady went on, and said:

"I've just got three thousand dollars I want some one to carry to a young man named Henry Wilbur. You look like an honest young man, and may be you can just run down with it to him."

"Three thousand dollars for Henry Wilbur, did you say?"

"Exactly!"

"I am Henry Wilbur, old lady, but, upon my word, you astonish me!" And the same instant Henry recollected himself, and added: "Great Heaven! Am I talking with my benefactor of last night?"

A low laugh came from behind the green veil, and the words:

"You are."

"I would never have known you."

"Here is the money; make good your account. Be careful in doing so that you do not betray yourself in making restoration."

"Heaven bless you!" murmured Henry Wilbur, as tears of gratitude filled his eyes.

"Never mind about blessing me; it's all right. We must not be seen talking together. I may want your assistance in a day or two. Hold yourself in readiness"—and after the hurried words recorded, the old woman resumed her screechy way of speaking, and continued:

"Well, I'm much obliged to you, young man. I kin git along all right now, and when you git old and half blind, may ye find good friends to lead you right through the crowded city!"

An instant later, and Henry Wilbur was standing alone.

The old lady had mysteriously disappeared in the crowd.

Our hero stood with the money in his hand; his salvation from disgrace, from punishment; ay, indeed, from death at his own hands! and he owed all to the mysterious and extraordinary creature who had so strangely become his friend.

The young man could hardly realize that he was not dreaming. It did not seem that the money was real, so wonderfully had it come into his possession.

He walked down a side street, and fastened his eyes upon it. It was there; he was awake; it was no dream, and he was saved!

He returned to the bank; an hour later, and his accounts were properly adjusted, and he could fix his handsome eyes upon any man living in their old-time fearless manner.

Extraordinary are the dealings of fate.

That same afternoon, Mr. Cameron came to Henry Wilbur, and said, in a cool, business-like manner, that he would go over certain accounts with him.

Mr. Cameron had once been book-keeper of the house, and had been promoted to junior partner.

He was an expert accountant.

The accounts that he demanded to go over would have exposed the defalcation.

Thanks to the angel who had come to our hero's rescue, he was able to say in a cheerful voice:

"Certainly, Mr. Cameron, my books are open for your inspection!"

A cold gleam shone in Mr. Cameron's eyes, and had one read his secret thoughts, the reading would have been:

"He thinks he has doctored those books. Well, well, see if I can be deceived."

The examination took place, and everything was found correct.

A person having an inkling of certain facts, who might have been watching Mr. Cameron's face, would have observed an expression thereon that plainly expressed:

"By George! I have been baffled!"

It was evident that Mr. Cameron had gone into the examination prepared to make a startling discovery.

His words to Mr. Comstock after the examination betrayed him.

"Hang it!" he said, addressing his partner in an undertone, "I do not understand it! The fellow's books are as straight as a string; it would be impossible for him to deceive me, as I studied just those points where deception would be attempted."

Mr. Comstock's remarks let out another secret concerning Mr. Cameron, proving that the latter individual was the original party to direct suspicion toward Henry Wilbur as the robber of the bonds.

"It may be possible that young Wilbur is as innocent of the theft of the bonds as he is of being deficient in his accounts?"

A dark frown came over the junior partner's face as he answered:

"I do not know how you can express such a doubt of his guilt after the facts I have furnished."

"Of course your facts leave no doubt of his guilt, and yet he is a young man whom I have always admired, and the last one whom I should have suspected, had it not been for the evidence you have furnished."

That same evening Mr. Cameron called upon a lady living in magnificent apartments, in a certain fashionable neighborhood.

The lady sat in the midst of the gorgeous furniture placed in the room.

She was a stately looking woman, remarkably handsome, and yet there was a coldness about her face and a steely glance in her eyes not at all attractive to a keen observer.

The latter also, despite the lady's beauty and the magnificence of her apparel, would have detected an underlying coarseness about her, proving that she had not been born to high breeding and culture.

Mr. Cameron, the junior partner of the great banking firm, was shown into the lady's presence.

At the office he had proclaimed her a relative, but the manner in which he approached, at the time of which we are writing, and his salutation, were hardly that which a male relative might render to a niece or a cousin.

Mr. Cameron advanced and clasped her in his arms, and essayed to imprint a kiss upon her red lips.

With a disdainful toss of her head, the magnificent woman drew her face back, and rudely untwining herself from his embrace, pushed him from her.

"Why, Julia, are you offended with me?"

"I am."

Mr. Cameron turned pale; passion of the most flaming type gleamed in his eyes, and it was evident that his sensitive heart was alarmed, as, in an anxious tone, he exclaimed:

"My precious darling, what have I done now to merit your disfavor?"

"You treat me in the most miserly manner. I want money—money! You promised me wealth, all that my heart could desire, when I yielded to your love, and how have you fulfilled your promise?"

As the magnificent woman spoke, she raised her handkerchief to her eyes, and her bosom heaved as though she were struggling to suppress the ready sobs bursting from her lips.

"Julia, have you any idea as to the amount of money I have supplied you with during the last few months?"

"A few thousands! Bah! had I not loved you, and had I accepted another love that was offered to me, I might have had millions even, had I wished."

"And so you shall in time; just wait until I have carried through a certain speculation I am engaged in, and every wish shall be gratified."

At this moment a neat-looking maid entered the room.

In a tone of alarm, Mr. Cameron whispered:

"Who is that?"

CHAPTER IX.

DEEP PLAY.

"My new maid," was the answer of the woman who went by the name of *Mrs.* Cameron.

"How long have you had her in your employ?"

"Two days."

"Discharge her at once!"

"Discharge her?"

"Yes."

"Why, pray?"

"I will tell you, Julia. I am a man governed by impressions. When that girl entered the room I felt a cold chill run through me. I feel that in some way she will prove inimical to me. You must discharge her."

"How ridiculous, and how superstitious!"

"Never mind—it is my wish."

"And you expect me to discharge the most skillful maid I ever had, simply because you feel chilly at the moment she entered the room?" and Mrs. Cameron laughed in a satirical manner.

"I had hoped you would show more attention to my wishes."

"Why, Tom, I would sooner surrender you than part with that French girl! She is invaluable! She is just the party I have been longing to secure all my life."

"A French girl, is she?"

"Yes; and she can not speak one word of English."

"Are you sure?"

"I am. Why, dearie, she has not been in this country two weeks yet!"

"Well, I do not mind, then, if what you say is true; but you know maids are great eavesdroppers, and that girl, if she understood English, might overhear certain admissions from me that would prove ruinous."

"You need have no fears."

Had those two people known that the party they were speaking about was at that moment bending with her ear at the key-hole, with a look of intelligence upon her face that betrayed the fact that she understood every word that was being spoken at that very moment, it is more than likely that Mr. Cameron would have experienced a second chill that would have almost frozen his heart's blood.

Mr. Cameron was a shrewd, cunning man, and he did not exactly feel satisfied that the new maid did not understand English, and he determined to fully satisfy himself upon this point.

"Julia," he said, "call that girl into the room on some pretense."

"Why?"

"I wish to satisfy myself that you have not been deceived in some way."

"Nonsense!"

"It is a small favor."

"Lydia!" called Mrs. Cameron.

The maid came into the room, looking as innocent and demure as a coy school-girl.

Mrs. Cameron addressed some words to the maid in French, while Mr. Cameron said, in a loud voice, and in English:

"Why, Julia, where did you get that girl from? She is a thief!—her picture hangs in the rogues' gallery!"

When Mr. Cameron made this terrible charge his keen eyes were fixed upon the maid's face.

Not the least sign did she give of understanding the fearful charge that had been made against her.

Her eyes looked straight before her; not a change of color came to her cheeks; she could not have been more perfectly indifferent if she had been deaf and dumb.

Indignation beamed, however, upon the countenance of Mrs. Cameron, and she exclaimed:

"What do you mean?"

"I mean that I shall send for a policemen, and have that girl arrested at once!"

Still the girl looked as coy and unconcerned as she had upon first entering the room.

Mrs. Cameron, in French, dismissed her, and, turning to her pretended husband, said:

"What do you mean by such language?"

"Oh, I was only in fun!"

"But why insult the girl?"

"If she can not speak English, how can it be an insult?"

"Oh, thank you. I see now you were testing her. Well, what is your conclusion?"

"I'll swear that she does not understand one word of English. It would have been impossible for any woman living not to have made some sign, if she had understood the nature of a charge so suddenly made."

Had Mr. Cameron heard that same maid murmur in good English a moment later when beyond his presence:

"It was a cunning ruse, Mr. Cameron; but I was prepared for you, and am glad you tested me, my man. I will have less trouble in running you down."

After the episode described, Mrs. Cameron returned to the subject of money.

"When can you let me have a few thousands, Tom?"

"Not until I have carried through my speculation."

"Can not a rich banker like you draw a check for a few thousand?"

"You must remember that I am but a junior member of the firm. I have drawn so much money lately that I fear every day my seniors will call my attention to the fact; and to draw a few thousand more just at present would most certainly invite the catastrophe I dread."

"See here, Tom," said Mrs. Cameron, in a low, decisive tone, "I must have five thousand dollars this week."

"I can not let you have it."

Mrs. Cameron lowered her voice, and said, in what was almost a whisper:

"Why not negotiate one of the bonds?"

"It would be a fatal act, woman!" said the man, in a husky whisper, while a deathly pallor overspread his face.

"I could get one of them cashed, Tom, without any risk."

"No, no, woman, do not tempt me: it would ruin us both."

"I have a scheme. I know a plan that would work snug and safe."

"I tell you, do not tempt me."

"Then you and I must part! Thousands have been laid at my feet as an offer to leave you, and you know, Tom, our marriage vows lie so lightly upon us that it would be easy to get a divorce; remember that even your own partners do not know me as your wife."

"Oh, Julia! you will drive me mad!"

"And I will go mad unless I have the money; if you would but listen to my plan all would be well!"

"What is your plan?"

"It is one that would bring the whole matter to a head: send a man whom you know to be a rogue to jail and give you a chance to work up the bonds, all of them!"

"Who is the man who is a rogue?"

"That fellow Wilbur."

"Hang it! I fear that fellow is innocent!"

"Nonsense! Have you not yourself beheld him lose a thousand dollars at the faro-table on a salary less than two thousand?"

"But I dropped on him to-day, examined his books, and found his accounts all right."

"Indeed!"

"Yes."

"Well, Tom, you are green!" said the woman, in a sarcastic tone.

"How?"

"Do you not know that a faro-bank owner would loan him a few thousand to show up with for a day or two? Examine his books one week from now; do it unawares, and you will catch him."

"There is something in that."

"You will find that I am right."

"What is your plan, Julia?"

"I know a man who for a few hundred dollars will take one of these bonds, and negotiate it."

"And would be detected!"

"Exactly!"

"What are you driving at?"

"Why, that is just the contingency he would be prepared for: the man would swear that he got the bond from Henry Wilbur; and what is more, we can arrange to have him in the man's company for a few days, so as to have disinterested witnesses to corroborate the man's story."

"Should the man fail us in the end?"

"He would die before he would fail us."

"I would fear even if the man were my brother."

"I would fear your brother, but not mine."

"Is the man you would employ your brother?"

"I would trust no other man."

"By George, Julia! you are a genius, to confess the truth; although a member of the firm, my accounts would not stand an overhauling. I must have money."

"When will you be prepared to meet my brother?"

"Any time."

"All right. I will arrange for you to meet him to-morrow night. He will carry this matter through nicely."

"Why do you not make the arrangement with your brother?"

"I am a woman. I could suggest a plan; I could not carry it out."

Cameron remained some time longer with the siren who had lured him to the robbery, and who was again luring him to certain destruction.

Having carried her point, she was pleasant and agreeable, and during the remainder of his visit she resorted to all those little endearments calculated to charm an already infatuated man to his destruction.

The two conspirators had well laid their plan as they supposed; but had either of them seen the smile of triumph upon the face of the French girl in the adjoining room, they would both have recoiled as though the gulf of perdition had yawned before them.

Half an hour after the departure of Mr. Cameron, another man was shown into the presence of Mrs. Cameron, showing that she too had need of a French maid who could not speak English.

CHAPTER X.

A LITTLE SCHEME IN THE BONDS.

"WELL, has the old lamb gone?" was the remark of a fashionably dressed young man, as he sauntered into the room.

"He has gone, Dick, and I have brought him around to let one of the bonds go flying in the air."

The young man, Dick, was a good-looking fellow, although his beauty, when closely scrutinized, would have panned out the same as Mrs. Cameron's, of the vulgar sort.

Again the French maid entered, when the fellow, Dick, like his predecessor, asked, the moment she had left the room:

"Who in thunder is that gal, Jule?"

"My new maid."

"By George! and she is a beauty. Where did you pick her up?"

"Oh, she came recommended to me; she is a French girl, and can not speak a word of English."

A strange light beamed in Dick's eyes, but he made no further remark concerning the girl at that moment; he had more important business on hand.

"You say your old lamb is going to let one of the bonds fly?"

"Yes."

"Who negotiates?"

"I have arranged for that little matter to be intrusted to you."

"It's risky; the Wall Street 'kites' are 'hovering close in' just now."

"Are you a coward?"

"Oh, no, sis, I'll run the string out; only you know you must let your lambie understand that he must come down handsome when it's a 'tickler.'"

"You're a fool, Dick!"

"How's that?"

"Don't you know that I intend to get every dollar of that little 'lift,' and then you and I will take the grand tour?"

"Very nice, my darling, but I tell you that you underrate your lamb. Cameron is awful soft on you, I'll admit, but his eyes are love-dusted just at this moment; if ever he gets over his infatuation, look out; he's a stocky man, keen as a whistle, and game; at the last moment he will astonish you, my dear."

"I will take all risks, and now to business; to-morrow night he is to meet you, and hand over a part of the swag. Where shall the meeting be?"

"At Doric's."

The place named was the same where Kate Goelet, the lady detective, had held her interview with Henry Wilbur, after having saved the young man's life.

"What room?"

"Room 20."

"What hour?"

"Ten o'clock."

"Say later."

"Why?"

"Well, it is better for mice to move when all in the house are asleep."

"Make it twelve."

"Good."

* * * * * * *

In a former chapter we mentioned that Kate Goelet had followed Mr. Cameron's visitor upon the first occasion when the lady detective saw her leave the banking-house.

Our heroine had tracked the woman to her home, but speedily reappeared in the vicinity and was just in time to see Mrs. Cameron leave her house.

The latter lady reached the corner of the street when she

beheld a young, lady-like-looking girl, standing against the iron rail of a fence weeping.

Mrs. Cameron stopped to inquire the cause of the girl's sorrow.

The weeping maiden indicated that she could not speak English, and made a reply in French.

It chanced that Mrs. Cameron's father had been a Frenchman, and the woman spoke the language well.

In a tearful manner the weeping girl told how she had come from Paris, and how on the steamer, in the steerage, she had been robbed of all her effects, and, further, how she had paid her board for one week by the sale of a few ornaments, but that now all her money was gone, and she had been turned penniless from her boarding-house.

"What brought you to this country?"

"To get a situation as lady's-maid."

"Are you a skillful hair-dresser?"

"Oh, madame, I have served the best ladies in Paris."

Mrs. Cameron was a woman who cared little about recommendations, and, as shrewd as she was in one sense, could be easily imposed upon.

She believed the French girl's tale, and determined to employ her.

That same evening her skill as a hair-dresser was put to the test, and her wonderful manipulation of the madame's hair won the latter's heart.

The French girl had asked permission to go away that night and return the following afternoon, stating that she had some little business to arrange.

Permission was granted, and the lady detective managed to accomplish all that has been related, and at the proper time returned to her mistress.

The following night, at twelve, the one bond was to be put on the fly.

Kate Goelet knew that she must be on hand.

The day following the scenes related, Mr. Cameron called again upon the woman who bore his name.

The details for the midnight meeting were arranged, and the sly Kate Goelet secured all the points of the intended conspiracy.

The lady detective had laid well her plans, and was prepared to take long chances.

At about half past eleven, four men entered the house of the man whom Dick Coulter had denominated as "Doric."

The whole party were under the leadership of a little man, whom the sitters around the place addressed as "Frenchy," and it appeared that his companions were Frenchmen also.

The party proceeded to room 19, and at once a singular scene occurred.

They all removed their boots; two of them produced strange-looking little glasses, and the chairs and table were arranged against the wall separating room 19 from No. 20.

The party of four had been in the room but a few moments, when steps were heard in the hall, and a party entered the adjoining room.

At once the four Frenchies leaped noiselessly upon the chairs and table, and assumed a suspicious position, indicating that they were bent upon watching some little transaction about to occur in room 20.

Among the number in room 20 was Dick Coulter; the latter had made no effort to conceal his identity.

The second party was a stranger, and the third man was none other than Mr. Cameron, junior partner in the banking firm of Attry, Comstock & Co.

Dick Coulter was the first spokesman, and in an easy, off-handed tone, he said:

"I believe you have a few bonds you want to convert, Mr. Cameron?"

"Conditionally."

"Ah! what are your conditions?"

"A knowledge, in the first place, as to how you intend to dispose of them."

"I shall place them in the hands of a man who is up to the racket from beginning to end."

"What is the man's name?"

"Young."

"What Young? the broker whose office is in New Street?"

"The same."

Mr. Cameron appeared surprised. He knew Mr. Young was a man who bore a fine reputation on the street as an honest, straightforward man.

"Do you mean to tell me that Young deals in off-color bonds?"

"He deals in nothing else—only at times, as a blind."

"You know who I am?"

"Yes, sir."

"By what name would you address me if you saw me on the street?"

Dick Coulter winked, and said, in a significant tone:

"It would be strange if I did not know Henry Wilbur, the man I have spent a good many nights in company with, tiger-hunting."

"Has any one seen you in my company?"

"Yes."

"When?"

"Last night."

"They are all well dusted who saw us together?"

"You bet! I know my business right up to the handle."

"Your friend there—he knows me?"

"He could swear to you on a stack of law books as high as the court-house, without winking."

"How long do you suppose it will be before the bonds are dropped on after Young has them?"

"You must arrange that yourself."

"How?"

"You must set a detective on Young's track."

"Then he will be arrested."

"Of course."

"And he will 'squeal'?"

"Certainly."

"And to save himself, expose the whole affair?"

"No, sir; he can only 'squeal' on me. I will be arrested, and then I can turn State's evidence, and prove from whom I received the bonds."

Mr. Cameron was thoughtful awhile, and at length said:

"It's a magnificent scheme; but, after all, it depends upon your gameness."

"I run no risk in the matter, and the whole affair will go through like oil."

CHAPTER XI.

THE MEETING IN "ROOM TWENTY."

MR. CAMERON exchanged a few more words with his cool confederate, and then handed over a number of bonds.

While in that room the three rogues presented a splendid life-like tableau.

Dick Coulter and Cameron sat in such a manner that both their faces were plainly revealed toward the partition dividing them from the adjoining room, No. 19.

Had the conspirators known of the extraordinary little occurrences transpiring so near them they would have recoiled in horror.

At the proper moment our readers shall be informed of the wonderful detective operation performed in that room.

Having delivered the bonds, after a few more words of caution, Mr. Cameron departed.

A few moments later, and the mysterious occupants of room No. 19 also departed.

The day following the scene above recorded the French girl was serving her mistress as quietly and demurely as though nothing extraordinary was going on.

At a late hour in the afternoon Mr. Cameron called at the home of the lady who pretended to bear his name.

He was always a quiet, cunning man, sly as a cat, and on the alert to make discoveries.

He was an exceedingly jealous and suspicious man, and as he was passing through the hall toward the front room of the apartments occupied by Mrs. Cameron, an impulse caused him to stop in front of the door of the rear room and peep through the key-hole.

He saw the French maid seated at a table writing.

The circumstance, though but a trifling one, aroused his suspicions.

He changed his position several times, and at length walked away, with a very troubled look upon his face.

Mr. Cameron carried a night-key to the apartments, and inserting it in the lock, he turned it noiselessly, and stole into the room as a sneak-thief would.

He found the room unoccupied, when he performed a very singular act; he removed his boots without making any noise, and on tiptoe moved through the passage leading from the front to the back room.

The door opening into the latter was ajar.

Opposite the opening, hanging upon the wall, was a mirror.

By looking into the mirror he could see the reflected form of the French maid, and what was more startling, he saw reflected also the paper upon which she was writing.

A cold chill passed over his frame as a suspicion flashed across his mind.

From his pocket he drew a small pocket-glass; the latter he held in such a manner that the written page in front of the French maid was reflected.

His face assumed the hue of death.

He could decipher but a few words, but they were *English*.

After all, his first suspicions were correct.

The supposed green French maid was a fraud.

It was certain she could write English if she could not speak it, but the most certain conclusion was that she could do both.

Mr. Cameron moved back into the front room, replaced his boots, and for an instant considered what he should do.

At length he resolved to boldly enter the room, seize the written page, and to her face accuse the cunning French girl of duplicity.

Ere he could carry out his resolution a most remarkable little incident occurred.

He heard the French girl coming through the passage.

She was warbling a tune as innocently and happily as a bird.

As she entered the room and saw Mr. Cameron she uttered a pretty little scream of surprise, started to leave the room in confusion, returned as though to approach him, turned about again, and still again returned, and approaching Mr. Cameron, in a pretty, timid manner, and while blushing to the temples, said, at the same moment, holding forth a written page:

"Ah, monsieur! I bes bold! you loak at ze lisson in English, eh?"

Mr. Cameron glanced at the written page. It was the same he had seen reflected in the mirror, and it was scribbled over alternately with French and English sentences.

The man was amazed.

He spoke to her, and she held toward him a French and English dictionary.

He spoke to her again, and she shook her head negatively, and in the most frank and innocent manner said, "I learn English quick."

Mr. Cameron felt that he had been mistaken, and his fears were allayed.

It was not possible that the girl was acting; such a conclusion would have been too extravagantly improbable.

The cunning man did not dream that the tell-tale mirror had reflected two ways, and that he was at that moment the victim of the finest piece of acting ever performed by a human being.

The scene had just closed when Mrs. Cameron entered, and the French girl, uttering a few words of explanation in French, left the room.

While talking to Mr. Cameron she held concealed in her pocket the fragment of a note, addressed to Henry Wilbur.

"I have had quite a fright!" observed Mr. Cameron, when he and the woman were alone.

"What frightened you? Has my maid been making love to you?"

"No, but I had, as I thought, proof that she was an impostor."

"Nonsense!" exclaimed the woman, while Mr. Cameron proceeded and related what had occurred.

Mrs. Cameron said, "Oh, nonsense!" and pretended to pass the matter off as a great joke, but she was herself a deep and cunning woman.

She resolved to watch that innocent French girl.

No suspicion entered her mind as to the real truth, but she had other little private reasons.

If the stranger was playing a part it was a deep game, and the designing woman within the moment had framed in her mind some very startling deductions.

After the departure of Mr. Cameron, she sat down, and soon commenced some very profound thinking.

The wicked and treacherous are always suspicious, and a suspicious woman will let her feelings, when once aroused, run away with her reason, as a prairie fire rushes roaring madly through the dry grass.

When she came to think, it struck her as strange that the girl should have met her so conveniently; then, again, it was strange that Mr. Cameron should have *suspected* the girl without cause.

The woman was now in a perfect frenzy of suspicion.

It was suggested to her mind that Mr. Cameron's singular suspicions were only a pretense and a "blind," that he had gotten up the scene to lure her to more security, and, to cap all, while her suspicions were once thus keenly alive, she considered it a singular circumstance that she should have suddenly entered and caught her lord and her maid talking together.

The story Mr. Cameron had told her was an extraordinary one—a tale too singular for belief. For a woman to suspect is, in most cases, to believe.

Mrs. Cameron had heard Dick Coulter say that her lord was a deep and cunning man. She knew that, as far as her relations with her dupe were concerned, she could not stand watching.

The result of all her thinking was the conclusion that the French maid was a fraud, and that she was in the pay of Mr. Cameron.

"I am equal to the occasion," she muttered, "and if I find that my suspicions are correct I'll silence that girl's tongue! She will discover that she has placed her head in the lion's jaw. I'll silence her," added the woman, in a husky voice, while a terrible expression came over her face.

In a moment the expression passed, and she called the maid in her most ordinary tone.

The girl came tripping into the room, and Mrs. Cameron asked suddenly in English:

"Were you writing a letter?"

The girl assumed a confused look, and shook her head.

Mrs. Cameron had tried Mr. Cameron's tactics, and had been baffled.

In French she asked some ordinary question, and was quickly answered.

That night, about two hours after the supposed French maid had retired, Mrs. Cameron on tiptoe stole into her room.

The cunning woman had provided herself with a bottle of clear-looking liquid and a silk handkerchief.

It was evidently her intention to prevent the maid from awaking during the prosecution of a thorough search of her clothing and baggage.

It had become a game of deep play between two deep and cunning women.

Mrs. Cameron had provided against surprise, and with a Lady Macbeth step, stole toward the room where her startling discoveries were to be made.

With careful hand she turned the door-knob, and glided into the room.

Once within she prepared her handkerchief, and stepped lightly beside the bed.

Deftly her hand wandered over the pillow, a cold chill ran over her frame, her hand encountered only a smooth and unruffled surface.

With trembling hand she turned on the gas and lit it, when a sight met her gaze that caused her to utter an exclamation of surprise.

The bed *was unoccupied;* in fact, had not been touched that night.

There was now no more reason to doubt. Mr. Cameron had set a spy upon her. Little did that guilty woman dream of the real truth!

CHAPTER XII.

AN ODD DISCOVERY.

WHILE Mrs. Cameron was exploring in the room of her French maid, that mysterious person was the heroine of an adventure destined to have an effect upon her fate ever after.

Kate Goelet had played her cards so well, and had gathered so much information, that she felt satisfied that she could lay her hand upon the whole bulk of the bonds.

She did not wish to make certain moves until she had secured them.

The words uttered by Dick Coulter had served as a warning to her; and she feared that in case a certain blow should fail, the victim would escape by his own hands, but that the property would never be recovered, and her work would

not be complete unless they were restored to their original owner.

On the night when the scenes occurred that we have depicted, she had retired to her room at the proper hour, but only remained a moment, when she performed a most singular act.

She passed up the scuttle-way, and, ascending to the roof, walked along lightly until she came to a scuttle-way a few doors below, which she raised, and descended to the first floor, when, inserting a key in the lock of one of the rooms, she entered a handsomely furnished apartment.

That our readers may not be bothered with any mystery, we will state that about the same time the French maid entered the service of Mrs. Cameron a modest-looking woman hired furnished apartments on the top floor of a house a few doors below Mrs. Cameron's residence.

It is hardly necessary to state that Miss Kate Goelet was the woman in question, and the securing of the room was a simple but necessary part of her programme.

Kate Goelet had led a strange and romantic life; but within the few weeks that she had been acting as a detective to discover the stolen bonds, she had fallen upon the real romance of a woman's existence.

It was not alone the hope of a reward that was inciting her to work up the mystery.

Ever since the night she had first met Henry Wilbur a new motive had agitated her.

Like a sudden gleam of sunlight flashing into a dark corner, a radiant hope had blazed away down in her heart.

She was but a woman, and women are strange beings when the affairs of the heart are concerned.

It was but ten o'clock when she left the apartment she had hired for a purpose, and she was robed in the most magnificent garments when she appeared.

Half an hour later a carriage stopped in front of a well-known public hall.

At the moment a select *bal-masqué* was in full progress.

A lady, heavily masked, alighted from the carriage, and, presenting a card at the door, passed into the hall.

A few moments after her entrance the mysterious masker issued from the ladies' room and mingled with the merry maskers, disguised as a gray nun.

From group to group she sauntered.

As is well known, the mask, serving as an *incognito*, permits a universal salutation among those who have never met before and who may never meet again.

The cavalier will address the peasant, and the latter will fire his familiar shot at the king.

The nun may be seen arm in arm with the harlequin, while some jolly friar argues theology with a seeming Satan in person.

Upon the removal of the masks, all fall back to the ordinary decorous reserve that distinguishes the association of strangers; but during the hours while the masks are held the merry, unrestrained fun and freedom goes on.

Diamonds of purest water glittered in the ears of the gray nun, and upon her fingers sparkled rings of great value—such gewgaws illy becoming the somber character she had assumed.

But what the real nun might eschew the mimic maiden of the convent can wear.

The gray nun moved from group to group, addressing a gay word to this peasant on one hand, and that cavalier on the other.

Then to the king, in all his royal splendors, she would address a word, and next to some gowned monk she passed a merry jest.

It was a matter of remark that all her salutations were confined to men.

At length she appeared discouraged, and retired to a seat, while a number of the gay revelers formed for the dance.

The gray nun had thus been seated for a few moments, when a cavalier came and seated himself beside her, and, in a bantering tone, said:

"Ah! ha! I'll whisper to the lady superior of thy little dissipation this night."

"Indeed, sir," answered the nun, in a sharp tone, "'tis easy to see thou art some lackey rigged out in his master's plumes."

"Prithee, but thou'rt sharp of tongue!"

"Nay, nay; not because I know thee in thy disguise."

"Why hast thou set me down as one in borrowed plumes?"

"'No true cavalier would be a tale-bearer; but 'tis the lackey's trade to tell tales, and his master's robes do not bring with them the master's honor.'"

The above conversation was carried on with mock solemnity, and in a merry, bantering tone.

Had the cavalier been as watchful and as keen of sense as the gray nun he would have noticed a slight tremulousness in the lady's tones.

It may have been that he was so charmed by her skillful repartee that he thought of naught else; as keen-witted as he was he received a Roland for an Oliver every time, and the word-play of the mysterious gray nun was much keener than his own.

A moment and the cavalier was beckoned away, and as he crossed the room he muttered:

"My heavens! if yon merry nun is as beautiful as she is witty, it were a pleasure indeed to see that mask set aside."

As the cavalier moved away the gray nun laid her jeweled hand over her heart, and murmured:

"I can not be mistaken! Oh, heavens! it is he."

The festivities continued for some time, when a second time the cavalier approached the gray nun.

The latter saw him start to come toward her, and in an under-tone, remarked:

"'Twill be good game; he shall see my face; I know 'tis for that he seeks me again."

As the cavalier approached, he said, in a gallant tone:

"I know thou art beautiful, and to speak fairly I have wagered that thou wert; now prithee, am I to have a glimpse of that fair face?"

"Indeed, thou dost know me?"

"On my honor I do not."

"Thou hast seen me before; thou shouldst know my voice."

"Indeed," said the knight, as he raised his gauntleted hand to his brow, "I can not recall one familiar tone, and I boast a good ear, and my memory is most excellent."

"Thou art a good actor, and wouldst mislead me to think that thou hast forgotten the tones of my voice. If 'tis true, thou dost me no compliment."

In their merry humor the cavalier and nun assumed the form of address peculiar to the age when gallant knights paid their *devoirs* to ladies fair and wore their colors at the tournament.

"Now, really, art thou making me thy sport, or have we really met before?"

"We have."

"Then pray remove thy mask, thou hast but whetted my curiosity."

"Nay, thou must test thy memory, and recall first the tones of my voice."

"I am at a loss."

"Hast not the least suspicion?"

"Not the least."

"And thou wouldst see my face?"

"I beseech that I may."

"Well, follow me; thy earnestness hast won for thee the favor thou cravest."

Little did either of the merry people dream of the fate that overhung the removal of that mask.

CHAPTER XIII.

A STRANGE UNMASKING.

THE gray nun led the way to one of the retiring-rooms.

Once away from the crowd of maskers, Henry Wilbur, who was the cavalier, exclaimed:

"So my disguise has been penetrated within the first half hour of my arrival?"

"How know you that your disguise has been penetrated?"

"It needs not a second guess to so decide; and now, pray who may be the fair lady whose keen glance has shot beneath my mask?"

"One who would warn you of danger."

"Warn me of danger?"

"Yes."

"Pray, what danger threatens me?"

"The danger of bad associates!"

"Indeed! but you are taking liberties with my mode of life!"

"I have reason."

"Now, by George! your language entitles me to demand to see your face."

"You have seen my face?"

"Well, I would see it again, to refresh my memory as to the benevolent countenance of one who appears to take such a warm interest in my fate!"

"Should you see my face, the charm and romance of my wizard warning would be all lost!"

"Why?"

"Simply, if you do not see my face, your imagination may picture it as being beautiful; if you do see it, you will learn the stern reality!"

"Begone, then, false imaginings, and let me stand face to face with the *stern* reality!"

"No, no; it is enough that I have warned you to give up your bad associates!"

"But, mysterious stranger, in self-defense I must declare that I do not claim to have any bad associates!"

"That is because you are blinded."

"How blinded?"

"You think them good!"

"Now, by Heaven, I'll tear aside your mask unless you grant me one glimpse!"

The masker uttered a pretty little laugh, and began naming a number of places where Henry Wilbur had been in the habit of going, which betrayed a most extraordinary acquaintance with his habits and modes of life generally.

Henry was completely mystified.

Matters were related that he supposed no human being was cognizant of besides himself.

"Are you some second-sight seer, or seventh daughter of a seventh daughter?" he asked, in a perplexed manner.

"I am but a simple person who has had eyes and ears open."

"Let me see your face."

"Why, you foolish man, know that I am an old woman! The young and giddy do not volunteer such advice as I have been administering to you."

"I am assured that you are not old, but young and beautiful."

"Nonsense!"

"It is not nonsense. I have my eyes about me as well as yourself. That pretty hand toying with that fan is not the property of one old and wrinkled."

"Well, good-bye, Sir Cavalier. I have warned you— take heed. And now once again, adieu."

The gray nun rose from the seat where she had thrown herself upon entering the room, and moved as though to go away.

Henry Wilbur, laid his hand upon her arm lightly, and said:

"No, no; you can not go! You have said words to me that make it absolutely necessary that I should see your face."

"You must let me pass!"

"No. I do not wish to be rude; but you know all is fair in love and war. You have played a little romance upon me, and I must see—"

"Hold!"

The cavalier had seized the lady's mask, when she caught his arm, and exclaimed, in a sharp tone:

"Hold!"

Henry was not to be baffled, however, and he did force the mask aside, actually tearing it completely off the lady's face.

In his astonishment, when that beautiful face was revealed, he recoiled, bearing the mask in his hand.

At the same moment a gentleman entered the room.

The latter was attired in a fancy costume, and he entered just in time to behold the unmasked face of the beautiful woman.

Henry Wilbur returned the mask, and noting an offended look on the lady's face, he said:

"You certainly must excuse me, but your extraordinary knowledge of my affairs emboldened me to act with seeming rudeness."

The look of indignation faded, and a smile, roguish and ravishingly sweet, overspread her lovely face, as she said:

"I forgive you."

During this whole scene, the man who had entered the room stood near the threshold an interested witness.

The lady returned the mask to her face, and Henry Wilbur, stepping up beside her, said:

"I recognize you."

"Indeed?"

"Yes."

"Where have you seen me before to-night?"

"You are the lady toward whom I acted so rudely in the street one night some time back."

A further conversation ensued of a pleasant character, and Henry invited the beautiful woman to dance.

Two hours followed of gay fun.

Henry Wilbur was charmed as he had never been charmed in all his life.

The face of the girl whom he had met upon that night had haunted him ever since as a pleasant dream, and now that he had seen her again, radiant in all her extraordinary beauty, a wonderful impression had been left upon his heart.

The hour approached when the assembly were to unmask.

Henry was still charmed by the wit and sparkle of his companion's conversation, when suddenly she exclaimed:

"I must go!"

"No, no: I must accompany you to your home."

"You can not."

"And why?"

"I can give no explanation."

A sudden suspicion of the most terrible character flashed over Henry's mind.

"May I ask you one question?"

"You would know my name?"

"Yes; but that is not the question I would ask."

"I am listening."

"Are you a *married woman*?"

A merry laugh came from behind the lady's mask, and she answered:

"I am not!"

"Your name?"

"I can not tell you my name."

"Why this mystery?"

"You shall know some day."

The mysterious girl rose to go to the dressing-room, and Henry would have detained her, when she exclaimed:

"I pray you do not follow me! Promise on your honor, you will not!"

"On one condition."

"What is the condition?"

"That you will meet me again."

"When?"

"To-morrow."

"Where?"

"Anywhere."

The lady named a place and hour, and hastened away.

Henry Wilbur was a remarkably handsome man, but, owing to the fact that he was a poor man, he had never allowed his attention to be seriously attracted by any woman.

At last, however, an impression had been made upon his heart that he began to realize could never be effaced.

The romantic circumstances under which he had met the mysterious beauty aided in exciting his imagination, and as there are moments liable to come to the coldest hearts when all their iciness melts before the blaze of some sudden destiny, so all our hero's indifference had vanished away, and he did not deny to himself that he had been wounded just where he thought himself for the time being invulnerable.

He would have liked to have followed the masked beauty, but having promised not to, he consoled himself with anticipations of the meeting on the coming day.

In the meantime the gray nun had resumed her wrappings, and was passing the entrance leading from the hall when a voice whispered in her ear:

"The French maid has acquired a knowledge of English in a marvelously short space of time!"

The party addressed turned to see who had spoken such strange words in her ear, but no one was near, save a number of masked females.

Kate Goelet remembered that at the time Henry Wilbur had removed her mask, a stranger disguised as a cavalier, had been standing in the door-way.

She knew at once that the party who had penetrated her disguise must have been that cavalier.

She was greatly astonished that any one had been able to identify her and was assured, from the fact that such identification had taken place, that some shrewd and keen party was upon her track.

She could remember but one person whom she had met during her late adventures to whom she could ascribe sufficient keenness for such a discovery.

CHAPTER XIV.
DEEP TREACHERY.

THE matter annoyed her considerably.

If her disguise had been penetrated, her little game in one direction was necessarily blocked.

Still thinking over the matter, she walked down to the street from the hall and entered her carriage.

As the man who drove her was supposed to know her, she said nothing to him more than to find out that it was the same coachman who had brought her to the hall.

Once in the carriage, she gave herself to intense thought, and so absorbed was she that she failed to observe that the carriage was being drawn at a tremendous pace, and that she was being carried a long distance.

Suddenly, however, she was recalled to herself, and chanced to glance out of the window, when she gave a start, and one expressive word fell from her lips.

"Treachery!" she muttered, and settled herself back like one resigned to some adverse fate, over which she had no control.

An ordinary woman would have screamed and made a great ado upon making such a discovery, but the lady detective was perfectly cool, and commenced to think over what she should do under the circumstances.

Had she chosen, she could have opened the coach-door and leaped forth, but that, as she thought, might not prove the best plan.

After thinking a moment, she muttered:

"All right! I will sit still and let them play out their little game: I will at least learn thereby just what they are up to, and from what quarter I have to apprehend danger."

Kate Goelet was not at all alarmed concerning her personal safety.

She had resources for self-protection ingeniously arranged, and felt perfectly able to take care of herself, although but a young and delicate woman.

It was not long before she discovered that she had left the city, and was being driven along an unpaved road.

A few moments longer, and the carriage was stopped in front of a villa, situated in the midst of a large park filled with trees.

As the carriage stopped, two men appeared at either door of the coach, and one of them, as he opened the door, remarked:

"Do not be afraid; you shall be returned unharmed."

"I am not at all afraid," was the cool reply.

"Will you alight?"

"Certainly."

The lady detective stepped from the coach, and, glancing up toward the driver's box, remarked, in a perfectly cool tone:

"Haven't you made a mistake, Mr. Driver?"

"No, madame; the gentleman, your husband, ordered me to drive here!"

"Ah! you have found a husband for me, eh? Well, my man, I know who you are, and you will be held responsible for my safe return!"

"Ain't this your home, ma'am?"

"You know it is not, and you will wait here to drive me home when I am ready to go. You will drive away at your peril." Then, turning toward one of the men standing at her side, she said, coolly, "Now, sir, I am ready to have you carry out your little joke!"

"This way, madame!" said the man, in a confused sort of tone.

The lady detective prepared to follow him, when she heard the driver whisper to the other man:

"Look here, 'cully,' that 'ere lady has got me down fine; now I want yer to understand that no harm must come to her till I take her back to where I got her from, do you mind?"

Kate Goelet was led up a broad flight of steps, and was standing before a massive front door, when suddenly a man came behind her, and a hood or shawl was thrown over her head.

She made no resistance.

It was plain that they meant to mask her, yet she did not utter a single cry or show the least alarm.

She felt herself a match for the conspirators, cunning as they thought themselves.

One of the men whispered, as the hood was thrown over her head:

" Do not be afraid!"

"I am not afraid; sharper men than yourselves are watching over me!"

She was led within the house, up a flight of stairs, and into a room carpeted in the richest manner, as she discovered the moment her feet touched it.

A few moments passed, when, discovering that she was alone, she removed the hood from her head.

She found herself in an elegantly furnished apartment.

The gas was turned low, but sufficient light was afforded for her to discern every object in the room.

Fully ten minutes passed, when a door opened, and a man, closely masked, entered the room.

The lady detective did not speak, but waited for the chief conspirator to open his business.

After a moment the masked man said:

" Madame, I suppose you are surprised at the innocent little trick that has been played upon you?"

" Not at all," was the cool reply.

" You are not surprised?"

" No."

" Nor alarmed?"

" No."

" You are very brave!"

" I was born so."

" You are in my power!"

" Indeed?"

" Yes."

" Well, I do not know as that disturbs me. You appear to be surrounded with every luxury; and, of course, having brought me here, you must intend that I should enjoy them?"

The man muttered an ejaculation under his mask, expressive of his astonishment at the strange woman's imperturbable coolness.

" I did not bring you here to enjoy yourself, madame!"

" Indeed! Then you are very ungallant!"

" I have a few questions to ask you."

" Proceed."

" You are the French maid who is in service with a lady known as Mrs. Cameron, are you not?"

" None of your business."

" I know that you are."

" Then why do you ask me the question?"

" I wish to proceed in a regular manner, that's all."

" All your proceedings have been very regular to-night."

" What is your game in engaging with Mrs. Cameron as a French girl who can not speak English, when you are as glib as a Yankee girl?"

" None of your business."

" You are not courteous, madame," said the man, in a mocking tone.

" I do not know that your underhand kidnapping of my person entitles you to courteous treatment."

" We will drop this comedy-play, madame, and come down to business."

" You are stage-manager, order on what you please."

" You may never leave this house; it may prove your tomb."

" Indeed! But that is a clean leap to the tragic."

" You will change your tone in a moment."

" Have we not already changed from comedy to tragedy?"

" In plain words, madame, I know your little game!"

" Indeed!"

" Yes; and now I want to know first what you are up to?"

" I thought you knew."

" Who employs you?"

" Employs me for what?"

" To act as a spy on the movements of Mrs. Cameron?"

" None of your business."

" You may as well answer me at once."

" When you know my game so well, why do you ask so many questions?"

" Simply because I mean to get answers to my questions, if I wring them from your throat."

" You threaten, eh?"

" I do; and now who employs you as a spy on the movements of Mrs. Cameron?"

" I am not acting as a spy on the movements of Mrs. Cameron."

" You are."

" I am not!"

" It is useless for you to attempt to deceive me, I tell, you."

" You have deceived yourself; I am acting as a spy on the movements of some one else."

" Who?"

" Mr. Cameron."

CHAPTER XV.

A MASKER MATCHED.

THE masked man recoiled, as though something fearful had suddenly been revealed to him.

" Great Heaven!" he ejaculated; " what does the woman mean?"

" I mean to follow my fancy."

" And what is your fancy?"

" To answer some of your questions; and it appears that my first answer does not sit well on your stomach."

" By heavens! you will come down from your high horse in a moment!"

" All right!"

" I think the best thing I can do is to dungeon you for awhile!"

" I wouldn't try it, if I were you."

" Why are you spying upon Mr. Cameron?"

" That is my business."

" I may as well tell you that Mr. Cameron is a friend in whom I am greatly interested."

" Yes; you are more interested in Mr. Cameron than any one else, so pull off your mask, as that little matter is perfectly plain."

" What little matter?"

" Your interest in Mr. Cameron."

" What do you know about Mr. Cameron?"

" Do you suppose I have been watching him so long without ' piping ' him well enough to penetrate a flimsy mask?"

" What do you mean?"

" I mean that I am talking to Mr. Cameron; so pull off your mask, and meet me face to face, and may be we will get along better."

" Curse you for a she-devil! who are you?"

" The French maid!"

" See here, woman, I see that you're no ordinary person, and that you have some game."

" I thought you knew my game?" came the taunt, in a satirical tone.

The man paid no heed to the taunt, but continued, " You must be paid for your game. Now listen to me; I will give you five thousand dollars right here, this moment, to betray your employer."

" That's plain talk."

" I mean to talk plain."

" Then you must meet me on an equality."

" In what manner?"

" Conduct me to the carriage waiting below, and meet me when I come voluntarily."

" What is the difference?"

" I do not like your present mode of procedure; it's a little too summary."

The masked man was silent a moment, but at length said:

" You will drive me to violence."

" You had better not attempt it."

" Now, then, will you listen to my proposition?"

" I will not, scoundrel!"

" Then, by Heaven, I'll compel you to answer all my questions."

" Do so, if you can!"

The masked man was a tall, powerful individual, and he suddenly leaped forward, and caught the woman by the wrists.

" Unhand me, sir!"

A struggle ensued.

A groan burst from the masked man's lips; the powerful man writhed and struggled in the hands of the small and delicate woman.

At length, pale and fainting, he fell to the floor.

The woman released her hold upon him, and drawing a pocket-handkerchief, saturated it from a bottle, and held the silk to the man's nostrils.

The latter's eyes closed, and he stiffened out upon the floor like a dead man.

The woman coolly left the room and descended the stairs.

The hall was dimly lighted, and she walked down slowly, taking a keen survey of her surroundings as she descended.

She had just opened the door to go out, when a man presented himself.

"Hold! you are not to go," he said.

"Oh, yes, I am!"

"But what will my master say about it?"

"He told me what to say to you."

"What did he tell you to say to me?"

"He told me to say this to you," and the bold, cool woman clapped her handkerchief right in the man's face.

The latter uttered a cry and fell back.

Kate Goelet passed through the door-way and descended toward the carriage, still standing under the arch.

"Are you there?" she said to the driver.

"Yes, madame."

"All right; you drive to the city, and you attempt to play treacherously and you will rue it. Whatever money the owner of this house paid you for your little game you can keep, and I'll say nothing about it; but try any more capers, and you will be in trouble."

"Look yer, madame; the man who hired me to drive you here deceived me, I reckon."

"What story did he tell you?"

"He told me you were his wife, that you were off on a little lark, and that he wanted to get square by a little lark on the other side. I meant no harm, only went into the joke."

"Have you been paid?"

"Yes, ma'am."

"All right! let her go! Take me to the spot where I first engaged you."

"All right, madame. You can depend upon me now, you bet!"

The carriage drove away, and in a few minutes the man at the door got up and ran upstairs to the room where the masked man lay upon the floor.

The latter had just recovered from the effects of the dose that had been administered from the handkerchief.

The servant raised his master to his feet, removed the mask, and disclosed the pale, marble face of Mr. Cameron, the banker.

"Oh, sir!" he cried, in terror, "are you murdered?"

"No, no! Where is that woman?"

"Gone, sir!"

"Gone!"

"Yes, sir."

"Why did you let her go?"

"Why, sir, she nearly smothered me! See here, master, I've a suspicion."

"What is your suspicion?"

"I don't believe that was a woman at all!"

"What was it, then?" asked Mr. Cameron, as he proceeded to examine his wounds.

"It was a man!"

"Nonsense! It was a woman; and by Heaven, I'll match her yet! But next time I will be prepared for her."

Mr. Cameron found that his wrists had been badly lacerated, but that he was not seriously injured.

CHAPTER XVI.

DARK SUSPICIONS.

WHILE the scenes previously recorded were in progress, Mrs. Cameron was carrying on her investigations concerning the strange disappearance of the mysterious French maid.

The girl had come to her with absolutely no baggage, and a search in every nook and corner failed to discover the least trace of anything tending to convict her of treachery.

Her mysterious absence was the only clew against her.

"Well, well, miss, when you make your appearance to-morrow, with your pretty little French airs and simperings, I reckon I will force the truth out of you."

"Suppose she does not come?" again thought the woman, and in audible tones she muttered:

"The creature has not left even a rag behind her. I fear that she has forestalled me by taking 'French leave.'"

Mrs. Cameron retired to her bed, and on the following morning, at the usual hour, the French maid put in an appearance.

A dark frown settled upon Mrs. Cameron's face, and in good plain English she said:

"Well, miss, you have dared to show your treacherous face here again, have you?"

The French maid shook her head, and said, in French: "Madame forgets; I do not understand."

"You do not understand, eh? well, I know better; you do understand; you were out of this house last night, and now I want to know just where you were all the time."

The maid stood mute.

"You might as well answer me, you understand me well enough."

The maid still made no response.

"I tell you, you vixen, that your employer, Mr. Cameron, has been compelled to confess that he sent you into this house to act as a spy over me!"

The girl still answered not.

Mrs. Cameron rose from her bed, and allowed the maid to assist her in robing.

After partaking of her coffee, the lady quietly proceeded, and locked every door leading from the room.

The maid was a witness of these strange movements, but appeared as quiet and demure as ever.

Having closed and locked all the doors, Mrs. Cameron said, as a glitter shone in her eyes and her face assumed the pallor of suppressed rage.

"Now, then, miss, you and I will come to an understanding!"

In French the maid asked:

"Is madame unwell, or what does she say?"

The madame now spoke in French, and said:

"You understand me well enough in English; but, as you are determined to cling to your little deceit, I will address you in a language that you admit understanding; and now I want to know where you were last night."

"I can not tell the madame."

"You can not tell me, eh? Well, I will see whether you will tell me or not! I want you to understand that your little game has been exposed. Mr. Cameron last night was compelled to confess that he procured your admission into this house, and that a perfect understanding exists between you and him."

"If Mr. Cameron made any such confession, madame, he told what is untrue. I never exchanged a word with Mr. Cameron except in this house."

"It is useless for you to tell any more falsehoods. You may be a smart, cunning woman, but you will find I am a match for you."

"I have nothing to tell madame of any collusion with Mr. Cameron, even though she kills me."

"Listen! I will give you one chance. Mr. Cameron does not employ you without promising you money. Now, then, no matter how great his reward may be, I will pay you just double the amount if you will leave his service and enter mine."

"I tell you, madame, that I am not in Mr. Cameron's service."

"And I tell you that I know you are!"

"I can say no more, madame."

"Remember, I warned you."

"I can say no more."

"One moment. Did you understand that I would pay you three times the amount promised you by Mr. Cameron, if you will betray him?"

"I can not betray him. I have nothing to betray."

Mrs. Cameron decided to change her tactics.

She was a cunning woman, and a determined foe.

"If you are innocent, forgive me."

A few moments' silence followed.

Mrs. Cameron was a large, powerful woman physically, and thinking that she had been fooled, she still resolved to force a confession from her maid.

Suddenly she rushed across the room, and attempted to seize the French girl.

A struggle ensued.

Again was Mrs. Cameron baffled; the slender, gracefully formed maid appeared to possess muscles of steel, combined with most extraordinary activity and strength.

She prevented her assailant from catching her by the throat, and pinioning her hands, held her writhing in impotent fury.

In the midst of the strange scene above described, there came a knock at the door.

"Heavens!" exclaimed Mrs. Cameron, "who can it be? Release me, girl!"

In French, the maid said:

"Madame, I came to you poor, and you gave me a home. I would have been a friend to you; now I must leave you. Remember I am in your service no longer; and, believe me, I never was in the service of Mr. Cameron; I know no more of him than I have learned since I lived in this house."

Mrs. Cameron appeared convinced, and she exclaimed:

"You must forgive me. And I pray you do not leave my service; and if that should prove to be Mr. Cameron at the door, do not let him know what has transpired between us."

"Madame can rely upon me that I will be silent."

The doors were unlocked, and the one leading to the hall opened, when Mr. Cameron entered.

The latter had his wrists bound with cloths and flannels, and his face was pale.

The French maid started to leave the room, when Mr. Cameron said, hastily, to his wife:

"Do not let that vile creature leave the room. I wish to ask you some questions in her presence."

Mrs. Cameron was bewildered; she did not know exactly how to act under the circumstances, but she said:

"I can summon her after you have offered me some explanation of your strange request, Mr. Cameron."

"I command you to keep that girl in the room!"

There was a decision in Mr. Cameron's tone that the lady had never before observed.

"I can call her," she repeated.

With a violent oath, Mr. Cameron exclaimed:

"Keep her here, I say; do you understand?"

The French girl had started to leave the room at the beginning of the talk, but Mrs. Cameron had bid her remain, and during the above dialogue she had stood with a look of pretty surprise upon her face.

Turning toward her, the man said:

"You deceitful hussy! do you see those wrists?"

Mrs. Cameron uttered a cry of amazement, when her assumed husband, addressing her, said:

"I warned you in the beginning that you had a spy in your house. That girl was out all night past, was she not?"

"I do not understand you!" answered Mrs. Cameron, who had begun to see the dawning of certain startling revelations.

"Yes, you do understand. I tell you that schemer there was out of the house all night!"

"And I tell you," answered Mrs. Cameron, "that she was not outside the door last night."

CHAPTER XVII.

EXPLANATIONS.

A DARK scowl overspread Mr. Cameron's face, supplemented with a look of perplexity as he said:

"How do you know she was not out all night?"

"Simply because I was not well last night, and she slept with me," answered Mrs. Cameron, with the utmost coolness.

The man was completely bewildered.

He knew no reason why his wife should make a misstatement, and yet he felt assured that he had seen the French maid at a certain entertainment the night before, and later at a certain house by the river-side.

If the woman he had procured to be conveyed to that house was not the French maid, who then could she be?

Mr. Cameron ordered the woman to let the girl leave the room.

He then sat down and calmly related all that had occurred.

He said that the French girl had a scar just under her plait of front hair, and that upon the previous night, while at the ball, where he had gone to watch the movements of a certain man, he had entered a room just as a female, dressed as a gray nun, had her mask torn aside.

Continuing his statement, Mr. Cameron said:

"When the mask was rudely thrust aside, her front hair was raised, and I saw the same scar on the forehead of the gray nun that I once accidentally saw on the forehead of your French maid."

Mrs. Cameron uttered an exclamation of astonishment.

Suddenly all suspicions concerning Mr. Cameron's collusion with the French maid ceased, and an entirely new idea crossed her mind.

Mr. Cameron proceeded, and told how he had bribed the driver of the gray nun's coach, and had her conveyed to a house belonging to him on the river-side, together with a minute account of the startling scene that occurred in the house.

"Who was the man you were 'piping'?" asked Mrs. Cameron.

"Henry Wilbur."

"And was he the man who tore the mask from the French maid's face?"

"I could not discover, although I have every reason to believe that Wilbur was her companion."

Mrs. Cameron now owned up that the French maid had been out all the night before, and went on and stated how she had been led to believe that the girl was a spy set over her by Mr. Cameron.

"Why should I wish to set a spy over you?" asked Mr. Cameron.

"Well, you know, dear, all men are so jealous, and I thought that possibly you had become infected, and the thought maddened me, and I denied the absence of the girl, supposing that you were only trying to throw dust in my eye."

"As I live, I never saw that mysterious creature until I met her in this house; and from the first I suspected her honesty."

"What do you suppose is her motive? Why should she come to spy over me?"

"I do not believe that she is a spy over you."

"Who, then?"

"Myself."

"Great Heaven! for what purpose?"

"Those bonds."

"Who could employ her?"

"Henry Wilbur."

"Do you suppose he has any suspicion of the truth?"

"We can not tell; but one thing is certain, that French girl is a fraud, and is here for some purpose inimical to our interests."

A dead silence followed this last remark.

Gradually a dark look stole over Mrs. Cameron's face, and at length, in a low tone, she said:

"I am sorry we let the girl know we suspected her."

"Why?"

"It will place her on her guard."

"You can drive her from your house."

"That would never do."

"Would you keep her here to watch us?"

"No."

"What would you do then?"

"She knows too much already."

"That is what I fear."

"That woman must be hushed somehow," remarked Cameron—and, after some further talk, these two wicked conspirators separated.

They were in dire alarm, and, as a matter of course, one crime had hurried them on to another.

Before the conversation above recorded had taken place, Mrs. Cameron had made sure, as she supposed, that no one could overhear.

In fact, both had spoken in such a subdued whisper, that one standing in the room could not have distinctly heard what was being said.

Once aroused, they were cunning; but there was one they had to deal with still more cunning, and, despite their low whispering, every word that they spoke was distinctly overheard.

A cunning scientific little instrument had been inserted in the key-hole, and an ear, keen and sensitive, was at the other end of it.

Mrs. Cameron came into the room where the French girl was sitting, immediately after the departure of Mr. Cameron.

The woman was as soft and kind in her manner as the low soughing of the breeze just before the outbreak of the coming tempest.

The matter had been reduced down to a desperate game of cunning between two bold and wily women.

That same afternoon, at dinner, Mrs. Cameron pressed the French maid to drink a cup of tea.

The latter declined, when once more Mrs. Cameron, seeing that she was baffled, lost her temper, and accused the maid of understanding English, and of having been an "eavesdropper;" and upon the inspiration of the moment she also accused her servant of having stolen a sum of money.

When this latter charge was made, a peculiar smile came to the French girl's face.

The latter had been waiting for a good excuse to resign her situation, and at once announced that she should go away.

The announcement had just been made, when again the conversation between the two women was interrupted by a rap at the door.

Mrs. Cameron hastened to open the door, and ushered in the rowdy and bully, Dick Coulter.

The appearance of the latter at once inspired the enraged woman with courage, and she told the French maid that she should not leave the house until she had submitted to a search for the missing money.

The girl positively refused to submit to a search, and proceeded to her own room to make arrangements for her departure.

Mrs. Cameron improved the interval of her absence by telling Dick Coulter all she suspected.

The man listened with eyes distended with astonishment, and finally he said:

"That gal can cut us out of a fortune!"

"She can."

"See here, my good gal, are you game?"

"How do you mean?"

"The folks who dwell in this house, all beside yourself, are out of town!"

"No; there is a family on the first-floor."

"A family on the first-floor?"

"Yes."

"Never mind; we can work it."

"You must remember one thing: that girl, if your suspicions are true, must have confederates who would raise a row should she be missing."

"It will not disturb us how much row they make, if you are only a game woman. You know we are playing for a million; if that gal goes abroad, our game is up! Now, then, the question is, shall we play on or give up beat?"

The woman was silent a few moments, but at length she said, in a low, husky tone:

"Dick, we can not lose our game, when it is so near played out."

CHAPTER XVIII.

THE BEGINNING OF TROUBLE.

DICK COULTER was a man who had traveled all over the world, and everywhere that he had been he had always associated with the criminal classes, and he had learned every little device known to criminals.

Mrs. Cameron went to the door of the French maid's room, and called her.

No answer came to the summons, and Mrs. Cameron called again.

The woman's voice was husky, and a look of terror rested upon her pale face, while within the adjoining room Dick Coulter waited.

Mrs. Cameron rapped at the door and called in a louder tone, and, as no answer came, she returned to the room where her companion was, and said:

"I can get no answer from her."

"If she has 'sloped,' we are gone up!" said the man.

"She has not gone; she could not pass out of that room without our knowing it."

"Then you wait here, and I will go into her room."

Trembling from head to foot, Mrs. Cameron threw herself into a chair, and Coulter went to the door of the girl's room.

He tried the knob; it yielded, and he pushed open the door.

There was sufficient light reflected from a gas-burner in the hall for him to see plainly about the room.

It was unoccupied—the bird had flown.

Kate Goelet had overheard sufficient, and having nothing particular to gain by remaining in that dangerous proximity, she determined to leave.

The astonishment and chagrin of the two was great, and their terror also began to increase.

Dick Coulter was smart enough to know that the mysterious French girl was in disguise, and his first exclamation was,

"We're ruined!"

"Not quite," answered Mrs. Cameron. "We will hunt up that girl."

"No, no, you will never see her again as the French girl; she has been in this house in disguise!"

"Mr. Cameron recognized her, however, and so can I, whenever and wherever I see her!"

"All right! hunt her down and the advantage is in our hands; but as it is, we are in danger every moment."

A week passed. During that time, Kate Goelet had occupied her quarters in the house a few doors distant from where Mrs. Cameron resided.

The latter had boasted that she would know the girl wherever she saw her, when in fact she had seen her a dozen times, and had failed to recognize her.

The lady detective had "dropped" to the scar identification mark, and had fixed that so that it would take sharper eyes than Mrs. Cameron's to discover it.

In the meantime Kate Goelet had several times met Henry Wilbur.

She was not deceived, concerning the truth; she had charmed the young man, and he loved her, and yet she was not happy.

Sitting alone in her room one day, she indulged her thoughts by audible expression of them.

"He loves me now," she soliloquized, "although he knows that there is some mystery surrounding me, but he is a refined and delicate-minded man. What will his feelings be when he learns that I am the famous lady detective? When he learns the person who he supposed was an unsophisticated girl is a woman, who, from necessity, has penetrated amidst all manner of scenes of vice and crime?"

Kate Goelet was a beautiful woman, and not by half as old as she, in her self-accusing mood, would make it appear.

Although she had become famous as a detective under an assumed name, she was really but twenty-five summers old.

As intimated in our opening chapters, she was a child of destiny.

At last, during her career, she had met a man whom she loved, and she had gained that man's love under false pretenses, and now she feared that, when the truth became known, he would despise her, and treat her with contempt and scorn—even worse—absolute hatred, for having deceived him.

She felt that when that hour came she would wish to die.

Kate Goelet was a woman of intense feeling, and as the hours sped by her passion increased, and her fears and dread of the result of the final discovery grew apace also.

One day the lady detective and Henry Wilbur were strolling in the park together.

Henry had noticed that his companion was strangely sad.

She had told him her name was Kate, and, calling her by that name in an endearing tone, he said:

"You are sad and silent to-day?"

"Yes; I have been thinking about you."

"And should thoughts about me make you sad?"

"Yes."

"Why, darling?"

"You have professed to love me."

"I do love you with all my heart."

"You have made the profession without having heard my true story."

"I care not about your true story."

"I fear you do not believe me when I tell you I am a person of humble origin."

The young man turned and caught Kate's hand; his fine handsome eyes glowed with a noble enthusiasm as he exclaimed:

"Kate, you are beautiful, and pure, and truthful! I ask no more! You have often hinted that some disclosure might cause my love to vanish! Now, darling, listen to me; as long as I know that you are a pure woman, I care not whether your father was a ragpicker! I love you for yourself, and not for your estate!"

"You may lose all your enthusiasm when the truth is told, and your love is put to the test."

"You are putting my love to the test now, more severely than I deserve."

The two young people had strolled away from the fr°

quented part of the park, and had wandered off to a lonely spot.

Little did either of them dream, while indulging their fond talk, that a pair of keen-eyed, strong-limbed, determined men were sneaking close upon their heels, and watching their movements.

A few moments Henry had been lost in deep thought, but at length he broke the silence by saying:

"Kate, you may not be the only one who has a disclosure to make."

"What do you mean, Henry?"

"I mean that at any moment I may be brought into disgrace. The sword of Damocles is hanging over my head, and may fall at any moment. If it were not so, I should urge our immediate marriage."

"You are threatened with disgrace?"

"Yes."

"Of what nature?"

"At any moment I may be accused of a terrible crime."

"But you are innocent?"

"As innocent as yourself!"

A moment Kate was silent, then, in a voice "full of tears," she said:

"No matter what may come, Henry, I will trust you as I have trusted you; and I believed in you from the first. And—"

At this moment two men burst through the hedge and advanced toward them.

Henry at once thought that he was waylaid by highwaymen, and he drew his pistol with the exclamation "*Robbers.*"

Kate laid her hand on his arm, and said:

"Put up your pistol."

A strange look came over his face, and he exclaimed, in a husky voice:

"Oh, Kate! Are you the confederate of—"

Kate Goelet raised her hand warningly, and only said:

"*Hush!*"

CHAPTER XIX.

OLD REBECCA BROWN AGAIN.

OUR readers will recollect that Henry Wilbur had met Kate Goelet under strange circumstances.

Her face was beautiful, and bore the impress of truth and virtue, and yet she had remained a mystery to him as far as her standing in society was concerned.

The fact that they had wandered far from the frequented paths, and the sudden springing forth of the two men, led Henry to think on the spur of the moment, as though a sudden revelation had burst upon his mind, that, after all, he had been played as the mere dupe of a charming adventuress and possible criminal.

In a few brief seconds the human mind can pass, lightning-like, though a number of startling emotions, and in those few brief seconds Henry Wilbur experienced astonishment, rage, and a sudden hatred.

He was under the firm impression that the two men were common foot-pads, and that Kate was the accomplice who had lured him to a convenient spot for the purpose of robbery.

In a few seconds, however, his emotions changed completely, and as, in a despairing manner, he gazed at Kate, it was to implore her pardon for the foul suspicion that he had permitted to cross his mind.

One of them stepped forward toward our hero, while the other covered him with a pistol.

"Is your name Henry Wilbur?" came the question.

"That is my name."

"You are my prisoner."

"Your prisoner?"

"Exactly."

"On what charge?"

"Robbery."

"There must be some mistake."

"Oh, yes!" laughed one of the detectives, "there is always a mistake made when we make an arrest."

"Who prefers the charge against me?" asked Henry.

"I have nothing to do with that, young man; all I have to do is to take you to the Tombs, and if you offer any resistance, it will be all the worse for you."

"Innocent men have no reason for offering resistance to the law; I am your prisoner."

The detective produced a pair of handcuffs.

"Oh, not those!" exclaimed Henry, with a shudder. "I will go quietly with you!"

"All right, my friend; if you are innocent, your arrest will only be a momentary inconvenience; and if you are guilty—well, so much the worse for you!"

"Can I speak in private to this lady one moment?"

The officers exchanged glances.

There was one terrible contingency they had to fear—suicide.

"You can speak to her on one condition—you must first submit to a search."

Kate stepped forward at this moment, seeing the blush of shame on Henry's cheek, and she said, in a strong, confident voice:

"Never mind speaking to me now, Henry; I will visit you at once. And remember, no matter what the charge, or by whom made, I have perfect confidence in your innocence, and the same confidence that it will be speedily proved; so keep up good courage, for *my* sake!"

"By George! you need have no fears; I'll prove my innocence if I have to pass through the tortures of hell in doing so!"

Two hours later and Henry Wilbur was in the Tombs.

The morning following, the news of the great robbery was spread abroad.

Five of the stolen bonds had been negotiated, and finally had been offered to a banking-house who had recognized them as part of the stolen bonds.

They were traced back from one possessor to another, until the man was found who had first put them upon the market.

The last individual stated that he had received them from a man, whose appearance he described, and an hour later the detectives had arrested Dick Coulter.

The latter when arrested was perfectly cool, and asserted his innocence, claiming that he had secured the bonds in good faith from one of the most respectable banking-houses in the city.

During further revelations, he admitted that the bonds had been given to him to be disposed of by Henry Wilbur, a clerk in the house of Attry, Comstock & Co., and that he had been led to believe that the transaction was perfectly regular and legitimate.

The banking-house named was communicated with, and they at once declared that the bonds were portion of a million dollars' worth that had been stolen from them.

A warrant was at once sworn out, and Henry Wilbur was arrested as stated.

The trick to fasten the robbery upon Henry Wilbur had been most coolly and cunningly carried out.

The district attorney had expressed himself as considering it one of the deadest cases he had ever had to prosecute.

The detectives were lauded to the skies as usual for their acuteness and promptness in making the arrest, and it looked as though the chances were set for Henry Wilbur to go to Sing Sing for the remainder of his natural life.

Upon the day following Henry's arrest, a strange-looking old woman presented herself at the Tombs with a permit to see the prisoner.

As the permit was from head-quarters, the strange-looking old creature was admitted.

As she was shown into the cell, her first exclamation was: "Well, sakes alive, young man, how could you go and do such an awful thing as to steal your employer's money?"

Our hero recognized the old woman as the mysterious Rebecca Brown who had done him such a wonderful service.

The moment the keeper had gone beyond ear-shot, the old woman changed her tone, and said, in a quick, earnest manner:

"Well, it's come; but do not be discouraged. You shall be brought out all right. The rogues have played a deep game, but a deeper game has been played against them!"

"Who are you?" asked Henry.

"You remember me?"

"I do."

"Well, then, you know who I am, and what my purpose is; I am on the track of the real robber."

"You may be on the *track* of the real robber, but before you catch the real robber, I may be convicted."

"You will never be convicted; you can take things as easy as you choose on that score."

"I am very thankful to you for the interest you have shown in my case, but you may be overhopeful."

"I could open your prison-door inside of twelve hours, if I thought proper; but you must remember that you promised to aid me in recovering those bonds."

"I will keep my promise."

"Then you must rest quietly in prison until the proper moment arrives for opening your prison doors."

"Why not at once?"

"I could put my hand on the real thief to-day, but not upon the bonds; I must recover them."

"Have you any hope of succeeding?"

"I have."

"How soon?"

"Possibly within a few hours, or a few days at most."

"I have no need to employ counsel?"

"No."

"I have been overrun with men offering their services."

"As a matter of course, they think a million dollar bond-robber must have plenty of money."

"Will you do me one favor?" asked Henry.

"What is it?"

"Go and see my mother."

"I saw your mother within two hours after your arrest."

"Mysterious woman! how did you know of my arrest so soon?"

"I was expecting that you would be arrested; I knew that the game of the conspirators against you was ripe for the final drop, as they thought it."

"I owe my life and my honor to you."

"Well, you can pay me some day," remarked the lady detective, in a strange, sad tone.

"I may pay you some day?"

"Yes."

"How?"

"Well, I may have something to ask of you."

"Whatever you ask, if it be in my power to grant it, it shall be so."

"Do not make a rash promise."

"I swear it!"

"Give me some pledge that you will keep your word."

It was a moment when Henry was filled with gratitude; it may be that a suspicion crossed his mind as to what the request might be, as he was aware that the appearance of an old woman was a disguise, and that his strange benefactor was young and comely; yet from his hand he drew a ring, and, handing it to her, said:

"I am not a king, to remind myself of a royal promise by the token of a ring, but I am a man of honor, and as you have only appeared to me in disguise, I present this with a reminder of my promise, and I'll not fail my word."

Receiving the ring, the lady detective said:

"Having settled our little romance, we will attend to business."

The detective had commenced asking a few questions, when the prison-keeper appeared at the door, accompanied by a gentleman.

The visitor was a member of the firm that had suffered such a heavy robbery—none other than Mr. Cameron.

CHAPTER XX.

IN THE LION'S DEN.

A LOW, startled exclamation burst from the old lady's lips, and at the same moment she said:

"Well, well, young man, I am sorry that you were tempted of the devil to commit so great a crime; and I hope it will be a lesson to other evil-doers."

The old lady started to leave the cell, when Mr. Cameron fixed a glance upon her so fearful in its import that even the keeper was induced to inquire:

"Do you know that woman, sir? Is she one of the outside gang?"

"No, no," answered Mr. Cameron; and, after a moment, he added: "I do not think I could bear seeing this young man at this moment. I thought more of him than any one in our employ, and his downfall has caused me the greatest sorrow; I will defer my visit."

Mr. Cameron turned to follow the old woman.

A startling recollection, and a no less startling suspicion, had flashed across his mind.

He lived in constant dread of some sudden and awful exposure; he would have given half the proceeds of his great crime to have known that the mysterious French maid was in the East River.

He did not feel that he was safe as long as that cute, mysterious being was moving above ground.

A hint of the real truth concerning her identity had taken possession of his mind, and at that very moment, in order to cover one crime, he was prepared to commit another.

The old woman passed from the gloomy prison, and, upon descending the great stone steps in Center Street, started down town.

A few squares, and she wheeled about and walked toward the river.

Mr. Cameron was close upon her heels.

The desperate man had resolved upon a desperate expedient should an opportunity offer.

The old lady reached South Street, and passed over and entered the Roosevelt ferry-house.

Mr. Cameron followed a moment later, and was just in time to see his game enter the ladies' waiting-room.

The man took up a position, determined to wait until she came forth again.

Not more than a minute had passed since seeing the old lady enter the waiting-room, when a young and neatly dressed lady came forth.

Ten minutes passed, and the party for whom Mr. Cameron was waiting did not come out.

It was an hour of the day when there were but few passengers.

Mr. Cameron began to grow weary, and advanced to the window of the waiting-room and peeped in.

There was no one in the room.

The man began to grow uneasy, and then a most daring scheme flashed across his mind.

He sneaked into the ladies' waiting-room, and, rapidly crossing, actually peered into a quarter where he had no business; but he saw no one.

The place was totally deserted—in some strange and mysterious manner the bird had flown, and he had been fooled once again.

He then remembered the young lady who had come forth so soon after the entrance of the supposed old one, and, with a curse, he muttered:

"Somebody kick Injun for a fool!"

He was now satisfied that he was playing against a detective—a female detective, one of the most wily and cunning women, as he believed, in existence.

In the meantime, Kate Goelet, who always went prepared to make just such wonderful transformations in her appearance, got well away, and commenced preparations to carry out a most daring scheme.

The lady detective was satisfied in her own mind that the bonds were concealed in the house to which Mr. Cameron had had her conveyed on the night of the masquerade.

As our readers know, she had in reserve evidence of Mr. Cameron's guilt sufficient to have released Henry Wilbur; but she had an idea that by letting the young man remain in prison, with every prospect of ultimate conviction, his enemies would become less guarded, and she would have a chance to pounce down upon the booty.

There were reasons why the lady detective wished to secure the large reward dependent upon the finding of the bonds.

As many times hinted, she had a secret in her life, and she felt that the hour was approaching when her whole destiny would be changed.

A week passed.

During the interval Henry Wilbur had been arraigned, and had pleaded not guilty to the charge against him.

Mr. Comstock and Mr. Cameron had called upon him in company, and the latter, with a coolness most remarkable, had hinted that there might be some chance for Henry's release, if he would surrender the stolen bonds.

Little did Mr. Comstock dream of the actual coolness of his partner's proposition, but the day was fast approaching when he would fully realize the stupendous villainy of the man whom at the moment he considered the soul of honor.

One night, as stated, after a week had passed, a slenderly formed man, about midnight, might have been seen, mounted on a swift horse, riding along the road leading to Mr. Cameron's mysterious country residence.

On the afternoon of the day preceding the excursion of

the mysterious horseman, Mr. Cameron had received a singular note, which read as follows:

"MR. CAMERON,—SIR: You appear to think that I had some design in becoming a servant to the woman who in public bears your name.

"Frankly you were right in your suspicion. I have a most extraordinary revelation to make to you. You are being 'played for an angel.' I expect to be paid for the services I may render you, but you will find it a great service, while necessity demands that our meeting should be a secret one; meet me at No. — S—— Street, and I will open your eyes to a little scheme wherein it is intended that the 'second thief shall be the best owner.' Do not fail to come, at your peril. From this note you will see that I am 'upon points' necessary to your safety.

"As I am watched, you will have to time your visit so as to reach the house named about two o'clock in the morning; and should you fear bodily harm, you can take any precautions you choose, even to the bringing of an officer with you; but it is necessary, I repeat, for your own safety, that you do not fail to be on hand.

"Yours, in haste,
"THE FRENCH MAID.

"P.S.—They are working to 'blow' in the real bond-thief after 'raking in the swag.'   F. M."

As the mysterious rider rode along, he muttered to himself:

"Cameron will not fail to attend the mandate of the letter, the road will all be clear for me. While he is looking for the French maid, I will be looking for the bonds."

It was after one o'clock in the morning when the horseman picketed his animal to the fence surrounding the residence of Mr. Cameron.

As our readers have ere this surmised, the midnight rider was the lady detective disguised as the little French maid.

Having secured her horse, Kate leaped the fence and stole along across the lawn toward the house.

The building was an ordinary summer villa, with heavy porticoed balconies and verandas, and bay windows at every story.

Our heroine passed round to one of the bay windows, and opening a small bag that she carried, disclosed quite an assortment of burglars' tools.

With the readiness and skill of an expert burglar, she pried open one of the windows, and in as agile a manner as a gymnast, raised herself from the ground, crept through the raised window and stood within the parlor.

She had a stout cord attached to her bag of tools, and when once in the room, she drew it up, selected a number of articles, and disposed them about her person.

The brave woman was prepared for any sort of interruption, and moving stealthily across the parlor, passed out into the broad hall, and, as noiselessly as a cat, ascended the stairs toward the second story.

The lady detective proved her remarkable powers of observation, by proceeding direct to the room where she had held that memorable interview with Mr. Cameron on a former occasion.

At the time she had been a forced visitor in the house, and yet in the few brief moments when leaving the house at that time, she had taken in the whole plan of the interior.

She turned to the knob of the door, and found that it was locked.

From her pocket she drew a cunningly contrived instrument, and had just inserted it in the lock, when she was startled by hearing a succession of heart-rending and piercing shrieks.

CHAPTER XXI.

AN APPARITION.

KATE GOELET possessed a wonderfully cool, strong nerve, and yet those screams, so piercing and so suddenly falling upon her ear, for the instant unnerved her.

It was a woman's voice she heard, and the screams proceeded from some room in the house. Kate stood and listened, but a dead silence had followed the first most extraordinary noise.

"Another mystery, and more villainy!" reflected the lady detective.

She had other business on hand, however, just at that

moment, and again directed her attention toward gaining an entrance into the room.

It took her but a moment to spring the lock-bolt and gain an entrance.

Once in the room, she drew a masked lantern from her pocket, lit it, and, raising it aloft, let the bright ray of light shoot on different objects as she took a deliberate survey of the room.

"There is no escritoire here where the stolen bonds could be concealed. We will try the next room," she murmured.

The door leading into the adjoining room was unlocked.

The lady detective passed through, and found herself in a sleeping-room.

An elegant bedstead stood in one corner of the large apartment, and other toilet furniture of the most gorgeous description.

The article that most pleased the eyes of our heroine, however, was a heavily carved desk.

Crossing to the latter, she made a most thorough examination of it, and, when fully satisfied, set about exploring its interior.

A pleased smile was on the detective's face, as she felt around, that at last her efforts were to be rewarded with the most satisfactory success.

Knowing what she was to encounter, she was provided with the proper instruments, and, understanding her business, she soon had the desk open.

A most exact and thorough examination followed.

She found an abundance of papers, and some of value, but not the least sign of the missing bonds.

An hour passed, and the lady detective was just despairing of success, and had determined to replace every article back in the desk and resume her search in some other direction, when she was startled by hearing a light footfall.

Less keen ears than her own would have failed to detect the approaching step, so light was the tread.

In an instant the slide of the masked lantern was shut to its place, and the lady detective sought a place of concealment behind the heavy folds of the curtains hanging across the bay window alcove.

She was not a moment too soon, and had but just concealed herself, and secured a position from whence she could peep forth, when a most extraordinary and astounding apparition met her gaze.

A female, dressed in a loose wrapper, with long, blonde hair stealing down to her waist, entered the room with a slow measured tread.

The female's face was beautiful, but pale and death-like, and her eyes glared in a preternatural manner.

In one hand she carried a light, the rays of which she carefully shaded as she peered over toward the bedstead standing in the far corner of the large apartment.

In fact the latter was so large, and the bed was standing so in the shadow, that, from where the strangely appearing female stood, it would have been impossible for any one to have seen whether it was occupied or not without approaching to within a few feet of it.

The strange, weird creature stood the lamp upon the floor in a corner.

A cold chill stole over the lady detective's form.

It was plain that the woman had a desperate purpose.

The chill of horror, however, passed off with the recollection that the bed was unoccupied.

A most strange and wonderful coincidence was it, however, that, in fooling Mr. Cameron to an absence from his home upon that particular night, she had most probably saved him from being assassinated in his bed.

The woman stole on tiptoe across the room toward the bed.

A moment she stood and gazed, when a fierce exclamation burst from her lips, followed by a low wail.

The lady detective was amazed at the singular scene occurring before her, but was cute enough to guess the true story.

The victim of a villain was seeking revenge after years of wrong and suffering.

Was the poor creature insane? was the question suggested to the lady detective.

The woman was beautiful and youthful.

A moment passed, and the weird woman turned and walked toward the corner where she had left her lamp.

Our heroine glanced keenly at her face.

It had a strange expression, and was worn with sorrow and evident suffering; but the bright, strangely staring eyes, despite their singular expression, appeared to reflect the thoughts of a sane soul.

A desperate idea was suggested to the detective.

If this beautiful desperate woman could kill the man who had wronged her, she could not be his friend.

Kate Goelet uttered a low "Hist!"

The woman stopped and listened.

The detective stepped forth.

Our readers will remember that the detective was disguised in the habiliments of a man.

As she stepped forth Kate raised her fingers to her lips and motioned silence.

The woman did not appear either surprised or frightened, and consequently made no outcry.

The detective moved toward her, when the woman raised her hand in a menacing manner, and asked:

"Who are you, and what are you doing in this room?"

The question was asked in a low, guarded whisper, showing that the woman was as anxious to avoid discovery as the detective.

"I am an enemy of Mr. Cameron; I am no thief, but he is a villain."

"You must leave the house at once."

"Why?"

"Mr. Cameron is reserved for my vengeance."

"But I can assist you in revenging yourself upon him."

"I want no assistance, and you must depart at once."

"No; I shall remain."

"It will be worse for you."

"Why?"

"I shall give an alarm!"

"One moment; you are a woman?"

"Certainly."

"Mr. Cameron has wronged you."

"How do you know?"

"I have been in this room for half an hour; I saw all your movements since you have been here, and besides, your own mouth betrayed you when you said he was reserved for your vengeance alone."

"The latter is the reason why you must go away; I will protect Mr. Cameron against any *man*; I will warn him of danger."

The lady detective drew close to the woman that had been Cameron's victim, and said, in a low tone:

"Listen, I am a woman like yourself."

"A woman?"

"Yes."

"Why tell me that, when I see with my own eyes that you are a man?"

"I am in disguise."

Suddenly a look of fury appeared in the woman's face, and she toyed, in a menacing manner, with her lantern as she assked in a sharp tone:

"Did Cameron ever pretend to love you?"

"No."

"Did you ever pretend to love him?"

"No."

"Why do you wish to revenge yourself upon him?"

"I am not seeking for revenge, but I want to bring him to justice."

"For what crime?"

"A terrible one."

"Is he a murderer?"

"Not that I know of."

"Why do you, a *woman*, seek to bring him to justice? You can not deceive me."

"I am not trying to deceive you."

"Then why are you, a woman, seeking to bring him to justice?"

An idea suddenly struck the detective, and she said:

"I do not love Cameron. I never loved him; I never saw him until during the last few weeks."

"It is easy to deny and assert."

"Let me tell you; I love a brave and noble man, and as handsome as he is noble and brave."

"Well?"

"Cameron is the enemy of my beloved, and he has woven a net-work around an innocent man to make him suffer for a crime he never committed."

"Who is the really guilty man?"

"Cameron."

"And you come to the house to capture him?"

"No."

"What, then?"

"I come to procure evidences of his crime to save the innocent."

"Are you telling me the truth?"

"I am."

A moment's silence followed, when the strange woman took up her lamp, and said:

"I think I know what his crime is, and I think I can assist you in the purpose that brought you to this house. Follow me."

The lady detective started to follow the apparition-like looking woman, when a strange incident occurred.

CHAPTER XXII.
A STRANGE REVELATION.

As stated in our previous chapter, the lady detective started to follow the apparition-like figure of the woman she had so strangely met, when suddenly her conductress came to a halt and said, in a terrified manner,

"Lay low! the fiends have missed me, and are on my track."

A shade of disappointment flashed over the detective's face.

This strange cry of her conductress appeared as though, after all, she was but following some maniac who had enjoyed but a moment's respite from her ordinary paroxysms of madness.

In an instant, however, the impression was removed.

The woman said:

"I am represented in this house as a mad person, and for a purpose I have favored the idea: you hide and I will surrender myself, throw my keepers off their guard, and then come down here for you again."

The above was spoken in a hurried whisper in the lady detective's ear.

The latter said:

"You may not be able to get away again to come to me."

"You need have no fears; I am not mad, and I can come and go when I please."

The lady detective heard footsteps approaching.

The pretended maniac had extinguished her light on the first alarm, and the two women were standing in total darkness.

"I will await you," said Kate, and she glided from the woman's side.

Half an hour passed, and the waiting detective heard a low, "Hist!"

She stepped forward from her place of concealment and met the woman, who had returned according to promise.

The latter led our heroine up the stairs to an apartment on the attic floor.

A light was burning in the room, and as the lady detective glanced around, she saw every indication of a prison cell.

The windows were barred, and an iron-barred door was inserted inside the door leading from the apartment. Every precaution had been taken to make the place as secure as the most massively constructed prison.

The pretended maniac closed both the wooden and iron doors, and, leading the lady detective to a seat, said:

"I will now tell you my story."

The story listened to by the detective was the old, old narrative of beguilement, betrayal, and wrong.

It is the story whose incidents have occurred since the days of old, and which will occur until the incoming of the millennium.

Florence Clarke was a girl born and bred in the country; an orphan who had been adopted by distant relatives of her mother.

She had been reared as an own child, and had the benefit of the best teachers, so that she became an adept in all the accomplishments peculiar to a young lady's education.

Alas! she had one lesson yet to learn, and that was that the despoiler is ever nigh with flattering tongue to deceive, and false heart to betray.

Florence Clarke met a young man, the confidential clerk in a great banking firm.

He had visited the town where she lived to transact some business with the local banking institution.

From the first moment that the man Cameron met the beautiful Florence, he pretended to be desperately in love with her.

He was a handsome man, of high social position seemingly, and in every way just calculated to attract the fancy and heart of a susceptible girl.

The man remained some weeks in Florence Clarke's native town, and finally declared his love, at the same time cautioning the unsuspecting girl from making his declaration known.

He stated that he was just about to be taken into the firm as a junior partner, and that it might damage his chances if his seniors knew that he was going to be married, as he had reason to know that one of them was very anxious to have him for a son in-law.

It is sufficient to add that by one story and another he finally induced the beautiful Florence to consent to a clandestine marriage.

A number of years followed.

The deceived girl, during all that time, was as one dead to the kind friends who had reared and lavished their affections upon her.

As always happens under similar circumstances, the deceiver at last tired of his victim; then followed slights and faults; at length personal abuse, and finally a cruel confession.

In a moment of rage, George Cameron declared to his supposed wife, Florence, that she was not his wife, that he had a legal wife living at the time he pretended to marry her.

"But my certificate, George?—the ceremony?"

"The first was a forgery; the latter was a farce!"

The victim fell insensible at the deceiver's feet.

When she returned to consciousness, Florence Clarke found herself a prisoner in the room where she sat at the moment while she was telling the sorrowful tale of wrong and injury.

"How long have you been confined in this room?"

"A number of years."

"Have you never sought to escape?"

"I did at first; not lately."

"Does George Cameron ever come to see you?"

"Never."

"Why have you not sought to escape, since you have discovered a means to go from these rooms?"

"Why should I go forth? I would be a homeless wanderer, it is thirteen years since I was beguiled from the home of my guardians."

"What would you have done had you succeeded last night in working out your revenge?"

"I should have killed myself!"

"Then you love this man still?"

"Love him!" exclaimed Florence Clarke as her face assumed a look of fury. "I love him as the bird loves the cobra!"

"Will you let me be your friend?"

"Who are you?"

Kate Goelet explained certain incidents in her career.

The woman listened, and at the conclusion said:

"So George Cameron is a common criminal after all?"

"He is a criminal of the deepest dye."

"You must recover those bonds to convict him?"

"Yes."

"I can assist you."

"How?"

"Come here to-morrow night, and I will tell you; but you must go now. Should you be discovered here, you would be in the greatest danger."

"I am prepared for ruffians," said Kate, in a confident tone.

"Discovery would defeat our plan, and morning draws near."

The two women, thus strangely met, exchanged a few more words, and the lady detective returned to the parlor and made her exit from the house.

She was crossing the lawn, when she suddenly came upon a man, dodging from tree to tree like herself.

The man evidently discovered her presence at the same moment that she had seen him.

He leaped toward her, with a curse and the exclamation:

"Ah! I've got you at last!"

The next instant the man reeled and fell to the ground.

The lady detective had dealt him a blow with a curious sort of instrument that she carried in her hand.

Kate Goelet did not stop to discover who the man was, but pursued her way to where she had picketed her horse.

She found the animal all right, and, mounting, started on her homeward journey just as the first streaks of day began to illumine the eastern sky.

Half a mile from the scene of her night's adventures she met a buggy in which sat a man.

One glance was sufficient—the occupant of the carriage was George Cameron.

On the following morning Henry Wilbur was brought before the judge for a preliminary examination.

He had pleaded "Not guilty," and said that he had nothing to say concerning the charge against him.

The members of the banking firm that had been robbed were present, including Mr. Cameron.

When in the court-room, as the prisoner was being led away, Cameron remarked to his partner, Mr. Comstock:

"It's strange that we have had such a hardened wretch in our employ so long without having suspected his character."

As the man spoke, another voice was heard, saying, in clear, distinct tones:

"It's more strange that Mr. Comstock has had such a hardened villain for a partner for so long a time without having suspected his character."

The two bankers turned, upon hearing the voice, and discovered that no one was standing within ten feet of them.

George Cameron, however, had heard the voice, and at the same moment had observed a female form disappear through the side-door.

"What is the meaning of that?" asked Mr. Comstock.

"I am as much puzzled as you are."

Half an hour later the banker was standing at the door of a low groggery, talking to a pale-faced, slender-formed man.

After talking for some time, the banker turned to walk away, after having remarked:

"Succeed in your work and I will make you a rich man!"

CHAPTER XXIII.

FOILED AGAIN.

IN a previous chapter we intimated that Mr. Cameron was a deep, cunning man.

He had been played against for a long time by a foe hidden in the dark, but at last he had unearthed his antagonist.

On the very day that he had received the note from the pretended French maid, he had been "piping" down the mysterious woman, who, by some secret web-work, had dropped to his true character and crime.

He had hired the services of a detective, and the latter, belonging to that class of the profession who care more for money than honor, had "piped to the facts," and let Mr. Cameron into the knowledge that the French maid was a certain Kate Goelet, a sharp and cunning lady detective.

The officer did not drop to the French maid business, but supplied sufficient data for Mr. Cameron to locate the facts himself.

The banker did not let the male detective know his purpose or fear, but invented a story to account for his interest in the singular woman who had proved herself so inimical to his interests.

It was diamond cut diamond. McGuire, the man employed by Mr. Cameron, was a shrewd, cunning fellow, and he got the points down so fine on the woman, that Mr. Cameron knew just where to put his hand on her for a purpose he had conceived.

His first move was to try bribery, and, in case of failure, he had determined to resort to a most cunning method for removing her from his path.

Kate Goelet, in a most singular manner, had a note put in her hand requesting an interview on the part of a party who could aid her in the game she was playing.

When the lady detective received this note, it caused her a great deal of uneasiness.

It told her that some person as cunning as herself was playing against her, and that to a certain extent her little game had been uncovered.

The note showed considerable knowledge as to her methods, as it instructed her to come to the interview in the guise of a man for "convenience and better security's sake."

The tryst was appointed for midnight, and at a place where it would require a person of nerve to go.

Our heroine pondered well upon the subject, and at length determined to brave all dangers and see the adventure through to the end, come what might.

The interview was named for the night of the same day that she had received the note.

At half past eleven o'clock, under cover as the Frenchman, a rôle she had so often assumed, she proceeded to the spot where the meeting was to take place, which was upon an unfrequented street in the lower portion of the city.

She started early, but did not show up on the ground.

For a time she lay low, to take the measure of the party who had called for the meeting.

She had been for some time in her place of observation, when she saw a roughly dressed man pass along the street.

"That's Cameron," was her quiet remark, as she left her hiding-place and proceeded to meet the banker, whose identity she had "dropped to," despite his disguise.

The banker was leaning against a lamp-post, looking around in every direction, when suddenly, like a shadow, the little Frenchman stood before him.

"Ah! you have come?"

"Certainly."

"I am glad."

"Well, what is your business with me?"

"You got my note?"

"I did."

"From that you know that I have perceived your several disguises."

"Well?"

"Now I want to know what your game is that you are playing against me?"

"Can you not wait until the game is played out?"

"No, Miss French Maid; since you have made such wonderful progress in English, I have concluded not to wait."

"Well, do the next best thing."

"You are very defiant."

"I can afford to be."

Mr. Cameron placed his hand behind him, when he was startled by hearing his companion say in a peculiar tone:

"Look here!"

Mr. Cameron did look, and saw that he had been forestalled.

"I am a woman, but I am used to this kind of play, and there are two reasons why you should not attempt any treachery. I came prepared, and you will find that I am the quicker of the two."

"I have no mind to bring on any encounter, especially with a woman."

"What is your business, then?"

"I wish to secure your services in my behalf."

"In plain words, you wish to bribe me to let up on you."

"What have you got to let up on me about?"

"You will learn when the game is played out: in fact, I've got the true history of all your villainies, and I will run you to earth before I am through."

"Taking your word for the truth of what you say, I will give you twenty-five thousand dollars to leave New York for Europe to-morrow."

"A good bribe certainly."

"Will you accept it?"

"No."

"If I make it fifty thousand?"

"No."

"If you do not, you will never be able to play your game out."

"I do not scare."

"Curse you!" yelled Mr. Cameron; and in the fury of the moment, he leaped forward to catch his companion.

It was evident that in the excitement of the moment he had forgotten a former experience, as in a moment he was brought to his knees writhing in agony.

Cameron was a powerful man, and, after the first shock, would have recovered his self-command, and would most probably have overcome his lighter antagonist; but, as he

fell to his feet, the lady detective released her hold, and glided away.

Fearful was the rage of the man, as he rose, with his bleeding arms, and started in pursuit; but, alas! the singular woman who had so strangely got the better of him glided out of sight.

The day following the adventure above recorded, Kate Goelet became aware that she was being followed by a pale-faced, slenderly built man.

She tried several dodges, to make sure that she was not mistaken, and then, with a courage that was extraordinary in a woman, she struck a line for a secluded part of the town, in order to give the man a chance to overtake her and show his hand.

She at once concluded that he was some instrument of Cameron's, and, with a shudder, conjectured that his purpose was bad.

She had first met the man down-town, and he had dogged her away beyond the limits of the city.

There is a certain district lying between the city and Harlem, where, along the river front, it is as wild as some spots on the Sound far beyond.

Especially after nightfall is this locality a particularly lonesome and deserted place.

Night had fallen when the lady detective turned toward the river bank.

She had not taken the step through a spirit of fate-daring venturesomeness, but in a belief that it was a matter of safety to run the man to the end of his string while she was on her guard, so as to provide against being taken at some other moment when unprepared for the peril.

On the bank of that river, under cover of the darkness, a most tragic and thrilling incident occurred; but the necessities of our narrative demand that we should defer a record of the adventures until a later period in our tale.

Two hours and a half subsequent to the moment when our heroine was recorded as passing toward the river, followed by the emissary of Cameron, a man might have been seen pacing to and fro across the apartment, along the North River road, where the lady detective had had the adventure with Cameron on the night of the masquerade.

It was well on toward midnight, and Mr. Cameron's face was expressive of great anxiety and concern as he rapidly traversed his room.

At length there came a great ring at his front door bell.

"Heavens!" exclaimed the banker; "that must be my man, as I told him to report the moment he had any news."

A servant soon appeared at the banker's door, and announced that a man, a stranger, was very anxious to see him.

"What kind of a looking man is he?" asked Mr. Cameron.

"A slender man, with a pale face, poorly dressed, and he appears to be very excited, like a man who had just been frightened."

"Show him up to this room at once!" exclaimed Mr. Cameron, in a tone and manner going to prove that he had absorbed some of his strange visitor's excitement.

The visitor was shown up to the room where the banker for hours had paced to and fro.

The latter closed the door securely, turned the gas down, and in a low, husky voice asked:

"Well?"

"It is done!" said the man.

"Is she shut up?"

"Yes."

CHAPTER XXIV.

THE CONFEDERATES.

THE man who had thus intruded himself upon the banker, was the same pale-faced party with whom he had been talking in front of the low groggery, and again was the same fellow who had been dogging the steps of the lady detective toward the river.

The banker's face wore a ghastly expression as he again asked:

"Have you really succeeded?"

"I have."

A moment he remained silent, but at length he asked:

"What proof have you brought me?"

The man produced a number of articles, and among

other things the very letter which the banker had written to the detective.

"How did you accomplish it?"

"I dogged her all day, and at last some fatal idea drove her to take a course toward the river. I followed close upon her heels, and when she came to a halt just over the bank I rushed upon her."

The banker's face could not assume a more ghastly hue, but a fit of trembling seized him.

At length he said:

"You must come to me some other time for your pay."

"Oh! I can wait for my pay: it is a large sum, you know."

"I promised you five thousand dollars!"

"More than that!"

"More than five thousand dollars?"

"Yes, sir."

"What did I promise you?"

"You promised to make me a rich man."

"Five thousand dollars would make you a rich man!"

"You think so?"

"I do."

"See here, Mr. Cameron, you used me for a purpose. I know why you were afraid of that woman. I didn't take the chances on a job like that without knowing my business."

"See here, fellow, I do not like the way you are talking."

"You will have to like it."

A look of rage came upon the banker's face. Should the proud millionaire be compelled to listen to the insolent talk of a common ruffian?

"How dare you talk to me in that manner?"

"I dare do anything with you now."

"What do you mean?"

"Why, my dear sir, you must not forget that you and I are 'pals!'"

"You and I are what?"

"'Pals.'"

"What do you mean by 'pals'?"

"Why, 'pards.'"

A ghastly look succeeded the expression of rage that had rested upon Mr. Cameron's face.

A terrible realization of the truth came over him.

He began to see in all its enormity the extent of his crime, and in that moment he would have surrendered all the bonds if he could have been loosened from the bond that bound him to the grinning wretch, who, by his manner, indicated that he knew well his power, and intended to use it.

The thought came to him that he must cow down his confederate at once, and he made a motion toward him.

"Hold on, boss! Don't go and try to come any gumgames over your 'pard,' you know. You see I'm jist up to them 'ere games, and I don't take 'em!"

"What do you require to conclude your business with me forever?"

"Well, I guess I'll be satisfied to let you alone on condition that you give me fifty thousand dollars' worth of those bonds you just yanked out of your partner's safe."

With a yell Cameron rushed toward the man, but was brought to a sudden halt.

"Won't work, nobby! I've got you down fine. I didn't go into this 'ere job without knowing the whole lay of the land."

"I would like to know how a scoundrel like you knows anything about my business!"

"See here, boss, we don't go into any fine discussions. You've got those bonds, and you can hand 'em over, if you choose; and if you do, you'll never have any more trouble or annoyance from Frenchy Joe."

"What guarantee have I that you will not come upon me with other demands?"

"Men like me with plenty of stamps get out of a place where they may meet with an accident. You just give me the bonds, and I'll flit."

"I've no bonds. I will give you ten thousand dollars in money."

"It won't do. I wants the fifty thousand, and I wants it in the bonds."

"You go away, and come here to-morrow, and I will see what I can do."

"No, no, boss. I know you, now; you see, you could

get some other chap to slit my gizzard for about five hundred, and save forty-nine thousand five hundred dollars. Won't do; and, besides, I ain't got no license to linger around here; that 'ere stiff may come to the top at any time, and make it hot for the surgeon."

"I have nothing in the house to give you."

"Well, go to where you got it."

"See here, my man, come here in the morning, and I will conclude terms with you."

"Can't wait; you know I'm a thief, and might be nipped any moment; I must 'lite out.'"

Mr. Cameron would gladly have given the fifty thousand in bonds to have got rid of the fellow, Frenchy Joe.

In fact, the banker had at last learned the bitterness of crime, and he would have given up all his plunder to have got out of the horrid scrape into which he had been led.

Already had he learned that even successful crime brings no pleasure, but, on the contrary, a load of miseries, under which the strongest man must in time succumb.

He remembered that he held twenty thousand dollars' worth of bonds that were not a part of the stolen ones.

The latter had but that day come into his possession.

He feared to give the others, lest in trying to dispose of them Frenchy Joe might precipitate a grand catastrophe.

"I have twenty thousand dollars in bonds; if you will take them and leave, you shall have them."

"When?"

"To-night."

"At once?"

"Yes."

"All right! I will take the twenty thousand."

"Where will you go to?"

"Well, may be South America."

"I will never see you again?"

"Never on this business, I reckon."

Mr. Cameron went into the adjoining room and closed and locked the door behind him.

Frenchy Joe stole across the room toward the door through which the banker had passed, and a most wonderful and remarkable scene followed.

CHAPTER XXV.

THE BONDS "HOCKED."

FRENCHY JOE drew from his pocket a little instrument of most singular construction and inserted it in the keyhole of the door.

A few moments passed, and then he removed his instrument, and with a satisfied grunt stole away.

An instant later the room door opened and George Cameron came forth.

In his hand the banker carried a number of bonds; addressing Frenchy Joe, he said:

"Now, then, if I give these to you, you will leave the town at once?"

"I will."

"Will you so swear?"

Frenchy Joe laughed and answered:

"You might as well swear a rattlesnake as force an oath from a scoundrel; all you have to do is to give me the bonds and take my word."

"You must swear."

"I will not swear to-night; keep your bonds, I know a way in which I may make more money out of certain information I possess than by making any promises."

The banker was bothered as to what he should do, but at length he said:

"Here, take the bonds; I will trust you."

Strangely enough the thief suddenly displayed a great reluctance to receive the bonds which a few moments before he had been so anxious to become possessed of.

"I can call on you to-morrow and we will talk matters over," he said.

"No, no, take the bonds; I promised them, and I choose to keep my word."

Frenchy Joe received the bonds, and moving toward the door, said:

"I will go now."

"I will not see you again, I trust."

"You will see me once more, and after that I will make myself scarce."

Frenchy Joe, after having delivered himself of this evasive answer, left the room, passed down through the hall and out of the front door.

It was a singular fact, however, that he did not leave the grounds, but skulked away between the rows of trees, and when a good distance from the house dropped down in the grass and showed a disposition to hang around awhile, as though he had some fell purpose in view.

An hour passed, and the mysterious Frenchy Joe rose from his hiding-place, and crept around to that part of the house where the light had gleamed from George Cameron's room.

All was still and dark.

Then the man stole back to the parlor window, produced a number of burglar's tools, and opened a passage through into the parlor.

Once within the house, he proceeded upstairs to the door of the room adjoining the one where George Cameron slept.

The skillful use of an instrument, provided for the purpose, admitted him into this room, when from a bag which he had brought with him he produced several articles suggestive of a most extraordinary proceeding.

Having arranged the articles, he stole into George Cameron's bedroom.

The banker was in bed. The robber stole beside his bed, and after saturating a handkerchief with some colorless liquid, he put it to the sleeping man's nostrils.

Having stupefied his victim, the man placed a gag in the banker's mouth, adjusted handcuffs upon his wrists, and securely bound his feet, thus leaving him bound, gagged, and helpless.

Having made everything secure against interruption, the robber produced a dark lantern, and at length disclosed the main purpose of his most extraordinary maneuvers.

He arranged his light so that the rays fell upon a certain portion of the floor, over which an elegant mat had been spread.

The man drew aside the mat, removed a piece of carpet which, singularly enough, needed no cutting.

When the carpet had been removed, a piece of the flooring was raised, and a little secret closet, or a place used as a secret depository was reached.

From the secret place the man drew forth a middling-sized box.

The box he placed directly under the rays of light from his dark lantern, and a grim smile broke over his evil face as he remarked:

"The second thief is the best owner."

A key was in the box, and when it was opened a large number of bonds and papers were disclosed.

"Not a moment to spare!" now muttered the man, as he shut down the lid of the box, turned the key, and stole out of the room.

Upon the day following the scene above described George Cameron arrived at the banking-house at a late hour.

The man looked fully twenty years older than he had when he left the office the night before.

His partner, Mr. Comstock, noticed his appearance, and, in a tone of astonishment, exclaimed:

"Why, Cameron, what on earth is the matter with you? You are a sick man!"

"I have passed a bad night," answered Mr. Cameron, and he showed no disposition to answer any more questions or give any explanations.

After remaining a short time at the office, he went out.

Ten minutes later Kate Goelet entered the office.

"It's done," she said, in her short, direct, sententious manner.

"What is done?"

"The bonds are recovered intact, and the thief is run down."

"You have recovered the bonds?" almost screamed Mr. Comstock.

"I have."

"Then Henry Wilbur has confessed?"

A strange smile played over the lady detective's face.

"You have something to tell me?"

"I have—a long story."

"I am ready to listen."

The lady detective related her whole experience in the recovery of the bonds.

The banker could hardly believe his own ears.

When the story was concluded, he exclaimed:

"I never did believe it possible that Henry Wilbur was a thief." At this moment Mr. Cameron re-entered the office.

All hands entered an inner room, and a long consultation ensued.

Mr. Cameron had been run to earth, and begged for mercy.

What followed our readers can readily anticipate.

A dissolution of the firm immediately followed.

For certain reasons no prosecution followed against Mr. Cameron.

The man was furnished money to retire to Europe.

In the meantime Henry Wilbur was released, and from Mr. Comstock subsequently heard the whole story of the faithfulness of the lady detective.

But one mystery remains to be explained: Kate Goelet had overcome the fellow who had followed her on the rocks, and getting herself up to represent him, had appeared to Mr. Cameron, and had recovered the bonds as described.

CHAPTER XXVI.

THE END.

UPON the day following the scenes above depicted, Kate Goelet, the lady detective, called at the banking-house of Attry, Comstock & Co., and made a formal surrender of the recovered bonds.

Her reward, after a division with the detective office, amounted to twenty-five thousand dollars.

Subsequently, in the office of Chief Young, she said:

"I have closed my career as a detective."

"How is that?" asked the chief. "Keep at it, and in a few years you will be a wealthy woman."

"No; it was necessity that drove me to engage in so unlady-like a trade, and now that the necessity is removed, I shall leave the business."

"You have a snug sum enough to live on?"

"Yes; I have made enough to settle my mother and her family comfortably for the rest of their lives, and I have these last earnings for my own support."

"When you leave the service, Miss Kate Goelet, one of the best detective brains that ever hunted a rogue will be withdrawn!"

"I thank you for the compliment, and yet I must say, despite my success, the duty has always been distasteful."

The next day Kate Goelet went down east to visit her mother.

She had departed without one word of warning to Henry Wilbur, not even dropping him a note saying good-bye.

Henry called to inquire about her, and was told she had returned to her home.

He asked where that home was.

The chief could not tell him; and all he could say was that it was somewhere in the vicinity of Boston.

Henry determined to turn detective.

He resolved to hunt up Kate Goelet, the beautiful and wonderful woman who had done him such extraordinary service.

Henry was a shrewd young man, but, do his best, he could not discover the home of the woman he sought.

At length he determined to return to New York.

On one of the Sound boats he noticed a veiled lady enter a state-room.

There was something that struck him as familiar in the lady's form, and he watched that state-room until he saw her come forth.

It was late, and most of the passengers had retired to their state-rooms, when the lady whom our hero was watching passed along and seated herself in one of the arm-chairs on the rear upper deck.

Henry followed, and, advancing toward her, said:

"I can not be mistaken. I am addressing Miss Goelet, the lady who has placed me under so great an obligation."

"My name is Goelet," answered the lady detective, coldly.

"Heaven! is it possible that you do not recognize me?" exclaimed Henry.

"Yes; I recognize you. I did so when you first came on the boat."

"And you would not address me?"

"I did not."

84

"And I have been searching all over the State of Massachusetts to find you."

"To find me?"

"Yes."

"Indeed! and why do you wish to find me?" answered Kate, still in a cold, chilling tone.

"Can you not guess?"

"I can not."

"Will you not try?"

"I would not know how."

"You certainly must suspect."

"I do not."

"Kate, I love you, and that is why I have been searching for you."

Henry could see behind the veil that his companion showed considerable agitation, but it was in the coldest of tones that she said, after a moment,

"What wild nonsense is this?"

"It is no nonsense; I speak from the bottom of my heart."

"The idea!" ejaculated Kate, in a contemptuous tone.

"What idea?"

"That the refined, highly cultured, well born and bred Henry Wilbur could honestly profess love to a woman who had associated in all kinds of rough company, and mixed in all kinds of horrid scenes while performing her duty as a professional detective!"

"Your life only proves what a noble and virtuous woman you are."

"You love Mary Clarkson, and it is only a feeling of gratitude that prompts you to come and offer your love to me. Why, I am almost an old maid!"

Henry was silent.

"Ah, ha! you dare not answer when I tell you that you love Mary Clarkson?"

"I tell you that I love you."

"No, no; you can not deceive me, it is Mary Clarkson you love!"

"I may have fancied the lady you mention, once upon a time, but I tell you that I love you!"

"And I tell you that it is me that you fancy, and that it is Mary Clarkson that you love."

"Even if I did love that woman, she has gone away. I know not where to find her, and I certainly shall not attempt to hunt her up, especially when my heart is really given to you."

"And you really love me?"

"I do."

"But the moment you meet Mary Clarkson again all your love for me would vanish."

"Never!"

"I would like to see you put to the test. I tell you I understand human nature pretty well."

"I wish I could be put to the test."

"You really would like to be put to the test?"

"I would."

"Then you shall. Mary Clarkson is a friend of mine, and I will arrange for you to meet her without informing her of the object of the meeting."

"And if I stand this test, will you really believe me when I assert that I love you alone?"

"I will," answered Kate, in a constrained voice.

Two days succeeding the events above recorded, Henry Wilbur started one night to go to a house where he was to meet Mary Clarkson, in accordance with a plan that had been arranged by Kate Goelet.

Arrived at the house, he was shown into the parlor, and a few moments later Mary Clarkson entered the room.

The situation would be an awkward one to a less self-possessed person than our hero, but he at once arose and greeted the lovely woman in a frank and hearty manner.

Miss Clarkson, however, appeared greatly ill at ease, and only answered him in monosyllables.

After remaining for some time, Henry arose to take his departure, when suddenly Mary placed her hand upon his arm, and gazing into his eyes in the most winning manner, said:

"You are not going to leave me thus abruptly?"

"Yes," answered Henry, coldly.

"And have you forgotten all the professions you once made to me?"

"Yes," answered Henry, with the same cool nonchalance.

"And you are going to desert me?"

"Yes."

"Why?"

"Well, I have discovered that I love another."

"Ah, you heartless man! and you tell me this in such a cruel manner."

"I must tell you the truth."

"And who is the lady you love?"

"Well, her name is Kate Goelet; I believe you are already acquainted with her."

"And do you really love Kate Goelet?"

"I love her as man never loved woman before," answered Henry, in an enthusiastic and earnest manner.

"Henry," murmured Mary, in a tone different from any she had used before, "are you really sincere, and on your honor is it not a feeling of gratitude instead of love that animates you?"

"When Kate Goelet becomes my wife, it will take me just two seconds to convince her that it is not gratitude, but the warmest and most passionate love."

"Henry!"

"Well?"

"I have deceived you."

"Indeed?"

"Yes; can you forgive me?"

There was a strange expression upon Mary Clarkson's face, and yet it was beaming with happiness.

"I can forgive you; but how have you deceived me?"

"I am Kate Goelet. I have used my art to appear to you in two characters."

"And you thought you had succeeded?"

"Why, Henry, what are you going to tell me?"

"I am going to tell you, darling, that I have never been deceived for one moment. A lover's eyes can not be so easily blinded. I have known you all along, in all your disguises, as my beautiful, brave, patient, heroic and loving Kate!"

"Ah, Henry!" murmured the lady detective, as she fell into the strong, brave arms outstretched to receive her in their warm embrace.

*   *   *   *   *

Henry Wilbur and his wife are well known in New York society; and Kate Goelet's husband is constantly heard to say that, if his wife had been born a man, she would have rivaled Napoleon the Grand. And he does say that she is the best, handsomest, and smartest woman in the world.

THE END.

OLD SLEUTH WEEKLY

A Series of
THE MOST THRILLING DETECTIVE STORIES
EVER PUBLISHED

MAR 14 1923

| No. 161 | THE ARTHUR WESTBROOK COMPANY, CLEVELAND, U. S. A.
Published Weekly. By Subscription, $2.50 per year; $1.25 for 6 months. | Vol. IV |

Madge The Society Detective,

or

A Strange Guest Among The Four Hundred

BY "OLD SLEUTH"

PRINCIPAL CHARACTERS IN THIS STORY.

MADGE NELSON—A brilliant and clever detective who works in unusual ways and accomplishes great things.
ARDMORE SANGSTER—A broker and millionaire.
COURTNEY SANGSTER—His wayward son.

ALICE VANCAMP—A beautiful and accomplished young society woman.
AGNES WARWICK—A thief by compulsion.
SPINDLE WARWICK—A deep-dyed villain and crook.

CHAPTER I.

AN INTERRUPTED RECEPTION.

"Miss Alice, won't you listen to me?"

Beautiful Alice VanCamp, society favorite, brilliant woman of the world laughed good naturedly.

"Am I not listening?"

"But," protested Courtney Sangster, "you do not listen in the right way."

"I do not?"

"You know you do not."

"How would you have me listen, then?"

"Seriously."

"Very well, now I am serious. See, I am listening. You shall not be able to again say that I have not given you serious consideration. You are such a serious boy, anyway, for——"

"There you go again."

"Pray, what have I done now?" pouted the beauty. "A boy? I am no boy, I am a full-grown man."

She surveyed him keenly for one brief moment with

a glance that seemed to shoot through the young man like a sharp weapon. What she saw was a somewhat boyish face that might have been handsome had it not been for certain weak lines, the natural beauty of the features marred by dissipation and excesses.

However, for all this, young Sangster, son of Ardmore Sangster, millionaire broker, clubman, yachtsman and promoter, passed for a handsome man. His manners were all that could be desired; that is, when in the society of his father and mother's guests or their proper circle.

For a long time Courtney had professed to be in love with Alice VanCamp. This gifted young woman was said to be the handsomest woman in the social set known as the Four Hundred. Left an orphan by a supposedly wealthy father some few years before, she had lived in the family mansion on lower Fifth avenue with a few old servants ever since. She was believed to possess a comfortable fortune.

Some said there was a mystery about Miss Van-

Camp, but it was admitted that besides being a brilliant woman, not a breath could be said against her. She was a masterful woman, and yet possessing all those delicate feminine ways that so endear a woman to the opposite sex. She was as dainty as she was beautiful, with a figure that artists raved over.

"Yes, you are a man, aren't you? Pardon me for not having observed this before. But you see we have known each other for so long that I still think of you as the child in short trousers that I knew, oh, ever and ever so many years ago."

The eyes of the the young woman twinkled merrily, all unobserved by young Courtney. His face was sour.

"You make me feel like a kid," he answered, petulantly.

"Why not leave it at that. Let's us forget that we are not children just for this once," begged the beauty.

They were sitting in the conservatory. The occasion was the wedding of Courtney's adopted sister Margaret. The latter had been adopted when a child, after the death of Mr. Sangster's only daughter, it was said, though there were few in the set in which the Sangsters moved, who possessed any definite knowledge about this phase of their lives. Margaret had been married at six that evening and the reception was then going on, one of those brilliant functions seldom seen outside of the great Metropolis, in this country.

Courtney's shifty eyes were glancing apprehensively out into the reception room where some of the younger set had begun to dance to the strains of the orchestra provided for the occasion. The reception proper had been interrupted by the dance, but the two young people in the conservatory appeared to feel no inclination to join the merrymakers.

"I do not want to leave it at that," replied Courtney in answer to Miss VanCamp's last question.

"Very well, being a man you have the privilege of suiting yourself, I suppose. This is a very enjoyable occasion. However, you will miss your sister."

"Yes, sis is a good sort, but she is a prude."

"A prude?" wondered the beauty.

"Yes."

"With reference to what?"

"She preaches."

"Well?"

"I don't like to be preached to."

"You don't?"

"No, I don't."

"Perhaps that is because you really need it. People object to having the truth told about themselves," she added, half maliciously.

He fixed his shifty eyes upon the young woman for a brief instant, then permitted his glance to fall to the floor of the conservatory.

"What do you mean by that remark?"

"You laid yourself open to the retort," she laughed.

"But you wished me to tell you what I meant. I have done so. Are you satisfied?"

"No, I am not. I should like to know what you meant by that remark?"

"About the coat fitting or words to that effect?"

"Yes."

"Let's not get personal."

"It strikes me that it is you who are indulging in personalities. I did not start the conversation in this direction, you will remember."

"Courtney, you are right. I beg your pardon. It was unkind of me. There, we will forget it. Am I absolved now?"

There was an irresistible sweetness in her tone. It brought a deep flush to the face of the young man. He raised his eyes to her face, holding her in one long, devouring glance.

The color slowly surged to the face and neck of Miss VanCamp, then disappeared suddenly.

"Yes," he murmured. "I could not deny you anything."

"You are very kind. Come, had we best not join the others? They will wonder at our absence. Even though we are old, old friends, people will wonder at our hiding ourselves away in this fashion."

"Not yet. I have something to say to you."

The girl sank back resignedly.

"I love you Alice!"

"What, again?" murmured the girl, half wearily.

"I always have. Ever since the days when you and I were little toddlers together——"

"Please don't go back into ancient history. It makes me feel old, an old woman," she begged with a short laugh.

"I tell you I love you. I want you, Alice. I never wanted anything so badly in my life. You always put me off in this way when I try to tell—when I try to tell you this. Why won't you be serious and listen to me?"

"I have been listening. It were better for you if I did not."

"Better for me?"

"Yes."

"No, it were better for me if you did."

Courtney was plunging ahead to his fate. He would not be warned. He was determined to possess the beautiful Alice VanCamp for his very own.

"Come, listen to me, ere we are interrupted, as we always are when I try to tell you of my love. I love——"

A woman rushed into the conservatory, interrupting the fervent declaration of love. Miss VanCamp breathed a sigh of relief. Then her beautiful eyes narrowed. The figure was all in white, a handsome girl, but whose beauty was marred by a death-like pallor.

"Margaret, what is it?" demanded Alice.

"Go away, we are busy, Margaret," demanded

Courtney, petulantly. He did not observe that his adopted sister was laboring under a great mental strain at that moment. This fact had not escaped the keen eyes of Alice VanCamp. She saw at once that something was wrong. For the moment she forgot the very existence of Courtney Sangster.

"What is it, Margaret?" she repeated.

"I've been robbed," gasped Margaret.

"Robbed?"

"Yes."

"Robbed of what?"

"Of everything."

"Surely, it is not so bad as that," protested Alice. "Please be more explicit. What have you been robbed of?"

"My jewels!"

"Your jewels?"

"Yes," gasped the pale-faced girl. "My diamonds, all the beautiful jewels given to me on my wedding day."

"There must be some mistake about that."

"No, there is no mistake. Think of it, Alice, a half a million dollars' worth of beautiful jewels, all gone, all gone."

Margaret broke down and wept. Miss VanCamp turned to look at Courtney Sangster. His face was pale and the hand he raised to his forehead trembled perceptibly.

"God, that's hard luck," he muttered thickly.

CHAPTER II.

THE ROBBERY OF THE GEMS.

"The police must be informed at once," decided the young man with more decision than Alice had ever before seen him exhibit. Courtney rose.

"Wait," said Alice, laying a restraining hand on his arm. "What would you do?"

"Notify my father then call the police."

"And alarm your guests?"

"It can't be kept from them."

"It must be."

"Must be?"

"Yes."

"Why?"

"You should know why, without asking that question."

"Margaret, have you told father?"

"Not—not yet," breathed the young girl tremulously. "I—I couldn't."

"Take my advice," suggested Alice, "say nothing about it to any one save possibly your father. You must not appear out in the other room. Come to your rooms and I will accompany you. After you have composed yourself we will send for your father, telling him all. Believe me, my dear, that will be best. Courtney, not a word of this until I give you leave,"

commanded Miss VanCamp with a strong note of authority in her voice.

Young Sangster had never heard her assume a tone like that before, and he glanced at the young woman in surprise.

"Very, well, if you think you know better about how to handle these things than I do."

"I did not say so. I know what is best for Margaret, and I know that a scene should not be made here. Think of the scandal that will follow——"

"You are right," murmured Margaret. "You are always right. That is why I sought you out. I knew you would know what to do."

"Courtney, go out and mingle with your guests. If any questions are asked about Margaret, say that she is with me, that I am assisting her in some matters that need attention."

Young Sangster nodded. He made no verbal reply. Now he stood watching the calm, resourceful girl to whom he had proposed only a few minutes before. He stood thus until Alice and Margaret had disappeared from view, then Courtney wiped the perspiration from his forehead. Instead, however, of going directly to the ball room, he stepped out on the veranda and walked off into the yard at the rear of the mansion.

In the meantime, Margaret had accompanied her friend up to the young bride's apartments. Margaret was all atremble.

"Now, Margaret, compose yourself. It will do no good to allow yourself to become so upset, and especially on your wedding night. What will your husband think to find you in tears?"

"Oh, Alice, I can't help it. Just think, all my beautiful jewels gone, gone——"

"Never mind, perhaps we shall be able to recover them. Surely the police will have little difficulty in recovering jewels of such great price. The thieves will have difficulty in disposing of them without attracting attention. Therein lies your best chance of getting your treasures back again."

"You make me almost believe you," answered the bride smiling through her tears.

"Believe me wholly. Now tell me all about it. Do so as quickly as possible, for we are liable to be disturbed at any moment."

"What shall I tell you? I have told you all there is to be told,"

"Oh, no, all you have told me is that your jewels have been stolen."

"What else is there to tell?"

"A great deal. Are you quite sure that they have not been mislaid?"

"I know they have not."

"Where were they?"

"In my jewel safe."

"Where was that?"

"Yonder."

A small, heavy iron safe stood at one side of the room. The door was open. In a center compartment where had been a wooden drawer or receptacle, Alice saw that the wood had been crushed in with some blunt instrument.

"Lock the door, Margaret," she said in a sharp, business-like tone.

The bride complied wonderingly. In the meantime Miss VanCamp had gone down on her knees in front of the open safe. With deft, careful fingers she went through the safe itself, then turned to an examination of the broken door of the inner compartment.

This done the young society woman cast a keen glance over the carpet in front of the safe.

"This drawer was locked, of course?"

"No, it was not."

"Ah!"

"Why do you ask?"

"Because the person who stole your jewels took for granted that it was. You are quite sure on that point, are you?"

"Yes. Why?"

"Because whoever did this deed had been told that the receptacle would be locked and that they would have to break in the end of the drawer. Otherwise, any thief would have first tried the drawer to learn whether it was locked or unlocked."

"Is it possible?"

"Yes, it is a fact, and we shall find it to be so when we get to the bottom of the affair."

"It all seems like a dream."

"The robber came here well prepared. He was well informed as to the lay of the land. How about your servants?"

"What do you mean, Alice?"

"Have they all been long in your employ?"

"Oh, yes, for a very long time, ever since I was a child."

"None of them could have had a hand in this, you think?"

"The idea is preposterous."

"That is what I think, Margaret."

The bride looked at her friend, wonderingly.

"You talk like a detective, Alice."

"You seem to know all about them," answered Miss VanCamp with a laugh, but her eyes were keenly glancing about the room taking in everything in quick, sharp, comprehensive glances.

Alice fixed her eyes on a door at the rear of the bride's chamber.

"Where does that lead to?" she demanded.

"To the hall way."

"And thence?"

"To the rear of the house."

"Remain here."

"Where are you going?"

"To look at something at the end of the hall," answered the society woman, slipping silently from the room, leaving Margaret wondering vaguely.

CHAPTER III.

BEAUTY ON THE TRAIL.

Miss VanCamp moved along the hall directly toward the rear of the house and though the doors of the rooms on that floor stood open, she did not even glance into them. The young woman seemed led by some inner instinct that was not of herself.

At the end of the hall on the right was the bathroom. To the left, as one stood facing the bathroom, was an open window.

Alice leaned from the window, to find herself looking down the sloping roof of an addition. For a moment she gazed out over the low roof, then turned to an examination of the window sill.

"It is here," she murmured scarcely above a whisper. "I felt sure I should find it here. It was all well planned and cleverly executed. I do not recognize the work at all. Well, it was fortunate that I was here and that I have had a chance to help my friends before the police came in to upset everything. I must go back to Margaret. The poor child is nearly crazed with her loss, and I do not know that I blame her. A half a million in jewels is a loss that would make me feel rather badly, I am sure." The words were accompanied by a quiet smile of amusement.

Miss VanCamp hurried back to where her friend was impatiently awaiting her.

"Where have you been, Alice?"

"To the bath room," answered the beauty, and with truth, for she had truly glanced into the bath room as she stood at the end of the corridor.

"I thought you were looking for something."

"I was."

"Did you find it?"

"Yes."

"What was it?"

"The bath room, dear."

Margaret smiled in spite of herself.

"You are such a funny girl."

"Yes, I should have made a great success as a humorist. I have often thought I might profitably have adopted that as a career. Who was up here besides yourself this evening?"

"Why, no one that I know of save my bridesmaids and the servants."

"Who of the servants?"

"My maid and the housekeeper."

"How along ago were they here?"

"I think when I came up after the ceremony. Why do you ask?"

"Merely my interest in you and your loss, that is all."

"Now I am going below. I will send your husband to you, through one of the servants. You are to remain here until he arrives. When he does tell him all. Don't break down and weep, but just tell him the facts. Have your husband see your father and bring him here, where your father will be told the story of your loss. That will be the best course to follow and the guests will know nothing about what has happened."

"You think of everything."

"So would you under ordinary circumstances, but you have reason to feel upset and excited this evening."

"Where are you going?"

"I am going down stairs for a few moments. I shall return. You may say to your husband and your father that you have sent for me. That will excuse me for intruding on your privacy when I return. But Margaret, be good enough to say nothing about my having been here, even to your husband for the present. You may tell him all when you are alone with him later on. I do not wish them to know of my apparent unusual interest in this affair. Not a word of it ever to your brother, only to your husband when the proper moment arrives."

" I will do as you wish," murmured Margaret.

" I knew you would, dear."

Miss VanCamp left the room, making her way down the staircase. Calling a servant she told her to inform Margaret's husband that his bride wished to see him in her apartments at once.

Having performed this duty, the society beauty strolled to the conservatory where, in the dim light, she stood surveying the gay throngs out in the ball-room. Her eyes were travelling over the assemblage, resting now and then on some face that seemed to claim her attention.

Alice's eyes lighted up and a smile suffused her face as she made out Courtney Sangster making violent love to a demure society bud off behind a spreading palm at the far side of the ball room.

" He is easily consoled," murmured the young woman, a sarcastic smile curling her lips as she noted the situation. She noted another thing, too. Courtney's face was pale and he appeared excited.

" I don't understand that young man at all. I have often wondered if he were not addicted to the use of some drug. I don't know what else would account for his erratic behavior. I am glad he is well out of the way. He was strolling out to the veranda when I went upstairs," showing that the young society woman used her eyes and her ears to excellent advantage.

Margaret turned suddenly and glided from the conservatory. Instead, however, of making her way out among the gay throngs she, too, went out upon the veranda. For a moment she leaned over the rail as if enjoying the fresh balmy night air.

Soon, she glided along the veranda with noiseless steps, holding up her handsome gown daintily that it might not be soiled by contact with the floor. Alice hastened down the steps with the perfect confidence of one who not only knew the way well, but who also knew where she was going and for what purpose.

Reaching the yard she hastened around the far end of the house after a quick glance about to make sure that she was not observed.

A moment later found her directly in the rear of the addition which so short a time before she had been gazing out over from the end of the corridor on the second floor.

That part of the rear yard was in darkness. A high board fence separated the yard from the adjoining one leading out onto another street.

After a brief survey of the surroundings, the handsome young society woman did a strange thing. She drew a dark object from her pocket and flashed a ray of light over the ground about her.

" Ah!" she muttered dropping to her knees. " I thought so."

A sheet of paper was extracted from some other part of that wonderful gown, and with it an exact copy of a footprint—of the shape of it—that she found there was made.

" I wish I had some plaster of Paris to make a cast of that," murmured the girl. " It is too bad, but I shall have to get along with what I have. I have made a great discovery. But what a terrible risk I am making. Ah, what is that?"

Alice crouched down in the shadows.

CHAPTER IV.

MATTERS GROW COMPLICATED.

" It is Margaret's husband," muttered the woman.

At that instant the gentleman halted in a listening attitude. It was evident that he realized some one else was near him.

Alice took the bolder course. Rising while his back was turned she walked toward the gentleman, uttering a merry, musical laugh as she did so.

" Why, Mr. Walker, are you out star-gazing instead of consoling your bride?"

Walker started. He peered into the shadows.

" Who is it, please?"

" Miss VanCamp, at your service," laughingly answered the young woman.

" And out here alone?"

" Oh yes, I am a poet by nature, you know. I love to commune with the stars, and you?"

" Perhaps I was imbued with the same motives. I came out here to think."

" Over the prize you have won? I do not blame you. Margaret is the dearest girl in the world."

" Naturally, I share your opinion."

" Have you been to Margaret?"

" Been to her?"

" Yes."

" Why no. I am waiting for her to come down."

" Then you did not get the message?"

" What message? I received no message," demanded Mr. Walker eagerly.

" A servant was asking for you as I came out. He said Margaret wished you to come to her at once."

The gentleman waited to hear no more. He started at a brisk walk, that was almost a run, for the house.

Alice VanCamp laughed softly.

" I wonder if he will be so devoted ten years from now. No, it does not last. There is an end to all things, love with the rest."

The young woman sighed deeply.

" Now that he has gone I will go on with my investigations. But I must hasten. There is no telling what Margaret will be doing if she finds no one is coming to her. But I wonder what Mr. Walker was doing out here?" mused the young woman thoughtfully. " Surely a strange mood to possess a man on his wedding night. Rather would he be waiting for the summons to go to his bride. It is a strange combination of circumstances all around, that I have been thrown in with on this night. Nor did I expect that my talents would be called into play. I came here for a pleasant social evening and now I find myself in the thick of a mystery that bids fair to be more than an ordinary mystery. Ah!"

Alice's exclamation was called forth by the sight of another figure in the grounds of the mansion. Like the first this, too, was that of a man. She could only make out the general outlines of the figure, but the young woman's shrewd eyes supplied what her instinct prompted.

" It is Courtney Sangster," muttered the young woman. " Now, what is he out here for? It seems as if the whole household had suddenly taken to star-gazing. I must confess that I do not understand it at all."

Young Sangster did not appear to be star-gazing. In fact he was standing with his back to Miss Van-

Camp, hands thrust deep in his trousers pockets gazing moodily at the ground.

The young man maintained this position for several
minutes. Then, heaving a deep sigh, he turned and
made his way back to the house.

Miss VanCamp was not far behind him. She made
sure that she was not caught, but it was her desire to
get in so close after Courtney that she would, for self-
protection's sake, be able to keep him in sight.

This the young woman accomplished easily. One
of the servants did see her entrance, however, but apparently set no special significance on the fact. Alice
was so close behind the young man that one would
have been led to believe she had entered with him
after a stroll on the veranda.

Instead, however, of proceeding on to the ball room
to join the merry throng there, the girl sat down in the
conservatory where, screened from view by the tall
tropical plants, she sat awaiting the moment when it
would be proper for her to go back up stairs to join
Margaret.

Meanwhile, Alice VanCamp was pondering over the
strange combination of circumstances that had beset
the Sangster household on that memorable evening.

"A quarter of a million in jewels gone," she murmured. "Quite a neat little fortune and I doubt not
that there was more taken. A secretary in the room
has been gone through hastily. It is reasonable to suppose that the thief also had information regarding the
presence there of other valuables, perhaps money. I
should not be at all surprised if such were the case.
I must be careful or I shall direct suspicion to myself.
That would not suit me at all. I cannot afford to expose my own hand, else my efficiency would be quite
at an end. Then Alice VanCamp surely would have to
go to work," added the girl with a grim smile curling
the corners of her pretty mouth.

After a few moments of reflection the girl rose and
made her way to the floor above. She waited at the
head of the stairs to gaze down into the ball room, all
unnoticed by the brilliant throngs there. Then she
proceeded on to Margaret's room.

A half-timid knock was responded to by a faint,
"Come in."

Alice entered. Her eyes rested on a picture. Margaret was seated on a divan her face buried in her
hands. Before her stood Mr. Sangster and her husband. It needed nothing more than the serious expressions on the faces of the two gentlemen present
to tell one that something serious had occurred.

"Did you send for me, Margaret?"

"Yes," came the sobbing reply from the hidden face
of the young bride.

"I am here at your service. Why, what makes you
all look so sober?"

Alice VanCamp was a privileged character in the
Sangster home, where she had been a visitor for
many years.

"It is not what one would expect on so joyous an
occasion as this."

"Our joy has turned to sorrow, Miss VanCamp,"
answered Mr. Walker.

"Indeed?"

"Alice, something very serious has occurred here to-
night." spoke up Mr. Sangster, turning to the girl.

"Something very serious?" wondered Alice innocently.

"Yes."

"You surprise me."

"Your surprise will be genuine when I tell you
what it is."

"My curiosity is consuming me, Mr. Sangster."

"My dear, it is no jest."

"No jest?"

"No, we have been robbed!"

"Impossible!"

"It is true, nevertheless. Margaret can attest to the
truth of that statement."

"This is most surprising. Was very much taken?"

"Quite enough for one evening. Margaret's jewels
have been taken."

"Oh, is that all?" smiled the society woman, easily.
"I thought something really serious had occurred."

Had there been no ladies present, Ardmore Sangster
would have sworn. As it was he bit his lip until it
whitened.

"I call it quite serious enough when more than a
quarter of a million dollars in jewels have been taken."

"A quarter of a million?" breathed Miss VanCamp.
"Is that all?"

"Yes."

"Are you sure?"

"It is enough. Why do you ask?"

"Because it struck me that perhaps something
might have been taken from the secretary there. I observe that it has been broken into," answered the girl,
calmly.

Margaret sprang up with a gasp. As she tore open
the drawer gazing within she staggered back, half-
fainting, into the arms of her husband.

CHAPTER V.

THE MYSTERY OF THE SECRETARY.

"What is it? What is it?" cried the young bride's
husband.

"It is nothing."

"Yes it is. I demand to know what it is that has so
suddenly upset you again?" exclaimed the father.

"Some trinkets that I prized highly and a five-hun-
dred dollar bill that you slipped into my hand last
night, father."

Margaret's face was deathly in its pallor. Alice Van-
Camp eyed her keenly.

"I probed deeper than I knew," thought Alice. "I
am sorry I spoke."

"Never mind, child," soothed Mr. Sangster. "There
are other bills where that came from. We will forget
it all. I do not wish you to be unhappy on your wedding night. No, you shall not be. Here, Walker, take
your wife below. Her guests will be wondering what
has happened to keep her from them thus long."

"No, I can't go just yet. I could not stand it to face
them all."

"But you must," protested her husband. "Think
how it will appear."

"Yes, you must hide your trouble and come below."

"Perhaps I can straighten her up," suggested Alice
with one of her rare smiles. "I know how to bring
the smiles to Margaret's cheeks, then I will turn her
over to her husband. He will continue the good work,
I am sure."

Mr. Walker flashed a keen glance at Miss VanCamp,
but her face revealed nothing of what was in her mind.

"Very well. Your plan is a good one. I am glad
you are here tonight, Alice. You always are so self-

reliant. We have learned to depend upon you. I want to speak with you when you have gotten Margaret back to her old self again."

Alice nodded.

"We shall be down to join you in a few minutes."

The gentlemen left the room almost at once. Once outside, they began discussing the strange robbery which was a mystery that neither man was able to solve.

In the meantime, Alice stood looking down at her friend.

"Why—oh, why did you do it?" murmured Margaret.

"Why did I do what?"

"Why did you speak of the secretary?"

"Was there anything so wrong in that?"

"Oh, you don't know."

"No, I don't know, but perhaps I might make a shrewd guess."

Margaret glanced up at her friend with a half frightened expression on her face.

"You—you guess?"

Miss VanCamp nodded.

"What do you guess?"

"That yonder secretary held a mystery. It was not the loss of the money that caused you to nearly faint —no Margaret, it was not that. I have no desire to pry into your private secrets. But if there is anything you want to tell me, you know I am your friend."

"I can't, oh I can't," wailed the stricken bride. "It is too terrible."

"Look here, Margaret, I cannot believe that your honor is in any way compromised by what that secretary contained. If so, in any event, I have but one suggestion to offer, tell your husband all, tell him everything."

"I can't, oh, I can't."

"Then tell me. I have no doubt I shall be able to straighten the tangle and set all to rights. This is no way for you to act on your wedding night. It is shameful. Think of your husband."

"I do, that is why I cannot tell you nor him."

"Very well, if that is the way you look at it, matters will have to remain as they are. But I warn you, you are laying up great unhappiness for yourself at this, the beginning of your married life. It is wrong. You will regret it. But whatever you may have done, I propose to stand back of you and do for you what you refuse to do for yourself."

"You cannot help me. How can you help me?" demanded the bride, looking up with a hopeless expression on her face.

"That is for me to decide. Go on, enjoy your honeymoon and perhaps by the time you return I shall be able to return those precious——"

"Precious what?"

"Oh, whatever it may be," laughed Alice.

"I don't understand you at all, Alice. You are a strange woman. You do and say such strange things that at times I am almost afraid of you."

"You need have no fear of me. I am wholly and shamefully human just like yourself. But, dear, I do not like to see my friends suffer when I know that I can help them."

"I wish I were dead," wailed the girl.

"Now that will do. Get up, bathe your face, then stand before the mirror and straighten your face. That is the way actors do when they are getting ready to go

on, you know. Mold their faces into those of the characters they are about to play."

"But this is a tragedy," protested Margaret.

"No, this is a comedy. You are about to go on in the character of the deliriously happy bride and you are going to carry it off in a way that will make me proud of you. What time does your train leave?"

"At midnight, I believe."

"You have two and a half hours yet, then."

"Yes. I shall be glad when it is over, when this strain is off my mind. I shall be glad to get away from this terrible house."

Miss VanCamp looked her surprise.

"You have not been happy here, Margaret?"

"Oh, please do not ask me."

Alice gripped the arm of her friend and led her to her dresser.

"Now get busy before I take matters into my own hand. I shall not let you move from this spot until you have made yourself presentable and have made up your face into that of a happy bride."

Margaret stood surveying herself in the French mirror for a full five minutes, now and then stealing a glance at the figure of Miss VanCamp reflected in the same glass just behind her.

At last a faint smile rippled over the pale face in the mirror, then a spot of color appeared.

"That's right, my dear. You are doing splendidly. You are really beautiful now. I feel sure that your husband will fall in love with you all over again when you go down stairs. I have never seen you look so lovely. You have magnified your troubles, but they are disappearing now like a mist before the morning sun. There. Straighten your hair at the back and you will be ready to make your second appearance this evening."

"You are splendid, Alice," muttered the girl. "What a wife you would make for some man."

"Yes, perhaps for some man. But some man never has asked me," laughed Miss VanCamp. "I do not expect that he ever will. In fact I am not sure that I should accept him if he did. Men do not want to marry me."

"I know some who would like to?" retorted Margaret, with a touch of the old spirit.

Alice did not ask who the men were to whom her friend referred. Perhaps she knew without asking. A faint smile curled her lips.

"Are you ready, dear?"

"Yes."

"Remember your lines."

"What do you mean?"

"Remember that you are the happiest girl in New York at this minute."

"I shall try to," answered the bride, faintly.

"You are. And you are going to be. Remember, too, that your husband is entitled to your brightest, happiest mood on this of all nights. Come, dear."

CHAPTER VI.

THE INTERVIEW WITH THE BROKER.

"Here we are," announced Miss VanCamp, brightly, as the two young women approached Mr. Sangster and his new son-in-law.

The two men turned to meet the smiling, happy face of Margaret Walker.

" You are a dream," breathed the girl's husband with glowing eyes.

" Thank you. I made a silly exhibition of myself upstairs, but I am myself again. Have our guests asked any questions."

" No, love. Come we must speak with some of them."

Margaret linked her arm within that of her husband and the two moved across the brilliantly lighted ball room, the envied of all eyes, for they made a very handsome couple.

Miss VanCamp in the meantime had discreetly dropped into the background.

" You are a wizard, Alice," said a voice at her side.

The young woman turned to find herself face to face with Ardmore Sangster, who was gazing at her admiringly.

" I wish I were," laughed the young woman.

" It isn't necessary to wish. You already have gotten your wish. I am happy that you are here tonight."

" Have you told Mrs. Sangster?"

" No, not yet."

" That is wise."

" So I thought. It is unnecessary to disturb her tonight, at least not until our guests have left."

" Wait until tomorrow," advised Alice, wisely.

" I think I shall take your advice."

" It would be best, if you will pardon my saying so. I seem to be interfering with matters that do not concern me, altogether too much this evening," smiled the girl.

" I do not know what we should have done without you. Come into the conservatory, we can talk there without interruption."

Miss VanCamp obeyed without a word. The couple seated themselves where Alice and young Courtney had been sitting earlier in the evening.

" Alice you have a wise little head on your shoulders. You are one of the most remarkable women I have ever known."

" Thank you, sir. You are very complimentary."

" I mean exactly what I say. What do you think of this affair?"

The girl elevated her eyebrows ever so little.

" What do you mean Mr. Sangster?"

" What do you think of it?"

" I think there has been a robbery committed," replied the girl, with a twinkle.

" Come, be serious. You are a shrewd observer. You ought to have been a detective. I have said it before. You would have been a wonder had you adopted that profession. I was speaking of you to a detective friend of mine some time ago, and saying just what I have told you tonight."

" May I ask who this detective friend of yours is?"

" His name is Jeff Clayton, have you ever heard of him?"

" Yes, I have heard of him," replied the girl, the suspicion of a smile lurking about the corners of her mouth. " I understand he is a most remarkable man."

" He is more than that, he is a marvel."

" Why do you not get him to take up this mystery of the robbery?"

" Unfortunately, Jeff is not in the country at present. He is in Europe on some mysterious mission. But to return to the original question, how did you ever deduce that Margaret's secretary had been broken into?"

" Oh, that is my secret," laughed the girl. " I never speak of my methods, you know."

" We will not discuss that phase of it, then. What I want from you is advice."

" Advice?"

" Yes."

" But surely you do not need advice from me. You are better able to decide what is best to do, than am I."

" What would you do, were you in my place?"

" Were I in your place, I undoubtedly should send for the police."

" That is what I am going to do."

" But, were I in your place, I should wait until the guests have departed, for the police do make such a stir when they come to a place. They seem to want every one to know what they are about, and as a rule, everybody does know."

" Yes, the guests will be going very shortly. But you have not told me what you would do were you in your own place instead of mine?" questioned the broker, shrewdly.

Miss VanCamp laughed.

" I didn't give you credit for it, sir."

" Credit for what?" he demanded, bending a keen glance upon her.

" Oh, never mind. I should not send for the police, to answer your question."

" You would not?"

" No."

" Why not?"

" I might be silly enough to think I could work up the case myself."

Mr. Sangster laughed heartily.

" I haven't the least doubt in the world that you would do that very thing. However, keen as you are, I think you would find that this mystery was too much for you."

" Perhaps," answered the girl dryly.

" I wish, however, that you would go over it in your mind. If you will drop around tomorrow I will meet you here at two in the afternoon and go over the situation with you. You see, I place great reliance on your judgment. I know of no other person who is so well fittted to give advice as yourself."

" You overrate my ability, sir."

" I think not."

" Very well, I shall be glad to meet you as requested, but it will not be at all necessary, so far as any investigation of our own is concerned."

" Not necessary?"

" No."

" And why not?" demanded the broker in surprise.

" Because I already have made an investigation on my own account," replied the girl with a soft laugh.

" You have?"

" Yes."

" And did you learn anything?"

" Perhaps."

" You amaze me."

Miss VanCamp was looking off toward the ball room with a faraway expression in her eyes. The girl seemed to be looking far into the future as it were, trying to pierce the veil that enveloped the mystery.

" What did you discover?"

" I cannot tell you all," answered the girl in a low voice. " I know how the crime was committed and perhaps something of the motive that prompted it. I might name one of the participants in it, though I shall not do so. It would not be best at this stage."

The broker stared with amazement unable to speak for the moment.

CHAPTER VII.

THE POLICE GET BUSY.

"Alice, as I have said so many times before, you are a strange and remarkable girl. Do you still advise me to send for the police?"

"Most certainly. What else is there for you to do?"

"True," muttered the broker thoughtfully. "And will you tell them what you suspect, what you have learned?"

"No, at least, not yet."

"Do you not think it is your duty to do so?'

"I owe no duty to the police."

"But in the interests of justice—in the interest of your friends."

"Permit me to serve my friends in my own way. There are some things you do not understand, Mr. Sangster. All may be made plain in time. Let the police come, give them all the data you have and set them at work. Perhaps they may recover the jewels, who knows. Stranger things than that have happened within even my recollection," added Alice, with a touch of sarcasm in her voice.

Mr. Sangster laughed.

"It shall be as you suggest. You will remain with us until I report?

"That depends when you do so. I certainly shall not remain after the guests have departed. What would people say? No, I think perhaps you had best see them alone or in the presence of your wife."

"She is not to be told, you know."

"Why not—but never mind."

"Say it, please."

"I was going to suggest your driving to headquarters, but that would not simplify matters any, as the police will wish to make an investigation here at the house."

"Yes. I think I shall send for them now," said the broker with emphasis.

Rising he hastened to his library where he telephoned the chief of police with instructions how the men who came in answer to the summons, were to enter the house so as not to attract attention. This was in compliance with a suggestion on the part of Alice.

Half an hour later, a lieutenant and two plainclothesmen entered by way of the basement door. The lieutenant was in citizen's clothes, also, and the other two did not look like the ordinary sleuths. Each was in full evening dress.

Miss VanCamp nodded her approval of this when she set eyes on them.

"If only they knew how to wear the clothes it would be all right. However, few men know how to wear evening dress well. It is an art——"

"Alice, I wish you would come to the library with us. I want you to hear all that passes. I have told Mrs. Sangster that you are going to do so, that we are to discuss some matters relating to the house with a couple of gentlemen, so nothing will be thought of the matter."

"I will go to the library in advance. You beg me to stay. That will be more natural."

He at once saw the point of her shrewd plan and nodded his approval. So that when the broker and the three officers entered the library, Margaret was found lounging over an album of foreign photographs. She glanced up rather apprehensively. Then, when she saw Mr. Sangster was accompanied by three men, the girl rose hastily as if she would leave the room.

"I pray you be seated, Margaret," said the broker with a wave of the hand. "Gentlemen, this is Miss VanCamp a very close friend of the family who is even more conversant with this affair than am I. It might be advantageous for you to ask her some questions, which I am sure she will be very glad to give."

"Certainly, if I may be of assistance," answered the girl with one of her rare smiles.

"It seems to me that I have met you before, Miss VanCamp," said the lieutenant. "But, somehow, I cannot recall it."

"Quite possibly." The girl drew herself up with a slight gesture of indifference.

Mr. Sangster started in to relate all that he knew of the robbery, to which the police listened attentively.

"How much were the jewels worth?"

"Something more than a quarter of a million."

The officers exchanged meaning glances.

"Where were these jewels kept?"

"In a safe in my daughter's room."

"Shall we visit the scene?" suggested the lieutenant.

Mr. Sangster rose, leading the way.

"Come, Alice," he said. "I want you to accompany us."

The girl did so with evident reluctance. These men did not interest her. She knew them almost as well as they knew themselves and she knew their methods fully as well.

The officers took a keen survey of the room, examining the safe much as the young woman herself had done. They went about it in a very professional, self-confident manner that made Miss VanCamp smile to herself.

"Who was on this floor during the evening?" demanded the lieutenant.

"I shall have to ask my daughter."

"Your daughter said her maid and the housekeeper were the only persons up here," volunteered Alice.

"Then we shall have to see the two later. May we see your daughter?"

"Certainly not. This is her wedding night. Besides it is not at all necessary. We are able to say all that she would say and more."

"Was anything else taken?"

"Some money belonging to my daughter, I believe. It was a small sum."

"How much?"

"I think something like five hundred dollars."

The lieutenant grunted.

"Where was it?"

"In the secretary yonder."

The officer made a quick examination of the secretary.

"Anything else?"

"Nothing that I know of."

"Are you keeping anything back from us, Mr. Sangster?"

"What do you mean by that remark, sir?"

"I mean, is there anything further that might enlighten us, perhaps matters of a personal and family interest?"

"You have been told all that we have to say," answered the broker sharply. "There are no skeletons in this family, needing to be hidden away."

"No offense meant, sir, I assure you."

"I should hope not."

The two detectives had been sitting side by side on the divan in the room while their superior had been carrying on the conversation. The two detectives' faces had assumed a most mysterious and knowing expression. Miss VanCamp, as she surveyed them from beneath half-veiled eyelids, could scarce repress a laugh.

"It is ludicrous," she murmured.

Every now and then the lieutenant would glance in her direction with a puzzled expression in his eyes, as if he were trying to recall something in connection with her. His memory was elusive, he could not place the beautiful but tantalizing face before him. In fact, he was sure that he never had seen the face before, yet there was an air, an atmosphere about the young woman that appeared to arouse some seemingly long-forgotten memory in the little police officer. She saw and understood.

"Well, sir, do you wish to make an examination of the house?"

"Oh no," answered the lieutenant, promptly "We have learned quite sufficient as it is."

"You have?"

"Yes."

"Then what is your conclusion?"

"That this is an inside job!"

"Meaning?"

"That we may look for the robber in this very house. Call on your servants."

CHAPTER VIII.

EXAMINING THE SERVANTS.

Mr. Sangster's face flushed.

"It is preposterous!" he exclaimed with some heat.

"That is what people always think. You will find that I am right."

"And that one of my household committed this crime?"

"There can be no doubt of it. You see how impossible it would have been for a second-story worker to make his way up here and get into this room without detection. Besides, who would have known where the jewels were, unless it were a servant? The case is perfectly plain. We shall have the jewels before another twenty-four hours have passed, if not sooner, believe me, Mr. Sangster."

Alice's lip curled. The broker's face was still red.

"I shan't submit to anything of the sort. My servants are beyond reproach."

"You will have to submit, sir. The matter is now in the hands of the authorities."

"I think the lieutenant is right regarding his rights, sir," interposed Alice. "Let him talk with them at the proper time. I am sure he will be convinced of their innocence."

"Very well, if you suggest it. Go ahead, lieutenant. But hold—you cannot do that until the guests depart."

"Very well. We shall set a watch to see that none of the servants communicate with outside parties in the meantime. Where are the servants' quarters?"

"On the upper floor."

"See that none of them go to their rooms within the next hour."

"Very well."

The party retired to the library, that is, all but one did. One of the detectives, at a signal from his chief, dropped behind unobserved by any save Alice. She saw the move and understood. The moment he found himself alone the detective hurried to the top floor where he began a systematic search of the rooms of the servants. He was engaged in the task for an hour, after which he, too, descended to the library.

At midnight the bride and groom took their departure amid shouts and merry laughter, then the guests followed rapidly.

As soon as they had gone, Mr. Sangster took his wife aside and explained what had occurred. It had been made necessary by the determination of the lieutenant to examine the servants. This was done in the library.

One after another of the household servants appeared before the police officers, trembling, frightened and halting in their speech. Did appearances count for anything, one would have thought every one of them had had a hand in the robbery.

The lieutenant appeared to center his attentions on the maid, who had not accompanied her mistress. The maid was French. Her name was Mlle. Corinne. The officer left her until the last, until he had examined all the other servants singly.

"After dressing your mistress what did you do?" questioned the officer.

"I remained in the room to put away her wedding gown, monsieur."

"How long did you remain in the apartments?"

"I did not look to see. I should say about twenty minutes, monsieur."

"Who was with you?"

"I was alone."

"Who did you see while you were in the room?"

"I saw no one."

"You are sure of that?"

"Yes, monsieur."

"Now Corinne was the safe open or closed at the time?"

"It was closed."

"Ah, you looked at the safe then?"

"I saw that it was closed."

"Did you know the jewels were in the safe?"

"I put them there, monsieur."

"Now we are getting at something real," declared the lieutenant, rubbing his hands together. "Did your mistress see you place them there?"

"Yes, monsieur."

"Did you lock the drawer?"

"No, I had not the key."

"Where was the key?"

"Madame had misplaced it, she said. She said it would not be necessary to lock the drawer as she would take the gems before her departure this evening."

"Then the drawer was open?"

"Yes, monsieur."

"And anyone could have helped themselves to the jewels in the box?"

"I suppose so."

"Did any of the other servants know of the presence of the jewels?"

"I do not know. I think not, monsieur. No other

servants came to madame's apartments, unless, perhaps, the housekeeper."

"And she was not in the room after that?"

"I did not see her here."

"Now miss, I know you are keeping something back from me. You might better make a clean breast of what you know about this affair. It will be much better that you do."

"What does monsieur mean?" questioned the girl, looking the lieutenant squarely in the eyes.

"I mean that you can help us to unravel this tangled skein if you will do so. You are making it necessary for us to adopt more stringent measures by your evasion."

The girl went white.

"Does monsieur mean that I—that I took the jewels?"

"Oh no, I have not said so. We are trying to find out who did, and when we do, the one who has helped us will be favored. Corinne, who took those jewels?"

"I do not know, monsieur."

"You mean, you won't tell whom you suspect did?"

"I do not know."

"Who is your friend?"

The girl colored.

"Ah! I see we are getting at something. Put on your things, miss."

"What does monsieur mean?" questioned the girl tremblingly.

"That you will have to accompany us to headquarters," answered the officer, sternly.

"I protest. This is an infernal outrage!" exploded Ardmore Sangster.

CHAPTER IX.

THE ARREST OF THE MAID.

"I shall have to be the best judge of that, sir," answered the lieutenant. "Will you be good enough to call a carriage? Corinne, have some one fetch your things and we will be going."

The girl burst into tears, burying her face in her hands.

"Oh, monsieur, believe me, I never did the terrible thing," she pleaded, turning to Mr. Sangster.

"I am satisfied that you did not, Corinne."

"Then save me, save me," begged the maid, piteously. "I shall die of shame and grief."

"Have patience for a little while, child. I shall see what can be done. I have no doubt that matters may be arranged so that you will be back here before the night is ended. It is all a terrible mistake—a beastly blunder. I am ashamed of my part in it, but at the moment I am powerless to help you. Lieutenant, is there no way—can not I give bail for the young woman and spare her this humiliation?".

"That matter lies wholly with the court. You will have an opportunity to make application in the night court. I have nothing to do with it. Come, girl, are you ready?"

Corinne did not answer. At a signal from the lieutenant, his assistants took each an arm of the stricken maid and led her away.

"I bid you good night," said the officer, nodding as he left the room.

"Well, Alice, we have gotten ourselves into a nice mess," broke out Mr. Sangster, after a moment of silence.

"You mean we have gotten the maid in a mess."

"Yes, and I think you ought to have come out and told what you knew of the matter."

"What good would that have done?"

"The girl would not have been arrested, that's what good would have been done. It is an outrage."

"I agree with your last statement, but not with the former."

"How so?"

"The lieutenant would have arrested the girl just the same. He had made up his mind to do that before he saw her. I observed that early. I knew he had settled upon her as the victim."

"But she never did it."

"Of course not."

"He knows she didn't."

"He probably has made himself believe she is the guilty one."

"What can we do?"

"Engage a lawyer and have him make application for bail pending trial, or pending the grand jury's action. I hardly think she will be admitted to bail. The offense is too great a one for that. However, we shall have the girl out in good time."

"I do not see any prospect of it. Matters look very dark. This has been about the worst evening I ever put in in my life."

"I will see what can be done."

"You?"

"Yes."

"What can you, a woman, inexperienced in the ways of the world, hope to accomplish?"

Alice laughed softly.

"If I remember correctly, it was but a short time ago that you were telling me what a really remarkable person I was. Have you changed your mind so soon?"

"No, but this is different. This is a man's affair, not a woman's."

"Only a woman's work?" repeated Alice absently. "Yes. What would you do were you to act?"

"I should get the best private detective whom I could employ and have him work up the case."

"I know of none save Clayton, and he cannot be gotten."

"Perhaps I might be able to find some one for you," suggested the girl meekly.

"You?"

"Yes, why not?" demanded Miss VanCamp.

"Do you know any detectives?"

"Yes."

"Who?"

"I can't tell you now."

"You can't tell me?"

"No."

"And why not—why all this mystery?"

"Mr. Sangster, I have my reasons and they are good reasons. But I have a friend, a detective whom I am sure would be just the person to run down this crime. I have implicit confidence in the ability of this person to do all that I have promised."

"You surprise me."

"This detective friend of mine is somewhat peculiar—I might say that this detective has certain peculiarities. The detective always works secretly. The detective never comes in contact with the person whom he is working for until perhaps the case has come to a close, and not always then."

"This is very strange."

"It would appear so to the uninitiated."

"Do you mind giving me the name of this wonderful person, in the strictest confidence, of course?"

"I am not at liberty to do even that, Mr. Sangster."

"Most peculiar, indeed. I do not know what to say."

"Why should you say anything? Leave the management of the entire matter to me. I will make all the arrangements. From time to time I may be able to report progress to you. In any event the detective can do no more than fail."

"No, that is true. You are a strange girl, Alice."

"So you have said before."

"How much money will this friend require to start the inquiry going?"

"None at all."

The broker gazed at her in perplexity.

"I will confess that I don't seem to get hold of the thing at all. However, I am going to take you at your word. Set this human sleuth hound on the track and if he is successful, I will reward him handsomely."

"Thank you. He will be pleased at that, though I am not so sure about his being willing to accept any reward from you. Do not employ any one else. Let the police go on in ignorance of the fact that any one else is working on the case."

"When shall I see you again?"

"Oh, frequently. I am afraid that I shall have to cancel my engagement with you tomorrow. I shall be rather busy. You will hear from me soon."

"Very well, Alice. As I have said before, I do not understand you at all, but somehow, I seem to feel instinctively that you know what you are talking about."

"Good night," said Miss VanCamp, rising and extending a hand to her host.

CHAPTER X.

THE SOCIETY DETECTIVE AT WORK.

Alice VanCamp was none other than Madge, the Society Detective, known as Madge Nelson, one of the most brilliant and clever detectives in the great Metropolis.

Alice, upon the death of her parents, found her father's affairs in such bad shape that she realized the necessity of at once doing something for herself. She was proud and it was her ambition to retain the family name and the old home on lower Fifth avenue, unsullied.

With that in view, the young woman cast about for something to do. Crime and criminals had always held a strange fascination for her. In fact, it had been one of her hobbies to study crime. She began with following the crimes as reported in the daily papers, working out theories of her own and eventually, when the police having failed, taking her theories to the chief of police.

It was but a very short time before the head of the great police force began to realize that he had made a find, that Madge, as she called herself, possessed one of those rare instincts seldom found in even a detective. He offered her a place on the force, which offer was declined.

However, the young woman did agree to take up certain cases for the chief, as they might present themselves. This she did. From the start her work was a brilliant success. She never received nor asked credit for what she had accomplished, but the satisfaction and the remuneration received from the work appeared to wholly satisfy her.

Madge excelled in another way. Her muscles due to long and skilful training were of iron. Under the graceful lines of figure, was a lithe, supple body, and the slender, artistic hands when clenched, could deliver a blow that had put more than one ruffian to sleep.

The society detective was a strange and unusual combination. Yet withal, she was a refined and lovable creature, one whom many admired, but whom none could possess for his own.

As Madge Nelson, none would have recognized her as Alice VanCamp, the favorite young society woman. This was due to her marvelous skill at make up. Then, again, the voice, the factor that indentifies almost every one, was so changed in Madge as to be wholly unrecognizable.

Madge soon found that she was able to find cases enough to make a splendid living for her. She had carried through successfully one case alone that had paid her thousands of dollars. This enabled her to pay off the mortgage on the family home with a good balance to spare.

Not one of the young society woman's friends suspected that she was leading what they would have called a double life. This very fact enabled her to get closer to many mysteries than would otherwise have been the case. When Madge the Detective got a society case to investigate, Alice VanCamp usually worked it up as a favored guest. Hers was a clever and brilliant mind.

Madge in the brief time she had spent in looking into the robbery at the Sangster mansion had formed certain well defined ideas. She knew full well that Corinne was wholly guiltless. She knew too—as the police officers did not—that the thief had gained an entrance to the house through the rear hall window, which he had reached over the addition at the rear of the house.

Madge had discovered something else, too. She had a copy of the footprint which it was reasonable to suppose the thief had left on the ground at the rear, and beyond this was another and most important clue. A slender bit of dark cloth of peculiar though almost invisibly pattern now rested in the detective's pocket.

The young woman had found it clinging to the lower corner of the safe door, where it had been torn from the costume of the thief, without doubt, as no one in the Sangster household wore goods of that pattern.

With these faint clues in her possession, Miss VanCamp hastened home in her own carriage. In her library she spread her clues out before her on the library table and examined the cloth under a magnifying glass.

"Of fine quality. Evidently worn by a person who is used to good clothes. I should say that that dress was worn by a person of about eighteen years of age."

Madge mused with half closed eyelids for a long time.

"Yes, I am sure of my ground now. The next thing is to find the thief. I see I shall have something to do on my own account, for this is no ordinary crime. Then there is another feature. Where did the thief obtain his exact information about the house and the jewels? That is an even more serious thing than all the rest. Some one in the household gave the information away, but doing so may have been purely accidental. I am inclined to the belief that it was."

Still thinking about the case, Miss VanCamp called Sarah, her faithful servitor, and told the woman she would retire. Sarah was an old servant and was wholly in the confidence of her mistress. Alice had found the old woman very useful in many of the cases on which the detective was engaged.

While preparing for bed the young woman related all that she knew about the case in hand.

"I am going to have you take a position in that house for a few days, Sarah," announced Madge.

On the following morning, Sarah presented herself at the Sangster mansion with a letter from Alice VanCamp which readily gained her a place. Perhaps the broker sensed something of the reason for this move, for he was a very shrewd man, but if he did so, he kept his own counsel well, and Sarah settled down to the routine of the household, which, however, was quiet after the wedding.

Nothing of the robbery got into the papers, owing, perhaps, to the fact that the broker had seen the authorities and properly induced them to keep silence. The maid was still locked up and there seemed no immediate probability of obtaining her release.

On the following morning Madge was up early. An hour or so later as Madge the Society Detective she left the house by the servants' entrance and proceeded up town. From then until evening nothing was seen of the beautiful young detective in her usual haunts.

Night came on. Madge made her way down Broadway, scanning the people she met with more than ordinary keenness. She was giving as much heed to the clothes the passersby wore as to their features.

At last she turned off to pass through a side street to Sixth avenue.

When half way across she halted suddenly. Coming toward her was a girl running. She could hear the young woman's heavy breathing many yards before the girl reached her.

"Hold on, my dear, where so fast?" demanded Madge, barring the progress of the other.

The girl dodged and would have fled on, but Madge laid a firm hand on the younger woman's shoulder.

"Wait, my dear. You are in trouble. Tell me what it is."

"Let me go, I tell you, let me go!" cried the girl struggling with all her might.

CHAPTER XI.

A GOOD SAMARITAN.

"Be still, child. I would befriend you. Come, if you fear to remain here. We will go to some place and you will tell me your trouble. I am your friend."

The girl glanced up apprehensively into the face of the detective. What she saw there seemed to reassure her in a measure. But almost instantly a hard expression appeared in her face and eyes.

"I have nothing to do with you. I will go my way."

"No, you will not."

"Why will I not?"

"Because I want to talk to you."

"You want to talk to me?"

"Yes."

"What do you wish to say to me?"

"To find out how I can help you."

"You cannot help me—no one can help me. I will be going."

"No, I have something to say to you," insisted Madge. "Come with me where we can talk and you shall tell me your troubles. I will help you."

"You cannot help me. No one can help me now."

"Not so bad as that. See, you are excited. I soon will make you feel better and then we will talk."

Madge released her grip on the arm of the girl and linking her own arm within that of the younger woman started on. The girl sought to draw away, but the pressure of the detective's arm grew firmer and more insistent.

"Who are you?" demanded the girl, glancing up suspiciously, half fearfully at Madge.

"Like yourself, I, too, need sympathy and help. We shall help each other."

The detective led the way on, then turning, proceeded down town.

"Where is your home, child?"

"I have no home—that—that is, not now."

"Ah. Are you hungry?"

"No, no."

"I thought if you were that we would go to some quiet place and have a bite to eat."

The girl seemed to shrink at the idea of it. Madge instantly scented the reason. The girl was fearful of being discovered.

"Tell me, child are you fleeing from the police or from some danger that besets you?" urged the detective.

"It is worse than the police. I almost wish it were the police!"

"Why?"

"Because then my troubles would be ended."

"Ah! here we are!"

Madge had paused before a two-storied brick house of very ordinary appearance. The blinds were tightly drawn and the place might have been deserted for all appearance that the outside gave.

"We will go in here. You will be safe here and comfortable——"

"Where are you taking me?" demanded the girl, sharply.

"I am taking you to one of my homes. This is where I frequently stay. I promise you that you shall find happiness and safety here."

The girl wrenched herself loose almost savagely.

"I know! I know why you have taken me up like this. I am not that kind of a girl. Let me go, I tell you!"

"Child, child, are you mad?" exclaimed Madge. "Look at me. Do you think I am one to lead a young girl into any place where she ought not to go. Come. I am strangely drawn to you. I want to help you. I am going to help you, in spite of yourself. There is no person in that house save one—a good motherly old soul who will take you to her heart of hearts and make you happy. If the place does not please you then you may go at your will. I promise you that."

Somewhat mollified, the young woman surveyed the house once more, then turning, said:

"I will go."

"You trust me?"

"I am not sure. I think so."

"You will after a little. I can be an all powerful friend to you, and I give you my word that I shall be."

Madge led her charge up the steps and pulling the bell waited. A middle aged, kindly-faced woman opened the door.

"Good evening, Mrs. Gates."

"Oh, Miss Madge, is that you?"

"Yes. I have a friend with me."

"I am glad to see you for——"

Madge gave Mrs. Gates a warning signal, whereat the woman quickly bridled her tongue. Then the detective led the way to the parlor.

"We wish to be alone for a little while, Mrs. Gates. If I wish you I will call."

"All right, dearie."

The woman of the house disappeared down the stairs to the basement.

"Now, my dear, to reassure you, let me say that Mrs. Gates is a fine woman. She keeps this house for me to use when I need. No one ever comes here save myself and no one save Mrs. Gates knows that I do come here."

"You do not live here?"

"Some of the time. I am a very busy woman and occasionally I am away for days at a time."

"It looks to be all right."

"It is all right. If you are in trouble perhaps it would be best for you to remain right here. You would do well to do so until you have recovered from your fright at least."

"From my fright?" demanded the girl sharply.

"Yes."

"How do you know I am frightened?"

"It is quite plain that you are. It must have been something very much out of the ordinary to have upset you so, too."

The girl did not answer. For several minutes Madge sat studying the face of the girl before her.

It was a face of great beauty, native refinement and intelligence, but here and there harsh lines told the story of bitter hours.

"Where have I seen that face before?" thought the detective. "I know it and yet I don't know it."

Try as she might, Alice VanCamp could not call back where she had seen the face of the girl before. Just at the moment when memory seemed about to reveal the secret it would be whisked away from her as if on wings.

"It will come to me. I shall catch the recollection sooner or later," thought Madge.

"Now, dear, tell me your troubles."

"I cannot."

"You must." There was an insistence in the tone that there was no denying. At last the girl looked up, studied the face of her new-found friend, after which her glances dropped to the carpet and a dull flush suffused her cheeks.

CHAPTER XII.

HER STRANGE STORY.

"Why should I tell you my story?"

"Because I am your friend," replied Madge.

"You may not be. You may be trying to entrap me, to get me into deeper trouble. God knows, I have enough as it is."

"You know that is not true."

"Forgive me, I did not mean it."

"What is your name, child?"

"Agnes."

"Agnes what?"

"Warwick."

"Why were you running away when I met you to-night?"

"I won't tell you."

"Oh, yes you will, you know you must tell me."

"I won't," emphasized the girl.

"Then I will tell you. You were running to the river where you thought to end your sorrows."

Agnes glanced up with a frightened expression on her face.

"How do you know that?" she demanded sharply.

"Never mind how I know. That I do know, is sufficient. Why were you doing that?"

"For reasons."

"What reasons?"

"I was unhappy."

"Come, come, dear, don't try to evade me. I must have your story, then we shall plan something for you to help you. Tell me all, dear."

Alice VanCamp rose and stepping over beside the girl, stroked the latter's head gently. All at once, Agnes burst into a flood of tears. With bowed head, she wept out her bitter sorrow, Madge the Detective making no effort to restrain the younger woman's grief.

At last Agnes raised her head.

"Why did you make me cry?" she asked weakly.

"I did not, child. But it is better for you that you should. I am sure you feel relieved now. Tell me where you live?"

Agnes gave the address of a house not far from where they were at that moment.

"With whom do you live?"

"With my father."

"Is your father unkind to you?"

"Yes."

"He beats you?"

"Sometimes," was the half-articulated reply.

"What for?"

"To make me do his bidding."

"Have you a mother?"

"I don't remember that I ever had one. Sometimes I have a faint recollection of a sweet, motherly face that I have thought might be that of my mother."

"Does your father never speak of her?"

"No, he never does. He forbids me to ask questions about her. But I am sure if I ever had a mother that she must have been good and sweet and noble. Perhaps I would have been, too, under other circumstances."

"Tell me about your father, why does he beat you?"

"I have told you. To make me do things he wants me to."

"What things?"

"Steal!"

It was out at last. Madge had suspected the truth long before, but she preferred to have Agnes tell her in her own way.

"He makes you steal?"

"Yes, I am a thief."

"But I am sure it is not because you want to be, my child?"

"No, I loathe it. I had determined to kill myself. I told my father to-night that I should steal no more. I begged him to let me go away, where I might earn an honest living. He beat me with a razor strop. See, see!"

The girl bared her left arm where livid streaks testified to the welts of the strop as it had been laid over and about her.

The eyes of the Society Detective glowed with a

strange light. Yet there was no other sign to indicate that her emotions had been aroused. The white hands lay passive in her lap, her position one of ease and perfect grace.

"How long have you been doing this?" asked Madge in a quiet voice.

"Since I finished school. I was educated fairly well, but before I had finished at the boarding school I was attending, father took me away. I was taught to steal. I was beaten and flogged. It is a wonder that I did not kill him." A fierce light sprang into the eyes of the girl. "Perhaps I should have to-night, had I not made up my mind to end it all by making away with myself."

"Why have you not appealed to the police or to some one for relief?" questioned the detective.

"I should have been arrested and sent to prison."

"Are you a skilful thief?"

"I think so. I have never been detected. I can do almost anything in stealing—but why am I telling this to you? You will betray me?"

"No, my child I will not betray you."

"You will not?"

"No, I will save you."

"You cannot do that."

"You do not know either my power or my resources."

"But I am a thief," protested the girl.

"By force of circumstances only. You are not a thief at heart."

"No, I loathe it, I abhor it. I shall surely kill myself if I ever have to steal again."

"You shall not."

"But he will kill me, if I do not."

"You shall never go back to him, child. He is an inhuman father, if he is a father at all, which latter fact I very much doubt."

"But he will find me?"

"I shall see that he does not. I will see your father myself."

Agnes' face went pale.

"No, no, you must not. He would surely kill you, too, then all would be lost. No, I must think it all out for myself."

"See here, Agnes, you will leave all of that to me. I will think the matter out and when I have decided upon the right course, I shall follow it and this inhuman father of yours will have done with his control over you. It may be necessary for you to remain here quietly for a time, after which you may face the world again and without fear or favor."

"It is impossible."

"Child you do not know who I am?"

"No, I do not."

"Have you ever heard of Madge, the Society Detective, so called?"

"Yes."

"How have you heard of her?"

"She once sent a friend of father's to prison."

"Who was that?"

"Dick Sparling."

Madge's eyes sparkled. Well did she remember the case.

"Then you will appreciate what I am about to tell you."

"What is it you wish to tell me?"

"My dear, I am Madge, the Society Detective."

The face of the beautiful thief went ghastly pale.

"You—you are—are Madge?"

"Yes."

"Then, God help me, I am lost!"

CHAPTER XIII.
BEAUTY IN DISTRESS.

"Child, child, be calm."

Agnes had risen. There was a wild, menacing look in her eyes. She appeared to be upon the point of doing something desperate.

"Sit down; did I not tell you I am your friend?"

"No, no, you are a detective! You have trapped me! You will betray me! Oh, why did I trust myself to you?"

The girl swayed unsteadily.

"Sit down!"

Miss VanCamp's tone was commanding.

"I have told you that you have nothing to fear from me. I am your friend. I will prove to you that I am your friend, and you will thank God for the moment that gave you to me. Now, be calm, child, and listen to reason."

"And you will not arrest me?"

"Arrest you? No, certainly not."

"Not if I told you, confessed my crimes?"

"No. But you need not confess them to me. It is not for me to know. What you have done has not been of your own free will, therefore, it is not you who have done these things, it is the monster whom you call father and whom I do not believe is your father any more than am I. No father could act like that toward his own flesh and blood. Agnes, I want to ask another and more personal question of you."

Miss Warwick nodded faintly.

"Are you a good girl?"

A faint color surged to the cheeks of Agnes, mounting to her forehead. Her eyes grew luminous.

"Yes, I am."

"I believe you. Nothing else matters. Now I shall work for you. You will see what I can do and how well I can do it. What other reason had you for leaving home so suddenly?"

The question was hurled at the girl with such unexpectedness that she colored, this time violently, to the roots of her hair.

"What other reason?"

"Yes."

"How do you know there was another reason?"

"I know, that is sufficient. There was a man in the case?"

"Yes."

"His name?"

"Rex Chapin."

"Tell me about him?"

"He made father's acquaintance, I know not how. They became great friends, though I knew father despised him and that he was tolerating the fellow only for what he could get out of him. Well, Rex was a handsome fellow; that is, he would have been, ordinarily. At first, I felt rather sorry for him, knowing that sooner or later father would finish him. For that reason, perhaps, I showed more consideration for the man than I otherwise should have done."

"Yes, go on."

"I soon saw that he had taken a violent liking for me. Then I avoided him. But he pursued me continually. One day he made me very angry by something he said to me. After that I avoided him."

Madge nodded understandingly.

"A robbery was planned. It seemed he gave the information to father on which father acted, or on which I acted, for I was the one who, as usual, had to do the real work."

"How long ago was this?" interrupted the detective eagerly.

"A long time ago."

"Oh! Proceed."

"I did the work and did it successfully. I got away with more stuff than I ever had before that. It was a dandy haul," added the girl with sparkling eyes. But the expression soon faded from them and her face grew pale.

"Yes?"

"Well, afterwards, that is, some time afterwards, father told me what the bargain was. In payment for the information that made the haul possible, he was to give this fellow Rex a number of thousand dollars and throw me in to boot."

"Marry you to the wretch?" demanded Miss Van-Camp.

"No, worse."

"The hound!" breathed the beautiful detective. "You rebelled?"

"With all the strength that was in me."

"Was the young man present at the time?"

"He was."

"What did you do?"

"I forgot myself in my terrible anger. I struck him with a chair. I knocked him down. He lay upon the floor like one dead. His face was bleeding. With a terrible oath, father started for me. Then I fled."

"You poor, poor, child," murmured Alice in her soft, sympathetic voice, as she took the slender figure of Agnes in her arms and pressed her lips to the hot feverish cheeks of the younger woman. "How you have suffered. That there should be such monsters allowed to live, almost passes human comprehension."

Agnes impulsively threw her arms about the neck of her new-found friend. Such tender sympathy the girl never had known before, within her memory. It opened the flood gates of sympathy and awakened the tender emotions that had so long remained dormant in her heart. Together the two women sat in silence for a long time.

"Agnes, you have no affection in your heart for this human monster, have you?"

"My father?"

"Yes?"

"I loathe him. I could see him torn limb from limb without stirring any other emotion than joy in me."

"That settles it," nodded Madge, with emphasis.

"Settles what?"

"He is not your father. No daughter could feel that way toward a parent, no matter how bad the parent might be. Blood is thicker than water, as the old saying goes. It is a true saying. There never was a truer one."

"You think he is not?" asked the girl with pleading eyes.

"I am positive."

"Oh, I hope he is not."

"And my love, it shall be my happy task to find your real father if he be alive and restore you to his arms. I promise you that, if he lives, I shall find him. Madge Nelson makes no idle boasts. What she promises she does."

An impulsive kiss was the reward of the detective's declaration.

CHAPTER XIV.
A STRANGE VISITOR.

"Now, my dear, I want you to go to your room. You may retire or not as you wish, but make yourself perfectly at home. No harm can come to you here, so long as you do not show yourself at the windows or venture upon the street."

"Are you going to leave me?"

"Yes."

"Please don't," pleaded the girl.

"I must. I have much to do. You should know that."

"Then let me go with you."

"No, that would not be possible. Where I go would be no place for you. Have no fears. Rest content. You are in good hands, and if you wish anything, you will feel perfectly free to ask the housekeeper for it. I shall give her orders before I leave, though that is not at all necessary. This is your home fully as much as it is mine. Use it in that light and you will please me."

"When shall I see you again?"

"I cannot say. It may be to-night, in the morning or possibly days. I can be no more definite. It will be hard for you to remain in doors all the time during my absence, but I must have your promise that you will do this. Will you make that promise?"

"Yes, I shall do exactly as you want me to."

"That is a dear. Now I shall go away perfectly contented in mind. Come, I will show you to your room."

Agnes found her room a cheerful, cosy little place at the rear of the house looking out onto a well-kept back yard of the conventional city type. At the back was a warehouse with closed iron blinds, so that the girl could sit there and see the fresh sunshine without danger of being observed. Madge warned her, however, against showing herself at the street windows in the front of the house. Agnes promised to be good.

After attending to all the girl's little requirements, Madge kissed the girl good night and left the house, first having called the housekeeper to give the latter full instructions.

An hour later, Spindle Warwick, as he was known among his associates, was startled by a ring at his door. He occupied rooms on the second floor back of a building used for stores on the lower floor and offices in most of the rest of the building.

Spindle glanced at the clock. The hour was very late for visitors.

"Who the devil——" muttered the man. Then taking a revolver from the drawer of the table before him, slipping the weapon in his pocket he strode to the door, throwing it wide open, as if he had nothing to fear.

There, before him, stood a very pretty young woman, slender, fair of face, dark-haired and keen-eyed.

"Is this Mr. Warwick?" she asked sweetly.

"Yes, what do you want?"

Miss VanCamp, for it was herself, gave the man a quick, comprehensive glance. He looked to her more like a college professor at first glance, but in the next second she saw deeper. The man though he wore spectacles, had the shifty eyes of the professional crook. The eyes took on an Oriental slant and set unusually close together.

"A dangerous man," was the mental summing up of the young woman.

"I should like to see you alone a moment."

The man regarded her keenly for a brief moment.

"Come in," he said, closing and locking the door behind her.

"Thank you!" answered Miss VanCamp, sweetly.

"Sit down," demanded Warwick, almost roughly.

Madge did so.

"Now what do you want?"

"I should like to see Agnes."

"Agnes?"

The word came out with explosive force.

"Yes, sir."

"And who might Agnes be?" he demanded, sarcastically.

"Your daughter, so she says, though I must confess that I fail to observe any marked family likeness between you."

Warwick's eyes narrowed.

"What do you know about my daughter?" he demanded in a quiet tone, that, to the keenly attuned ears of the caller, conveyed a subtle warning.

"She is my friend."

"And who are you?"

"I am known among our class as—but it does not matter who I am known as. We are friends."

"When did you meet my daughter?"

"Some weeks ago at the Charity Bazar at the Waldorf."

"What were you doing there?"

"Much the same that Agnes was," laughed the young woman. "We found congenial companionship in each other's company from the first. I asked her if she would be at liberty to help me sometime when I had anything worth while on."

"She said no, she wouldn't."

"Well?"

"I have something on hand. I thought perhaps I might be able to induce her to give me a hand. I need some one who can work delicately."

"You are very frank, madame, I must say. How do you know but I may decide to turn you over to the police?"

Madge laughed.

"I am not at all fearful."

"You are not?"

"Certainly not."

"May I ask why?"

"You may."

"Well?"

"Thieves seldom give one another away."

An angry light flashed into the eyes of Warwick.

"Be careful, young woman. I am not in the habit of being talked to in this manner."

"I have said nothing that is not the truth. Why not call a spade a spade in the presence of spades? We are both spades, aces or deuces as the case may be, at that."

Warwick laughed this time. He was becoming interested.

"You say you have a game on hand?"

"I think I intimated something of the sort."

"Is there much in it?"

"Something like a fortune," answered the girl carelessly.

The crook started, then there flashed into his narrow eyes a crafty look.

"A fortune, eh?"

CHAPTER XV.

NOT SO DELICATE, AFTER ALL.

A crafty light had sprung into the eyes of Spindle Warwick. He eyed the girl narrowly for several minutes.

"What is the nature of this game you wanted my daughter to participate in?"

"Oh, you are really interested in it, are you?" laughed the girl, tantalizingly.

"A father has to be careful where his daughter is concerned," replied the hypocrite, piously.

A ripple of laughter greeted the words, bringing a flush to the cheek of the bespectacled, serious-looking, gaunt face. Warwick came near losing his suavity of manner.

"Are you making sport of me, young woman?"

"Making sport of you? Why, my dear fellow, I do not see anything humorous in you. You are the most serious-looking person it has ever been my pleasure to gaze upon. But, you wanted to know what the nature of the game is on which I have come here to enlist the services of your daughter?"

"It will be best for me to know. You surely cannot speak of it to my daughter until I know all the details of it."

Madge knew better about this than did Warwick. She alone, was in a position to speak to Agnes at the present time.

"By the way, what has become of Agnes's young man?" asked the woman, casually.

"What?"

"Agnes's young man?"

"I do not know what you mean. To whom do you refer?"

"I don't know his name. Let me see Reginald, Reg—no that was not it. She told me the young man was very sweet on her, but that she hated him. Curious I have forgotten the name. From what she said it struck me that he might be available for a certain thing I want done."

"Young woman, what have you come here for?" demanded Warwick steadily.

"I thought I had made myself plain. I have told you exactly what I came here for."

"You have told me nothing. I demand to know all the facts in the case you have referred to."

"The young man?"

"To the devil with the young man. The game you spoke of some time ago before you began beating around the bush."

"You wish me to tell you all about it, eh?"

"I not only wish, but I insist."

"And supposing I refuse?"

"Then I shall find a way to make you speak out."

"Supposing you begin now," suggested the caller, calmly, leaning both elbows on the table and looking the man squarely in the eyes. "You are a man and I a weak woman. Try to make me say something I don't want to and note the results."

Madge leaned back after a moment and laughed.

"You have got a yellow streak in you haven't you?" she scoffed. "I thought as much. That makes it all the more certain that Agnes is not of

your blood. I didn't believe her, when she told me
she was your daughter. Now I am sure of it."

"You hussey!" hissed the man.

"You shouldn't indulge in such expressions in the
presence of ladies," warned Madge. "It doesn't become you, though it fits your character most excel-
lently. Further than this I am not in the habit of being addressed in such terms. You will have to speak
in a more gentlemanly way if you wish me to remain."

"You don't have to remain."

"Don't I?"

"No."

"Thank you."

"I didn't ask you to come here. I don't want you
here. I'd be much better pleased if you got out."

"I think I will stay then," decided the girl, settling
down in her chair in apparent perfect contentment.

"What do you want here?" demanded the man.

"I think you asked me that question before. I told
you that for one thing, I was here to see Agnes."

"You can't see her."

"I can't?"

"No."

"Why not?"

"That is my business."

"You are very discourteous. I ask you again why
I am not to see your daughter?"

"Because she isn't here, curse you!" exploded Warwick.

"Thank you," replied Madge, demurely.

"Now, I hope you are satisfied and that——"

"Satisfied—no."

"Well, what is it now?"

"Where is Agnes?"

"That is none of your affair."

"For argument's sake, we will say that it is my affair. Where is she?"

"She is not here."

"So I think you have already said. I am very anxious to see her."

Warwick regarded the detective shrewdly.

"You say you came here to interest her in the
work?" he questioned.

"Yes."

"Will you tell me what you want her to do?"

"Why should I?"

"Because, perhaps I may be able to give you some
help."

"I don't want you to. I want a woman or a young
man. The latter will do. What I want is a dissipated
young blade who can be molded to suit my requirements. If you can furnish me with what I want, I
can put a lot of money in your pocket or his or both,
whichever way you may wish to work it out."

The eyes of the crook glowed.

"How much?"

"Well, if I were able to get hold of Agnes and
have her help me it would be worth a great deal more
to you as well as to me. Do you not think you could
find her?"

"Find her? Did I say she was lost?" demanded
Spindle with narrowing eyes.

"I do not remember that you did. You impressed
me as not knowing, however."

"Come, you are here for business. Let us settle
down and talk business," suggested the man.

"Very well, we will talk business," answered
Madge the Detective.

CHAPTER XVI.

HER WITS AGAINST HIS.

"First, tell me what the lay is?"

"It is, or will be, a second story job, as the case
looks now."

"Where?"

"Oh, in a house I know about."

"What shape is the fat in?"

"Principally diamonds."

"Paste, probably," sniffed Warwick, contemptously.

"These will not be."

"You seem to know a great deal about it?"

"I do."

"What makes you so sure they will be the real dew-
drops."

"Because they are going to be a present to a bride."

"Ah!"

"There is going to be a bushel of them, more or
less."

"Then, this bride is a swell?"

"Yes."

"Who is she?"

"I haven't said."

"You will have to."

"Who will make me?"

"I will."

Madge laughed lightly.

"Better men than you have tried it," she said, without a suggestion of boasting in her tone. "And they
have failed. You will fail. You are treading on dangerous ground, Spindle Warwick."

The crook started at the words.

"You know my title?" he demanded, suspiciously.

"I ought to."

"Why?"

"I have had you held up as a model ever since I
got into the game, and that wasn't yesterday!" she
added.

The suspicion of a smile appeared on Warwick's
face.

"Is this game you speak of a safe one?"

"No, no games are safe."

"That's right," agreed the crook.

"This one is as safe as any one I know of, because
the people will be otherwise engaged."

"It is to be at a wedding, eh?"

"Yes. You have worked that kind of a game before
and you know how easily it can be done."

He shot a shrewd glance at her, but Madge's face
possessed no guile. She seemed absorbed in her subject to the exclusion of all else.

"Never mind what I have done. It is what may be
done in the future that we are interested in at the
present moment. Will the jewels be guarded by the
police or by specials?"

"I don't know. I have not been able to learn. I
shall find out all of that in good time."

"Good. I hope you don't overrate your ability to
do things."

"I never have. There always comes a time in our
business when we take a bite more than we can digest."

Warwick laughed.

"You are a keen one."

"Thank you. All compliments gratefully received."

"When does the wedding come off?"

"Tuesday, week."

"When do you propose to make the sortie?"

"I didn't say I proposed to do it."

"Well, when is the sortie to be made, if that suits you better?"

"It does. The sortie will be made on the night of the wedding, of course."

"Can it not be made before?"

"Yes, that would be possible, but were we to do so, we should not be making as good a haul. All the presents will not be in. For instance, the groom's present to his bride will be a rope of diamonds worth a king's ransom in themselves."

Warwick's eyes twinkled avariciously, his hands clasped and unclasped and Miss VanCamp noted that they were white and slender. The man though a brute, was artistic, clever and dangerous. She knew that full well. She knew that he would not hesitate to shoot her where she sat, did he have reason to believe she was not what she seemed.

But Madge the Detective had no fear. She had passed through too many perilous situations to feel fear. The girl was amply able to take care of herself under almost any circumstances, no matter how critical.

"What is the worth of the whole swag?"

"What share would you demand, were Agnes to do the job for me?" replied Madge without answering the question.

Warwick wrinkled his forehead and thought for some moments.

"You have got to have somebody to help you?"

"I didn't say so."

"Not necessary. It is the fact, or you would not have come here for assistance."

"Well, for the sake of argument, we will say that I do need help. Naturally, I am not calling here at this time of the night for the mere pleasure of gazing upon your manly countenance."

Warwick frowned.

"Cut it out!" he growled.

Madge laughed softly and aggravatingly.

"You have not answered my question yet?"

"Who disposes of the gems?"

"That remains to be settled between us if we make a deal. We can each take our share and dispose of them. Perhaps that would be best."

He nodded his approval of this plan. It seemed to strike him with much favor.

"I will agree to that."

"What per cent?" she urged.

"Eighty."

"Eighty for me, and you will be satisfied with twenty per cent?" questioned the girl demurely.

"No, not by a jug full!" shouted Warwick.

"Indeed? You surprise me. What do you mean?"

"It's the other way around. You get twenty per cent and we get eighty."

"Mister man, you've got another guess coming," replied the girl rising and buttoning the glove on her left hand. "You and I can't talk business, I see."

CHAPTER XVII.

SHADOWED!

"Hold on there!"

"Well?"

"Don't be so touchy."

"I am not touchy."

"Yes you are."

"No."

"Then why are you leaving in a huff?"

"Why should I remain longer? We have nothing further to discuss. You want the whole of the swag, even though I am making it possible for you to make a fortune that you would not even have had a look-in at had it not been for me."

"But you want us to do all the work," protested Warwick.

"Hardly. I think I have already done some of it, and much more will be done before I am ready to call you and your daughter into the case. When the bubble is ready to burst, then I shall call upon you to do your part."

"How much of a haul is it likely to be?" again asked the crook.

"It may total up to a big figure."

Madge was urging the crook on, and he was jumping at the bait now.

"How big?"

"Oh, perhaps half a million dollars."

Spindle Warwick fairly leaped out of his chair.

"Half a million dollars?" he gasped.

Madge smiled tolerantly.

"You seem interested?" she laughed.

"Heavens, it's a fortune!"

"Of course, it is. Didn't I tell you it was? Now, will you let me have Agnes to help carry the thing through?"

"I can't just now."

"Why not?"

"I tell you she is not here, and I don't know where the little hussey is."

"Tut, tut. She does not deserve to be called such names. Agnes is a fine girl and I shall not listen to such language directed at her. You do not know where she is?"

"No."

"How does that happen?"

"No matter how it happens. She isn't here and that's all there is about it."

"But you will find her?" questioned the woman.

"Oh, I'll get her all right, no doubt about that. I'll have her in hand pretty soon and I'll teach her a lesson she won't soon forget."

The lips of the detective compressed and a dangerous light flashed into her eyes.

"When do you think I shall be able to come here to see her?"

"I'll let you know. What address?"

The girl laughed.

"I am not giving away my address. I will come back in a day or so and see what you have to offer. But we have not yet decided on the terms. You, of course, did not mean to hog eighty per cent of the swag? You know well enough that I wouldn't fall for that."

"I'll make a great concession," said the crook, as Madge smiled tolerantly. "I'll say share and share alike. How does that strike you?"

"It doesn't strike me at all."

"That is the best I will do. I wouldn't think of touching the case for any less."

"And if you don't get Agnes, what then?"

"I'll pull off the thing myself."

"Very well, I accept your terms. I can get plenty of people to help me, but I don't want them. I want somebody that I can depend upon, somebody on whom I have a hold."

"On whom you have a hold?" exclaimed Warwick, explosively.

"Yes."

"What do you mean, woman?"

The girl laughed easily.

"Oh, that's all right."

"It isn't all right. I want to know what you mean?"

"If you insist I will tell you."

"Do so."

"Well then, here it is. I know all about that last haul of yours, how much you got and all about it. That was a fine second-story game. I was in for that job myself, but you got the best of me there."

The detective laughed harshly.

"I said to myself, a fellow who can pull off a game as neatly as that is the man for my purposes, and so I came to you. You needn't tell Agnes that I know anything about it, though. It isn't necessary for her to know."

"You devil!" cried Warwick, his face suddenly flushing with anger.

For a brief instant he appeared to be struggling with himself.

All at once he sprang toward the girl.

"Stand back!" warned Madge.

"I'll take it out of you, you hussey! I'll show you you can't trifle with me!"

The next second Warwick gripped the left arm of the young woman with a grip that would have made any other woman cry out with pain.

"Mister man, will you let go of my arm?" she demanded, coolly.

"No, by Heaven, I'll hang onto you this time! I'll make you eat those words, and I'll——"

The man was working himself into a towering rage.

"I don't permit men to take such liberties with me. Will you release me?"

"No!"

Biff!

The blow landed fair and square on the point of Spindle's jaw. He dropped like a beef under the slaughterer's ax. The falling body carried a chair down with it, upsetting the table at the same time.

"There, I guess that will teach the brute a lesson. It's one for Agnes at the same time."

With that Madge unlocked the door, stepped out and made her way down stairs. For a moment or so she stood thoughtfully at the door on the street, then she started away. The girl had not gone far before a dark figure slunk out of the doorway she had just left, skulking along in the shadows behind her. Had the detective not been so absorbed in her thoughts she would quickly have discovered the shadow, but as it was, Madge went along all unconscious of the peril that lurked on her trail.

CHAPTER XVIII.
MEETING THEIR MATCH.

But Madge Nelson was a shrewd girl. It was a clever shadow, indeed, who could long remain on her trail without discovery.

All at once some inborn instinct seemed to warn the girl that danger threatened. She raised her head as if scenting the air, but Madge did not make the mistake of turning around. She continued on steadily as if nothing had occurred to excite her suspicions.

"I am being followed," she murmured. "Warwick must have woke up sooner than I thought. This is strange, there are two of them. Very well, let them follow. Perhaps I shall be able to show them a trick they never saw worked before. I wonder what the game is?"

Madge made several short turns, then, changing her mind turned and took the back track again.

This soon brought her face to face with two men. She did not appear to see them, as she went hurrying on. Suddenly she bumped fairly into one of the shadows.

"I beg your pardon, sir," murmured Madge. "I did not see you."

"Hold on, miss, not so fast!" commanded one.

"Permit me to pass, please," begged the girl, with dignity.

"Not much. I'm wise to your game."

"What do you mean?"

"You know well enough what I mean."

"Better let her go, Berg."

"Let her go? I guess not. She's got my watch!" cried the shadow.

"So, that's her game, is it?"

"You bet it is. I was wise to her the minute she bumped into us."

The fellow had fixed a firm grip on the arm of the woman detective. Madge was making no effort to release herself.

"What are you going to do with her?"

"I reckon we had better take her in."

"Yes, I guess that would be a good thing to do. Shall we call a cop?"

"No, we'll take her in ourselves."

"You had better not," warned the girl.

"It ain't for you to dictate, girl. We'll do as we think best."

At that, one ranged himself on each side of her and began leading Madge along.

"You come along quiet like, girl, and you won't have any trouble with us, but make any row and there will be more trouble than you ever had in your life."

"Why are you doing this to me?"

"Because you are a thief. You are a fine bird, you are, even if you are a woman. I reckon the chief will be glad to get his hands on you."

"And you are a precious pair of rogues yourselves. No honest man would use a woman in this manner."

"Shut up!" commanded one of the men. "You will force us to call the police."

Madge appeared to tremble under this threat. From that moment on she went along, apparently, willingly enough. But her strange willingness did not appear to arouse the suspicions of the men. They were congratulating themselves on the ease with which they had obtained possession of the young woman. Hurrying her along, they turned into a side street, then made their way across town toward the East river until Second avenue had been reached. There they turned uptown.

"Isn't this an unusual way to take for a police station?" questioned the girl.

"Never mind, you'll find out when we get there," answered one of her captors.

"Yes, I'll find out," replied Madge, significantly. "You will find out, too, if you aren't playing on the square with me. You don't suppose I'm going to let you lead me to a police station, do you?"

"Where do you think we are taking you, then?"

"That remains to be seen. I shall know when I get there, perhaps. However, I may not reach there at all."

"You may not?"

"No."

"What makes you think you won't?"

"I may manage to make my escape before that."

"No danger of that," laughed the scoundrels.

"No, I guess not. You've got me this time, but my turn will come later. I'll see that you fly cops, or whatever you are, get yours after I get free, and if I don't I have friends who will look after you for me."

"That's all right, girlie. Your friends won't get a chance to find out where you are right away, I am thinking."

"Perhaps they are not as slow as you think. They will know soon enough, and then look out. Things will begin to happen."

The men laughed easily. What could a delicate woman hope to accomplish against the powerful band to which Spindle Warwick belonged? It was a band possessing more far-reaching power than even the police dreamed. Miss VanCamp, in the character of Madge the Society Detective, did have an inkling of the truth. In fact, she had correctly analyzed the situation. She saw that she had inadvertently stumbled upon a vast criminal machine, one whose ramifications and branches were too numerous to take account of.

"I will break them up. I know what I am about now," she thought as the men led her along. "And when I am ready to move—when I do move, there will be an exodus of thieves from this town. They will be taking their hurried departure for Chicago and other parts of the Union. I am on the right track. I know, now."

"What is that you were saying?" demanded one of the captors.

"Perhaps I was thinking out loud," laughed Madge. "It is a bad habit I have fallen into."

In the meantime the delicate fingers of the detective had been skillfully probing the pockets of the men who were leading her along. There were weapons in those pockets. These she did not disturb. She possessed weapons of her own. However, there were other things that the sensitive fingers found and deftly removed, without, in fact, so much as moving the muscles of the upper arms.

At last the party halted before a building that appeared to be a private house. One of the old-time mansions of Second avenue.

The men started up the steps with their prisoner.

"What is this?" demanded Madge, suspiciously.

"This is the station."

She peered up, caught the number of the house, which she fixed in her mind for future reference.

"You are mistaken," said the girl.

"No matter, in you go!"

While one hastily opened the door the other thrust Madge in, then followed. The instant the second man had entered, things began to happen.

Suddenly releasing herself from the fellow's grip, the girl dealt him a powerful blow that felled the man to the floor.

Biff!

Ere the other man was able to recover from his astonishment, he caught a sledge-hammer blow on the neck that sent him spinning across the floor, landing him in a motionless heap against the wall.

"There, I think I have taught you loafers a lesson that you will not soon forget," muttered Madge.

Her words fell on deaf ears, for the men were unconscious, wholly knocked out by the girl's powerful blows. Miss VanCamp very calmly stepped out, closing the door behind her, but in her hand lay the key that she had taken from the lock.

CHAPTER XIX.

AN UNEXPECTED SETBACK.

The girl quickly hurried from the scene, slipping around a corner and disappearing from view. When the villains finally awoke and hurried out, their intended victim was nowhere to be seen.

Very shortly after that, Spindle Warwick came down the street. He gave a signal rap on the door. It was opened by one of the two men.

"Well, did you get her?" he demanded.

"Yes, we got her."

"Good! Where is she?"

"That's what we should like to know," answered the man, ruefully.

"What? You don't mean to say that——"

The fellow nodded.

"The girl got away."

"Got away?"

"Yes."

"You fools! You have made a mess of it! But, I felt sure you would. I told you she was a sharp one—sharp as lightning, but you didn't believe me. It serves you right. I am only glad she didn't connect me up with the affair. Still, she may suspect at that. Tell me about it."

"Well, we got her on the street. Played right into our hands and bumped into us. We accused her of picking my pocket, then we took her along."

"Did she resist?"

"No, she led as fine as you please, she appeared to be thoroughly halter-broke."

A sarcastic smile curled the lips of Spindle Warwick.

"You are a couple of mutton-heads," he scoffed. "Didn't you know enough to realize what that meant?"

"I don't see that it meant anything in particular."

"Why, you idiots, she was on to your little game all the time. She was playing you for a couple of suckers. Well, you are easy. You deserve all you got and that is nothing. I promised you a good price if you would land her here without bringing me into the case. I had hoped to get some valuable information out of her. She's worth money, that woman is."

"We'll get her yet," protested one of the men.

"No, thank you. I'll do my own getting, at least, I shall not trust you to go against the young woman again."

"Who is she, boss?"

"Never mind who she is. That doesn't concern you. But you have not told me how she managed to give you the slip?"

"No." It was very ruefully said.

"Explain? Did she give you the slip on the way here after fooling you into believing that you had her scared?"

"No, that wasn't the way of it."

"Come, speak out. How did it happen?"

"It was this way. We had got here with the gal."

"You got here with her?"

"Yes. Bob opened the door and I pushed her right into the hallway here. Bob came in closing the door behind him, then something happened."

"What happened?"

"She slugged me."

Warwick laughed outright.

"Then she slugged Bob. We both went down. I'm ashamed to confess it, boss, but that woman has got a punch like a Missouri mule. Ain't never seen anything like it. You can see how my face is swelled up——"

"She used a billy, that's what she did," interrupted the other ruffian.

"Nothing of the sort. She used her fists, she did, and I never see a man who could use his mauleys any better. She'd make Mr. Johnson sick at his stomach with one friendly little love tap, you bet. No more of them slender white hands for mine. No, sir, never again."

"I thought you said you would get her?" sneered Warwick.

"I'd get somebody to do it."

"No, thank you. We do not want any more people mixed up in this deal. And besides, I don't want any harm done to the woman. She is worth too much money to me just at present. I can't afford to lose her for a spell yet. Later on perhaps we might forget that she was on earth. Just now she's worth more alive than in the river. So she got in here, did she?"

"Yes."

"Was there a light here?"

"No, it was dark here then."

Warwick nodded, then he went out on the stoop where he took a survey.

"The visit won't do her any good. I shouldn't like to think she had got the place spotted. Did she seem to be looking about her much when you came in?"

"Not at all. She had her head down. I thought it was so we couldn't get a good look at her face."

"She is a pretty slick young woman, Berg. You have learned that to your surprise and at your expense, for losing her has lost you quite a bit of money."

The other man nodded sadly.

"Yes, I suppose that's so. It's a rotten fluke we've made of it."

"It is," agreed Spindle. "It is the worst ever. I have another job that I want you men to get out on."

"All right, boss, we'll try to do better next time. Is there a woman in this case, too?"

"Yes."

The man looked solemn.

"I dunno about that."

"Who is it?" demanded the other fellow.

"My daughter, Agnes."

"The deuce, you say. What has she been doing?"

"Nothing that will interest you."

"But what is it you want us to do?"

"Find her. She has either run away or been picked up. I think she has run away. She got in a temper over some fancied wrong last night and left the house. I want her found and brought back. But mind you, there must be no unnecessary force used."

"Sure, of course. Shall we take her home if we get her there?"

"I'll tell you where to take her after you get her. That will be time enough. You haven't got her yet, and judging from the success you have had in this case, I don't think you will get her right away."

"Can you give us a steer?"

"No. Keep outside, especially at night. I don't think you'll find her around in the daylight much. But at night keep a sharp lookout. No doubt she'll be over on Broadway working the crowds there for she's got to live and I know she didn't have a cent when she went away."

"You don't think she's jumped into the river or anything, do you?" questioned one shrewdly.

Warwick's face darkened.

"Hardly," he answered dryly. "No reason for that and you ought to know better than ask the question. It's near morning, now. Nothing can be done tonight. Get to bed and sleep. Let me hear from you tomorrow sometime if you get any news."

With that Warwick took his departure abruptly. But the coming day was to be replete with surprises, and even the crook was to be gratified.

In the meantime, Miss VanCamp had gone to her own home for a few hours of well-earned rest.

CHAPTER XX.

MADGE MEETS WITH A SURPRISE.

That afternoon Miss VanCamp, in her coupé, dressed elegantly, made a call upon the Sangsters. The young woman was in her sweetest mood. There was no trace of the woman of the previous night, Madge the Detective, had so valiantly fought her own battles.

"Well, did you get in touch with your friend the detective?" asked Mr. Sangster.

"Oh, yes, I did that last night."

"And will he take up the case?"

"He not only will, but has."

"You lost no time?" smiled the broker.

"No."

"Of course, it is too early yet to expect any results.

I was about to ask if your friend had made any report?"

"He had made distinct progress, sir. I may say that he is going to clear up this mystery in a very short time if I am any judge, at least, basing my opinion on what he tells me."

"You surprise me, Alice. Tell me all."

"No, I shall have to ask you to bear with us a little longer. The information is not mine to give just yet. In due time, you no doubt will learn all. Have you heard from Margaret yet?"

"No, that is, nothing more than a telegram from Washington where they are stopping for a few days. She asked me to tell you that she had taken your advice."

Alice's face was instantly wreathed in smiles.

"I knew she would forget about her loss after she got away. How is Mrs. Sangster to-day?"

"Tired, but well. She is driving in the park this afternoon."

"Then I will be going. I have several other calls to make this afternoon, then, too, I have some business matters to attend to."

"You are a very busy woman."

"Oh, yes."

"But I have never been able to figure out just what you do to occupy your time so fully."

"Perhaps it is just as well that you don't know, my dear, sir. You might not approve of my various avocations."

"Oh, yes, I should. I believe in every one having some distinct and definite purpose in life. Work is the only thing worth while. If we don't keep our minds occupied with some healthful occupation, we get into trouble."

"That is true," answered Alice thoughtfully. "Remember me to Mrs. Sangster. I will leave a card, but you deliver the message to her."

Alice was on too friendly a footing with the Sangster family to call for formalities. Mr. Sangster escorted her to her carriage and shortly after that the young society woman drove away. That afternoon she devoted to calling on her friends, at the same time as she lounged back among the luxurious cushions of her carriage, keeping a sharp eye on all that passed in the street. No face that was worth while, escaped her keen glance.

Thus the day was spent until near dinner time when the young woman returned home where she dined simply. Sarah had returned for the evening, and after dinner, Alice had a long talk with her. The young woman was very well satisfied with what she learned. For the first time she examined certain papers that she

had extracted from the pockets of the men who had pretended to arrest her on the previous night.

It will be seen that Miss VanCamp was a skilful worker as well as a clever woman. Her plans were by this time well laid, and while she had not solved the mystery she had obtained certain information that led her to believe the solution would be reached ere many days had passed.

"I shall go out again this evening, Sarah," she said, after having finished the evening's duties.

"For the night?"

"Perhaps, I don't know. I have that matter still in hand. I look for some developments this evening."

"Be careful, dearie," warned Sarah.

Miss VanCamp laughed lightly.

"You need have no fears for me."

"But you do take such terrible risks."

"That is part of the profession, Sarah. Still, I am reasonably careful. When do you return, tonight?"

"Yes. I had intended to remain away all the evening, but now that you are going out I shall go back very shortly."

"Keep a sharp lookout. I hardly think it will be necessary for you to remain beyond the week's end. There is nothing further to be learned there that I do not already know."

Miss VanCamp, as Madge the Detective, soon after that, took her departure. Her first visit was to a well-known music hall where the men and women of the underworld did congregate. There she met Courtney Sangster. The young man was in gay company, and having a glorious time. Madge took pains to attract the attention of Sangster. But there was no look of recognition in his eyes as he gazed admiringly at her. It was plain that he did not believe he had ever seen the woman before.

Miss VanCamp chuckled softly to herself. It was a compliment to her skill that he had unwittingly paid her.

For an hour or more the detective remained in the music hall, observing carefully all that went on about her. She saw many faces that interested her, some well known criminals. None of them appeared to be acquainted with Sangster, which gave the girl a new line of thought.

During the evening one of the men who had arrested her on the previous evening appeared. It was evident that he was looking for some one. Yet though he looked at Madge he did not recognize her. Her appearance had been changed from the previous evening.

From that to other places the young woman journeyed, remaining a short time at each stopping place.

It was late in the evening when finally she turned her footsteps to the little house where Agnes had found a refuge. First taking a survey to make sure that she was not observed, Madge let herself in with a key, and proceeded down stairs to Mrs. Gates' apartments. The woman was still up.

"How is Agnes?"

"Well and contented. She is in her room."

Alice made her way upstairs. Somehow the house seemed to her to be deserted. She paused just outside the young girl's door, listening. All was silent within.

Alice opened the door and stood gazing in. The room was brightly lighted, but there was no one there.

"*Gone!*" muttered the young woman. "*What does this mean?*"

CHAPTER XXI.

TURNING THE TABLES.

"What does this mean?" muttered Madge.

For a moment longer she stood gazing into the room. Then she stepped within. A faint aroma filled the air, smiting her nostrils familiarily.

"Chloroform!" muttered the girl. "So that is the way of it, eh? I wonder how they got wise to her presence here?"

With no apparent emotion, Madge went to the basement.

"When did the child leave the house?" she demanded.

"When did she leave? What do you mean?" replied the housekeeper.

"I mean that your charge is not here."

"Not here?" repeated Mrs. Gates, her face growing pale.

"No."

"Then she has run away."

"No, she has not run away. She has been taken away."

"You—you don't mean it?"

"I do. Some one has entered this house, chloroformed the child while she lay sleeping on the divan, and abducted her. Have you heard any noise this evening?"

"N-n-no."

"How long ago did you see Agnes?"

"I think it was an hour and a half ago."

"Where?"

"In her room. She said she was going to lie down for a little while, but that she would not undress as she rather thought you might be in during the evening."

Madge nodded.

"I cannot understand how any one could have got-

ten in and carried the girl away without your having heard them."

"It must have been while I was in the cellar."

"When was that?"

"Oh, something like an hour ago. I was doing some work down there, knowing that the girl was in her room and all right. You see, I had no reason to feel worried over her, knowing just where she was."

"I am not blaming you, Mrs. Gates. We are dealing with some very shrewd men. But what disturbs me is, how did they know she was here?"

"I don't know, unless perhaps, they followed you here."

"They did not follow me here?" replied Madge, with a firm compression of the lips. "The girl must have showed herself at a window or something of the sort. She has not been out, has she?"

"Oh, dear me, no."

"Then she has been seen at a window. I am sorry. It complicates matters considerably at this stage of the game."

"What shall you do?"

"Why, go find her, of course."

"But you have no idea where they have taken her?" protested the housekeeper.

"No, but I shall know, I shall find her, never fear, and I shall go about doing so first of all, before I attend to any of the other matters that are pressing me."

"I—I hope you find her. I feel that I am to blame," muttered Mrs. Gates.

"Do not worry. All will come out right in the end. Be sure to double-bolt the doors after I leave the house, and do not open them under any pretext unless you get the proper signal. I am going up to my room to dress. In the meantime go to the observation room and make sure that there is no one watching this house. It would be strange if some one were not."

The detective went to her room, first having examined the lock carefully to make sure that no one had entered there. It was a lock that the ordinary crook would not be likely to succeed in picking, being of peculiar and unusual type.

Satisfying herself on this score, Madge entered and proceeded with her dressing. This time she worked a complete change in her appearance.

Half an hour later a slender young man emerged from the house, Mrs. Gates having assured her mistress that the street was clear. Madge, in her new disguise, looked like a youth of sixteen or eighteen, and a very handsome boy she made. Her hair twisted into a small knot was hidden beneath a soft fedora hat. Her delicate hands were gloved by loose fitting gloves, that could be withdrawn instantly and that only slightly impeded the action of the fingers.

Madge made her way directly to the second avenue house. Some instinct told her that this was the most likely place to go. She reasoned that, had Warwick caused the girl to be kidnapped, which undoubtedly was the case, he would not have Agnes taken directly home.

Whether or not that reasoning was correct, the reader will learn very shortly.

Miss VanCamp passed the house on the opposite side of the street. The shades were tightly drawn, but from under one she saw a faint glimmer of light.

"Some one is at home," murmured the girl. "I shall have to proceed with extreme caution. But I am going to get into that house, whatever the risks I take."

The young man, or girl, as it was in reality, turned back at the next corner and upon reaching the house, dodged up the steps noiselessly and so quickly that even though one were looking out of the window he might have thought it a mere shadow.

Madge was at the door. There she crouched, listening at the key-hole. She could make out no sounds from within. For several minutes the girl maintained her position there, then drawing a key from her pocket, she softly unlocked the door, opening it ever so little.

As on the previous evening, the hall was in darkness. But, from an adjoining room, she could hear voices. The door to that room was closed. The detective listened attentively, but could make nothing out of the conversation being carried on within.

Drawing her flash-light, she looked about her. There was nothing in the hall to claim her attention. Madge turned and made her way softly up the stairs. All was quiet there. Several closed doors greeted the flash from the hand lamp. She tried each of these cautiously, each yielding to her touch, until she had reached the lower end of the upper hall.

There she encountered a locked door.

"This promises something, even if no more than rousing some one out of bed," she murmured.

The detective unlocked the door and opened it. The room was in darkness. The flash lamp shot a slender ray about the room. Miss VanCamp uttered an exclamation.

CHAPTER XXII.

IN THE NICK OF TIME.

As stated at the close of the preceding chapter, Madge uttered an exclamation of surprise. Forewarned as she was, she was not prepared for the sight that met her gaze.

On the low divan lay the figure of Agnes Warwick. The girl was gagged and bound. But this was not all. The eyes were open wide and staring. She might have been dead, for all signs of life that were observable.

The eyes of the detective flashed menacingly. With a spring she was at the side of the unhappy girl. A hand laid over the latter's heart, and Madge uttered a chuckle of satisfaction.

"The poor child is laboring under the influence of some powerful drug. I must get her out of here and give her attention at once, or I may be too late."

The next question was how this should be done. There appeared to be but one way, and this way the detective determined to follow, namely, carry the unconscious girl out.

Miss VanCamp stepped out into the hallway where she stood listening for a few seconds. There were no disquieting sounds, so she returned to the room. At first, she was about to remove the gag and the bonds.

"No, it is not best," decided the woman. "She may moan and thus arouse the others in the house. I shall have to leave her as she is for the present."

Freeing her revolver and placing it on the table, Miss VanCamp, with apparent ease, lifted the girl from the divan, placing the unconscious figure over her shoulder. The detective did not even stagger.

Next Madge picked up her revolver which she carried in the right hand, and with her burden and weapon ready, descended the stairs to the lower hall.

Behind the closed doors were heard the voices of two or three men conversing. Madge imagined that she recognized the voice of Spindle Warwick, but she could not be sure.

She managed to get the front door open without attracting attention. Reaching the outside, she cautiously closed the door, then hurried down the steps with her burden.

The rest was not so easy. Were passers-by to observe the woman carrying a bound and gagged girl over her shoulders, trouble might follow, at least, inquiry, and the woman detective did not wish to be delayed by anything of this sort, for time was precious.

She hurried on until she came to a drug store around the corner on a cross street. There she quickly made herself know to the druggist, exhibiting her authority and stating her wants.

While the druggist was telephoning for a taxicab, Madge was removing the bonds from the unconscious victim. The cab reached the store in record time. The druggist assisted in placing Agnes in, then at the risk of being stopped by traffic policeman the taxi tore down town fairly humming over the smooth pavement in Fifth avenue.

The cab drew up before Alice VanCamp's own home. The driver was paid his regular tariff, with an extra allowance for keeping his mouth shut.

Alice bore her burden up the steps of her handsome home and a few minutes later, laid the child in her own fresh sweet bed. In the meantime, a physician had been hastily summoned. He pronounced the girl to be suffering from an overdose of some powerful drug. It was fully two hours later when Agnes awoke from her death-like sleep.

At first the child was too dazed to take account of her surroundings. At last she fixed her eyes inquiringly on those of her friend.

" Where am I? " she asked.

" In my own home. This time you will not be disturbed. But do not try to think or talk. You must rest for the remainder of the night. In the morning we will have a long talk. I have much to say to you. I will leave you in good hands. Have no fears, your troubles are nearly at an end now."

" How did I come here? "

" I brought you here."

Madge saw that the girl had no recollection of what had happened to her. The child had been asleep when she was overpowered by her abductors and probably did not even know that anything of the sort had taken place.

Madge retired to her library and there telephoned to a well-known detective, a friend of old, requesting him to meet her at a certain place within the next thirty minutes where she would pick him up with a cab.

This done, the woman paid another visit to Agnes, after which she hurriedly left the house.

Bob Collins was the detective friend. To him she explained her plans, briefly sketching the history of the case that she was engaged upon.

" You say you want me to keep this man until you are ready to make disposition of him, Madge? "

" Yes."

" Why not hand him over to the police? "

" It may be possible to avoid the publicity of it. I want to spare my friends if possible."

" Very well, it shall be as you say. Will he be alone? "

" If he is there, he probably will be. I hope he is not, for I want to do something."

" Anything I can help you at? "

" Yes. If the man is not at home, I want you to stand guard outside while I make my investigations. I reckon I know where I want to look. I had that pretty well sized up last night."

Shortly after that the young woman ordered the cab to halt. The two detectives alighted. They were a block from the home of the man Warwick. Madge led the way. The two spoke in subdued tones now.

" We will go up together, then we can make our arrangements afterwards."

Arriving in front of Warwick's door, the pair halted,

taking turns at listening at the door. All was silent and dark within.

" I think the coast is clear. Stand aside while I pick the lock," announced the resourceful Madge.

With scarcely a sound save a single faint click, she performed the operation of picking the lock. An interval of silence followed. Madge opened the door, throwing a flash into the room from her lamp.

" It is all right. You remain near the head of the stairs. If he comes up, down him and put the irons on. I shall not be long."

" Very well, you may depend upon me."

Miss VanCamp entered the room, closing the door behind her. For a moment she remained in the center of the room, flashing her light about.

Suddenly she started forward and pulled a couch from the wall.

CHAPTER XXIII.

CLOSING IN.

The instant the couch came clear of the wall the slender white hands of Alice VanCamp ran over the cloth backing.

" I saw him looking at it. His eyes kept continually wandering to this piece of furniture and I was sure— Ah! "

A knife quickly ripped through the tough canvas that backed the couch and the hands of the detective were thrust in deeply. With a triumphant chuckle the detective drew forth a metal box.

" This is indeed good fortune."

It was good fortune. Quickly opening the box and flashing her light into it, the box burst into a perfect blaze of light.

" The missing jewels. I knew I could not be wrong," murmured the wonderful girl. " Now for the man. I hope he doesn't keep us waiting long. I have still much to do before the morning. I——"

A warning tap on the door, signaled her that someone was approaching. Madge quickly thrust the box into her pocket, buttoning a flap over that the box might not slip out in a scrimmage, then sprang out into the hall.

A man was heard hurriedly running up the stairs.

" It is he. Wait until he gets a foot or so ahead then land on him! "

Warwick dashed by. He was going for the jewels. He had discovered the fact that his daughter had been kidnapped from his other hiding place, and he knew that a powerful enemy was upon his track.

Suddenly Warwick measured his length upon the floor. A billy thrust between his ankles had done the business. The male detective was upon him in an instant. At the same time Madge was down on her knees and before the desperate crook knew what had occurred, she had clapped the irons on him.

"Help me carry him down."

A few moments later and Warwick was in a cab being hurried toward Bob Collins' home. There he was placed in a cell in the basement and there Madge Nelson the Detective visited the man alone.

"The game is up, Spindle," she smiled.

"What game?"

"This!"

Madge held up the box of jewels.

"Who are you?" he demanded.

"Madge the Society Detective!"

"O, Lord help me, I am undone!"

"You are."

"I'll make you rich if you will let me out of this."

"I can't be bribed, Warwick. You should know that without my telling. However, there may still be a way out. I want you to tell me everything, make a clean breast of the whole affair. To save my people publicity I may be able to set you free, providing you will clear out and never show your face in America again. Now talk."

Warwick did talk. He talked, led on by the skilful questioning of Alice VanCamp until the first streaks of dawn shot through the grated window of Bob Collins' cellar.

It was then that Madge took her leave. Going directly home she found Agnes up and dressed, pale, but with a smile of welcome on her beautiful face.

"I am so glad you have come, dear?" breathed Agnes. "I want you to tell me all that happened last night."

"No, not now. But I will say that I think this will prove the happiest day of your life. What would you say, were I to restore you to your real parents?"

"I should be the happiest woman in the world. But you—you cannot mean it."

"It is possible. I shall not promise. I have something to do yet before I can be certain. If you will excuse me I will hasten on to the final chapter of your wonderful history."

An hour later found Alice closeted with Mr. Sangster.

"Well why this early call?" he demanded jovially.

"To report progress."

"What progress have you made?"

"This!" Alice placed the box of jewels before the astonished broker.

He was speechless with amazement.

"When you have recovered from your surprise I wish to ask you some very personal questions. I think I have earned the right to do that."

"Indeed you have. I too wish to ask you some questions. Proceed."

"Did you ever have a daughter who was lost to you?"

An expression of pain passed over the face of the broker.

"Yes," he answered in a low voice.

"What became of her?"

"She disappeared one day when about eight years of age. We have never seen her since."

"That would make her about eighteen years of age were she alive now?"

"Yes."

"Mr. Sangster, what would you say were I to tell you that I had found your real daughter?"

"My God, you can't mean it!" exclaimed the broker, springing from his chair.

"But I do mean it."

Mr. Sangster's agitation was so great that he could not speak for a few moments. He paced back and forth during the time, then turning to her, said:

"Bring her to me! My God I can't stand this uncertainty!"

"Carry the glad tidings to your wife and by the time you have composed her, I shall have the young woman here. Be cautious, do not break the news too suddenly," she warned.

Nearly an hour later Madge entered the drawing room of the Sangster home with a veiled girl at her side. Mr. and Mrs. Sangster were awaiting them there, standing in the middle of the room, their faces ghastly in their pallor.

Agnes began to tremble violently.

"My dear remove your veil," requested the sweet voice of Alice VanCamp.

The girl did so.

"My daughter!" cried the father and mother in one voice as they sprang to the side of the long lost child, clasping her tightly in their arms.

Miss VanCamp discretely withdrew to another room. There she remained for more than an hour. Finally Mr. Sangster entered.

"Alice words fail me. I can't say a thing that I want to say."

"Don't try," said the smiling Miss VanCamp.

"I must. I want to know what all this means? There is something almost uncanny about it. Who in God's name are you that you work such miracles?"

" I think you know me pretty well? "

" I thought I did, but I don't."

" Can't you keep a secret? "

" I can."

" Then listen. When my father died I was forced to earn my living. I followed my natural bent and took up detective work. That in brief is the story. I have been at the work for some years now and in that time have earned a reputation and fortune for myself. I have of course acted under an assumed name. No one knows me in the profession as Alice VanCamp."

Mr. Sangster had listened in speechless wonder.

" Who in Heaven's name are you when you are at work then? "

" I am known as Madge Nelson, Detective," answered the girl smilingly.

" Good Lord, is it possible! "

" Yes, but there are other things to be discussed. I must tell you the whole of this miserable tale and leave you to act as your best judgment dictates."

Alice did tell the story, not sparing a single detail nor minimizing the part that the man Rex Chapin, otherwise Courtney Sangster had played in it. She did impress upon the broker that Courtney was not a bad boy at heart, and advised that he be sent abroad to straighten himself out, otherwise, to inform him that he would have to suffer for his crimes.

Mr. Sangster was not long in deciding. He even went so far as to give Spindle Warwick a liberal bunch of money to take him to the far corners of the earth.

" I owe him that for making it possible to recover my daughter," said the broker. " He did not steal her. He picked her out of the street. If he had been the man who kidnapped her, I should kill him."

And so it was left. Courtney was sent abroad after a stern talk both from his father and Miss VanCamp, to return a few years later a changed and better man. Agnes was united with her family and took her rightful place a few months after the reunion. At first her return caused a great sensation in the social set where the Sangsters moved, but the real story was never known. The maid was released from prison on the following day.

Alice VanCamp had won her greatest case. She had triumphed and she had brought happiness to several people, but Madge the Society Detective neither was offered nor expected a fee for her splendid work.

THE END.

The next issue will be

Old Sleuth Weekly, No. 162,

Entitled

THE MASTER ROGUE,

or

OLD SLEUTH SOLVES THE PUZZLING VAULT MYSTERY.

By " Old Sleuth."